PERSPECTIVES IN
PROBABILITY AND STATISTICS

PERSPECTIVES IN
PROBABILITY AND STATISTICS

Papers in honour of

M. S. BARTLETT

on the occasion of his sixty-fifth birthday

Edited by

J. GANI

Published by the

APPLIED PROBABILITY TRUST

Distributed by

ACADEMIC PRESS · LONDON · NEW YORK · SAN FRANCISCO

Published by the
APPLIED PROBABILITY TRUST
The University
Sheffield S3 7RH
England

Library of Congress Catalogue Card Number: 74–28567

ISBN: 0–12–274450–0

Printed in Israel by
JERUSALEM ACADEMIC PRESS
P. O. Box 2390
Jerusalem

Distributed throughout the world by
ACADEMIC PRESS INC. (LONDON) LTD.
24/28 Oval Road
London NW1 7DX

Preface

Maurice Bartlett, Professor of Biomathematics in the University of Oxford, celebrates his sixty-fifth birthday on 18 June 1975. We, his colleagues and friends, welcome this opportunity of honouring a remarkable probabilist and statistician; his very broad interests and catholic taste have been an inspiration to several generations of research workers. It is also fitting that we express our high personal regard and affection for him on this happy occasion.

I first met Maurice in 1956 at the University of Manchester, where I had journeyed as a young Nuffield Research Fellow from Australia. The Statistical Laboratory, of which he was then head, was housed in a small building at the North end of the campus; among the staff at that time were Jo Moyal (now at Macquarie University, Sydney), Harold Ruben (now at McGill University, Montreal), Maurice Priestley and Peter Wallington (both now at UMIST, Manchester). We were a happy group, busy with our lecturing and research duties, and presided over benignly by Maurice, whose shy thoughtfulness was a byword among us. We were learning a great deal from him: his wide range of interests and his multifarious research activities sustained us all in our endeavours. Every problem we raised inevitably called forth a ready and learned response from the wide stock of his experience.

It is difficult to describe the magnitude of Bartlett's contribution to the fields of probability and statistics. His earliest work was on moment-generating functions, multiple regression, the meaning of probability, mathematical genetics, some classical statistical problems and their applications to agricultural experiments, psychology and biology. He gradually became more comprehensively interested in multivariate analysis, and later in stochastic processes; here his work included inference problems for Markov chains and time series. While developing these new fields, he did not relinquish his previous concern with statistical applications in physics and psychology. His interest in stochastic processes found ready application in epidemic theory, where he made fundamental contributions to the understanding of the spread of measles. Point processes were a further interest, and with his appointment to the Oxford Chair came his increased activity in biological models. In every one of these areas, his contribution has been fundamental.

What we have attempted to do in this volume is to reflect the breadth of Bartlett's interests. All the contributors owe Bartlett a debt both as a teacher and as a friend: all have benefited from his flair for relevant problems, and from his demonstration that breadth need not be the enemy of depth. Regrettably, not all who might have wished to join us in honouring him could be invited to contribute to this book; we know, however, that they will insist on joining us in wishing him a very happy sixty-fifth birthday.

In conclusion, may I thank all those who have helped to make this volume possible: Mavis Hitchcock, whose work on the layout and proofreading has been invaluable, Carol Nixon, Julie Musgrave and Kathleen Lyle, who have prepared the typescripts and proofread the printed material in its several stages of production, and last but not least the printers who have set up the type by their new electronic setting system.

C.S.I.R.O., Canberra   J. GANI
January 1975

Contents

vii

Publications of M. S. Bartlett

1932

[1] (With J. Wishart) Distribution of second-order moment statistics in a normal system. *Proc. Camb. Phil. Soc.* **28**, 455–459.

1933

[2] (With J. Wishart) Generalised product moment distribution in a normal system. *Proc. Camb. Phil. Soc.* **29**, 260–270.
[3] Probability and chance in the theory of statistics. *Proc. Roy. Soc.* A **141**, 518–534.
[4] On the theory of statistical regression. *Proc. Roy. Soc. Edinburgh* **53**, 260–283.

1934

[5] The problem in statistics of testing several variances. *Proc. Camb. Phil. Soc.* **30**, 164–169.
[6] The vector representation of a sample. *Proc. Camb. Phil. Soc.* **30**, 327–340.
[7] (With J.B.S. Haldane) Theory of inbreeding in autotetraploids. *J. Genetics* **29**, 175–180.

1935

[8] (With J.B.S. Haldane) Theory of inbreeding with forced heterozygosis. *J. Genetics.* **31**, 327–340.
[9] The statistical estimation of 'G'. *British J. Psychol.* **26**, 199–206.
[10] An examination of the value of covariance in dairy cow nutrition experiments. *J. Agric. Sci.* **25**, 238–244.
[11] Effect of non-normality on the t-distribution. *Proc. Camb. Phil. Soc.* **31**, 223–231.
[12] Some aspects of the time-correlation problem in regard to tests of significance. *J. R. Statist. Soc.* **98**, 536–543.
[13] Contingency table interaction. *J. R. Statist. Soc. Suppl.* **2**, 248–252.

1936

[14] Statistical information and properties of sufficiency. *Proc. Roy. Soc.* A **154**, 124–137.
[15] The information available in small samples. *Proc. Camb. Phil. Soc.* **32**, 560–566.
[16] Square-root transformation in analysis of variance. *J. R. Statist. Soc. Suppl.* **3**, 68–78.
[17] Some notes on insecticide tests in the laboratory and in the field. *J. R. Statist. Soc. Suppl.* **3**, 185–194.
[18] (With A.W. Greenhill) Relative importance of field and laboratory sampling errors in small plot pasture productivity experiments. *J. Agric. Sci.* **26**, 258–262.
[19] Note on the analysis of covariance. *J. Agric. Sci.* **26**, 488–491.
[20] Statistical probability. *J. Amer. Statist. Assoc.* **31**, 553–555.

1937

[21] Properties of sufficiency and statistical tests. *Proc. Roy. Soc.* A **160**, 268–282.
[22] Subsampling for attributes. *J. R. Statist. Soc. Suppl.* **4**, 131–135.
[23] Note on the derivation of fluctuation formulae for statistical assemblies. *Proc. Camb. Phil. Soc.* **33**, 390–393.

[24] Deviations from expected frequencies in the theory of inbreeding. *J. Genetics* **35**, 83–87.
[25] The statistical conception of mental factors. *British J. Psychol.* **28**, 97–104.
[26] Note on the development of correlations among genetic components of ability. *Ann. Eugen.* **7**, 299–302.
[27] Some examples of statistical methods of research in agriculture and applied biology. *J. R. Statist. Soc. Suppl.* **4**, 137–183.

1938

[28] Further aspects of the theory of multiple regression. *Proc. Camb. Phil. Soc.* **34**, 33–40.
[29] The characteristic function of a conditional statistic. *J. London Math. Soc.* **13**, 62–67.
[30] (With F. Crowther) Experimental and statistical technique of some complex cotton experiments in Egypt. *Emp. J. Exp. Agric.* **6**, 53–68.
[31] The approximate recovery of information from replicated field experiments with large blocks. *J. Agric. Sci.* **28**, 418–427.
[32] (With J. C. Drummond *et al.*) An experiment on the nutritive value of winter-produced 'summer' milk. *J. Hygiene* **38**, 25–39.

1939

[33] A note on tests of significance in multivariate analysis. *Proc. Camb. Phil. Soc.* **35**, 180–185.
[34] Complete simultaneous fiducial distributions. *Ann. Math. Statist.* **10**, 129–138.

1940

[35] The standard errors of discriminant function coefficients. *J. R. Statist. Soc. Suppl.* **6**, 169–173.
[36] A note on the interpretation of quasi-sufficiency. *Biometrika* **31**, 391–392.
[37] The present position of mathematical statistics. *J. R. Statist. Soc.* **103**, 1–29.

1941

[38] The statistical significance of canonical correlations. *Biometrika* **32**, 239–244.

1944

[39] Negative probability. *Proc. Camb. Phil. Soc.* **41**, 71–73.

1946

[40] The large sample theory of sequential tests. *Proc. Camb. Phil. Soc.* **42**, 239–244.
[41] On the theoretical specification and sampling properties of autocorrelated time series. *J. R. Statist. Soc. Suppl.* **8**, 27–41.
[42] A modified probit technique for small probabilities. *J. R. Statist. Soc. Suppl.* **8**, 113–117.
[43] (With D. G. Kendall) The statistical analysis of variance-heterogeneity and the logarithmic transformation. *J. R. Statist. Soc. Suppl.* **8**, 128–138.
[44] *Stochastic Processes.* (Mimeographed notes of a course given at the University of North Carolina.)

1947

[45] The general canonical correlation distribution. *Ann. Math. Statist.* **18**, 1–17.
[46] The use of transformations. *Biometrics* **3**, 39–52.
[47] Multivariate analysis. *J. R. Statist. Soc. Suppl.* **9**, 176–190.

1948

[48] (With J. E. Moyal) The exact transition probabilities of quantum-mechanical oscillators calculated by the phase-space method. *Proc. Camb. Phil. Soc.* **45**, 545–553.

[49] Internal and external factor analysis. *British J. Psychol. Statist. Sect.* **1**, 73–81.

[50] A note on the statistical estimation of supply and demand relations from time-series. *Econometrica* **16**, 323–329.

1949

[51] Fitting a straight line when both variables are subject to error. *Biometrics* **5**, 207–212.

[52] Probability in logic, mathematics and science. *Dialectica* **3**, 104–113.

[53] Some evolutionary stochastic processes. *J. R. Statist. Soc.* B **11**, 211–229.

[54] Statistical significance of dispersed hits in card guessing experiments. *Proc. Soc. Psychical Res.* Part **176**, 336–338.

[55] Tests of significance in factor analysis. *British J. Psychol. Statist. Sect.* **3**, 77–85.

[56] Mathematical statistics and the universities. *Univ. Quart.* **3**, 665–671.

1950

[57] Periodogram analysis and continuous spectra. *Biometrika* **37**, 1–16.

[58] (With P. H. Diananda) Extensions of Quenouille's test for autoregressive schemes. *J. R. Statist. Soc.* B **12**, 108–115.

[59] (With D. G. Kendall) On the use of the characteristic functions in the analysis of some stochastic processes occurring in physics and biology. *Proc. Camb. Phil. Soc.* **47**, 65–76.

[60] The frequency goodness of fit test for probability chains. *Proc. Camb. Phil. Soc.* **47**, 86–95.

[61] Teaching and education in biometry. *Biometrics* **6**, 85–98.

[62] *The Statistical Approach to the Analysis of Time-Series.* (Mimeographed Report, Ministry of Supply Symposium on Information Theory, London.)

1951

[63] An inverse matrix adjustment arising in discriminant analysis. *Ann. Math. Statist.* **22**, 107–111.

[64] A further note on tests of significance in factor analysis. *British J. Psychol. Statist. Sect.* **4**, 1–2.

[65] Some remarks on the theory of statistics. *Trans. Manchester Statist. Soc.* 1–27.

[66] (With appendix by W. Ledermann) The effect of standardization on a χ^2 approximation in factor analysis. *Biometrika* **38**, 337–344.

[67] The goodness of fit of a single hypothetical discriminant function in the case of several groups. *Ann. Eugen.* **16**, 199–214.

[68] The dual recurrence relation for multiplicative processes. *Proc. Camb. Phil. Soc.* **47**, 821–825.

1952

[69] A sampling test of the χ^2 theory for probability chains. *Biometrika* **39**, 118–121.

[70] The statistical significance of odd bits of information. *Biometrika* **39**, 228–237.

1953

[71] (With D. V. Rajalakshman) Goodness of fit tests for simultaneous autoregressive time-series. *J. R. Statist. Soc.* B **15**, 107–124.

[72] Approximate confidence intervals. *Biometrika* **40**, 12–19.

[73] Recurrence and first passage times. *Proc. Camb. Phil. Soc.* **49**, 263–275.
[74] On the statistical estimation of mean life times. *Phil. Mag.* Ser. 7 **44**, 249–262.
[75] Factor analysis in psychology as a statistician sees it. *Nordisk Psykologi*, Monograph Series 3, March.
[76] Estimation of mean life times from multiplate cloud chamber tracks. *Phil. Mag.* Ser. 7 **44**, 1407–1408.
[77] Approximate confidence intervals II. More than one unknown parameter. *Biometrika* **40**, 306–317.
[78] *The Meaning and Practical Importance of Stochastic Processes.* (Royal and Manchester Statistical Societies' Conference, Manchester.) Later published in *Applied Statistics* **2**, 44–64.

1954

[79] A comment on the use of the square-root and angular transformations. *Biometrics* **10**, 140–142.
[80] Processus stochastiques ponctuels. *Ann. Inst. Henri Poincaré* **14**, fasc. 1, 35–60.
[81] Problèmes de l'analyse spectrale des séries temporelles stationnaires. *Publ. Inst. Statist. Univ. de Paris* **3**, fasc. 3, 119–134.
[82] A note on the multiplying factors for various χ^2 approximations. *J. R. Statist. Soc.* B **16**, 296–298.
[83] The statistical analysis of stochastic processes. *Colloque sur L'analyse statistique, tenu à Bruxelles les 15, 16 et 17 décembre 1954.*

1955

[84] (With J. Medhi) On the efficiency of procedures for smoothing periodograms from time series with continuous spectra. *Biometrika* **42**, 143–150.
[85] Approximate confidence intervals III. A bias correction. *Biometrica* **42**, 201–204.
[86] *An Introduction to Stochastic Processes.* Cambridge University Press (2nd Edition 1966).

1956

[87] Deterministic and stochastic models for recurrent epidemics. *Proc. Third Berkeley Symp. Math. Statist. Prob.* **4**, 81–109.
[88] Comment on Sir Ronald Fisher's paper: 'On a test of significance in Pearson's *Biometrika Tables* (No. 11)'. *J. R. Statist. Soc.* B **18**, 295–296.

1957

[89] Measles periodicity and community size. *J. R. Statist. Soc.* A **120**, 48–70.
[90] On theoretical models for competitive and predatory biological systems. *Biometrika* **44**, 27–42.
[91] A note on tests of significance for linear functional relationships. *Biometrika* **44**, 268–269.

1958

[92] Some problems associated with random velocity. *Publ. Inst. Statist. Univ. de Paris* **6**, 261–270.

1959

[93] The impact of stochastic process theory on statistics. *Probability and Statistics, The Harald Cramér Volume*, ed. U. Grenander. Almqvist and Wiksell, Stockholm: John Wiley and Sons, New York, 39–49.

1960

[94] The critical community size for measles in the United States. *J. R. Statist. Soc.* A **123**, 37–44.

[95] (With J. C. Gower and P. M. Leslie) A comparison of theoretical and empirical results for some stochastic population models. *Biometrika* **47**, 1–11.

[96] *Stochastic Population Models in Ecology and Epidemiology*. Methuen and Co. Ltd., London.

[97] Some stochastic models in ecology and epidemiology. *Contributions to Probability and Statistics. Essays in honour of Harald Hotelling*, ed. Ingram Olkin *et al*. Stanford University Press. 89–96.

1961

[98] Monte Carlo studies in ecology and epidemiology. *Proc. Fourth Berkeley Symp. Math. Statist. Prob.* **4**, 39–55.

[99] Equations for stochastic path integrals. *Proc. Camb. Phil. Soc.* **57**, 568–573.

[100] *Probability, Statistics and Time*. (Inaugural lecture, University College, London.)

[101] The classification and properties of various types of statistical fluctuations in physics. *Bull. Inst. Int. Statist. (Tokyo)* **38**, 3, 429–434.

1962

[102] Probability and statistics in the physical sciences. *Bull. Inst. Int. Statist. (Paris)* **39**, 3, 3–21.

[103] *Essays in Probability and Statistics*. Methuen and Co. Ltd., London.

1963

[104] The spectral analysis of point processes. *J. R. Statist. Soc.* B **25**, 264–296.

[105] Statistical estimation of density functions. *Sankyā* A **25**, 245–254.

[106] (With N. W. Please) Discrimination in the case of zero mean differences. *Biometrika* **50**, 17–21.

1964

[107] The relevance of stochastic models for large-scale epidemiological phenomena. *Appl. Statist.* **13**, 2–8.

[108] The spectral analysis of two-dimensional point processes. *Biometrika* **51**, 299–311.

[109] A note on spatial pattern. *Biometrics* **20**, 891–892.

1965

[110] R. A. Fisher and the last fifty years of statistical methodology. *J. Amer. Statist. Assoc.* **60**, 395–409.

[111] Multivariate statistics. *Theoretical and Mathematical Biology*, ed. T. H. Waterman and H. J. Morowitz. Blaisdell, London, 201–224.

1966

[112] Some notes on epidemiological theory. *Research Papers in Statistics: Festschrift for J. Neyman*, ed. F. N. David, Wiley, New York, 25–35.

[113] *Introduction to Stochastic Processes*. Cambridge University Press, 2nd Edition.

1967

[114] Inference and stochastic processes. *J. R. Statist. Soc.* A **130**, 457–477.

[115] Spectral analysis of line processes. *Proc. Fifth Berkeley Symp. Math. Statist. Prob.* **3**, 135–153.

[116] Some remarks on the analysis of time series. *Biometrika* **54**, 25–38.
[117] Ronald Aylmer Fisher. *International Encyclopedia of the Social Sciences*, ed. D. E. Sills. Macmillan, U.S.A., p. 485.
[118] Biometry and Theoretical Biology. *Haldane and Modern Biology*, ed. K. R. Dronamraju. The Johns Hopkins Press, Baltimore, 203–216.
[119] *Biomathematics*. (Inaugural lecture, University of Oxford.)
[120] A further note on nearest-neighbour models. *J. R. Statist. Soc.* A **131**, 579–580.

1969

[121] Distributions associated with cell populations. *Biometrika* **56**, 391–400.
[122] (With J. Besag) Correlation properties of some nearest-neighbour models. *Bull. Inst. Int. Statist.* (*London*), **43**, 191–193.

1970

[123] Age distributions. *Biometrics* **26**, 377–386.
[124] Two-dimensional nearest-neighbour systems, and their ecological applications. *Proc. Int. Symp. Statist. Ecol.* (Yale), 179–191.

1971

[125] When is inference *statistical* inference? *Proc. Symp. on Foundations of Statist. Inf.* Waterloo, Canada, 20–31.
[126] Physical nearest-neighbour models and non-linear time-series. *J. Appl. Prob.* **8**, 222–232.
[127] (With Jennifer M. Brennan and J. N. Pollack) Stochastic analysis of some experiments on the mating of blowflies. *Biometrics* **27**, 725–730.

1972

[128] Epidemics. *Statistics: A Guide to the Unknown*, ed. Judith M. Tanur *et al.* Holden-Day, San Francisco, 66–76.
[129] Physical nearest-neighbour models and non-linear time-series II. Further discussion of approximate solutions and exact equations. *J. Appl. Prob.* **9**, 76–86.
[130] Some applications of multivariate point processes. *Proc. Symp. on Point Processes.* John Wiley and Sons, New York, 136–150.

1973

[131] Equations and models of population change. *The Mathematical Theory of the Dynamics of Biological Populations*, ed. M. S. Bartlett and R. W. Hiorns. Academic Press, London, 5–21.
[132] A note on Das Gupta's two-sex population model. *Theor. Pop. Biol.* **4**, 418–424.

1974

[133] The statistical analysis of spatial pattern. *Adv. Appl. Prob.* **6**, 336–358.
[134] Physical nearest-neighbour models and non-linear time-series: III Non-zero means and sub-critical temperatures. *J. Appl. Prob.* **11**, 715–725.

PART I

HISTORICAL INTRODUCTION

Bartlett's Work on Agricultural Experiments

W. G. COCHRAN

Abstract

A selection of Bartlett's work as an operating statistician in his first position as statistician 1934–38 at the I.C.I. agricultural research station at Jealott's Hill, Berks., is described. This illustrates some of the methods he used for the efficient detection of treatment effects and for an appraisal of the suitability of the experimental designs that were being used.

1. Introduction

From 1934 to 1938 Bartlett was statistician at the I.C.I. agricultural research station at Jealott's Hill, Berks., this being his first full-time job. His work involved dealing with the design and analysis of randomized experiments both in the field and laboratory. By 1934 the Fisherian methods for comparative experimentation had been produced in rapid succession — randomized blocks, latin squares, factorial design (including the confounding of interactions), with the analysis of variance and covariance as primary techniques in aiding the interpretation of the results. At that time we were just learning how to use these tools to best advantage. A selection of Bartlett's work in this process will show something of his methods as an operating statistician.

2. The efficient detection of treatment effects

In a section with this title, Bartlett (1937) notes that the more statisticians can condense the description of the treatment effects, the more likely they will be able to make efficient tests of these effects. In the

9

absence of any available theory of the mode of action of treatments, the statistician has to seek efficient *empirical* reduction methods.

Isolation of single d.f. This now standard device is illustrated in a 4×4 factorial on weights of sugar-beet tops, with 4 degrees of closeness of spacing (S) and 4 levels of complete fertilizer (M). Although the degrees of closeness are not in strictly equal steps, the S_L, M_L and $S_L \times M_L$ single d.f. are found to summarize adequately the performance of the 16 treatment combinations, there being little or no advantage from close spacing unless manure is given. Nowadays, standard computer programs for factorial designs usually allow a breakdown of main effects and 2-factor interactions into polynomial components of this type, but may not cover components of the non-polynomial type.

Observations repeated in time on each unit (plot). With observations taken at n successive times on each unit, the problem of a summary analysis is more difficult. One approach that is often natural is to fit a response curve $y(t)$ to each plot from the n available times, studying how the treatments affect the nature of this response curve or concentrating on its most important aspects in relation to the objectives of the experiment. Two examples, Bartlett (1937), will be cited.

The first came from experiments on the effect of shading and types of nitrogen on the herbage on a lawn in successive weeks. One response variable y was the percentage area covered by clover each week. For this the response curve $y(t)$ on a plot appeared graphically to be a declining non-linear function. Bartlett notes, however, that the rate of change of this percent with time will depend both on the amount of clover available to expand and on the area $(100 - y)$ available to expand into (or, with a negative rate of change, on the area of competing species). These comments suggest as an approximation the equation

$$\frac{dy}{dt} = Ay(100 - y)$$

giving

$$\ln(y/(100 - y)) = Bt + c.$$

This leads to the familiar logit transformation $x = \ln(y/(100-y))$ as a device usually effective in straightening the relation $x(t)$ of x against time. Analyses of variance were made of the linear regression of x on time, to give a compact empirical summary of the treatment effects.

The second example was an experiment (7 treatments, 6 blocks) on germination in peas. For each treatment, 50 seeds per replicate were placed in a pan on 5 May 1936, daily counts being made of the *total* number y_t germinated by day t. Here the key economic variables are the overall total number germinating and some measure of the earliness of germination. For the latter, Bartlett suggests a 'rate index' , which for the n days in the experiment is

$$\left(\sum_{1}^{n} y_t\right)\Big/ (ny_n).$$

The choice of this index may appear puzzling. But if d_j seeds germinate on day j, then $y_t = \Sigma^t d_j$, so that if we omit the divisor n, the index becomes

$$\{nd_1 + (n-1)d_2 + \cdots + d_n\}\Big/\left(\sum_{1}^{n} d_j\right).$$

This quantity can be described as the mean earliness of germination, the days being counted backwards, $1, 2, \cdots, n$, from the last date, as Bartlett points out. The quantities y_n (total number germinated) and the rate index then constitute the most important variables for a summary analysis. (In the data the counts were not entirely daily, one day having two counts, but Bartlett uses the index as an empirical measure that serves to denote earliness.)

An ingenious use of confounding. A 3^3 experiment on wheat was conducted in 1934, the factors being varieties, spacings and nitrogen in 4 blocks of 27 plots. In 1935 a 3^2 experiment on maize was planned on the same site, the treatments being the same 3 spacings and levels of nitrogen. It was desired in addition to measure any residual effects of the 1934 spacings and N levels, comparing them with the direct effects of these factors. By using three of the four 1934 blocks, Bartlett noted that he could construct a plan that was a single replication of a 3^4 (S_D, N_D, S_R, N_R) with 2 d.f. from the 4-factor interactions confounded with blocks, where D denotes the direct and R the residual effects.

The composition of the 1935 blocks (I, II, III) is given by the following diagram.

Residual factors				Direct factors				1935 blocks		
	S_0	S_1	S_2		S_0	S_1	S_2		X	Y	Z
N_0	X	Y	Z	N_0	A	B	C	A	I	II	III
N_1	Z	X	Y	N_1	C	A	B	B	III	I	II
N_2	Y	Z	X	N_2	B	C	A	C	II	III	I

Thus the 1935 block I had the 27 treatment combinations AX, BY, CZ where A denotes the three direct combinations N_0S_0, N_1S_1, N_2S_2 and X the corresponding three residual combinations N_0S_0, N_1S_1, N_2S_2. The error mean square was estimated from the remaining 4-factor interactions (14 d.f.) and the 3-factor interactions which contained a 2-factor residual interaction (16.d.f). Significant residual effects of N and S were found, but were negligible relative to the large direct effects.

Salt damage in experiments in Egypt. Accumulation of salt in the upper layers of the soil in Egypt can be a major source of variation in some experiments, reducing the cotton yield. In three experiments with serious spotty damage, a visual estimate of the degree of saltiness of the plot soil was made on each plot on a 0 to 10 scale, (Crowther and Bartlett (1938)). Since the regression of yield on this index appeared linear, a covariance adjustment for the regression of yield on salt was made. This device reduced the error mean square by 54% and 38% in two experiments though by only 5% in a third.

For many statisticians, analysis of the covariance-adjusted yields would be assumed to have removed the disturbing effects of salt damage. But Bartlett reminds us that covariance may not really *adjust* for salt damage, since severe salt concentrations might decrease the ability of the crop to respond to the treatments. To examine whether this effect of the salt was present, he recalculates the analysis, omitting the 12 plots most severely salty. In the re-analysis the linear response to nitrogen increased by 16%, so that his warning about the interpretation of covariance was justified.

Recovery of intra-block information. Bartlett (1938) examined an ingenious method proposed by Papadakis (1937) for handling patchy fields. The technique might be described as the recovery of *intra-block* information about fertility. First calculate for each plot yield y the quantity $y' = (y - \bar{y}_t + \bar{y})$, where $\bar{y}_t$ is the mean of the treatment on the plot. The quantities y' are regarded as estimates of the fertility levels of the plots, though nothing would be gained by a covariance regression of the y on the y'. Instead, a covariate x is found by using the fertility y' of neighboring plots to predict the fertility level of the plot. With long narrow plots, x is the mean of the two y' values contiguous to the long side of the plot. With squarish plots, x can be the mean of the y' for the four contiguous plots, with special rules for edge plots. The treatment yields $\bar{y}_t$ are adjusted for the covariance on x.

Bartlett's contribution has two parts. In the first, accepting the method at face value, he applies it to two $4 \times 3^2 \times 2$ factorials on cotton in blocks of 72 plots. The standard errors per plot are reduced from 12.0% to 8.6%, and from 8.9% to 7.0% — certainly worthwhile gains. He goes on to investigate the approximate theoretical validity of the technique by examining algebraically the first-order disturbances to the standard covariance formulas. He finds that the assumptions required are likely to be least disturbed when the blocks are large and suggests from his analysis that, when calculating the residual error mean square, 2 d.f. be allotted to the regression on x (instead of the usual 1 d.f.) He concludes that the method is approximately valid with, at my guess, at least 30 plots per block, and may occasionally be useful if an experiment has large blocks found to be internally heterogeneous.

3. Analysis as a guide to design

A notable feature of Bartlett's work was the use of supplementary analysis of the completed results of an experiment in forming a judgment as to whether the design used was the most suitable for its purpose, or whether an alternative should be tried for similar experiments in the future. This working habit, natural in the early stages of experimentation, is worth forming in any major program of experimentation. Some examples follow.

Split-plot experiments. Split-plot experiments were quite common in the 1920's and 30's, especially if a larger plot was more convenient for some factors than for others. A series of large-scale factorials on cotton in Egypt had two main-plot factors — varieties (3) and watering (2 levels) — and two sub-plot factors — spacing (3 levels) and nitrogen (3 levels). In appraising the suitability of the split-plot plans, Bartlett (1937) estimates, from the main-plot and sub-plot error mean squares in 10 experiments, what the efficiencies of main-plot and sub-plot comparisons would have been with ordinary randomized blocks on the same sites, relative to those obtained from the split-plot plans used. The median relative efficiencies were 3.2 for main-plot comparisons and 0.82 for sub-plot comparisons.

These figures suggest that there will be a net gain, as regards precision of main effects, from reverting to randomized blocks. This was done in two experiments in 1936, which showed satisfactory precision. Similarly, with factorials employing partial confounding of interactions, Bartlett estimates from the results the gains in efficiency for unconfounded effects and gains or losses for confounded effects as a check on the performance of the design versus randomized blocks.

Fertility diagrams. A further device used by Bartlett (Crowther and Bartlett (1938)) was the fertility diagram, in combination with the size of the standard error per plot. Construction of fertility diagrams from uniformity trial data was well known in agriculture as a guide to the suitability of the field and to the best method of blocking. Subject to the assumption of additivity of the effects, a fertility diagram that serves the same purposes can be constructed from the quantities $(y - \bar{y}_t + \bar{y})$, where y is the yield on an individual plot and $\bar{y}_t$ the mean yield of the treatment on that plot. As with uniformity data, these diagrams often revealed a patchiness in fertility with no regular pattern, from which geographically compact blocks seem the best protection, although the judgment might be to avoid some fields in future experiments or (with large blocks) to try the Papadakis method already described.

Experiments on dairy cows. The cow is an expensive animal for experimentation owing to the high variability of milk yield from cow to cow. Standard errors of 25% per cow in milk yield are not uncommon. One method used in the 1930's to circumvent this difficulty was to make the cow serve as its own control by using a cross-over or latin square design with the treatments given in succession to the cow for short periods during the lactation cycle. Bartlett (1935) notes two disadvantages of this method. The number of treatments is limited to two or three, and it is by no means clear that the performances of treatments in practice over the whole lactation cycle are predictable from their performance during a short period in that cycle. Thus, precision may have been obtained by asking the wrong question.

He takes advantage of an experiment that had no significant treatment effects to regard the data as a uniformity trial. The alternatives to the cross-over design that he wishes to consider are to give a cow uniform treatment during the first n weeks ($n = 1, 2, 3, 5$) and a single treatment during the remaining (20-n) weeks of the lactation period. He finds that a covariance adjustment for the early period yields reduces the s.e. per cow from 25.2% to around 8% for $n = 1, 2, 3, 5$, a level at which the measurement of treatment differences of economic value becomes feasible. This analysis indicates that one week's preliminary period is enough, but Bartlett suggests three weeks as a safer period to protect against temporary fluctuations. This method was used in a 1934 winter feeding trial, resulting in a standard error of 7.0%.

This experiment had one missing cow which ran dry early. He notes (Bartlett (1937)) that the exact least squares analysis of data with a missing value can be obtained by inserting any number y for the missing value and doing a covariance analysis on a dummy x-variate which takes the value 1 for the missing value and 0 elsewhere. This approach has recently been adapted (Rubin (1972)) as a computer method of handling analyses of data with missing values.

A non-linear response. In insecticide tests under controlled laboratory conditions, the proportion $\hat{p}$ killed out of n by a given dose can often be assumed to be binomial. Under a normal tolerance distribution, the theoretical proportion killed is assumed to be related to the log dose x by the relation

$$ p = \frac{1}{\sqrt{(2\pi)}} \int_{-\infty}^{(x-\mu)/\sigma} z(u)\,du, $$

where $z(u)$ is the standard normal ordinate at u. This is a two-parameter problem. For the estimation of μ, the median lethal dose, the Fisherian amount of information is well-known to be

$$ I(\mu) = \frac{nz^2}{\sigma^2 pq} = \frac{z^2}{\sigma^2 V(\hat{p})} $$

and to be maximized if x can be chosen to produce an expected 50% kill.

Bartlett's (1936) problem arose from insecticide tests in the field, not the laboratory. Leatherjackets (larvae that live in the soil and attack the roots of cereals and grass) are controlled by applying toxic emulsions to the plots, the experiment having 5 treatments, including a control. The surviving leatherjackets are counted by application of a standard emulsion which brings the leatherjackets to the surface, two square foot samples being counted per plot.

Still assuming the normal tolerance distribution, Bartlett notes that the number $n\hat{q}$ surviving in the field will not be binomial (further, n is unknown). The simplest assumption is that $n\hat{q}$ is Poisson, for which $V(n\hat{q}) = nq = m$ (say). But in the field the variance is often found to contain also a component in m^2. Consequently he writes

$$V(n\hat{q}) = \alpha m(1 + \beta m) = \alpha m(1 + \lambda q) \propto q(1 + \lambda q).$$

Consequently, for these field tests the information is more accurately expressed as

$$I(\mu) \propto \frac{z^2}{\sigma^2 q(1 + \lambda q)}.$$

He plots the curve of $I(\mu)$ against p (proportion killed) for a series of values of λ. For $1 \leq \lambda \leq 3$, the information is maximized by aiming at a percent kill around 80% instead of the 50% for a binomial model. (The experimental example presented suggests $\lambda \simeq 3$.)

He warns that this is a 'rough and ready' analysis and that other experiments may not follow this model, but gives this calculation as another example of the kinds of questions that should be asked in monitoring the efficiency of experiments.

4. Concluding remarks

In some respects the preceding examples do not do justice to Bartlett. They do not illustrate his originality and power in tackling unsolved problems in theory and they mostly concern techniques that now are, or should be, well-known. But they illustrate that he is equally at home in applied statistics, continually keeping in mind the objectives of experimental design and analysis, questions of feasibility and convenience, and ready to employ approximate theoretical methods when they would be adequate for his purpose.

References

BARTLETT, M. S. (1935) An examination of the value of covariance in dairy cow nutrition experiments. *J. Agric. Sci.* **25**, 238–244.

BARTLETT, M. S. (1936) Some notes on insecticide tests in the laboratory and in the field. *J. R. Statist. Soc. Suppl.* **3**, 185–194.

BARTLETT, M. S. (1937) Some examples of statistical methods of research in agriculture and applied biology. *J. R. Statist. Soc. Suppl.* **4**, 138–183.

BARTLETT, M. S. (1938) The approximate recovery of information from replicated field experiments with large blocks. *J. Agric. Sci.* **28**, 418–427.

CROWTHER, F. AND BARTLETT, M. S. (1938) Experimental and statistical technique of some complex cotton experiments in Egypt. *Emp. J. Exp. Agric.* **6**, 53–68.

PAPADAKIS, J. S. (1937) A statistical method for field experiments. *Bull. Inst. Amél. Plantes à Salonique* **23**, 1–30.

RUBIN, D. R. (1972) A non-iterative algorithm for least squares estimation of missing values in any analysis of variance design. *Appl. Statist.* **21**, 136–141.

PART II

PROBABILITY THEORY

Probability Functions which are Proportional to Characteristic Functions and the Infinite Divisibility of the von Mises Distribution

TOBY LEWIS

Abstract

Reciprocal pairs of continuous random variables on the line are considered, such that the density function of each is, to within a norming factor, the characteristic function of the other. The analogous reciprocal relationship between a discrete distribution on the line and a continuous distribution on the circle is also considered. A conjecture is made regarding infinite divisibility properties of such pairs of random variables. It is shown that the von Mises distribution is infinitely divisible for sufficiently small values of the concentration parameter.

0. Introduction

The discussion in Section 1 of this paper was originally motivated by the problem of whether Student's t- distribution on ν degrees of freedom is infinitely divisible for all values of the parameter ν; the discussion in Section 2 was motivated by the problem of whether the von Mises distribution is infinitely divisible for some or all values of its concentration parameter.

1. Reciprocal distributions on the line

1.1. Suppose X is an absolutely continuous (a.c.) random variable on the line with the following property: the probability density function (p.d.f.) of X, f say, is at the same time the characteristic function (c.f.), to within a norming factor $1/f(0)$, of another random variable Y on the line. We will call such a random variable X a 'characteristic variable'. The following results are easily shown:

19

(i) Y is also a.c., and X, Y are both symmetric about 0.

(ii) If f, g are their respective p.d.f.'s, then $f(0)$, $g(0)$ (which we shall write as f_0, g_0) are finite and non-zero, and g/g_0, f/f_0 are their respective c.f.'s.

(iii) f and g are reciprocal cosine transforms, i.e.,

$$g(y)/g_0 = \int_{-\infty}^{\infty} f(x) \cos yx\, dx$$

and

$$f(x)/f_0 = \int_{-\infty}^{\infty} g(y) \cos xy\, dy.$$

(iv) $2\pi f_0 g_0 = 1$.

Proof. Since f is proportional to a c.f., $0 < f_0 < \infty$; and since f is a p.d.f. it is real-valued on the real line, hence the c.f. f/f_0 is even, and the X-distribution is even. Further f, being a p.d.f., is absolutely integrable over $(-\infty, \infty)$, from which it follows (Lukacs (1970), Theorem 3.2.2) that Y, with c.f. f/f_0, is even and a.c. and has a continuous p.d.f. g given by

$$g(y) = \frac{1}{2\pi} \int_{-\infty}^{\infty} \{f(t)/f_0\} \cos yt\, dt.$$

Hence $2\pi f_0 g_0 = 1$, $0 < g_0 < \infty$, and the c.f. of X is $2\pi f_0 g = g/g_0$.

Clearly if X is a characteristic variable Y is also a characteristic variable, and there is a reciprocal relationship between the distributions of X and Y; we may call X, Y 'reciprocal characteristic variables' (on the line). Examples of reciprocal characteristic variables are:

$X_1 (N(0, a))$:
$$f(x) = \frac{1}{\sqrt{(2\pi a)}} \exp\left(-\frac{x^2}{2a}\right),$$

X_2 (Cauchy): $f(x) = \dfrac{1}{\pi} \dfrac{1}{1 + x^2}$,

X_3 (Triangular):
$$f(x) = \max(1 - |x|, 0),$$

$X_4 (\ln|\text{Cauchy}|)$: $f(x) = \dfrac{1}{\pi} \operatorname{sech} x$,

X_5: $f(x) = \tfrac{1}{2}a \operatorname{sech}^2 ax$,

X_6: $f(x) = \dfrac{x(e^a - \cos ax) - \sin ax}{\pi(e^a - 1)x(1 + x^2)}$,

$Y_1 (N(0, 1/a))$:
$$g(y) = \sqrt{\left(\frac{a}{2\pi}\right)} \exp\left(-\frac{ay^2}{2}\right)$$

Y_2 (Double exponential):
$$g(y) = \tfrac{1}{2}\exp(-|y|)$$

Y_3: $g(y) = \dfrac{1}{2\pi} \{\sin(\tfrac{1}{2}y)/(\tfrac{1}{2}y)\}^2$

Y_4: $g(y) = \tfrac{1}{2} \operatorname{sech}(\tfrac{1}{2}\pi y)$

Y_5: $g(y) = \dfrac{1}{\pi a}\left\{\left(\dfrac{\pi y}{2a}\right) \operatorname{cosech}\left(\dfrac{\pi y}{2a}\right)\right\}$

Y_6: $g(y) = \dfrac{e^{a-|y|} - 1}{2(e^a - 1 - a)}$ $(|y| < a)$,
$$= 0 \quad (|y| \geq a).$$

1.2. In the above examples, X_i and Y_i are both infinitely divisible (i.d.) in cases $i = 1,2,4,5$ and neither i.d. in cases $i = 3,6$. Such considerations suggest the following conjecture.

Conjecture C1.   Either both the characteristic variables in a reciprocal pair on the line are infinitely divisible, or neither.

This conjecture is to date unresolved. No counter-examples have been found; and the conjecture is also to some extent supported by the following consideration. It is well-known that the c.f. of an i.d. distribution has no real zeros. It is also true that the p.d.f. of an a.c. i.d. distribution has no real zeros; this result is stated below as Theorem A. Hence if X, Y are reciprocal characteristic variables and Y, say, is i.d., then its c.f. f/f_0 has no real zeros, thus X satisfies a necessary condition for being i.d., namely that its p.d.f. has no real zeros.

Theorem A (Sharpe).   The set of real zeros of the p.d.f. of an a.c. i.d. distribution is either empty or a closed half-line. In particular, the p.d.f. of an even a.c. i.d. distribution has no real zeros.

This was proved by Sharpe (1969), subject to the restriction that all positive powers $|\phi|^r$, where ϕ is the c.f. of the distribution, are integrable (thus excluding, for example, the double-exponential distribution). Details of the extension to the case of an even distribution not subject to this restriction will be given elsewhere.

2. Reciprocal distributions on the circle and on the integer lattice

2.1. The term 'lattice distribution' is commonly used for a discrete distribution on the line whose discontinuity points form a subset of a sequence of uniformly spaced points. In the particular case in which this sequence consists of the integers $\cdots, -1, 0, 1, 2, \cdots$ we will use the term 'integer lattice distribution'.

A reciprocal relationship analogous to that in Section 1.1 can be set up between a symmetric integer lattice distribution on the line — i.e., a *discrete* distribution supported on the integers $0, \pm 1, \pm 2, \cdots$, or a subset of them — and a symmetric *a.c.* distribution on the circle, noting that the c.f. of a distribution on the circle is defined only for integer values of the argument (see, e.g., Mardia (1972), p. 41), and that the c.f. of a lattice distribution having 0 as a lattice point is periodic. Suppose that X is an integer lattice 'characteristic variable', i.e., a lattice random variable with the following property: the probability function (p.f.) of X, f_x say ($x = 0$,

$\pm 1, \pm 2, \cdots)$, is at the same time the c.f., to within a norming factor, of a random variable Y on the circle. Then, as in Section 1.1, it is readily shown that

    (i) Y is a.c., and X, Y are both symmetric about 0.

    (ii)   If g is the p.d.f. of Y, then f_0, g_0 are finite and non-zero, and g/g_0, f/f_0 are the respective c.f.'s of X and Y.

    (iii) $g(y)/g_0 = \sum_{x=-\infty}^{\infty} f_x \cos yx, \quad f_x/f_0 = \int_{-\pi}^{\pi} g(y) \cos xy \, dy.$

    (iv) $2\pi f_0 g_0 = 1.$

For, since the c.f. of Y, which is proportional to f, is real, Y, and also X, must be symmetric about 0; thus f is even, $0 < f_0 < \infty$, and f/f_0 is the c.f. of Y. Since f is a p.f., $\sum_{x=-\infty}^{\infty} f_x^2 < \infty$, and it follows (Mardia (1972), pp. 42, 82) that Y is a.c. and has a p.d.f. g, periodic with period 2π, given by

$$g(y) = \frac{1}{2\pi} + \frac{1}{\pi} \sum_{r=1}^{\infty} (f_r/f_0) \cos ry.$$

Clearly $2\pi f_0 g_0 = 1$, $0 < g_0 < \infty$, and the c.f. of $X = f_0 + 2\sum_{x=1}^{\infty} f_x \cos tx = 2\pi f_0 g(t) = g(t)/g_0$. Since the c.f. of Y is f/f_0, $f_x/f_0 = \int_{-\pi}^{\pi} g(y) \cos xy \, dy$. The same results follow if we start with the assumption that Y is a characteristic variable on the circle, i.e., a random variable on the circle with p.d.f. g which is proportional to the c.f. of an integer lattice random variable X. There is again a reciprocal relationship; if Y is a characteristic variable so also is X, and *vice versa*. Examples of such reciprocal characteristic variables are:

X_7('Discrete normal'):

    $f_x = C \exp(-\tfrac{1}{2}\sigma^2 x^2),$
    $C = 1/\vartheta_3(0, e^{-\frac{1}{2}\sigma^2})$

Y_7 (Wrapped normal):

$$g(y) = \frac{1}{\sigma\sqrt{(2\pi)}} \sum_{j=-\infty}^{\infty} \exp\{-(y + 2j\pi)^2/2\sigma^2\}$$

X_8 (Double geometric):

    $f_x = \dfrac{1-q}{1+q} q^{|x|}$

    $X_9: f_x = e^{-k} I_x(k)$

Y_8 (Wrapped Cauchy):

$$g(y) = \frac{1}{2\pi} \frac{1-q^2}{1-2q\cos y + q^2}$$

Y_9 (von Mises):

$$g(y) = \frac{1}{2\pi I_0(k)} \exp(k \cos y).$$

2.2. The wrapped normal and wrapped Cauchy distributions Y_7 and Y_8 are clearly i.d. X_8 and X_9 are also i.d., X_8 being distributed as the difference between two independent geometric random variables each with parameter q, and X_9 as the difference between two independent Poisson random variables each with mean $k/2$. A problem of interest is whether or not the von Mises distribution Y_9 is i.d. Analogously to Conjecture C1 in Section 1.2 we may formulate the following conjecture (valid, e.g., for X_8, Y_8).

Conjecture C2. Of the characteristic variables in a reciprocal pair one on the circle and one on the integer lattice on the line, either both are i.d. or neither.

If Conjecture C2 were true, the infinite divisibility of the von Mises distribution would follow. We show below that the von Mises distribution is indeed infinitely divisible for some values at least of the parameter (Theorem B); but that Conjecture C2 is false.

It may be noted that close similarity has been shown to exist in various respects between the Y_7 and Y_9 distributions (Stephens (1963); Kendall (1974)). Note also that the analogue of Theorem A in Section 1.2 only holds in part. That is, an i.d. lattice random variable X unbounded in both directions has positive probability at every lattice point; but if X is a one-sided i.d. lattice random variable, with support confined say to points belonging to the sequence Σ: $(0, 1, 2, \cdots)$ and with $P(X = 0) > 0$, then there may be points of Σ, confined to a finite interval, at which X has zero probability. These results follow from the representation of an i.d. lattice distribution as a compound Poisson distribution and a result (Feller (1966), Lemma 2, p. 144) regarding the set formed by the points of increase of a distribution F on the line and its successive convolutions with itself, F^{2*}, $F^{3*}, \cdots$. A simple example of a one-sided i.d. lattice distribution with a 'gap' in its support sequence would be a compound Poisson mixture of random variables Z_n $(n = 0, 1, 2, \cdots)$ where $Z_n - 2n$ is (say) Poisson with mean $n\mu$; clearly $P(X = x) > 0$ for $x = 0, 2, 3, \cdots$, but $P(X = 1) = 0$.

Conjecture C2 *is false.* Proof by counter-example: Consider the reciprocal pair X_7, Y_7 defined above; Y_7 (wrapped normal) is i.d. We shall prove that X_7 is not i.d. Its c.f. is the entire function

$$\phi(t) = C \sum_{x=-\infty}^{\infty} \exp(-\tfrac{1}{2}\sigma^2 x^2)\cos xt$$

(1)

$$= \vartheta_3(t/2, q)/\vartheta_3(0, q)$$

where $q = e^{-\frac{1}{2}\sigma^2}$.

X_7 clearly has finite variance. If, therefore, it is i.d., $\phi(t)$ admits the Kolmogorov canonical representation

$$\ln \phi(t) = K(t), \text{ say}, = ict + \int_{-\infty}^{\infty} (e^{itx} - 1 - itx) \frac{dM(x)}{x^2}$$

where $M(x)$ is a non-decreasing bounded function such that $M(-\infty) = 0$; in other words $0 < M(\infty) < \infty$ and $M(x)/M(\infty)$ is a distribution function. Clearly $K(t)$ can be differentiated twice, giving

$$-K''(t) = \int_{-\infty}^{\infty} e^{itx} dM(x)$$
$$= M(\infty)\psi(t)$$

where $\psi(t)$ is a c.f. That is, a necessary condition for X_7 to be i.d. is that $-K''(t)$ should be proportional to a c.f.

In fact, (1) gives

$$K'(t) = \tfrac{1}{2} \vartheta_3'(t/2, q)/\vartheta_3(t/2, q) = 2\sum_{n=1}^{\infty} (-)^n q^n \sin nt /(1 - q^{2n}).$$

This series can be differentiated term by term since the derived series is uniformly convergent for $0 < q < 1$, hence

$$-K''(t) = 2\sum_{n=1}^{\infty} (-)^{n-1}\{nq^n/(1 - q^{2n})\}\cos nt.$$

This is the Fourier transform of a sequence on the integers whose signs are alternately positive and negative. It cannot therefore be proportional to a c.f., and the 'discrete normal' distribution X_7 cannot be i.d.

2.3. Reverting now to the von Mises distribution, we have the following theorem.

Theorem B.   The von Mises distribution with p.d.f.

$$(2) \qquad g(y) = \frac{1}{2\pi I_0(k)} \exp(k \cos y), \ y \in (-\pi, \pi], \qquad k > 0$$

is infinitely divisible for sufficiently small values of the concentration parameter k.

Consider first a function h which satisfies the following necessary conditions for being a c.f., whether on the line or the circle:

$$h(0) = 1, \ \bar{h}(t) = h(-t).$$

For any given positive integer n let $c = (c_0, c_1, \cdots, c_n)'$ be an arbitrary vector of complex quantities; let $t = (t_0, t_1, \cdots, t_n)'$ be an arbitrary vector of real quantities or an arbitrary vector of integers, according as the discussion relates to c.f.'s on the line or to c.f.'s on the circle; and write

$$S(n, c, t) = \sum_{i=0}^{n} \sum_{j=0}^{n} c_i \bar{c}_j h(t_i - t_j).$$

S is real. By Bochner's theorem, valid both on the line and on the circle, h is a c.f. iff

$$S(n, c, t) \geqq 0 \qquad \forall n, c, t.$$

For a real-valued function h, which must necessarily be even if it is to be a c.f., this condition reduces, on putting $c_j = a_j + ib_j$, $c = a + ib$, to

$$\sum_i \sum_j (a_i a_j + b_i b_j) h(t_i - t_j) \geqq 0 \qquad \forall n, \forall \text{ real } a, b, \forall t,$$

or equivalently

(3) $$\sum_i \sum_j a_i a_j h(t_i - t_j) \geqq 0 \qquad \forall n, \forall \text{ real } a, \forall t$$

or equivalently again to the statement that the matrix $\{h(t_i - t_j)\}$ is non-negative definite $\forall n, t$.

Now let $\phi(t)$ be a real-valued (and therefore even) c.f. on the circle, and suppose further that it is strictly positive, and hence has a real-valued logarithm, for all integer values of t. It will be i.d. iff

$$\{\phi(t)\}^r \text{ is a c.f. } \forall r > 0$$

which is clearly equivalent to

$$\{\phi(t)\}^r \text{ is a c.f. } \forall r \in (0, r^*]$$

for any positive r^* however small, since a distribution with c.f. $\{\phi(t)\}^s$ for any $s > r^*$ can be generated as the convolution of distributions whose c.f.'s have the form $\{\phi(t)\}^r$ with $r \in (0, r^*]$. Thus from (3) $\phi(t)$ is i.d. if, for any n, real a, and integer-valued t, there exists a positive r^* (which may depend on n, a, t) such that

(4) $$\sum_{i=0}^{n} \sum_{j=0}^{n} a_i a_j \{\phi(t_i - t_j)\}^r \geqq 0.$$

Denote $-\ln \phi(t)$ by $\lambda(t)$. $\lambda(t)$ is real, even, and non-negative $\forall\, t$, and $\lambda(0) = 0$. Since

$$\{\phi(t)\}^r = \exp\{-r\lambda(t)\} \geqq 1 - r\lambda(t),$$

$\phi(t)$ is i.d. from (4) if

$$\left(\sum_{i=0}^{n} a_i\right)^2 - r\sum_{i=0}^{n}\sum_{j=0}^{n} a_i a_j \lambda(t_i - t_j) \geqq 0 \quad \forall\, r \in (0, r^*],$$

i.e., if

(5) $$\sum_{i=0}^{n}\sum_{j=0}^{n} a_i a_j \lambda(t_i - t_j) \leqq 0 \quad \forall a \text{ for which } \sum_{i=0}^{n} a_i = 0.$$

Substituting $a_0 = -(a_1 + a_2 + \cdots + a_n)$, (5) becomes

(6) $$\sum_{i=1}^{n}\sum_{j=1}^{n} a_i a_j \{\lambda(t_i - t_0) + \lambda(t_j - t_0) - \lambda(t_i - t_j)\} \geqq 0 \quad \forall n, a_1, a_2, \cdots, a_n, t.$$

An equivalent statement is that the matrix

(7)
$$
\begin{bmatrix}
2\lambda(t_1 - t_0) & \cdots & \lambda(t_1 - t_0) + \lambda(t_n - t_0) - \lambda(t_1 - t_n) \\
\lambda(t_2 - t_0) + \lambda(t_1 - t_0) - \lambda(t_2 - t_1) & \cdots & \lambda(t_2 - t_0) + \lambda(t_n - t_0) - \lambda(t_2 - t_n) \\
\cdots\cdots\cdots & \cdots & \cdots\cdots\cdots\cdots \\
\lambda(t_n - t_0) + \lambda(t_1 - t_0) - \lambda(t_n - t_1) & \cdots & \cdots\, 2\lambda(t_n - t_0)
\end{bmatrix}
$$

is non-negative definite $\forall n$, $\forall t$.

Now particularise to the von Mises distribution (2). Its c.f. is

(8) $$\phi(t) = I_t(k)/I_0(k) \qquad (t = 0, \pm 1, \pm 2, \cdots),$$

which is even and strictly positive $\forall t$. For $t \geqq 0$, and small k,

(9)
$$\phi(t) = \frac{(k/2)^t}{\Gamma(t+1)}\{1 + o(k)\}$$
$$\lambda(t) = t\xi + \ln\Gamma(t+1) + o(k)$$

where

(10) $$\xi = -\ln(k/2) > 0.$$

In (6), (7) the $\{t_i\}$ are integers. We may without loss of generality take $0 = t_0 < t_1 < t_2 < \cdots$. The typical term

$$\lambda(t_i - t_0) + \lambda(t_j - t_0) - \lambda(t_i - t_j)$$

becomes, from (9),

$$\xi\{t_i + t_j - |t_i - t_j|\} + O(1) = 2\xi \min(t_i, t_j) + O(1).$$

As $k \to 0$, $\xi \to +\infty$. Thus for sufficiently small k the sign of the determinant of a matrix such as (7) will be the same as the sign of the determinant whose (i, j)th element is $\min(t_i, t_j)$. This latter determinant is

$$\begin{vmatrix} t_1 & t_1 & t_1 & \cdots & t_1 \\ t_1 & t_2 & t_2 & \cdots & t_2 \\ t_1 & t_2 & t_3 & \cdots & t_3 \\ \cdots\cdots\cdots\cdots & & \cdots & \cdots \\ t_1 & t_2 & t_3 & \cdots & t_n \end{vmatrix}$$

$$= t_1(t_2 - t_1)(t_3 - t_2)\cdots(t_n - t_{n-1}) \geqq 1$$

on subtracting the $(n - 1)$th column from the nth, then the $(n - 2)$th from the $(n - 1)$th, and so on.

All principal submatrices of the matrix (7) (i.e., having their principal diagonal elements on the principal diagonal of the parent matrix) are of the same form as (7), and their determinants are therefore positive for sufficiently small k. The infinite divisibility of the von Mises distribution follows for such values of k.

Acknowledgments

I am grateful to Dr. M. S. Bingham and Professor D. G. Kendall for helpful comments. My thanks are also due to Professor G. E. H. Reuter and Professor E. Lukacs for drawing my attention to Sharpe's work.

Note added in proof

Dr. Michael Bingham has most helpfully pointed out that the proof I have given of Theorem B is defective, since it does not establish that the matrix (7) is uniformly non-negative definite over some k-range independent of n. I have now shown that this condition is met, and that the von Mises distribution is therefore i.d., at any rate when $k < 0.16$. Details are somewhat lengthy and will be given elsewhere.

References

FELLER, W. (1966) *An Introduction to Probability Theory and its Applications*, Vol. II. John Wiley, New York.

KENDALL, D. G. (1974) Pole-seeking Brownian motion and bird navigation. *J. R. Statist. Soc.* B **36**, 365–417.

LUKACS, E. (1970) *Characteristic Functions.* 2nd edn. Griffin, London.
MARDIA, K. V. (1972) *Statistics of Directional Data.* Academic Press, London.
SHARPE, M. (1969) Zeros of infinitely divisible densities. *Ann. Math. Statist.* **40,** 1503–1505.
STEPHENS, M. A. (1963) Random walk on a circle. *Biometrika* **50,** 385–390.

On a Problem of Fluctuations of Sums of Independent Random Variables

LAJOS TAKÁCS

Abstract

The author determines the distribution and the limit distribution of the number of partial sums greater than k $(k = 0, 1, 2, \cdots)$ for n mutually independent and identically distributed discrete random variables taking on the integers $1, 0, -1, -2, \cdots$.

Introduction

Let $\xi_1, \xi_2, \cdots, \xi_r, \cdots$ be mutually independent and identically distributed real random variables and write $\zeta_r = \xi_1 + \xi_2 + \cdots + \xi_r$ for $r = 1, 2, \cdots$ and $\zeta_0 = 0$. Denote by $\Delta_n(k)$ the number of subscripts $r = 1, 2, \cdots, n$ for which $\zeta_r > k$ and let $\Delta_0(k) = 0$. In particular, we write $\Delta_n = \Delta_n(0)$.

The problem of finding the distribution of $\Delta_n(k)$ and the limiting distribution of $\Delta_n(k)/n$ as $n \to \infty$ has been studied extensively in the case when $k = 0$. In this paper we shall be concerned with the case of $k \geqq 0$ and find explicit results for a class of discrete random variables.

In 1939 P. Lévy ([6], 303–304) demonstrated that if

$$P\{\xi_r = 1\} = P\{\xi_r = -1\} = \tfrac{1}{2}.$$

then

(1) $$\lim_{n \to \infty} P\{(\Delta_n/n) \leqq x\} = 2\pi^{-1} \arcsin \sqrt{x}$$

for $0 \leqq x \leqq 1$. In 1947 P. Erdös and M. Kac [4] proved that if $E\{\xi_r\} = 0$ and $E\{\xi_r^2\} = 1$, then (1) holds unchangeably. In 1954 E. S. Andersen [3] proved that if

29

(2) $$\lim_{n \to \infty} P\{\zeta_n > 0\} = \alpha$$

where $0 \leqq \alpha \leqq 1$, then

(3) $$\lim_{n \to \infty} P\{(\Delta_n/n) \leqq x\} = F_\alpha(x)$$

exists. If $0 < \alpha < 1$, then

(4) $$F_\alpha(x) = (\sin \alpha\pi)\pi^{-1} \int_0^x u^{\alpha-1}(1-u)^{-\alpha} du$$

for $0 < x < 1$, $F_\alpha(x) = 0$ for $x \leqq 0$, $F_\alpha(x) = 1$ for $x \geqq 1$. If $\alpha = 0$ or $\alpha = 1$, then $F_0(x) = 0$ for $x < 0$, $F_0(x) = 1$ for $x \geqq 0$ and $F_1(x) = 0$ for $x < 1$, $F_1(x) = 1$ for $x \geqq 1$.

In 1956 F. Spitzer [7] proved that (3) holds also if we replace (2) by the weaker condition

(5) $$\lim_{n \to \infty} \frac{1}{n} \sum_{r=1}^n P\{\zeta_r > 0\} = \alpha.$$

For another proof of this result see C. C. Heyde [5].

The distribution of Δ_n for $n = 1, 2, \cdots$ can be obtained by the results of E. S. Andersen [2], [3]. In 1953 E. S. Andersen [2] proved a general theorem which implies that

(6) $$P\{\Delta_n = j\} = P\{\Delta_j = j\} P\{\Delta_{n-j} = 0\}$$

for $0 \leqq j \leqq n$. In 1954 E. S. Andersen [3] showed also that

(7) $$\sum_{n=0}^\infty P\{\Delta_n = 0\} z^n = \exp\left\{\sum_{n=1}^\infty P\{\zeta_n \leqq 0\} z^n/n\right\}$$

and

(8) $$\sum_{n=0}^\infty P\{\Delta_n = n\} z^n = \exp\left\{\sum_{n=1}^\infty P\{\zeta_n > 0\} z^n/n\right\}$$

for $|z| < 1$. Formulas (6), (7) and (8) completely determine the distribution of Δ_n for $n = 1, 2, \cdots$.

For example, if the random variables $\xi_1, \xi_2, \cdots, \xi_r, \cdots$ have a continuous and symmetric distribution, then it follows easily from (6) that

(9) $$P\{\Delta_n = j\} = \binom{2j}{j}\binom{2n-2j}{n-j} 2^{-2n}$$

for $0 \leqq j \leqq n$. (See E. S. Andersen [1].)

If the random variables $\xi_1, \xi_2, \cdots, \xi_r, \cdots$ have a stable distribution function with characteristic function

(10) $$E\{e^{i\omega\xi_r}\} = \exp\{-|\omega|^\alpha (1 - i\beta\omega|\omega|^{-1} \tan(\tfrac{1}{2}\alpha\pi))\}$$

where $0 < \alpha < 1$ or $1 < \alpha \le 2$ and $-1 \le \beta \le 1$, or $\alpha = 1$ and $\beta = 0$, then for $n = 1, 2, \cdots$ we have

(11) $$P\{\zeta_n > 0\} = q = \tfrac{1}{2} + (\alpha\pi)^{-1} \arctan(\beta \tan(\tfrac{1}{2}\alpha\pi))$$

where $-\tfrac{1}{2}\pi < \arctan x < \tfrac{1}{2}\pi$ and thus by (7) and (8) we obtain that

(12) $$P\{\Delta_n = j\} = (-1)^n \binom{-q}{j}\binom{q-1}{n-j} = \binom{j+q-1}{j}\binom{n-j-q}{n-j}$$

for $0 \le j \le n$.

However, if we assume, for example, that $P\{\xi_r = 1\} = P\{\xi_r = -1\} = \tfrac{1}{2}$, then the determination of $P\{\Delta_n = j\}$ by (7) and (8) is somewhat involved. In this case (7) reduces to

(13) $$\sum_{n=0}^{\infty} P\{\Delta_n = 0\} z^n = \left[\frac{1 + \sqrt{(1 - z^2)}}{2(1 - z)}\right]^{1/2}$$

and (8) reduces to

(14) $$\sum_{n=0}^{\infty} P\{\Delta_n = n\} z^n = \left[\frac{2 - 2\sqrt{(1 - z^2)}}{z^2(1 - z)}\right]^{1/2}$$

for $|z| < 1$. Hence by Lagrange expansion we obtain that

(15) $$P\{\Delta_n = 0\} = \binom{2n}{n} 2^{-2n} + \sum_{r=1}^{[n/2]} (2r + 1)^{-1} \binom{4r}{2r}\binom{2n - 4r}{n - 2r} 2^{-2n}$$

and

(16) $$P\{\Delta_n = n\} = \binom{2n}{n} 2^{-2n} - \sum_{r=1}^{[n/2]} (4r - 1)^{-1} \binom{4r}{2r}\binom{2n - 4r}{n - 2r} 2^{-2n}.$$

It is not readily seen that (15) and (16) can also be expressed in the following simple forms

(17) $$P\{\Delta_n = 0\} = \binom{n}{[\tfrac{1}{2}n]} 2^{-n}$$

and

(18) $$P\{\Delta_n = n\} = \binom{n-1}{[\frac{1}{2}n]} 2^{-n}$$

for $n \geq 0$. Formulas (17) and (18) can be deduced from the general results of this paper.

2. The distribution of $\Delta_n(k)$

In what follows we assume that $\xi_r = 1 - \nu_r \; (r = 1, 2, \cdots)$ where $\nu_1, \nu_2, \cdots, \nu_r, \cdots$ are mutually independent and identically distributed discrete random variables taking on non-negative integers only. We write $N_r = \nu_1 + \nu_2 + \cdots + \nu_r$ for $r = 1, 2, \cdots$ and $N_0 = 0$. In this case $\Delta_n(k)$ is the number of subscripts $r = 1, 2, \cdots, n$ for which $r - N_r > k$. We shall determine explicitly the distribution of $\Delta_n(k)$ for $k = 0, 1, 2, \cdots$ and $n = 1, 2, \cdots$ and the limiting distribution of $\Delta_n(k)$ as $n \to \infty$.

The proofs are based on a simple theorem which was found in 1960 by the author [8]. By this theorem we have

(19) $\quad P\{N_r < r \text{ for } 1 \leq r \leq n \mid N_n = i\} = \begin{cases} (n-i)/n & \text{for } 0 \leq i \leq n, \\ 0 & \text{for } i \geq n, \end{cases}$

provided that $P\{N_n = i\} > 0$. This formula can easily be proved by mathematical induction.

Now let us define $\rho(k)$ as the smallest $r = 0, 1, 2, \cdots$ for which $r - N_r = k$, and $\rho(k) = \infty$ if there is no such r. By (19) it follows immediately that

(20) $$P\{\rho(k) = r\} = \frac{k}{r} P\{r - N_r = k\}$$

for $1 \leq k \leq r$.

Furthermore, let us define

(21) $\qquad P(n, k) = P\{N_r - r < k \quad \text{for } 1 \leq r \leq n\}$

and

(22) $\qquad Q(n, k) = P\{r - N_r < k \quad \text{for } 1 \leq r \leq n\}$

for $n \geq 1$ and let $P(0, k) = Q(0, k) = 1$ for $k \geq 0$.

By (19) we get

(23) $$P(n, 0) = \sum_{i=0}^{n} ((n-i)/n) \, P\{N_n = i\}$$

for $n \geq 1$.

Since $Q(n, k) = P\{\rho(k) > n\}$, it follows from (20) that

$$(24) \qquad Q(n, k) = 1 - \sum_{i=k}^{n} \frac{k}{i} P\{N_i = i - k\}$$

for $1 \leq k \leq n$, and $Q(n, k) = 0$ if $1 \leq n < k$.

Theorem 1.   Let $\nu_1, \nu_2, \cdots, \nu_r, \cdots$ be mutually independent and identically distributed discrete random variables taking on non-negative integers only. Let $N_r = \nu_1 + \cdots + \nu_r$ for $r = 1, 2, \cdots$ and $N_0 = 0$. Denote by $\Delta_n(k)$ the number of subscripts $r = 1, 2, \cdots, n$ for which $r - N_r > k$. Then we have

$$(25) \qquad P\{\Delta_n(k) = 0\} = Q(n, k + 1)$$

for $k \geq 0$ and $n \geq 1$,

$$(26) \qquad P\{\Delta_n(0) = j\} = P(j, 0) Q(n - j, 1)$$

for $j \geq 0$ and $n \geq 1$, and

$$(27) \qquad P\{\Delta_n(k) = j\} = P(j, 0)[Q(n - j, k + 1) - Q(n - j, k)]$$

for $j > 0$, $k > 0$ and $n \geq 1$ where $P(n, 0)$ is given by (23) and $Q(n, k)$ is given by (24) for $n \geq 1$ and $P(0, k) = Q(0, k) = 1$ for $k \geq 0$.

Proof.   Formula (25) is obvious and (26) follows from (6). To prove (27) let us observe that if $j > 0$ and $k > 0$, then the event $\Delta_n(k) = j$ can occur in such a way that $\rho(k) = r$ for some $r = k, \cdots, n - j$ and $s - N_s > r - N_r$ for exactly j subscripts $s = r + 1, \cdots, n$. Thus we get

$$(28) \qquad P\{\Delta_n(k) = j\} = \sum_{r=k}^{n-j} P\{\rho(k) = r\} P\{\Delta_{n-r} = j\}$$

for $j > 0$, $k > 0$ and $n \geq 1$. By (6) we can write that

$$(29) \qquad P\{\Delta_n(k) = j\} = P\{\Delta_j = j\} \sum_{r=k}^{n-j} P\{\rho(k) = r\} P\{\Delta_{n-r-j} = 0\}$$

for $j > 0$, $k > 0$ and $n \geq 1$. This formula already determines $P\{\Delta_n(k) = j\}$ by (25) and (26); however, we can simplify (29) further. If we take into consideration that $\rho(k + 1) > n$ can occur in such a way that either $\rho(k) > n$ or $\rho(k) = r$ where $k \leq r \leq n$ and $s - N_s \leq r - N_r$ for $r \leq s \leq n$, then we have

(30) $Q(n, k + 1) = Q(n, k) + \sum_{r=k}^{n} \boldsymbol{P}\{\rho(k) = r\}\, \boldsymbol{P}\{\Delta_{n-r} = 0\}$

for $k > 0$ and $n \geq 1$. By (30) we can express the sum in (29) as $Q(n - j, k + 1) - Q(n - j, k)$. Since $\boldsymbol{P}\{\Delta_j = j\} = P(j, 0)$ for $j > 0$, by (29) we obtain (27) which was to be proved.

3. An example

Let us suppose that $\boldsymbol{P}\{\nu_r = 2\} = p$ and $\boldsymbol{P}\{\nu_r = 0\} = q$ where $p > 0$, $q > 0$ and $p + q = 1$. In this case the random variables $r - N_r$ $(r = 0,1,2,\cdots)$ describe a one-dimensional random walk, and by the reflection principle we obtain easily that

(31) $P(n, k) = \boldsymbol{P}\{N_r - r < k\} - (p/q)^k \boldsymbol{P}\{N_r - r < -k\}$

and

(32) $Q(n, k) = \boldsymbol{P}\{r - N_r < k\} - (q/p)^k \boldsymbol{P}\{r - N_r < -k\}$

for $k \geq 1$ and $n \geq 1$. Obviously

(33) $P(n, 0) = q\, P(n - 1, 1)$ and $Q(n, 0) = p\, Q(n - 1, 1)$

for $n \geq 1$. These formulas determine the distribution of $\Delta_n(k)$ for $k \geq 0$ and $n \geq 1$ by (25), (26) and (27). If, in particular, $p = q = \frac{1}{2}$, then we have

$$P(n, 1) = Q(n, 1) = \boldsymbol{P}\{N_n - n = 0\} + \boldsymbol{P}\{N_n - n = 1\}$$

(34)

$$= \binom{n}{[\frac{1}{2}n]} 2^{-n}$$

for $n \geq 0$,

(35) $$P(n, 0) = Q(n, 0) = \binom{n - 1}{[\frac{1}{2}n]} 2^{-n}$$

for $n \geq 0$, and

$$Q(n, k + 1) - Q(n, k) = \boldsymbol{P}\{n - N_n = k\} + \boldsymbol{P}\{n - N_n = k + 1\}$$

(36)

$$= \binom{n}{[\frac{1}{2}(n + k + 1)]} 2^{-n}$$

for $k \geq 0$ and $n \geq 1$. Accordingly, if $p = q = \frac{1}{2}$, then

$$(37) \qquad P\{\Delta_n(k) = 0\} = \sum_{n-k-1 \leq 2s \leq n+k} \binom{n}{s} 2^{-n}$$

for $k \geq 0$, and

$$(38) \qquad P\{\Delta_n(k) = j\} = \binom{j-1}{[\frac{1}{2}j]} \binom{n-j}{[\frac{1}{2}(n-j+k+1)]} 2^{-n}$$

for $1 \leq j \leq n$ and $k \geq 0$. It seems this is a new result for a symmetric random walk.

4. Limit distributions

Let us write

$$(39) \qquad \gamma = E\{\nu_r\} = \sum_{n=0}^{\infty} n P\{\nu_r = n\}$$

and

$$(40) \qquad \pi(z) = E\{z^{\nu_r}\} = \sum_{n=0}^{\infty} P\{\nu_r = n\} z^n$$

for $|z| \leq 1$.

Theorem 2. If $k \geq 0$, then

$$(41) \qquad \lim_{n \to \infty} P\{\Delta_n(k) = 0\} = 1 - \delta^{k+1}$$

and

$$(42) \qquad \lim_{n \to \infty} P\{\Delta_n(k) = j\} = (1 - \delta)\delta^k P(j, 0)$$

for $j = 1, 2, \cdots$ where $P(j, 0)$ is given by (23) and $z = \delta$ is the smallest non-negative real root of the equation $\pi(z) = z$. If $\gamma > 1$, then $0 \leq \delta < 1$. If $P\{\nu_r = 1\} = 1$, then $\delta = 0$, and if $\gamma \leq 1$ and $P\{\nu_r = 1\} < 1$, then $\delta = 1$.

Proof. By the results of reference [9] p. 25, we have

$$(43) \qquad \lim_{n \to \infty} Q(n, k) = 1 - \delta^k$$

for $k = 1, 2, \cdots$. Thus (41) and (42) follow immediately from (25) and (27).

Theorem 3. If $j \geq 0$, then

$$(44) \qquad \lim_{n \to \infty} P\{\Delta_n(0) = n - j\} = [1 - \gamma]^+ Q(j, 1),$$

and if $k \geq 1$ and $j \geq 0$, then

(45) $\lim\limits_{n \to \infty} P\{\Delta_n(k) = n - j\} = [1 - \gamma]^+ \{Q(j, k + 1) - Q(j, k)\}$

where $[1 - \gamma]^+ = \max(0, 1 - \gamma)$ and $Q(j, k)$ is given by (24).

Proof. By (23) we have

(46) $\lim\limits_{n \to \infty} P(n, 0) = \lim\limits_{n \to \infty} E\{[(n - N_n)/n]^+\} = [1 - \gamma]^+$

and thus (44) and (45) follow from (26) and (27).

Accordingly, if $\gamma > 1$, then $\Delta_n(k)$ has a proper limiting distribution as $n \to \infty$, whereas, if $\gamma < 1$, then $n - \Delta_n(k)$ has a proper limiting distribution as $n \to \infty$. If $\gamma = 1$ then in order that the limiting distribution of $\Delta_n(k)/n$ exists as $n \to \infty$ it is necessary and sufficient that

(47) $\lim\limits_{n \to \infty} E(\{\Delta_n\}/n) = \lim\limits_{n \to \infty} \frac{1}{n} \sum\limits_{r=1}^{n} P\{N_r < r\} = \alpha$

where $0 \leq \alpha \leq 1$.

If (47) holds, then

(48) $\lim\limits_{n \to \infty} P\{(\Delta_n(k)/n) \leq x\} = F_\alpha(x)$

exists for $k \geq 0$ and is independent of k. Here $F_\alpha(x)$ is defined by (4) for $0 < \alpha < 1$ and $F_0(x) = 0$ for $x < 0$, $F_0(x) = 1$ for $x \geq 0$, $F_1(x) = 0$ for $x < 1$, $F_1(x) = 1$ for $x \geq 1$. If $k = 0$, then this follows from (3). If $k \geq 0$, then by (28) we can prove that (48) is independent of k. Conversely, if the limiting distribution (48) exists, then the limit (47) necessarily exists and is equal to the first moment of the limiting distribution function.

References

[1] ANDERSEN, E. S. (1949) On the number of positive sums of random variables. *Skand. Aktuarietidskr.* **32**, 27–36.

[2] ANDERSEN, E. S. (1953) On sums of symmetrically dependent random variables. *Skand. Aktuarietidskr.* **36**, 123–138.

[3] ANDERSEN, E. S. (1954) On the fluctuations of sums of random variables, II. *Math. Scand.* **2**, 195–223.

[4] ERDÖS. P. AND KAC, M. (1947) On the number of positive sums of independent random variables. *Bull. Amer. Math. Soc.* **53**, 1011–1020.

[5] HEYDE, C. C. (1967) Some local limit results in fluctuation theory. *J. Austral. Math. Soc.* **7**, 455–464.

[6] LÉVY, P. (1939) Sur certains processus stochastiques homogènes. *Compositio Math.* **7**, 283–339.

[7] SPITZER, F. (1956) A combinatorial lemma and its application to probability theory. *Trans. Amer. Math. Soc.* **82**, 323–339.

[8] TAKÁCS, L. (1961) The probability law of the busy period for two types of queuing processes. *Operat. Res.* **9**, 402–407.

[9] TAKÁCS, L. (1967) *Combinatorial Methods in the Theory of Stochastic Processes.* John Wiley, New York.

PART III

STATISTICAL THEORY

On the Geometry of Estimation

G. A. BARNARD

Abstract

The conditional inference approach is shown to extend to the general regression problem and to give exact inferences for entirely arbitrary distributions.

1. Introduction

Bartlett's paper (1934) on the geometry of a sample was a beacon of light amidst a somewhat murky gloom for many of us who were trying to work through the mathematics of statistics in the late nineteen thirties and forties, unaided (some might say, unhindered!) by the mass of textbooks now available. Since then we have all become much more familiar with matrix manipulation, and perhaps less familiar with geometry; but it still may be of interest to present, with geometrical interpretation, an extension of an argument due essentially to Fisher (1934), which has application to a problem of current interest—the treatment of regression theory when the distributions involved are non-normal.

2. Formulation of the problem

To simplify the exposition we shall make the unrealistic assumption that the scale parameter (usually, but not necessarily, the variance) of the error distribution is known. We shall indicate at the end how this assumption can be removed without seriously affecting the argument. At the same time, we generalise the usual model by taking the joint error distribution to be entirely arbitrary. Thus our treatment covers, for

41

example, the case of stable distributions with infinite variance discussed recently by Mandelbrojt and others, in connection with economic and meteorological phenomena, and the case of non-independent errors.

Suppose, then, that we have an $m \times 1$ vector Y of observations, linearly related to an $n \times 1$ vector of unknown parameters θ by

$$Y = X\theta + E$$

where X is a known $m \times n$ matrix of full rank, and E is an error vector whose distribution is known to have density function ϕ, a known function. Geometrically (Figure 1), in m-dimensional space the observations are represented by (the coordinates of) a point Y while the unknown point $X\theta$ is known to lie in the linear subspace $\{S\}$ spanned by the columns of X. The vector E is then represented by the line joining the point $X\theta$ to the point Y.

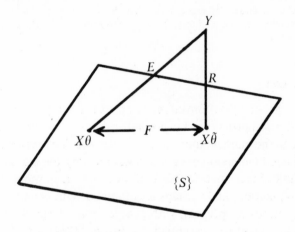

Figure 1

Now this vector E can be split into two parts

$$E = F + R$$

where F lies in $\{S\}$ and R lies in the orthogonal complement of $\{S\}$. Since F lies in $\{S\}$ there will be an $n \times 1$ vector $\tilde{\theta}$ such that

$$F = X\tilde{\theta} - X\theta$$

and then

$$R = Y - X\tilde{\theta}.$$

The point $X\tilde{\theta}$ will be the foot of the perpendicular from Y to $\{S\}$, i.e., it will be that point in $\{S\}$ whose squared distance from Y is least. In other words, $\tilde{\theta}$ will be the ordinary least squares solution of the equations

$$Y = X\theta + \text{residual},$$

namely

$$\tilde{\theta} = (X'X)^{-1}X'Y.$$

Since F is constrained to lie in $\{S\}$, it has n independent components, while R will have $m - n$ independent components.

Now suppose we were informed of the value of Y by first being told the vector R, and then being told $\tilde{\theta}$—and hence $X\tilde{\theta}$. Knowing R, we know that the observation point lies in a plane $\{S\} + R$, parallel to $\{S\}$ and obtained from it by shifting it through the vector R. The probability function for R will be obtained by integrating the probability function of Y, $\phi(Y - X\theta)$, over $\{S\} + R$ and this will not depend on θ. The information about θ will be contained in $\tilde{\theta}$. And since we know R, the relevant distribution of $\tilde{\theta}$ will be its conditional distribution given R.

Because the transformations leading from E to (F, R) are 1-1 and linear, their Jacobian is constant and the joint probability function of (F, R) is proportional to $\phi(E)$, with E expressed in terms of F and R as

$$\phi(R + X(\tilde{\theta} - \theta));$$

this expression will, after renormalisation, give us the conditional probability function of $\tilde{\theta}$ if we treat R as fixed as well as X. Thus the original m observations Y, with probability function $\phi(Y - X\theta)$ are equivalent to n observations $\tilde{\theta}$, with probability function proportional to

$$\phi(R + X(\tilde{\theta} - \theta)).$$

3. A numerical illustration

To illustrate numerically, let us suppose we have four observations

$$1.1 = \theta_1 - \theta_2 + E_1, \quad 2.3 = \theta_1 - \theta_2 + E_2,$$

$$0.2 = \theta_1 + \theta_2 + E_3, \quad 3.6 = \theta_1 + \theta_2 + E_4.$$

We easily find $\tilde{\theta}_1 = 1.8$, $\tilde{\theta}_2 = 0.1$, and then the residuals $R_1 = -0.6$, $R_2 = +0.6$, $R_3 = -1.7$, $R_4 = +1.7$. If the errors are independent Cauchy variables,

$$\pi^4 \phi(E) = \prod_i (1 + E_i^2)^{-1} \qquad i = 1,2,3,4,$$

and writing $D_1 = \bar{\theta}_1 - \theta_1$, $D_2 = \bar{\theta}_2 - \theta_2$, the joint conditional density of D_1 and D_2 is, apart from the normalising factor,

$$\{(1 + (-.6 + (D_1 - D_2))^2)(1 + (.6 + (D_1 - D_2))^2)(1 + (-1.7 + (D_1 + D_2))^2)$$

$$\times (1 + (1.7 + (D_1 + D_2))^2)\}^{-1} = \{((1.36 + (D_1 - D_2)^2)^2 - 1.44(D_1 - D_2)^2)$$

$$\times ((3.89 + (D_1 + D_2)^2)^2 - 11.56(D_1 + D_2)^2)\}^{-1} = \psi(D_1, D_2), \text{ say.}$$

If we write

$$K^{-1} = \int \int \psi(D_1, D_2) dD_1, D_2,$$

then the four observations given above are equivalent to two observations $\bar{\theta}_1 = 1.8$, $\bar{\theta}_2 = 0.1$ with joint density function $K\psi\,(\bar{\theta}_1 - \theta_1, \bar{\theta}_2 - \theta_2)$. If we wish to test whether the observations are consistent with the hypothesis $\theta_2 = 0$, in the absence of knowledge of θ_1, we can use the marginal distribution of $\bar{\theta}_2$, given by

$$\psi_2(\bar{\theta}_2 - \theta_2) = K \int \psi(D_1, \bar{\theta}_2 - \theta_2) dD_1$$

and the (one-sided) tail area for our data will be $\int_{0.1}^{\infty} \psi_2(t) dt$.

4. A further example

As another illustration, let us suppose, with the general set-up

$$Y = X\theta + E$$

that the joint density of the errors is

$$\phi(E) = (2\pi)^{-\frac{1}{2}m} |v|^{-\frac{1}{2}} \exp\{-\tfrac{1}{2}E' v^{-1} E\},$$

that is, that the errors are normally distributed but with covariance matrix v. We find in this case that the conditional joint density of $\bar{\theta} - \theta$ is proportional to

$$\exp\{-\tfrac{1}{2}[(R + X\bar{\theta} - X\theta)' v^{-1}(R + X\bar{\theta} - X\theta)]\}$$

which is proportional to

$$\exp\{-\tfrac{1}{2}[(\bar{\theta} - \theta)' X' v^{-1} X(\bar{\theta} - \theta) + wR' v^{-1} X(\bar{\theta} - \theta)]\}.$$

Recalling that if Z is normal with vector mean μ and variance w its density function is, apart from a normalising constant,

$$\exp\{-\tfrac{1}{2}(Z'w^{-1}Z - 2\mu'w^{-1}Z)\},$$

we can see that the conditional distribution of $\tilde{\theta} - \theta$ is normal with variance matrix $(X'v^{-1}X)^{-1}$ and mean $-(X'v^{-1}X)^{-1}X'v^{-1}R$. Thus, to obtain observations normally distributed about θ we should take

$$\begin{aligned}
\tilde{\theta} &= \tilde{\theta} + (X'v^{-1}X)^{-1}X'v^{-1}R \\
&= \tilde{\theta} + (X'v^{-1}X)^{-1}X'v^{-1}(Y - X(X'X)^{-1}X'Y) \\
&= (X'v^{-1}X)^{-1}X'v^{-1}Y
\end{aligned}$$

which is the usual maximum likelihood estimator in this case. The equivalence of the original observations to $\tilde{\theta}$ can, of course, be derived from sufficiency considerations; it should be noted that such considerations do not enter into the present form of argument. For instance, in the first example, when the observations have Cauchy distributions, no sufficient statistics having the dimension of the unknown vector θ exist; but the reduction to the equivalent observations is fully efficient. Apart from seeing that this must be true, since all transformations involved are 1-1 and hence information-preserving, while the only conditioning is upon known values having known distributions, it is also clear that there is no loss of information because the likelihood function derived from the observations $\tilde{\theta}$, with their conditional distribution, is the same as that derived from the original observations. This fact is easily verified from the form given above for the conditional probability function of $\tilde{\theta}$.

5. Case of unknown scale parameter

If the scale parameter σ is unknown, the distribution of R is no longer known, independent of unknown parameters, so that its use for conditioning involves losing information on σ. However, if we transform R to polar coordinates, $R = r \wedge$, where r is the length of R and $\wedge$ is a vector of direction cosines, the distribution of $\wedge$ does not involve σ and so fully efficient conditioning on $\wedge$ is possible. We are left with $\tilde{\theta} - \theta$ as before, except that this is now divided by σ, but in addition we have a further variable r/σ in the conditioned distribution. Also, since the transformation to polars is not linear, a factor $(r/\sigma)^{m-1}$ is introduced into the conditioned distribution. If probability statements about the θ are needed which do not involve the unknown σ, these can be obtained by a further transformation in the conditioned distribution to

$$t = ((\tilde{\theta} - \theta)/\sigma)/(r/\sigma)$$

and

$$z = r/\sigma$$

followed by taking the marginal distribution with z integrated out. If the original observations are normally distributed, this operation will give the usual set of Student's t variables; but of course we shall obtain different distributions if the original observations are not normal.

Reference

BARTLETT, M. S. (1934) The vector representation of a sample. *Proc. Camb. Phil. Soc.* **30**, 327–340.

FISHER, R. A. (1934) Two new properties of mathematical likelihood. *Proc. Roy. Soc.* A **144**, 285–307.

Prediction Intervals and Empirical Bayes Confidence Intervals

D. R. COX

Abstract

Approximate parametric prediction intervals are obtained for an unobserved random variable when the amount of data on which to base the estimation is large. Applications include the construction of approximate confidence intervals in empirical Bayes estimation.

1. Introduction

Most formulations of statistical inference focus on statements about unknown parameters. Sometimes, however, it is required to consider explicitly the value of an as yet unobserved random variable having a distribution related to the distribution of the data. Familiar examples are the prediction of a future observation in normal-theory linear regression and the prediction of time series.

The objects of this paper are first to give a rather general solution for prediction intervals when the amount of data is large and secondly to apply the results, in particular, to give confidence intervals in parametric empirical Bayes estimation.

2. Prediction intervals

It is useful to outline first a relation between prediction intervals and the theory of similar tests which sometimes leads to a simple 'exact' set of prediction intervals (Guttman (1970), p. 36). Let Y be an observed random variable with probability density $f(y; \theta)$, depending on an unknown parameter θ. Let Z^+ be an as yet unobserved random variable with probability density $g(z; \theta)$. We deal first for simplicity with the situation where Y and $Z^\dagger$ are independent. Both Y and $Z^\dagger$, and also θ, may be vectors.

A prediction region of size $1 - \alpha$ for $Z^\dagger$ is found by constructing a size α critical region, w_α, in the sample space of $(Y, Z^\dagger)$ for testing the notional null hypothesis $\theta = \theta^\dagger$ from observations on $(Y, Z^\dagger)$, where $Z^\dagger$ has density $g(z; \theta^\dagger)$. For a similar region is such that

$$\mathrm{pr}\{(Y, Z^\dagger) \in w_\alpha ; \theta^\dagger = \theta\} = \alpha.$$

Hence if

$$P_{1-\alpha} = \{z^\dagger; (y, z^\dagger) \notin w_\alpha\}$$

we have that for all θ

(1) $$\mathrm{pr}(Z^\dagger \in P_{1-\alpha} ; \theta) = 1 - \alpha.$$

The interpretation of (1) in terms of hypothetical frequencies is over repetitions of Y and $Z^\dagger$ and not over repetitions of $Z^\dagger$ for fixed $Y = y$. If the similar region has optimum power properties, the prediction region $P_{1-\alpha}$ has a corresponding property which is, roughly, that the region is chosen to discriminate as sharply as possible from the distribution that $Z^\dagger$ would have for $\theta^\dagger \neq \theta$. Different kinds of regions $P_{1-\alpha}$, e.g., intervals, upper limits, lower limits, etc., are obtained depending on the specification of notional alternative hypotheses. When θ is a vector, it will often be desirable or necessary to take $\theta^\dagger$ as differing from θ in just one component.

Unfortunately this 'exact' approach is applicable only to special rather simple problems.

3. An asymptotic solution

For an approximate solution it is natural to suppose that Y has a large number n of components, thus allowing precise estimation of θ, but that the dimensions of $Z^\dagger$ remain small. This precludes the use of the usual theory of asymptotic tests. In particular cases we can proceed directly with an approximate version of (1). For example, if θ is a location parameter for both Y and $Z^\dagger$, and V is an estimate of θ, then $Z^\dagger - V$ has a distribution not involving θ and to complete the solution an approximation to the distribution of $Z^\dagger - V$ has to be found.

For a general treatment it is, however, easier to proceed slightly differently. We suppose that $Z^\dagger$ is scalar and continuously distributed and that a lower limit at level α is required. Further, to begin with, suppose that $Z^\dagger$ and Y are independent. Let $G(z; \theta)$ be the cumulative distribution function of $Z^\dagger$ and $q_\alpha(\theta)$ its lower α quantile, i.e.,

$$(2) \qquad G\{q_\alpha(\theta); \theta\} = \alpha.$$

From Y we form an estimate V of θ with

$$E(V; \theta) = \theta + a(\theta)/n + o(1/n),$$

(3)

$$\text{var}(V; \theta) = b(\theta)/n + o(1/n).$$

If θ is a $p \times 1$ column vector, so too is $a(\theta)$ and $b(\theta)$ is a $p \times p$ covariance matrix.

If θ were known, we would take $q_\alpha(\theta)$ as the required lower limit. With θ unknown, a first approximation is $q_\alpha(V)$. To find a second approximation, we can either modify V or start from $q_\alpha(V)$ and then argue as follows. First, for $V = v$,

$$\text{pr}\{Z^\dagger \leqslant q_{\alpha'}(v); \theta\} = G\{q_{\alpha'}(v); \theta\}.$$

Therefore

$$(4) \qquad \text{pr}\{Z^\dagger \leqslant q_{\alpha'}(V); \theta\} = E[G\{q_{\alpha'}(V); \theta\}].$$

The expectation on the right-hand side of (4) can now be approximated via Taylor's theorem. If θ and hence V are scalars, we get, under some regularity conditions, that

$$\text{pr}\{Z^\dagger \leqslant q_{\alpha'}(V); \theta\} = G\{q_{\alpha'}(\theta); \theta\} + \frac{a(\theta)}{n}\left[\frac{\partial G\{q_{\alpha'}(v); \theta\}}{\partial v}\right]_{v=\theta}$$

(5)

$$+ \frac{1}{2}\frac{b(\theta)}{n}\left[\frac{\partial^2 G\{q_{\alpha'}(v); \theta\}}{\partial v^2}\right]_{v=\theta} + o(1/n)$$

$$(6) \qquad = \alpha' + c_{\alpha'}(\theta)/n,$$

say. If θ and V are vectors, the second and third terms of (5) have to be interpreted respectively as

$$n^{-1}\Sigma a_r(\theta)[\partial G/\partial v_r] \quad \text{and} \quad \tfrac{1}{2}n^{-1}\Sigma b_{rs}(\theta)[\partial^2 G/\partial v_r \partial v_s].$$

From (6) it follows that if we take

(7) $\alpha' = \alpha - c_\alpha(v)/n,$

the required probability property holds to higher order.

In applications to time series and empirical Bayes estimation, Y and $Z^\dagger$ are not independent. We suppose that there is a function U of Y such that

$$\mathrm{pr}(Z^\dagger \leqslant z \mid Y = y; \theta) = G(z, u; \theta).$$

The conditional quantile $q_\alpha(\theta, u)$ is defined by

(8) $G\{q_\alpha(\theta, u), u; \theta\} = \alpha$

and the argument leading to (6) can be repeated, conditionally on $U = u$, provided that we replace (3) by

$$E(V \mid U = u; \theta) = \theta + a(\theta, u)/n + o(1/n),$$
(9)
$$\mathrm{var}(V \mid U = u; \theta) = b(\theta, u)/n + o(1/n).$$

We end by amending (7) to

(10) $\alpha' = \alpha - c_\alpha(v, u)/n.$

Examples are given in Sections 4 and 6.

4. Some examples

While the procedure based on (7) and (10) is in principle very general, realistic examples tend to be complicated and therefore quite simple special cases are studied here.

First consider about the simplest prediction problem, where $Y = (Y_1, \cdots, Y_n)$ are independently and identically normally distributed with unknown mean θ and known variance σ_0^2 and $Z^\dagger$ has independently the same distribution. Of course, this has the simple 'exact' solution, obtainable for example by the procedure of Section 2, in which the required limit is

(11) $\bar{y} - k_\alpha^* \sigma_0 \sqrt{(1 + 1/n)},$

where $\bar{y} = \Sigma y_i/n$, $\Phi(k_\alpha^*) = 1 - \alpha$ and $\Phi(\cdot)$ is the standard normal integral.

To apply the approximate procedure of Section 3 we take $V = \Sigma Y_i/n$, $a(\theta) = 0$, $b(\theta) = \sigma_0^2$,

$$q_\alpha(\theta) = \theta - k_\alpha^* \sigma_0,$$

$$G\{q_\alpha(v); \theta\} = \Phi\left(\frac{v - \theta}{\sigma_0} - k_\alpha^*\right).$$

Thus

$$c_\alpha(\theta) = \tfrac{1}{2}\sigma_0^2\left[\frac{\partial^2}{\partial v^2}\Phi\left(\frac{v - \theta}{\sigma_0} - k_\alpha^*\right)\right]_{v = \theta}$$

$$= \tfrac{1}{2}k_\alpha^*\phi(-k_\alpha^*),$$

where

$$\phi(x) = \frac{1}{\sqrt{(2\pi)}}e^{-x^2/2}.$$

Therefore we take

(12)
$$\alpha' = \alpha - \frac{k_\alpha^*}{2n}\phi(-k_\alpha^*),$$

the required lower limit being

(13)
$$\bar{y} - k_{\alpha'}^* \sigma_0.$$

The agreement between (11) and (13) is close even for $n = 10$.

As a second simple example, which can also be treated directly but which is one where $Z^\dagger$ and Y are not independent, consider the Gaussian first-order autoregressive process in which

(14)
$$Y_s = \theta + \lambda_0(Y_{s-1} - \theta) + \epsilon_s.$$

We take a simple if unrealistic case where λ_0 and σ_0^2, the variance of the Gaussian innovation process ϵ_s, are assumed known, only the mean θ being unknown. From observations on $Y = (Y_1, \cdots, Y_n)$, it is required to predict $Z^\dagger = Y_{n+1}$. If we take

$$V = \sum_{i=1}^n Y_i/n, \qquad U = Y_n,$$

the previous discussion applies because if θ is known, the distribution of $Z^\dagger$ is determined once $U = Y_n$ is given. To apply (8)–(10), we need

(15)
$$E(\bar{Y}\,|\,Y_n = y_n) = \theta + (y_n - \theta)/\{(1 - \lambda_0)n\} + o(1/n),$$

$$\text{var}(\bar{Y}\,|\,Y_n = y_n) = \sigma_0^2/\{(1 - \lambda_0)^2 n\} + o(1/n).$$

With θ known, the required lower limit is

(16) $q_\alpha(\theta, y_n) = \theta + \lambda_0(y_n - \theta) - k_\alpha^* \sigma_0.$

When θ is estimated by $\bar{y}$, the limit is modified to

$$q_{\alpha'}(\bar{y}, y_n),$$

where

(17) $\alpha' = \alpha - \dfrac{\phi(-k_\alpha^*)}{n} \left\{ \left(\dfrac{y_n - \bar{y}}{\sigma_0} \right) + \tfrac{1}{2} k_\alpha^* \right\}.$

It is interesting that the correction $(y_n - \bar{y})$ enters to order n^{-1}.

For the more realistic situation in which λ_0 and σ_0^2 are replaced by unknown parameters, it would be necessary to evaluate the bias in the estimates to order $1/n$, conditional on $Y_n = y_n$. The effect on prediction limits of errors of estimation could then be compared with the results of Bloomfield (1972) on the effect of estimation errors on the mean squared error of prediction. This will not be investigated here.

5. Empirical Bayes estimation

A special application of the above results is to the construction of confidence intervals in parametric empirical Bayes estimation. One moderately general formulation is as follows; see, for example, Cox and Hinkley (1974), p. 400. Suppose that $Y_1, \cdots, Y_n$ are independently distributed, Y_j having probability density $f_{Y_j}(y; \psi_j, \lambda)$, where λ is a common nuisance parameter. Suppose further that $\Psi_1, \cdots, \Psi_n$ have independent and identical prior densities of the form $f_\Psi(\psi; \zeta)$, where ζ is a further unknown parameter, and that it is required on the basis of observations $y_1, \cdots, y_n$ to make inferences about one of the ψ's, say ψ_n. All distributions are assumed of known parametric form.

If λ and ζ are known an ordinary Bayesian analysis can be used; the posterior distribution of ψ_n depends only on y_n and is

(18) $f_{\Psi_n | Y_n}(\psi_n \mid y_n; \lambda, \zeta),$

say. In an empirical Bayes approach we estimate (λ, ζ) say by $(\tilde{\lambda}, \tilde{\zeta})$, these being for example maximum likelihood estimates based on the marginal distribution of $Y_1, \cdots, Y_n$, with the ψ's integrated out.

Previous work on empirical Bayes methods (Maritz (1970)) has dealt largely with non-parametric prior distributions and in any case has concentrated on point estimation. It would be possible to develop a theory of empirical Bayes confidence intervals from first principles, but we can subsume the problem under the discussion of prediction intervals. For this Ψ_n is taken as the unobserved random variable $Z^\dagger$, (18) as its distribution with $\theta = (\lambda, \zeta)$, and $Y = (Y_1, \cdots, Y_n)$ as the observed random variables from which θ is to be estimated and (18) computed. In a few very special cases, of which one is given below, it may be possible to use the 'exact' approach of Section 2. Otherwise in the approximate formulation V is the estimate $(\lambda, \tilde{\zeta})$, and U, the part of the data determining the distribution of $Z^\dagger$, is Y_n.

To apply the solution (10), we have to compute to order n^{-1} the asymptotic bias and covariance matrix of $\tilde{\theta}$, conditionally on $Y_n = y_n$. The difficulties associated with the conditioning can be avoided at the cost of a slight loss of precision, by basing the estimation of θ on $Y_1, \cdots, Y_{n-1}$. If, however, maximum likelihood estimation is used, general formulae are available for the required properties (Bartlett (1953), Rao (1963)) and these are easily adapted to take account of the conditioning.

We give below one illustration of an 'exact' solution and one of the use of the asymptotic theory.

6. An exact solution

As an example, admittedly unrealistic, of a problem for which exact empirical Bayes confidence levels are available, suppose that $Y_1, \cdots, Y_n$ are independently normally distributed with known variance σ_0^2 and with unknown means $\mu_1, \cdots, \mu_n$. Suppose further that the prior distribution is such that the corresponding random variables $M_1, \cdots, M_n$ are independently normally distributed with known variance ν_0^2 and unknown mean ξ. Suppose that μ_n is the parameter of interest.

To adapt this to the formulation of Section 2, note that $Y = (Y_1, \cdots, Y_n)$ is a set of independent and identically distributed normal random variables of mean ξ and variance $\sigma_0^2 + \nu_0^2$. Conditionally on $Y = y$, the random variable of interest $Z^\dagger = M_n$ is normal with mean and variance respectively

$$(19) \qquad \frac{\sigma_0^2 \xi + \nu_0^2 y_n}{\sigma_0^2 + \nu_0^2} \quad \text{and} \quad \frac{\sigma_0^2 \nu_0^2}{\sigma_0^2 + \nu_0^2}.$$

This is a specification for non-independent random variables. We now replace ξ in (19) by $\xi^\dagger$ and consider the construction of an optimum similar test of $\xi = \xi^\dagger$. In virtue of sufficiency we can condense Y to $\bar{Y} = \Sigma Y_j / n$ and then it is clear that similar tests are based on the distribution of

$$(20) \qquad M_n - \frac{\sigma_0^2 \bar{Y} + \nu_0^2 Y_n}{\sigma_0^2 + \nu_0^2}$$

which has zero mean and variance $(\sigma_0^2/n + \nu_0^2)\sigma_0^2/(\sigma_0^2 + \nu_0^2)$. Thus the optimum lower α limit for μ_n is

$$(21) \qquad \frac{\sigma_0^2 \bar{y} + \nu_0^2 y_n}{\sigma_0^2 + \nu_0^2} - k_\alpha^* \left\{ \frac{(\sigma_0^2/n + \nu_0^2)\sigma_0^2}{(\sigma_0^2 + \nu_0^2)} \right\}^{\frac{1}{2}}.$$

An alternative route to this is to show that if $\Sigma a_i Y_i$ is a linear combination of $Y_1, \cdots, Y_n$ with $\Sigma a_i = 1$ the mean squared difference $E(M_n - \Sigma a_i Y_i)^2$ is minimized by the combination $(\sigma_0^2 \bar{Y} + \nu_0^2 Y_n)/(\sigma_0^2 + \nu_0^2)$. Of course if ξ were known and equal to ξ_0, the weighted mean

$$(\sigma_0^2 \xi_0 + \nu_0^2 Y_n)/(\sigma_0^2 + \nu_0^2)$$

would be used in the estimation of μ_n. The form of (20) and (21) is thus not surprising although also not totally obvious because of the dependence between $\bar{Y}$ and Y_n.

7. An asymptotic solution

To illustrate the use of the asymptotic theory, we take the situation of Section 6, now supposing that the prior variance $\tau = \nu^2$, say, is unknown. We continue to assume the variance σ_0^2 is known or estimated with negligible error.

The parameter $\theta = (\xi, \tau)$ is estimated by

$$(22) \qquad \hat{\xi} = \bar{y}, \quad \hat{\tau} = \frac{\Sigma(y_i - \bar{y})^2}{n - 1} - \sigma_0^2.$$

We ignore the possibility that $\hat{\tau} < 0$; of course, in fact the estimate $\max(\hat{\tau}, 0)$ could be used. If θ is known, the required lower α limit is

$$(23) \qquad \frac{\sigma_0^2 \xi + \nu^2 y_n}{\sigma_0^2 + \nu^2} - k_\alpha^* \frac{\sigma_0 \nu}{(\sigma_0^2 + \nu^2)^{1/2}}.$$

Thus in the general notation $u = y_n$ and $v = (\hat{\xi}, \hat{\tau})$. To use (9) and (10), we need the asymptotic covariance matrix of V, which is

$$\text{diag}\{(\sigma_0^2 + \nu^2)/n, \ 2(\sigma_0^2 + \nu^2)^2/n\}$$

and the conditional bias of V, given $U = u$, which is

$$[(u - \xi)/n, \{(u - \xi)^2 - \sigma_0^2\}/n].$$

It then follows that the lower α limit for μ_n is

(24)
$$\frac{\sigma_0^2 \hat{\xi} + \hat{\nu}^2 y_n}{\sigma_0^2 + \nu^2} - k_{\alpha'}^* \frac{\sigma_0 \hat{\nu}}{(\sigma_0^2 + \hat{\nu}^2)^{1/2}},$$

where

(25)
$$\alpha' = \alpha - \frac{\phi(-k_\alpha^*)}{n} \left\{ \frac{k_\alpha^* \sigma_0^2}{2\hat{\nu}_0^2} - \frac{2(y_n - \hat{\xi})\sigma_0}{\hat{\nu}(\hat{\nu}^2 + \sigma_0^2)^{1/2}} \right.$$
$$\left. + \frac{(y_n - \hat{\xi})^2 \sigma_0^2 k_\alpha^*}{\hat{\nu}^2(\sigma_0^2 + \hat{\nu}^2)} + \frac{(y_n - \hat{\xi})^3 \sigma_0}{\hat{\nu}(\sigma_0^2 + \hat{\nu}^2)^{1/2}} \right\}.$$

8. Discussion

In practice the correction terms of order $1/n$ may often be negligible. Then the discussion provides some justification for ignoring errors in estimating θ.

Because of the relation between significance tests and prediction intervals outlined in Section 2, the asymptotic theory of Section 3 can be used to investigate significance tests with nuisance parameters in which asymptotic considerations are applicable to only part of the data.

Finally it must be stressed that a number of important considerations, such as robustness and the examination of the adequacy of the models, have been ignored.

References

BARTLETT, M. S. (1953) Approximate confidence intervals. *Biometrika* **40**, 12–19.

BLOOMFIELD, P. (1972) On the error of prediction of a time series. *Biometrika* **59**, 501–507.

COX, D. R. AND HINKLEY, D. V. (1974) *Theoretical Statistics*. Chapman and Hall, London.

GUTTMAN, I. (1970) *Statistical Tolerance Regions*. Griffin, London.

MARITZ, J. S. (1970) *Empirical Bayes Methods*. Methuen, London.

RAO, C. R. (1963) Criteria of estimation in large samples. *Sankhyā* A **25**, 189–206.

Direction and Dimensionality Tests Based on Hotelling's Generalized T_0^2

A. M. KSHIRSAGAR

Abstract

Bartlett and Williams have shown that the hypothesis of the goodness-of-fit of one or more assigned discriminant functions in the case of several groups can be tested using Wilks's Λ criterion. By factorizing this Λ criterion suitably, it is also possible to test whether the directions of the given functions are inadequate or whether the number of proposed functions is inadequate. Hotelling's T_0^2 statistic is a competitor of Wilks's Λ in multivariate analysis; previously its use for this hypothesis and also for the dimensionality and direction aspects of this hypothesis was unknown. The present paper derives the appropriate T_0^2 type statistics for this and also gives their exact null distributions.

1. Introduction

It is a pleasure to contribute to this dedicatory volume to one of the pioneers in the fields of multivariate analysis and stochastic processes. As is well known, Professor Bartlett has done considerable research in the area of Wilks's Λ criterion and canonical correlations analysis. I have therefore chosen this area on the present occasion for my contribution.

Consider $q + 1$ p-variate normal populations with the same variance-covariance matrix Σ but different means $\mu_1, \cdots, \mu_{q+1}$, of the (column) vector x of variables. If independent samples are available from these populations, we shall get the following multivariate analysis of variance table:

TABLE 1

Source	d.f.	$p \times p$ matrix of sum of squares (s.s.) and sum of products (s.p.)
Between populations	q	B_x
Within populations	$n - q$	W_x
Total	n	$B_x + W_x$

For testing the equality of the means of these $q + 1$ populations, the following multivariate test criteria are generally used:

(i) Wilks's $\Lambda : \Lambda = \dfrac{|W_x|}{|W_x + B_x|}$.

(ii) Hotelling's generalized $T_0^2 : T_0^2 = \operatorname{tr} W_x^{-1} B_x$.

(iii) Pillai's criterion: $V = \operatorname{tr}(W_x + B_x)^{-1} B_x$.

(iv) Roy's largest root criterion: largest eigenvalue of $(W_x + B_x)^{-1} B_x$.
When the μ_r's are all equal, the distributions of Λ, T_0^2 and V depend only on n, p and q, n being the degrees of freedom (d.f.) of $B_x + W_x, p$, the order of B_x or W_x and q being the d.f. of B_x. We shall denote these distributions by $\Lambda(n, p, q)$, $T_0^2(n, p, q)$ and $V(n, p, q)$ respectively. Percentage points of these distributions, large sample χ^2 approximations and explicit expressions of the density functions are available and may be found in the list of references in Kshirsagar (1972).

Professor Bartlett has many times expressed his preference for Wilks's Λ over the other criteria, because when the null hypothesis of equality of the means of the $q + 1$ populations is rejected, much useful information can be derived from factors of Λ, especially for discriminating among the populations. For example, consider the hypothesis,

$H : s$ given linear functions $L_1 x$ (where L_1 is of order $s \times p$ and rank s) of the variables x are adequate for discrimination.

This is the hypothesis of goodness of fit of s assigned functions. For testing this Λ can be factorized as

(1.1) $\Lambda = \Lambda_a \cdot \Lambda_R,$

where

(1.2) $$\Lambda_a = |L_1 W_x L_1'| / |L_1(W_x + B_x)L_1'|$$

is the Λ based on $L_1 x$ only and Λ_R, therefore, is the 'residual' Λ when $L_1 x$ is eliminated. When H is true, Λ_R has the $\Lambda(n - s, p - s, q)$ distribution and H can be tested by this test. Williams (1952) and Bartlett (1951) observed that Λ_R contains two types of deviations, one due to the number s of discriminant functions being wrong and another due to the specifications of the functions being wrong. The first is called deviation due to 'dimensionality' (because s discriminant functions are adequate only when $\mu_1, \cdots, \mu_{q+1}$ lie in an s-dimensional space) and the second one is called deviation due to 'direction' (as L_1 in the given functions $L_1 x$ represents the directions of the discriminant function). For this, Bartlett (1951) factorized Λ_R as

(1.3) $$\Lambda_R = \Lambda_D \cdot \Lambda_{C|D}$$

where Λ_D is the 'direction' factor and $\Lambda_{C|D}$ is the 'partial' 'dimensionality' factor. Under H, Λ_D has the $\Lambda(n - s, p - s, s)$ distribution and $\Lambda_{C|D}$ has an independent $\Lambda(n - 2s, p - s, q - s)$ distribution. An alternative factorization

(1.4) $$\Lambda_R = \Lambda_C \cdot \Lambda_{D|C}$$

where Λ_C is the 'dimensionality' factor and $\Lambda_{D|C}$ is the 'partial' direction factor is also possible. Under H, Λ_C has the $\Lambda(n - s, p - s, q - s)$ distribution and $\Lambda_{D|C}$ has an independent $\Lambda(n - q, p - s, s)$ distribution. Actually, Bartlett obtained these factors for the particular case $s = 1$ but they can be extended to the general case easily (see Williams (1961) or Kshirsagar (1970)). Explicit expressions for these factors in terms of W_x, B_x, L_1 are available in Kshirsagar (1970).

This kind of factorization of Λ is not available for the other two criteria T_0^2 and V and Bartlett is therefore right in preferring Λ. The distributions of these direction and dimensionality factors were derived by Bartlett, geometrically. However later Kshirsagar (1970) succeeded in expressing them in the following forms:

(1.5) $$\Lambda_R = \frac{|W_{22.1}|}{|W_{22.1} + B_{22.1} + S|}$$

(1.6) $$\Lambda_D = \frac{|W_{22.1} + B_{22.1}|}{|W_{22.1} + B_{22.1} + S|}$$

$$(1.7) \qquad \Lambda_{C|D} = \frac{|W_{22.1}|}{|W_{22.1} + B_{22.1}|}$$

$$(1.8) \qquad \Lambda_C = \frac{|W_{22.1} + S|}{|W_{22.1} + S + B_{22.1}|}$$

$$(1.9) \qquad \Lambda_{D|C} = \frac{|W_{22.1}|}{|W_{22.1} + S|}$$

where

$$(1.10) \qquad W = L\, W_x\, L' = \begin{bmatrix} \overset{s}{W_{11}} & \overset{p-s}{W_{12}} \\ \hline W_{21} & W_{22} \end{bmatrix} \begin{matrix} s \\ p-s \end{matrix}\, ,$$

$$(1.11) \qquad B = L\, B_x\, L' = \begin{bmatrix} B_{11} & B_{12} \\ \hline B_{21} & B_{22} \end{bmatrix}$$

$$(1.12) \qquad W_{22.1} = W_{22} - W_{21} W_{11}^{-1} W_{12}$$

$$(1.13) \qquad B_{22.1} = B_{22} - B_{21} B_{11}^{-1} B_{12}$$

$$(1.14) \qquad \begin{aligned} S = W_{21} W_{11}^{-1} W_{12} &+ B_{21} B_{11}^{-1} B_{12} \\ - (W_{21} + B_{21})(W_{11} + B_{11})^{-1}(W_{12} + B_{12}) &= FF', \end{aligned}$$

$$(1.15) \qquad F = (B_{21} B_{11}^{-1} - W_{21} W_{11}^{-1})(B_{11}^{-1} + W_{11}^{-1})^{-\frac{1}{2}}$$

and

$$(1.16) \qquad L = \begin{bmatrix} L_1 \\ \hline L_2 \end{bmatrix} \begin{matrix} s \\ p-s \end{matrix}\, ,$$

L_2 being so chosen that

$$(1.17) \qquad L \Sigma L' = \begin{bmatrix} L_1 \Sigma L_1' & 0 \\ \hline 0 & I_{p-s} \end{bmatrix}.$$

The matrices of order $p - s$, $W_{22.1}$, $B_{22.1}$, S have independent Wishart distributions under H of d.f. $n - q - s$, $q - s$, s respectively (Kshirsagar (1970)) and the distributional results of the direction and dimensionality results stated earlier then follow easily from this.

A direct decomposition of T_0^2 or V similar to that of Λ as described above does not seem possible. But the representations $(1.5) - (1.8)$ make it possible to construct alternative direction and dimensionality statistics, having either T_0^2-type distributions or V-type distributions. Thus corresponding to (1.5), the over-all T_0^2-type statistic to test the hypothesis H will be

$$(1.18) \qquad T_R^2 = \text{tr } W_{22.1}^{-1}(B_{22.1} + S)$$

having the $T_0^2(n - s, p - s, q)$ distribution under H and its direction and dimensionality parts corresponding to (1.6) and (1.7) or (1.8) and (1.9) will be

$$(1.19) \qquad T_D^2 \quad = \text{tr}(W_{22.1} + B_{22.1})^{-1} S$$

$$(1.20) \qquad T_{C|D}^2 = \text{tr } W_{22.1}^{-1} B_{22.1}$$

$$(1.21) \qquad T_C^2 \quad = \text{tr}(W_{22.1} + S)^{-1} B_{22.1}$$

$$(1.22) \qquad T_{D|C}^2 = \text{tr } W_{22.1}^{-1} S,$$

T_D^2 will have the $T_0^2(n - s, p - s, s)$ distribution, $T_{C|D}^2$ will have the $T_0^2(n - 2s, p - s, q - s)$ distribution, T_C^2 will have the $T_0^2(n - s, p - s, q - s)$ distribution and $T_{D|C}^2$ will have the $T_0^2(n - q, p - s, s)$ distribution, under H. However for practical purposes these statistics must now be expressed in terms of our original matrices W_x, B_x and the hypothetical functions $L_1 x$. This involves a lot of algebra and is accomplished in the next section, omitting uninteresting details of matrix algebra. (These details can be found in McHenry's dissertation.)

2. Expressions for the T_0^2-type statistics in terms of known quantities

We shall first consider T_D^2. For that, we observe that

$$(2.1) \qquad B_{22.1} = L_2\{B_x - B_x L_1'(L_1 B_x L_1')^{-1} L_1 B_x\}L_2'$$

which follows from (1.11) and (1.16). Replacing the L_2 in the above expression by the full matrix L, one can verify that

$$(2.2) \qquad L\{B_x - B_x L_1'(L_1 B_x L_1')^{-1} L_1 B_x\}L' = \begin{bmatrix} 0 & 0 \\ \hline 0 & B_{22.1} \end{bmatrix}.$$

Now define

$$(2.3) \qquad M = \begin{bmatrix} W_{11} & W_{12} \\ \hline W_{21} & W_{22} + B_{22.1} \end{bmatrix}.$$

But, on account of (2.2) and (1.10), this is also

$$(2.4) \qquad L\{W_x + B_x - B_x L_1'(L_1 B_x L_1')^{-1} L_1 B_x\}L'.$$

From the standard result about the inverse of a partitioned matrix,

(2.5)
$$M^{-1} = \left[\begin{array}{c|c} \cdots & \cdots \\ \hline \cdots & (W_{22.1} + B_{22.1})^{-1} \end{array}\right],$$

where the blank entries are submatrices not required specifically and hence are not fully spelled out.

From (1.10), (1.11) and (1.15),

(2.6)
$$S = FF' = L_2 F_x F_x' L_2',$$

where

(2.7)
$$F_x = \{B_x L_1'(L_1 B_x L_1')^{-1} - W_x L_1'(L_1 W_x L_1')^{-1}\}$$
$$\times \{(L_1 B_x L_1')^{-1} + (L_1 W_x L_1')^{-1}\}^{-\frac{1}{2}}$$

and so, replacing L_2 by L in (2.6),

(2.8)
$$L F_x F_x' L' = \left[\begin{array}{c|c} 0 & 0 \\ \hline 0 & S \end{array}\right].$$

Finally therefore, from (2.5) and (2.8)

(2.9)
$$T_D^2 = \operatorname{tr}(W_{22.1} + B_{22.1})^{-1} S$$
$$= \operatorname{tr} M^{-1} L F_x F_x' L'.$$

After a lengthy algebra the right hand side of (2.9) can be expressed as (using (2.4) and (2.7))

(2.10)
$$T_D^2 = \operatorname{tr}\{(L_1 B_x L_1')[L_1(B_x + W_x)L_1']^{-1}$$
$$\times (L_1 W_x L_1')[L_1 W_x (W_x + B_x)^{-1} B_x L_1']^{-1}\} - s.$$

Considering the partitioned form of W^{-1} (which has $W_{22.1}^{-1}$ in the last corner), it can be seen that the partial dimensionality statistic $T_{C|D}^2$ given by (1.20) is expressible as

$$T_{C|D}^2 = \operatorname{tr} W_{22.1}^{-1} B_{22.1}$$
$$= \operatorname{tr} W^{-1} \left[\begin{array}{c|c} 0 & 0 \\ \hline 0 & B_{22.1} \end{array}\right]$$
$$= \operatorname{tr}(L W_x L')^{-1} \cdot L\{B_x - B_x L_1'(L_1 B_x L_1')^{-1} L_1 B_x\}L'$$

on account of (1.10) and (2.2). This now reduces to

(2.11) $T_{C|D}^2 = \operatorname{tr} W_x^{-1} B_x - \operatorname{tr}(L_1 B_x W_x^{-1} B_x L_1')(L_1 B_x L_1')^{-1}.$

The alternative statistics T_C^2 and $T_{D|C}^2$ can also be dealt with in a similar manner. We define

(2.12)
$$K = \left[\frac{B_{11}}{B_{21}}\right] B_{11}^{-1/2}$$

and observe that this is also

(2.13)
$$(L\,B_x\,L\,{}_1')(L_1\,B_x\,L\,{}_1')^{-\frac{1}{2}}$$

on account of (1.11). Again

(2.14)
$$(W + KK')^{-1} = \left[\begin{array}{c|c} \cdots & \cdots \\ \hline \cdots & (W_{22.1} + S)^{-1} \end{array}\right] ,$$

but from (1.10) and (2.13),

(2.15)
$$(W + KK')^{-1} = [L\,(W_x + B_x L\,{}_1'(L_1 B_x L\,{}_1')^{-1}L_1 B_x)L\,']^{-1},$$

so, from (1.21), (2.2), (2.14) and (2.15),

$$T_C^2 = \operatorname{tr}(W_{22.1} + S)^{-1} B_{22.1}$$

$$= \operatorname{tr}(W + KK')^{-1} \left[\begin{array}{c|c} 0 & 0 \\ \hline 0 & B_{22.1} \end{array}\right]$$

$$= \operatorname{tr}[W_x + B_x L\,{}_1'(L_1 B_x L\,{}_1')^{-1}L_1 B_x]^{-1}[B_x - B_x L\,{}_1'(L_1 B_x L\,{}_1')^{-1}L_1 B_x]$$

which simplifies to

(2.16)
$$\operatorname{tr} W_x^{-1}B_x - \operatorname{tr} L_1 B_x W_x^{-1}(W_x + B_x)W_x^{-1}B_x L\,{}_1'(L_1 B_x L\,{}_1'$$
$$+ L_1 B_x W_x^{-1}B_x L\,{}_1')^{-1}$$

after some algebra.

To find the partial dimensionality statistic $T_{D|C}^2$ of (1.22) we consider $\operatorname{tr} W^{-1}LF_x F_x' L'$, which by (2.8) reduces to

(2.17)
$$\operatorname{tr} \left[\begin{array}{c|c} \cdots & \cdots \\ \hline \cdots & W_{22.1}^{-1} \end{array}\right] \left[\begin{array}{c|c} 0 & 0 \\ \hline 0 & S \end{array}\right] = \operatorname{tr} W_{22.1}^{-1} S = T_{D|C}^2$$

On the other hand, by (1.10) it is

$$\operatorname{tr}(LW_x L\,')^{-1} L\,F_x F_x' L\,' = \operatorname{tr} W_x^{-1} F_x F_x'$$

which simplifies to (on account of (2.7))

$$\text{tr} [(L_1 B_x L_1')^{-1} L_1 B_x W_x^{-1} B_x L_1'(L_1 B_x L_1' + L_1 W_x L_1')^{-1} L_1 W_x L_1']$$

(2.18)

$$- \text{tr} [(L_1 B_x L_1') (L_1 B_x L_1' + L_1 W_x L_1')^{-1}].$$

3. Discriminant functions in the dummy variables space

The matrix B_x of Table 1 can also be looked upon as the matrix of regression sums of squares and sums of products in the regression of x on q dummy variables y representing the differences among the k populations corresponding to some s ($s < q$) specified linear functions of y, denoted by t (an $s \times 1$ vector). The matrix B_x can be split up as $C_{xt} C_{tt}^{-1} C_{tx}$ representing the regression of x on t and the remainder $B_x - C_{xt} C_{tt}^{-1} C_{tx}$. This yields

(3.1) $$\Lambda_R' = \frac{|W_x|}{|W_x + B_x - C_{xt} C_{tt}^{-1} C_{tx}|}$$

as the overall Λ criterion with distribution $\Lambda(n - s, p, q - s)$ to test the hypothesis H' of the goodness of fit of t, which are known as discriminant functions of the dummy variables space (see Kshirsagar (1971)). This Λ_R' is also factorized into direction and dimensionality test statistics. The distributional problem here is different as y are not stochastic variables. Explicit expressions for the corresponding Hotelling's T_0^2-type statistics have been worked out by McHenry (unpublished thesis of McHenry) and the author and the details will be published somewhere else.

4. Other multivariate criteria

In Section 1, Pillai's V and Roy's largest root criterion are also mentioned. These also can be used to test the direction and dimensionality aspects of hypothesis H of Section 1 or the hypothesis H' of Section 3. Explicit expressions for these statistics along with their distributions have been worked out and will be published by McHenry and the author elsewhere.

As Bartlett (1973) has remarked, these direction and dimensionality statistics have not been exploited by the applied statisticians as much as they should to extract more information about the structure of the means of various multivariate groups. McHenry has therefore written a detailed computer program for these tests and it is hoped that this will make the tests more readily accessible to the users. The program is also being sent for publication.

5. Some remarks

In the case of Wilks's Λ criterion,

$$\Lambda_R = \Lambda_D \Lambda_{C|D} = \Lambda_C \Lambda_{D|C}$$

and $\Lambda_D, \Lambda_{C|D}$ or $\Lambda_C, \Lambda_{D|C}$ are factors of Λ_R and hence of Λ. Alternatively, by taking logarithms, we get the partitioning of the χ^2 statistic (pq d.f.)

$$- [n - \tfrac{1}{2}(p + q + 1)] \log_e \Lambda$$

first proposed by Bartlett, from this. Such a factorization or break-up for the other statistics T_0^2 or V does not appear to exist corresponding to the direction and dimensionality aspects of H. The criteria T_C^2, $T_{D|C}^2$ or T_D^2, $T_{C|D}^2$ constructed from the factors of Λ *do not* represent factors or partitions of T_0^2 or T_R^2. This is an unfortunate feature of these statistics. The only relationship one can see, from (1.18) to (1.22), is

$$T_R^2 = T_{D|C}^2 + T_{C|D}^2$$

and is difficult to interpret as $T_{D|C}^2$ and $T_{C|D}^2$ are both 'partial' test statistics of dimensionality and direction.

Contingency tables can also be analysed using canonical analysis between vectors of dummy variables (Williams (1967)) and goodness of fit assigned scores can be tested (Kshirsagar (1970)). The author (Kshirsagar (1970)) has given an 'approximate' break-up of Pillai's V for this problem, considering the large sample distribution of a certain matrix. This paper and the papers to be published on the basis of McHenry's thesis replace this approximate partitioning by exact statistics of the T_0^2 or V type.

Kshirsagar's (1970) results (1.5) to (1.9) have been proved by him under the assumption $q \geqq p$, so that the matrix B_x has a Wishart distribution. However all the results hold even when $q < p$, though the method of derivation is different. McHenry has given the details of this case in his dissertation and these will be published elsewhere.

The author is extremely grateful to McHenry for useful discussions during the preparation of this material.

References

BARTLETT, M. S. (1951) The goodness of fit of a single hypothetical discriminant function in the case of several groups. *Ann. Eugen.* **16**, 199–214.

BARTLETT, M. S. (1973) Some historical remarks and recollections in multivariate analysis. Conference on Multivariate Analysis at the University of Hull, England. 16–18 April 1973.

KSHIRSAGAR, A. M. (1970) An alternative derivation of the direction and collinearity statistics in discriminant analysis. *Calcutta Statist. Assoc. Bull.* **19**, 123–134.

KSHIRSAGAR, A. M. (1970) Goodness of fit of an assigned set of scores for the analysis of association in a contingency table. *Ann. Inst. Statist. Math.* **22**, 295–306.

KSHIRSAGAR, A. M. (1971) Goodness of fit of a discriminant function from the vector space of dummy variables. *J. R. Statist. Soc. Ser.* B **33**, 111–116.

KSHIRSAGAR, A. M. (1972) *Multivariate Analysis.* Marcel Dekker and Company, New York.

MCHENRY, C. (1974) *Direction and Dimensionality Statistics based on Hotelling's T_0^2, Pillai's V and Roy's Criteria.* Unpublished Ph. D. Thesis, Texas A & M University, College Station, Texas.

WILLIAMS, E. J. (1952) Some exact tests in multivariate analysis. *Biometrika* **39**, 17–31.

WILLIAMS, E. J. (1961) Tests for discriminant function. *J. Austral. Math. Soc.* **2**, 243–252.

WILLIAMS, E. J. (1967) The analysis of association among many variates. *J. R. Statist. Soc. Ser.* B **54**, 199–228.

Estimation of a Distribution Function from Incomplete Observations

PAUL MEIER

Abstract

The product-limit estimator for a distribution function, appropriate to observations which are variably censored, was introduced by Kaplan and Meier in 1958; it has provided a basis for study of more complex problems by Cox and by others. Its properties in the case of random censoring have been studied by Efron and later writers. The basic properties of the product-limit estimator are here shown to be closely parallel to the properties of the empirical distribution function in the general case of variably and arbitrarily censored observations.

1. Introduction

1.1 *Background*

In his monograph on stochastic processes [2] Bartlett observed that the empirical distribution function (EDF) has the same covariance structure as the Brownian bridge. Since, for large samples, the EDF is approximately normal, the distribution of this Brownian process could reasonably be taken as an asymptotic approximation to that of the EDF. The use of this analogy, Bartlett showed, leads to easy derivations of certain asymptotic distributions, such as that of the Kolmogorov-Smirnov statistic, and it should be helpful in other applications as well.

The same analogy was independently remarked upon by Doob [9], who pointed out the need for further conditions to justify the asymptotic equivalence. Formal justification in this case was provided by Donsker [8], and further work on these foundations led to a quite general theory of weak convergence of stochastic processes, comprehensively discussed by Billingsley [4].

1.2 The problem

A closely related problem, arising in many applications, is familiar from the life table calculation which is used in the analysis of follow-up data in studies of chronic disease. What this amounts to is the estimation of a distribution function from variably censored observations, and a serviceable solution (using arbitrary grouping intervals) to that estimation problem has been known, at least since 1912 [5].

A method for estimating the variance was given by Greenwood [11], and an extension of that method to give an estimated covariance function (and hence an estimated variance for the mean lifetime) was provided by Irwin [12].

In 1958 it was shown by Kaplan and Meier [13] that the arbitrary grouping was, in fact, unnecessary. They provided what they named the product-limit (PL) estimator, a step function appropriate to the presence of censored observations which reduces to the EDF when no censored observations are present; they discussed a number of its properties and compared it with alternatives.

1.3 Examples

The most common applications in which variably censored data arise are those of medical follow up, and those of industrial life testing. Should one wish to estimate the survival distribution for patients given a new treatment, one may have, after five years, some patients treated a full five years ago, and a great many others treated more recently. The interval from the time of treatment to that chosen for analysis is the censoring time, and these time intervals will usually be quite variable. Similarly, a large number of electronic components may be put on test simultaneously, but from time to time a number of yet unfailed units may be removed for special studies, and these, too, are censored observations.

Turning to ecology, a recent study of baboon behavior [17] included observations to determine the distribution of time of day at which the baboon colony descends from trees where they spend the night, to begin their daily activities. The observer arrives at his post at time a_i and, should he find the baboons already up and about, he has a (left) censored observation, rather than a complete one.

1.4 The objective

The PL estimator, defined for variably censored observations, is a generalization of the empirical distribution function; we undertake to show that it shares the important properties of the EDF. Thus, we seek

(a) to show that the process is asymptotically unbiased and normal at each point,

(b) to find the covariance function, and

(c) to prove weak convergence to an appropriately transformed Brownian Motion process.

The purpose is to develop an asymptotic theory, useful in estimation and testing, which is analogous to the general theory for the more familiar empirical distribution function.

1.5 Properties of the empirical distribution function

The results we present for estimators from incomplete observations are analogous to well-known results for ordinary random samples, and we state them for the latter case in a form suitable for generalization.

Suppose, then, that we have a distribution function (d.f.) $F(x)$, and n i.i.d. random variables, $X_1, \cdots, X_n$, each with d.f. $F(x)$. Purely for convenience we will assume that we are dealing with positive and continuous random variables, having finite second moment. It is convenient to use in place of $F(x)$ its complement, $S(x) = 1 - F(x)$, and, since we use S rather than F throughout in the sequel, we shall hereafter mean $S(x)$ when we refer to 'the distribution function'.

The following assertions are true, and are generally well known.

(a) Within the unrestricted class of all possible distribution functions, the one which maximizes the likelihood of the observations is the sample distribution function, $\hat{S}(x)$, which assigns probability $1/n$ to each of the observed values of the X_i. (On account of the fact that the class over which the likelihood is maximized is unrestricted, we call this the non-parametric maximum likelihood (NPML) estimator of $S(x)$.) For a functional, $g(S)$, which is defined for a suitable class of distribution functions, e.g., μ or $S(x_0)$, we define the NPML estimator of $g(S)$ by $\hat{g} = g(\hat{S})$. Thus, for example,

$$\widehat{S(x)} = \hat{S}(x) = \text{proportion of } X_i \geq x$$

$$\hat{\mu} = \int_0^\infty \hat{S}(x)dx = \bar{X}.$$

(b) The first two moments of $\hat{S}(x)$ are given by

$$E\{\hat{S}(x)\} = S(x)$$
$$E\{\hat{S}^2(x)\} = S^2(x) + \frac{S(x)[1 - S(x)]}{n}$$
$$= S^2(x)[1 + C(x)]$$

where $\sqrt{(C(x))} = [(1 - S(x))/nS(x)]^{\frac{1}{2}} =$ coefficient of variation of $\hat{S}(x)$, and $\hat{S}(x)$ is distributed as a binomial proportion, with parameters $(n, S(x))$.

(c) The function, $\hat{S}(x)$, converges uniformly in probability to $S(x)$. More specifically, the Glivenko–Cantelli theorem states

$$\lim_{n \to \infty} \Pr\{\sup_x |\hat{S}(x) - S(x)| > \epsilon\} = 0 \text{ for every } \epsilon.$$

(d) Viewed as a stochastic process indexed by x, $\hat{S}(x)$ is a Markov process with second moment function given by

$$E\{\hat{S}(x)\hat{S}(y)\} = S(x)S(y)[1 + C(x)] \text{ for } x \leqq y.$$

Further, given an arbitrary set of values $u_1, \cdots, u_k$ the random variables

$$\hat{S}(u_1), \hat{S}(u_2), \cdots, \hat{S}(u_k)$$

have an asymptotically normal joint distribution.

(e) The stochastic process $\sqrt{n}\,(\hat{S}(x) - S(x))$, indexed by x, satisfies the conditions for weak convergence to a transformed Brownian Motion. In consequence, asymptotic distributions for suitable functionals of $\hat{S}(x)$ may be derived from the distributions of the Brownian Motion process.

1.6 *Notation*

Our problem is to estimate a distribution function, where the observations are arbitrarily and variably censored. Rather than the more usual $F(y) = \Pr\{Y \leqq y\}$, we will find it convenient to use the complementary distribution function, $S(y) = 1 - F(y) = \Pr\{Y > y\}$. In order to avoid some points of detail we assume that $S(y)$ is absolutely continuous.

Without loss of generality we assume that the arbitrarily specified censoring values, $L_1, \cdots, L_n$ are indexed in increasing order of magnitude $0 < L_1 \leqq L_2 \leqq \cdots \leqq L_n$.

The observed variably censored sample is taken to be derived from a random sample, $Y_1, \cdots, Y_n$, i.i.d. with d.f. $S(y)$, and the set of arbitrary censoring values, $L_1, \cdots, L_n$, as follows. We observe

$$(X_1, \delta_1), \cdots, (X_n, \delta_n)$$

where

$$X_i = \min(Y_i, L_i)$$

and

$$\delta_i = \begin{cases} 1 & \text{if} & Y_i \leqq L_i \\ 0 & \text{if} & Y_i > L_i. \end{cases}$$

Thus, the pair (X_i, δ_i) is a specification of the random variable, Y_i, censored on the right at L_i.

In order to facilitate description we shall make free use of the concrete terminology appropriate in the medical context. Thus we refer to the variable, x, as 'time', we speak of an underlying 'survival' distribution, of 'observation time', of 'death' and of 'loss' from observation. We define functions of time x as follows:

$M(x)$ = number of $L_i \geqq x$, i.e., the number of items in the sample 'observable' to time x or beyond. (For the present case of arbitrary fixed L_i, $M(x)$ is a fixed, non-random, step function.)

$N(x)$ = number of $X_i \geqq x$, i.e., the number of items in the sample 'surviving' and still under observation at time x. (For each fixed x, $N(x)$ is a random variable and, viewed as a function of x, it is a stochastic process. It is evident from the definition that, for fixed x, $N(x)$ is binomially distributed with parameters $(M(x), S(x))$.)

$\mathcal{N}(x) = E\{N(x)\} = M(x)S(x)$.

$D(x)$ = number of $(X_i, 1)$ with $X_i < x$, i.e., the number of 'deaths' observed up to and including time x.

$L(x)$ = number of $(X_i, 0)$ with $X_i < x$, i.e., the number of 'losses' observed prior to time x.

We have, then, for all x, $N(x) + D(x) + L(x) = n$.

Many of our calculations concerning the estimation of $S(x)$ will involve the intervals between censoring values, and it will be convenient to define supplementary notation as follows.

For given fixed x, let k be the index such that $L_k < x \leq L_{k+1}$, where $L_0 = 0$ and $L_{n+1} = \infty$. Let $\Delta_1, \cdots, \Delta_{k+1}$, be the half-open intervals

$$\Delta_1 = [0, L_1), \ \Delta_2 = [L_1, L_2), \cdots, \Delta_k = [L_{k-1}, L_k), \Delta_{k+1} = [L_k, x).$$

There being no possibility of censoring, except at the end-points of such intervals, it is convenient to introduce the conditional probabilities

$$p_1 = S(L_1), \ p_2 = S(L_2)/S(L_1), \cdots, p_k = S(L_k)/S(L_{k-1}), \ p_{k+1} = S(x)/S(L_k)$$

i.e., p_i = conditional probability of survival over the interval, Δ_i, given survival to the start of that interval.

It follows that

$$S(x) = \prod_{i=1}^{k+1} p_i.$$

We introduce also the random variables

$$N_i = N(L_{i-1} + 0), \text{ the number alive and under observation after the start of } \Delta_i$$

$$\left. \begin{array}{l} D_i = D(L_i) - D(L_{i-1}) \\ D_{k+1} = D(x) - D(L_k) \end{array} \right\} \quad \begin{array}{l} \text{the number observed to 'die'} \\ \text{in the interval } \Delta_i. \end{array}$$

Also, we define $\mathcal{N}_i = E\{N_i\}$.

1.7 Fixed or random censoring values

A variety of models for censoring mechanisms are used in different applications [14]. For the development of theory, the choice of a purely random mechanism with $L_1, \cdots, L_n$ i.i.d. random variables is attractive, since the observed variables $(X_1, \delta_1), \cdots, (X_n, \delta_n)$ are then also i.i.d. In some important applications, however, such a mechanism is not realistic. Further, results which hold uniformly when $\mathcal{N}(x) \to \infty$, for the case of fixed L_i, carry over directly to the case of random L_i, but not vice versa. In particular, there are cases which are represented in the limit by degenerate distributions for the L_i, so that the random censoring model does not apply; but for these the present model provides appropriate asymptotic theory.

1.8 *The* NPML *estimators* $\hat{S}(x)$ *and* $S^*(x)$

As shown by Kaplan and Meier [13], an NPML estimator of $S(x)$ must be a discrete distribution with probability mass only at those points $(x_i, 1)$ where 'deaths' are observed. In fact, should the last observed individual be censored, say at x_m, rather than observed to 'die', we find $\hat{S}(x_m) > 0$, and $\hat{S}(x)$ may be defined arbitrarily for $x > x_m$, without affecting the likelihood. Following Efron [10] we define $\hat{S}(x)$ as follows.

Definition. The product-limit (PL) estimator of $S(x)$ is defined by

$$\hat{S}(x) = \begin{cases} \prod_{i=1}^{k+1} \hat{p}_i & \text{for} \quad x \leq x_m, \quad \text{where} \quad \hat{p}_i = \frac{N_i - D_i}{N_i} \\ 0 & \text{for} \quad x > x_m. \end{cases}$$

An alternative NPML estimator, needed purely as a computational convenience, we call the extended product limit (EPL) estimator.

Definition. The EPL estimator of $S(x)$ is defined by

$$S^*(x) = \prod_{i=1}^{k+1} p_i^*, \quad \text{where} \quad p_i^* = \frac{N_i^* - D_i^*}{N_i^*},$$

$$N_i^* = \begin{cases} N_i & \text{if} \quad N_i > 0 \\ 1 & \text{if} \quad N_i = 0, \end{cases}$$

$$D_i^* = \begin{cases} D_i & \text{if} \quad N_i > 0 \\ D_i + d_i & \text{if} \quad N_i = 0 \end{cases}$$

and d_i is a $(0, 1)$ random variable, independent of the sample, with $\Pr\{d_i = 0\} = p_i$. The effect of this definition is that $S^*(x)$ is identical with $\hat{S}(x)$, except when $x > x_m$. It is defined so as to be unbiased for every x.

2. Distribution of $\hat{S}(x)$

2.1 *The Markov property*

As is well known, the empirical distribution function is Markovian. That is, if $\hat{F}(x)$ is such an empirical distribution, the evolution of $\hat{F}(x)$ for $x > t$ is dependent on $[\hat{F}(x), x \leq t]$ only through the value of $\hat{F}(t)$. This is not the case for the function $\hat{S}(x)$, but provided we specify both $N(x)$ and $\hat{S}(x)$, the resulting process is Markovian.

Theorem. The processes $N(x)$, $[N(x), \hat{S}(x)]$, and $[N(x), S^*(x)]$ are Markovian.

To see this we undertake the following construction. Given an arbitrary set of censoring times, $L_1, \cdots, L_n$ (or equivalently, the function $M(x)$), we start with a random sample of size n, $Y_1, \cdots, Y_n$ from the distribution of $S(x)$, and record $N(x)$, the number of 'survivors' ($Y_i > x$) at time x, over the time range $(0, L_1)$. There are, then, $n - N(L_1 - 0)$ individuals remaining with $y_i > L_1$. With probability $N(L_1 - 0)/M(L_1 - 0)$, the individual censored at time L_1 is among the $N(L_1 - 0)$ survivors, and thus we let $N(L_1 + 0)$ be defined by a simple binomial experiment.

$$
N(L_1 + 0) = \begin{cases} N(L_1 - 0) & \text{with probability} \quad 1 - (N(x)/M(x)) \\[2mm] N(L_1 - 0) - 1 & \text{with probability} \quad (N(x)/M(x)). \end{cases}
$$

In the latter case we delete one of the remaining Y_i at random, and now continue as before. The evolution of the process so constructed is clearly Markovian. Thus, the process $N(x)$ is Markovian and in similar fashion it may be seen that $(N(x), D(x))$, $(N(x), \hat{S}(x))$ and $(N(x), S^*(x))$ are also Markovian.

2.2 First moments — the bias of $\hat{S}(x)$

In view of the fact that we set $\hat{S}(x) = 0$ in the indeterminate case, it may be expected that, for fixed x, $E\{\hat{S}(x)\} < S(x)$, and this is indeed the case.

Lemma. $E\{S^*(x)\} = S(x)$ for every x.

Proof.

$$
S^*(x) = p_1^* \cdots p_{k+1}^*.
$$

Although the p_i^* are not independent, they are uncorrelated and, conditional on N_i, each p_i^* is binomial (N_i^*, p_i). Thus taking successive conditional expectations we find that $E\{p_1^* \cdots p_{k+1}^*\} = p_i \cdots p_{k+1}$, as claimed.

Theorem. $\hat{S}(x)$ is a 'nearly unbiased' estimator of $S(x)$. Specifically,

$$
0 \leq S(x) - E\{\hat{S}(x)\} \leq e^{-N(x)}.
$$

Proof. From the definitions, $S^*(x) = \hat{S}(x) + B(x)$ with $0 \leqq B(x) \leqq 1$, and $B(x) = 0$ unless (a) the last surviving case is lost before death, and (b) this event occurs earlier than x.

Now $M(x)$ = number of cases for which $L_i > x$ and if at least one of these is a survivor at time x we have $B(x) = 0$. So $\Pr\{B(x) > 0\} \leqq (1 - S(x))^{M(x)} \leqq e^{-\mathcal{N}(x)}$ from which the stated result follows directly.

2.3 The asymptotic variance of $\hat{S}(t)$ — Greenwood's formula

In 1926 Major Greenwood [11] proposed that the variance of the familiar 'actuarial' estimator (for discussion see [3]) should be approximated as that of a product of independent binomials. Thus, taking

$$\bar{S}(x) = \prod_{i=1}^{r} \bar{p}_i,$$

we paraphrase his results as

$$\text{Var}\{\bar{S}(x)\} = S^2(x) \left[\prod_{i=1}^{r} \left(1 + \frac{q_i}{n_i p_i}\right) - 1 \right] \sim S^2(x) \sum_{i=1}^{r} \frac{q_i}{n_i p_i}.$$

In the simple case, with no censored observations, the estimator $\bar{S}^2 \Sigma \bar{q}_i / n_i \bar{p}_i$ reduces to $\bar{S}^2(1 - \bar{S})/n\bar{S} = \bar{S}(1 - \bar{S})/n$, the usual result for a simple proportion. This result follows from the identity $n_i = n \bar{p}_i \cdots \bar{p}_{i-1}$ so that

$$\frac{\bar{q}_i}{n_i \bar{p}_i} + \frac{\bar{q}_{i+1}}{n_{i+1} \bar{p}_{i+1}} = \frac{1 - \bar{p}_i \bar{p}_{i+1}}{n_i \bar{p}_i \bar{p}_{i+1}}.$$

The asymptotic equivalence of Greenwood's two formulas and their validity in the general case, assuming only that $\mathcal{N}(x) = E\{N(x)\} \to \infty$, is the content of the theorem and corollary which we now prove.

Theorem. Consider a fixed distribution function, $S(x)$, and a sequence of censored sampling processes each characterized by $S(x)$ and by the sample size function, $M(x)$, such that for a given value of x,

$$\mathcal{N}(x) = E\{N(x)\} = M(x)S(x) \to \infty,$$

and

$$0 < S(x) < 1.$$

Then, if

$$C(x) = \sum_{i=1}^{k+1} \frac{q_i}{n_i p_i},$$

(a)
$$C(x) \leq \frac{1}{\mathcal{N}(x)},$$

(b)
$$\lim_{\mathcal{N}(x) \to \infty} \frac{C'(x)}{C(x)} = \lim_{\mathcal{N}(x) \to \infty} \frac{C''(x)}{C(x)} = 1,$$

where

$$C'(x) = \prod_{i=1}^{k+1} \left(1 + \frac{q_i}{n_i p_i}\right) - 1$$

and

$$C''(x) = e^{C(x)} - 1,$$

(c)
$$\lim_{\mathcal{N}(x) \to \infty} E\left\{\left[\frac{S^*(x) - S(x)}{S(x)\sqrt{C(x)}}\right]^2\right\} = 1,$$

that is, $\sqrt{C(x)}$ is the asymptotic coefficient of variation of $S^*(x)$.

Proof. (a) follows from the fact that $M(x)$ is a decreasing function of x, by using the reduction identity above.

(b) follows from the observation that for $a_1, \cdots, a_k > 0$,

$$\Sigma a_i \leq \Pi(1 + a_i) - 1 \leq e^{\Sigma a_i} - 1 \text{ and that } \lim_{x \to 0} \frac{e^x - 1}{x} = 1.$$

To establish (c) we proceed as follows. The idea is that for $\mathcal{N}(x)$ large, the sequence $N_1, \cdots, N_{k+1}$ is 'close' to the sequence of expected values, $\mathcal{N}_1, \cdots, \mathcal{N}_{k+1}$, so that Greenwood's treatment of $\bar{S}(x)$ as a product of independent binomial proportions is asymptotically valid. We show first that

$$\lim_{\mathcal{N}(x) \to \infty} E\left\{\left[\frac{S^*(x) - S(x)}{S(x)\sqrt{C(x)}}\right]^2\right\} \leq 1$$

and to that end we define $W_i = 1$ or 0, according as $N_i^* < (1 - \epsilon)\mathcal{N}_i$ or not. Then

$$E\{(p_i^*)^2 \mid N_i\} = p_i^2\left(1 + \frac{q_i}{N_i^* p_i}\right) \leq p_i^2\left(1 + \frac{q_i}{(1 - \epsilon)\mathcal{N}_i p_i}\right) + p_i q_i W_i.$$

Observe that the first term is a constant, independent of the fluctuations of the process, and the second term, $p_i q_i W_i$ (which is a function of N_i) goes to zero in probability at a fast rate as $\mathcal{N}(x) \to \infty$. Taking successive conditional expectations as before, we obtain

$$E\{[S^*(x)]^2\} \le S^2(x) \prod_{i=1}^{k+1} \left(1 + \frac{q_i}{(1-\epsilon)\mathcal{N}_i p_i}\right) + \sum_{i=1}^{k+1} p_i q_i E\{W_i\}$$

so that

$$E\left\{\left[\frac{S^*(x) - S(x)}{S(x)\sqrt{C(x)}}\right]^2\right\} \le \frac{\prod_{i=1}^{k+1}\left(1 + \frac{q_i}{(1-\epsilon)\mathcal{N}_i p_i}\right) - 1}{C(x)} + \frac{1}{S^2(x)} \frac{\sum_{i=1}^{k+1} p_i q_i E\{W_i\}}{C(x)}.$$

As in the proof of assertion (b), the first term on the right approaches $1/(1-\epsilon)$ as $\mathcal{N}(x) \to \infty$. Recalling the definition, $C(x) = \Sigma q_i / \mathcal{N}_i p_i$ the second term is seen to converge to zero if max $\mathcal{N}_i E\{W_i\} \to 0$. Now from Chebyshev's inequality we can show that

$$E\{W_i\} = \Pr\{N_i - n_i < -\epsilon \mathcal{N}_i\} \le \Pr\{(N_i - \mathcal{N}_i)^4 > \epsilon^4 \mathcal{N}_i^4\}$$

$$\le \left(\frac{\text{const}}{\epsilon^4 (S(x))^2}\right) \left(\frac{1}{\mathcal{N}(x)}\right)^2,$$

since N_i is binomial, $(M(x), S(x))$, Thus max $\mathcal{N}_i E\{W_i\} \to 0$ as $\mathcal{N}(x) \to \infty$, as required.

Finally, we see that

$$\lim_{\mathcal{N}(x) \to \infty} E\left\{\left[\frac{S^*(x) - S(x)}{S(x)\sqrt{C(x)}}\right]^2\right\} \le \frac{1}{1-\epsilon} \qquad \text{for every } \epsilon$$

so that

$$\lim E\left\{\left[\frac{S^*(x) - S(x)}{S(x)\sqrt{C(x)}}\right]^2\right\} \le 1,$$

as stated.

A similar argument shows that

$$\lim E\left\{\left[\frac{S^*(x) - S(x)}{S(x)\sqrt{C(x)}}\right]^2\right\} \ge 1$$

and assertion (c) then follows.

Corollary. On account of the high probability that $\hat{S}(x) = S^*(x)$, the following hold.

(a) $\dfrac{\hat{S}(x) - S(x)}{S(x)\sqrt{C(x)}}$ converges in probability to $\dfrac{S^*(x) - S(x)}{S(x)\sqrt{C(x)}}$,

provided $\mathcal{N}(x) \to \infty$.

(b) $\lim_{\mathcal{N}(x)\to\infty} E\left[\dfrac{\hat{S}(x) - S(x)}{S(x)\sqrt{C(x)}}\right] = 0$, provided $\lim_{\mathcal{N}(x)\to\infty} \sqrt{C(x)}\,e^{\mathcal{N}(x)} = \infty$.

(c) $\lim_{\mathcal{N}(x)\to\infty} E\left\{\left[\dfrac{\hat{S}(x) - S(x)}{S(x)\sqrt{C(x)}}\right]^2\right\} = 1$, provided $\lim_{\mathcal{N}(x)\to\infty} C(x)\,e^{\mathcal{N}(x)} = \infty$.

Proof. The 'normalized' variables $(\hat{S}(x) - S(x))/S(x)\sqrt{C(x)}$ and $(S^*(x) - S(x))/S(x)\sqrt{C(x)}$ are identical, except possibly in the case where $N(x) = 0$. Since, as we have shown, $\Pr\{N(x) = 0\} \leqq e^{-\mathcal{N}(x)}$ which approaches zero as $\mathcal{N}(x)\to\infty$, the convergence in probability and the condition required for asymptotic unbiasedness are immediate. It may be seen that the derivation of the asymptotic variance used in the theorem above fails in the case of $\hat{S}(x)$ because the multiplier q_i (in the term involving W_i) no longer applies in the case of the bound for $E\{\hat{p}_i^2 \mid N_i\}$, and the condition specified is needed to guarantee the convergence. In fact, if the condition fails, as it may when $S(x)$ is constant, or nearly so, in the neighborhood of x, the bias resulting from assigning $\hat{S}(x)$ the value zero when $N(x) = 0$ may be comparable or greater in magnitude than the asymptotic standard error, $S(x)\sqrt{C(x)}$.

The asymptotic covariance of $\hat{S}(u)$ and $\hat{S}(v)$ may be dealt with in the same fashion, leading to the following result.

Theorem. Suppose that the conditions of the previous theorem are satisfied and that for a given value of x, say T, $\mathcal{N}(T)\to\infty$.

(a) The stochastic process, $S^*(x)$, $0 \leqq x \leqq T$ has second moment function, $\mathrm{Cov}\{S^*(u), S^*(v)\}$ such that

$$\lim_{\mathcal{N}(T)\to\infty} \frac{\mathrm{Cov}\{S^*(u), S^*(v)\}}{S(u)\,S(v)\,C(u)} = 1 \quad \text{for} \quad 0 < u \leqq v \leqq T.$$

(b) Also, the process $\hat{S}(x)$, $0 \leqq x \leqq T$ converges in probability to $S^*(x)$, $0 \leqq x \leqq T$, as $\mathcal{N}(T)\to\infty$ and

$$\lim_{\mathcal{N}(T)\to\infty} \frac{\mathrm{Cov}\{\hat{S}(u), \hat{S}(v)\}}{S(u)\,S(v)\,C(u)} = 1 \text{ for } 0 < u \leqq v \leqq T$$

provided that $\lim_{\mathcal{N}(T)\to\infty} C(T)\,e^{\mathcal{N}(T)} = \infty$.

Proof. Observe that for $u < v$, $S^*(u) = p_1^* \cdots p_{k_u}^* p_{k_u+1}^*$ and $S^*(v) = S^*(u)p_{k_u+1}^* \cdots p_{k_v+1}^*$ so that $S^*(u)S^*(v) = (S^*(u))^2 p_{k_u+1}^* \cdots p_{k_v+1}^*$, where the notation is the obvious extension of that introduced earlier. Following the same procedures as before, using conditional expectations, we find that

$$E\{S^*(u)S^*(v)\,|\,(N(\tau),\,S^*(\tau)),\,\tau \leqq u\} = [S^*(u)]^2\frac{S(v)}{S(u)}.$$

$E\{[S^*(u)]^2\}$ is given by the previous theorem, and the result establishes assertion (a). Part (b) follows from the fact that, with probability greater than $1 - e^{-\mathcal{N}(T)}$, $\hat{S}(x) = S^*(x)$ for all $x \leqq T$.

2.4 *Consistency of* $\hat{S}(x)$

With the above results we are now in a position to establish the convergence in probability to $S(x)$ for both $\hat{S}(x)$ and $S^*(x)$.

Theorem. (Glivenko–Cantelli) Given a fixed distribution function, $S(x)$, and a sequence of censored sampling processes such that $\mathcal{N}(x) \to \infty$ for all x such that $S(x) > 0$.

$$\lim \Pr\{\sup_x |\hat{S}(x) - S(x)| > \epsilon\} = 0$$

for every $\epsilon > 0$.

Note. The same result holds, of course, for $S^*(x)$. If $\mathcal{N}(x) \to \infty$ for $x \leqq T$, but not necessarily for all x such that $S(x) > 0$, we have

$$\lim_{\mathcal{N}(T) \to \infty} \Pr\{\sup_{x \leqq T} |\hat{S}(x) - S(x)| > \epsilon\} = 0$$

for every $\epsilon > 0$.

Proof. For the proof of the Glivenko–Cantelli theorem it is sufficient that

(1) $S(x)$ be bounded.
(2) $S(x)$ be monotone.
(3) $\lim \Pr\{|\hat{S}(x) - S(x)| > \epsilon\} = 0$ for every x and every $\epsilon > 0$.

Conditions (1) and (2) are immediate from the definition of $\hat{S}(x)$. Condition (3) follows from the asymptotic equivalence of $\hat{S}(x)$ and $S^*(x)$, and the asymptotic result for the variance of $S^*(x)$.

2.5 *Asymptotic normality of* $\hat{S}(x)$

From our earlier results concerning the first two moments of $S^*(x)$ and $\hat{S}(x)$ it seems plausible that

$$\frac{\hat{S}(x) - S(x)}{S(x)\sqrt{C(x)}}$$

might be distributed asymptotically $N(0, 1)$. The method we use to prove this, subject to appropriate conditions, is to show that $\hat{S}(x)$ is asymptotically equivalent to a sum of independent (although not identically distributed) random variables to which the Liapounoff Central Limit Theorem applies.

Lemma 1.   Given a fixed distribution function, $S(x)$, and a sequence of censored sampling processes such that for some fixed value of x, $\mathcal{N}(x) \to \infty$, then

$$\frac{S^*(x) - S(x)}{S(x)\sqrt{C(x)}} = \frac{1}{\sqrt{C(x)}} \sum_{i=1}^{k+1} \frac{p_i^* - p_i}{p_i} + o_p(\mathcal{N}(x))$$

(where $Z = o_p(\mathcal{N})$ means that Z converges to zero in probability as $\mathcal{N} \to \infty$).

Proof.

$$S^*(x) = \prod_{i=1}^{k+1} p_i^* = \prod p_i \prod \left(1 + \frac{p_i^* - p_i}{p_i}\right)$$

$$= S(x) \prod \left(1 + \frac{p_i^* - p_i}{p_i}\right).$$

Now, if we can be sure that all of the $(p_i^* - p_i)/p_i$ are of magnitude less than unity, we could establish the inequality (starting from $x - x^2/2 \leq \ln(1 + x) \leq x$)

$$S(x) \exp\left[\sum \frac{p_i^* - p_i}{p_i}\right] \exp\left[-\frac{1}{2} \sum \left(\frac{p_i^* - p_i}{p_i}\right)^2\right]$$

$$\leq S^*(x)$$

$$\leq S(x) \exp\left[\sum \frac{p_i^* - p_i}{p_i}\right].$$

Since p_i^*, conditional on N_i, is binomial (N_i^*, p_i) we have

$$E\left\{\sum \left(\frac{p_i^* - p_i}{p_i}\right)^2\right\} = \sum \frac{q_i}{p_i} E\left\{\frac{1}{N_i^*}\right\}$$

$$\leq \sum \frac{q_i}{p_i} \frac{2}{\mathcal{N}_i}$$

$$\leq \frac{2(1 - S(x))}{\mathcal{N}(x)S(x)} \to 0.$$

(The inequality, $E\{1/N_i^*\} \leq 2/\mathcal{N}_i$ is readily proved by the methods of Stephan [16], see also [13].)

Thus $\Sigma\{p_i^* - p_i)/p_i\}^2$ converges to zero in probability and it follows that the same is true for $\max[(p_i^* - p_i)/p_i]$. Hence, with probability approaching unity, the inequality for $S^*(x)$ is satisfied and, since $S^*(x)$ converges to $S(x)$ in probability, $\Sigma(p_i^* - p_i)/p_i$ converges in probability to zero. If we now write the corresponding inequality for $(S^*(x) - S(x))/S(x)\sqrt{C(x)}$ we can show that both the left and right hand sides converge to $\Sigma[(p_i^* - p_i)/p_i]/\sqrt{C(x)}$ and the lemma is established.

As we have seen, the $(p_i^* - p_i)/p_i$ are uncorrelated, but they are not independent. To show the equivalence of $\Sigma[(p_i^* - p_i)/p_i]$ to a sum of independent random variables we proceed by a familiar method. Let $p_1, \cdots, p_{k+1}$ be defined as before, and, for each $i = 1, 2, \cdots, k + 1$ we consider a sequence of Bernoulli variables $\{X_{ir}\}$, such that $\Pr\{X_{ir} = 1\} = p_i$, $\Pr\{X_{ir} = 0\} = q_i$, and all X_{ir} are jointly independent. On the sample space thus created we define $p_1^*, \cdots, p_{k+1}^*$ in accordance with the construction used in Section 2.1, that is $p_i^* = (\Sigma_{r=1}^{N_i} X_{ir})/N_i$. On the same sample space we define $p_1', \cdots, p_{k+1}'$ by choosing $\mathcal{N}_i' = [\mathcal{N}_i] + 1$ and

$$p_i' = \left(\sum_{r=1}^{\mathcal{N}_i'} X_{ir} \right) \Big/ \mathcal{N}_i'.$$

These definitions are chosen so that the p_i^* have the joint distribution specified earlier, and the p_i' are independent binomial proportions with sample sizes essentially equal to the expected values of the sample sizes for the p_i^*. As defined here, however, the p_i^* and p_i' are highly correlated, and the difference between them is, for our purposes, negligible.

The proof of the following lemma is straightforward and similar to those given earlier, and the details are omitted.

Lemma 2.   Let p_i^* and p_i', $i = 1, \cdots, k + 1$ be as defined above. Then

$$\frac{1}{\sqrt{C(x)}} \sum \frac{p_i^* - p_i}{p_i} = \frac{1}{\sqrt{C(x)}} \sum \frac{p_i' - p_i}{p_i} + o_p(\mathcal{N}(x)).$$

With these two lemmas we have established that $[S^*(x) - S(x)]/[S(x)\sqrt{C(x)}]$ is asymptotically equivalent to a sum of independent random variables — in fact, a linear combination of independent binomial random variables. This linear combination has mean 0 and variance 1, and one might expect that, provided $0 < S(x) < 1$ and $C(x) \rightarrow 0$, the asymptotic distribution will be normal. In fact, this need not be the case; the limit distribution may have a Poisson component as well (or instead).

The essential feature which leads to a combination of normal and Poisson components is an abrupt drop in the order of magnitude of $\mathcal{N}(x)$ combined with a very small rate of change of $S(x)$. This is by no means an unlikely situation in applications. For example, a large sample may be followed for a period of 3 years, in which most of the mortality occurs, and only a small fraction are followed up for an additional 2 years. Very little mortality occurs in the latter groups, and we may wish to place limits on $\hat{S}(5)$. The distribution in this case may be closer to Poissson than to normal. In order to insure that we reach a normal limit we must impose a condition which excludes this case.

Theorem. Given a fixed distribution function, $S(x)$, and a sequence of censored sampling processes such that for a given value of x, $\mathcal{N}(x) \to \infty$, then provided $\mathcal{N}^2(x)C(x) \to \infty$, the random variable

$$\frac{\hat{S}(x) - S(x)}{S(x)\sqrt{C(x)}}$$

converges in distribution to $N(0, 1)$, as $\mathcal{N}(x) \to \infty$.

Proof. We have shown that

$$\frac{\hat{S}(x) - S(x)}{S(x)\sqrt{C(x)}} \sim \frac{S^*(x) - S(x)}{S(x)\sqrt{C(x)}} \sim \frac{1}{\sqrt{C(x)}} \sum_{i=1}^{k+1} \left(\frac{p_i' - p_i}{p_i} \right)$$

$$= \frac{1}{\sqrt{C(x)}} \sum_{i=1}^{k+1} \sum_{r=1}^{i} \left(\frac{X_{ir} - p_i}{\mathcal{N}_i p_i} \right)$$

where the X_i are independent binomial $(1, p_i)$ random variables. We have $E\{X_i\} = p_i$, $\mathrm{Var}\{X_i\} = p_i q_i$,

$$E\{|X_i - p_i|^3\} = p_i q_i(p_i^2 + q_i^2) \leqq p_i q_i.$$

Let

$$Z_{ir} = \frac{X_{ir} - p_i}{\mathcal{N}_i p_i \sqrt{C(x)}},$$

then

$$E\{Z_{ir}\} = 0, \quad \sigma_{ir}^2 = \mathrm{Var}\{Z_{ir}\} = \left(\frac{1}{C(x)} \right) \left(\frac{q_i}{\mathcal{N}_i^2 p_i} \right)$$

$$\rho_{ir}^3 = E\{|Z_{ir}|^3\} \leqq \left(\frac{1}{[C(x)]^{\frac{3}{2}} \mathcal{N}_i^2 p_i} \right) \left(\frac{q_i}{\mathcal{N}_i p_i} \right)$$

and it is easily seen that

$$\sigma^2 = \sum_{i,r} \sigma_{ir}^2 = \frac{1}{C(x)} \sum_{i=1}^{k+1} \frac{q_i}{\mathcal{N}_i p_i} = 1$$

$$\rho^3 = \sum_{i,r} \rho_i^3 \leqq \frac{\sum_{i=1}^{k+1} \left(\frac{1}{\mathcal{N}_i p_i}\right) \left(\frac{q_i}{\mathcal{N}_i p_i}\right)}{\left(\sum_{i=1}^{k+1} \frac{q_i}{\mathcal{N}_i p_i}\right)^{\frac{3}{2}}}.$$

It is then easy to verify that the condition of the Liapounoff Central Limit Theorem, namely $\rho/\sigma \to 0$, is satisfied if $\mathcal{N}^2(x)C(x) \to \infty$. Thus, assuming $\mathcal{N}^2(x)C(x) \to \infty$, $(\hat{S}(x) - S(x))/S(x)\sqrt{C(x)}$ is asymptotically $N(0, 1)$, and the theorem is proved.

The following corollary is proved in the same way as the above theorem, using the decomposition into sums of independent random variables.

Corollary. As in the above theorem, suppose there is given a fixed distribution function, $S(x)$, and a sequence of censored sampling processes such that for a given value of x, say T, $\mathcal{N}(T) \to \infty$ and $\mathcal{N}^2(T)C(T) \to \infty$. Let $0 \leqq u_1 \leqq \cdots \leqq u_r \leqq T$. Then the random variables

$$\psi_1 = \frac{\hat{S}(u_1) - S(u_1)}{S(u_1)\sqrt{C(T)}}, \cdots, \psi_r = \frac{\hat{S}(u_r) - S(u_r)}{S(u_r)\sqrt{C(T)}}$$

are jointly asymptotically normal with asymptotic means μ_i, and asymptotic covariances σ_{ij}, given by $\mu_i = 0$, $i = 1, 2, \cdots, r$ and $\sigma_{ij} = C(u_i)/C(T)$ for $i \leqq j$.

3. Weak convergence of $\hat{S}(x)$

3.1 *Introduction*

Having determined the asymptotic covariance function of $\hat{S}(x)$, it is natural to ask about the distributions of simple functionals, such as $\hat{\mu} = \int_0^\infty \hat{S}(x)dx$. Thus, Irwin [12] gave an approximation to the variance of $\bar{\mu}_T = \int_0^T \bar{S}(x)dx$, based on the approximate covariance function. However, the proof of our analogous result requires that we establish a compactness condition called 'tightness' for the sequence of processes under consideration.

It is often easier to prove tightness for a sequence of slightly modified processes and, provided that the two sequences converge in probability, tightness for one implies tightness for the other.

Suppose, then, that $\{Y_n(x)\}$ is a sequence of stochastic processes for which we seek to prove tightness. A sufficient condition (see [4], p. 106) is that for every $u < t < v$ and for all sufficiently large n,

$$E\{(Y_n(v) - Y_n(t))^2(Y_n(t) - Y_n(u))^2\} \leq K(v - t)(t - u),$$

where K is some constant.

3.2 The modified process $S^\epsilon(x)$

Proof of the above condition for $\hat{S}(x)$ would be simpler were we able to guarantee that $N(x)$ remains of order n, for all x. It is not sufficient that it does so with high probability for each x. Accordingly, it is convenient to replace $\hat{S}(x)$ by a closely related process, $S^\epsilon(x)$, defined as follows.

For each sample path, let x_ϵ be the least x for which $N(x) < (1 - \epsilon)\mathcal{N}(x) + 1$.

Define

$$N^\epsilon(x) = \begin{cases} N(x) & \text{for} \quad x \leq x_\epsilon \\ \mathcal{N}(x) & \text{for} \quad x > x_\epsilon \end{cases}$$

and

$$S^\epsilon(x) = \begin{cases} \hat{S}(x) & \text{for} \quad x \leq x_\epsilon \\ (\hat{S}(x_\epsilon)/S(x_\epsilon))S(x) & \text{for} \quad x > x_\epsilon. \end{cases}$$

Clearly, $E\{S^\epsilon(x)\} = S(x)$ and $\text{Var}\{S^\epsilon(x)\} \leq \{(1 - \epsilon)\mathcal{N}(x)\}^{-1}$ for all x.

Theorem. Let $(N_j(x), \hat{S}_j(x))$ be a sequence of processes as defined in Section 1.5 and let $(N_j^\epsilon(x), S_j^\epsilon(x))$ be the modified version, as described above. Provided that $\lim_{j \to \infty} \mathcal{N}_j(T) = \infty$, the sequence

$$\sqrt{\mathcal{N}_j(T)}(S_j^\epsilon(x) - S(x))$$

is tight.

Proof. In this case $Y_n(x) = \sqrt{\mathcal{N}_j(T)}(S_j^\epsilon(x) - S(x))$ and the requirement becomes

$$\mathcal{N}^2(T)E\{[(S^\epsilon(v) - S(v)) - (S^\epsilon(t) - S(t))]^2$$

$$\times [(S^\epsilon(t) - S(t)) - (S^\epsilon(u) - S(u))]^2\}$$

$$\leq K(v - t)(t - u),$$

where K is a constant. If we define $p_1 = S(u)$, $p_2 = S(t)/S(u)$, $p_3 = S(v)/S(t)$ this may be rewritten in obvious notation as

$$\mathcal{N}^2(T)E\{[p_1^\epsilon q_2^\epsilon - p_1 q_2)^2(p_1^\epsilon p_2^\epsilon q_3^\epsilon - p_1 p_2 q_3)^2\} \leqq Kp_1^2 p_2 q_2 q_3.$$

The type of calculation used for second moments in Section 2.3 must now be extended to third and fourth moments. These calculations are tedious but straightforward, and they lead to the required inequality, verifying that the sequence is tight.

Corollary. Any sequence of processes which converges in probability to $\sqrt{\mathcal{N}(T)}(S^\epsilon(x) - S(x))$ is also tight.

3.3 *Conditions for convergence of* $\hat{S}(x)$ *and* $S^\epsilon(x)$

From the construction of $S^\epsilon(x)$ we should expect that, under reasonable conditions,

$$\Pr\{\sup_{x \leqq T} \sqrt{\mathcal{N}(T)} | \hat{S}(x) - S^\epsilon(x)| > \epsilon\} \to 0 \text{ as } \mathcal{N}(T) \to \infty.$$

Although more general conditions clearly could be found, the following lemma will serve for cases in which the fraction lost prior to T is bounded away from unity.

Lemma. Consider a sequence of censored sampling processes for which $\lim \sup \mathcal{N}(T)/n < 1$. Then

$$\Pr\{\sup_{x \leqq T} | N(x) - \mathcal{N}(x)| > \epsilon\} \to 0 \text{ as } \mathcal{N}(T) \to \infty.$$

Proof. As in Section 2.4, the conditions required for proof of the Glivenko–Cantelli theorem are satisfied by the function $N(x)/n$ and the conclusion therefore follows.

Corollary. Let $\{\hat{S}_i(x)\}$ be a sequence of censored processes for which $\mathcal{N}_i(T) \to \infty$ and $\lim \sup (\mathcal{N}(T)/n) < 1$. Then the sequence

$$\{\sqrt{\mathcal{N}(T)}(\hat{S}_i(x) - S(x))\}$$

is tight, and, in view of the already proved asymptotic normality, the sequence converges (weakly) to a suitably transformed Brownian Motion.

3.4 *An application*

The most immediate application of our weak convergence proof is to the restricted mean, $\mu_T = \int_0^T S(x)dx$. Following Irwin [12] we choose the restricted mean, since the censoring will generally preclude any serious attempt to estimate $\mu = \int_0^\infty S(x)\,dx$.

In this case it follows from the convergence just proved that if

$$\hat{\mu}_T = \int_0^T \hat{S}(x)\,dx, \qquad \text{(see [4] and [13])}$$

then

$$E\{\hat{\mu}_T\} = \mu_T$$

$$\text{Var}\{\hat{\mu}_T\} \approx 2 \int_0^T \int_u^T S(u)S(v)C(u)\,dv\,du$$

and

$$\frac{\hat{\mu}_T - \mu_T}{\sqrt{\{\text{Var}(\hat{\mu}_T)\}}} \sim N(0, 1).$$

Similar results apply to a wide class of functionals of $\hat{S}(x)$.

4. Historical note

The so-called 'actuarial method' for constructing a life table from censored data, a grouped version of the method elaborated here, has been in the literature for many years [5], [3]. Appropriate formulas for variances and covariances were put forward by Greenwood [11] and by Irwin [12].

In 1958 Kaplan and Meier [13] introduced the product-limit estimator and explored some of its properties. The estimator was studied further, this time under the assumption of random censorship, by Efron [10] in 1967. In 1967 the writer undertook a more detailed study of the estimator in the more general arbitrarily censored case. A manuscript [14] was prepared and given limited circulation which contains all results reported here, except for the material in Section 3, dealing with weak convergence. (I am indebted to Patrick Billingsley for helpful discussions leading to the results in that section.) Quite recently further work has been reported by Breslow and Crowley [6] dealing with the case of random censorship, and by Aalen [1], who extends the random censorship case to the general multiple decrement model. Meanwhile, extensions of these methods by Peto and Peto [15] and by Cox [7] have led to procedures of great importance, permitting the incorporation of covariate information into the analysis of censored data.

As indicated in Section 3, the general case of arbitrarily variably censored observations is important in practice and leads to some results not obtainable through the random censorship and multiple decrement models.

Acknowledgement

Support for this research has been provided in part by an NIH Special Fellowship award, by Research Grant No. NSF GP 32037X from the Division of Mathematical, Physical, and Engineering Sciences of the National Science Foundation, and by the Office of Naval Research, Contract No. N00014-67-A-0285-0009.

References

[1] AALEN, O. (1973) Nonparametric inference in connection with multiple decrement models. *Statistical Research Report* (*mimeo*), Institute of Mathematics, University of Oslo.

[2] BARTLETT, M. S. (1966) *An Introduction to Stochastic Processes with Special Reference to Methods and Applications.* University Press, Cambridge.

[3] BERKSON, J. AND GAGE, R. P. (1950) Calculation of survival rates for cancer. *Proc. Mayo Clinic* **25**, 270–286.

[4] BILLINGSLEY, P. (1968) *Weak Convergence of Probability Measures.* Wiley, New York.

[5] BÖHMER, P. E. (1912) Theorie der unabhängigen Wahrscheinlichkeiten. *Rapports, Mémoires et Procès-verbaux du Septième Congrès International d'Actuaires*, Amsterdam. **2**, 327–343.

[6] BRESLOW, N. AND CROWLEY, J. (1974) A large sample study of the life table and product limit estimates under random censorship. *Ann. Statist.* **2**, 437–453.

[7] COX, D. R. (1972) Regression models and life tables. *J. R. Statist. Soc. Ser.* B **34**, 187–220.

[8] DONSKER, M. (1952) Justification and extension of Doob's heuristic approach to the Kolmogorov-Smirnov theorems. *Ann. Math. Statist.* **23**, 277–281.

[9] DOOB, J. L. (1949) Heuristic approach to the Kolmogorov-Smirnov theorems. *Ann. Math. Statist.* **20**, 393–403.

[10] EFRON, B. (1967) The two sample problem with censored data. *Proc. Fifth Berkeley Symp. Math. Statist. Prob.* **4**, 831–853.

[11] GREENWOOD, M. (1926) The natural duration of cancer. *Reports on Public Health and Medical Subjects* **33**, H. M. Stationary Office, London.

[12] IRWIN, J. O. (1949) The standard error of an estimate of expectation of life. *J. Hygiene* **47**, 188–189.

[13] KAPLAN, E. L. AND MEIER, P. (1958) Non-parametric estimation from incomplete observations. *J. Amer. Statist. Assoc.* **53**, 457–481.

[14] MEIER, P. (1967) Nonparametric estimation from incomplete observations — II. (Unpublished MS.)

[15] PETO, R. AND PETO, J. (1972) Asymptotically efficient rank invariant test procedures. *J. R. Statist. Soc. Ser.* A **135**, 185–198.

[16] STEPHAN, F. F. (1945) The expected value and variance of the reciprocal and other negative powers of a positive Bernoullian variate. *Ann. Math. Statist.* **16**, 50–61.

[17] WAGNER, S. S. AND ALTMAN, S. A. (1973) What time do the baboons come down from the trees? (An estimation problem.) *Biometrics* **29**, 623–635.

On A Unified Theory of Estimation in Linear Models—A Review of Recent Results

C. RADHAKRISHNA RAO

Abstract

The paper deals with two approaches to the estimation of the parameters β and σ^2 in the General Gauss-Markoff (GGM) model represented by the triplet $(Y, X\beta, \sigma^2 V)$, where $E(Y) = X\beta$ and $D(Y) = \sigma^2 V$, when no assumptions are made about the ranks of X and V. One is called Inverse Partition Matrix (IPM) method, which depends on the numerical evaluation of the g-inverse of a partitioned matrix. The second is an analogue of least squares theory applicable even when V is singular, unlike Atiken's method which is applicable only for non-singular V, and is called Unified Least Square (ULS) method.

1. General Gauss-Markoff model

Consider the triplet

$$(1.1) \qquad\qquad (Y, X\beta, \sigma^2 V)$$

where Y is an $n \times 1$ vector of random variables, X is a given $n \times m$ matrix and V is a given $n \times n$ non-negative definite (n.n.d.) matrix. Furthermore $E(Y) = X\beta$ and $D(Y) = \sigma^2 V$, where β an $m \times 1$ vector and σ^2 are unknown parameters to be estimated. Note that D stands for dispersion or variance-covariance operator. We refer to (1.1) as the GGM (General Gauss-Markoff) model when no assumption is made about $R(V)$ and $R(X)$, the ranks of V and X.

We use the following notations throughout the paper. $\mathcal{M}(\cdot)$ with a matrix argument denotes the linear space generated by the columns of the matrix. $(V: X)$ is a partitioned matrix. $A^{\perp}$ is a matrix of maximum rank such that $A'A^{\perp} = 0$.

89

A^- is said to be a g-inverse of A if $AA^-A = A$ (see [16], [21]). The class of all g-inverses of A is denoted by $\{A^-\}$. The projection operator on $\mathcal{M}(A)$ is represented by P_A. Note that

$$P_A = A(A'A)^-A' \text{ when the inner product } (x, y) = x'y,$$
$$= A(A'DA)^-A'D \text{ when the inner product } (x, y) = x'Dy$$

where D is a positive definite matrix.

Let $K = V^\perp$ and $N = K(K'Y)^\perp$ where Y and V are as in the GGM model (1.1). Then the following are true.

(1.2)   (i) $Y \in \mathcal{M}(V: X)$ with probability 1.

(1.3)   (ii) $K'Y = C$ (Constant) with probability 1.

(1.4)   (iii) $Y \in \mathcal{M}(N^\perp)$.

(1.5)   (iv) $N'X\beta = 0$.

(v)   A linear function $L'Y$ is unbiased for a given parametric function $p'\beta$ iff $X'L - p \in M(X'N)$, i.e., there exists a vector λ such that

(1.6) $L'X - p' = \lambda'N'X$ or $p = X'(L - N\lambda)$.

Note that in literature on linear models the condition $p = X'L$ is implicitly assumed as necessary and sufficient for $L'Y$ to be unbiased for $p'\beta$. This is true only when V is non-singular. (See [14], [16], [17], [18].)

(vi)   If $L'Y$ is unbiased for $p'\beta$ in the sense of (1.6), then there exists a vector M such that

(1.7) $M'Y = L'Y$ with probability 1,

(1.8) $M'X = p'$.

This result implies that in seeking for unbiased estimators of $p'\beta$, we may consider the class $M'Y$ with the usual condition $M'X = p'$. (See [14], [16].)

Definition 1.   We shall say that $L'Y$ is the BLUE (best linear unbiased estimator) of $p'\beta$ if $L'VL = \sigma^{-2}V(L'Y)$ is a minimum subject to the condition $X'L = p$.

Definition 2.   We shall say that $L'Y$ is the BLUE (W) (W standing for wider class) of $p'\beta$ if $L'VL = \sigma^{-2}V(L'Y)$ is a minimum subject to the condition $X'L - p \in \mathcal{M}(X'N)$.

The representation of BLUE(W)'s is considered in detail in [17].

2. The IPM ('Pandora Box') approach

Let us consider the standard problem of minimizing $L'VL$ subject to $X'L = p$, which is the problem of the BLUE. With λ as a Lagrangian multiplier, the minimizing equations for L and λ are

$$(2.1) \qquad \begin{matrix} VL + X\lambda = 0 \\ X'L \quad = p \end{matrix} \quad \Leftrightarrow \quad \begin{pmatrix} V & X \\ X' & 0 \end{pmatrix} \begin{pmatrix} L \\ \lambda \end{pmatrix} = \begin{pmatrix} 0 \\ p \end{pmatrix}.$$

If

$$(2.2) \qquad \begin{pmatrix} V & X \\ X' & 0 \end{pmatrix} = \begin{pmatrix} C_1 & C_2 \\ C_3 & -C_4 \end{pmatrix}$$

is one choice of g-inverse, then $L_* = C_2 p$ is a solution for L of (2.1) giving the BLUE of $p'\beta$ as $p'C_2'Y$. Thus the solution depends on the numerical evaluation of an inverse of a partitioned matrix. If only the BLUE is needed, it is enough to compute the partition C_2 only. The following theorem gives the uses of the other partitions in drawing inferences on the unknown parameters.

Theorem 2.1. Let C_1, C_2, C_3, C_4 be as defined in (2.2). Then the following hold:

(i) [Use of C_2 or C_3] The BLUE of an estimable parametric function $p'\beta$ is $p'\hat{\beta}$ where

$$(2.3) \qquad \hat{\beta} = C_2'Y \text{ or } \hat{\beta} = C_3Y.$$

The condition for estimability of $p'\beta$ is

$$(2.4) \qquad p'C_3X = p' \text{ or } X'C_2p = p.$$

(ii) [Use of C_4] The dispersion matrix of $\hat{\beta}$ is $\sigma^2 C_4$ in the sense that

$$(2.5) \qquad V(p'\hat{\beta}) = \sigma^2 p'C_4p,$$

$$(2.6) \qquad \text{Cov}(p'\hat{\beta}, q'\hat{\beta}) = \sigma^2 p'C_4q = \sigma^2 q'C_4p,$$

where $p'\beta$ and $q'\beta$ are estimable functions.

(iii) [Use of C_1] An unbiased estimator of σ^2 is

$$(2.7) \qquad f^{-1}Y'C_1Y, \quad \text{where} \quad f = R(V:X) - R(X).$$

Theorem 2.2. Let $P'\hat{\beta}$ be the vector of BLUE's of k estimable parametric functions $P'\beta$, $R_0^2 = Y'C_1Y$ and f be as defined in (2.7). If $Y \sim N_n(X\beta, \sigma^2 V)$, i.e., n variate normal, then:

(i) $P'\hat{\beta}$ and $Y'C_1Y$ are independently distributed with

(2.8) $P'\hat{\beta} \sim N_k(P'\beta, \sigma^2 G), \ G = P'C_4P,$

(2.9) $Y'C_1Y \sim \sigma^2\chi_f^2,$

where χ_f^2 denotes the central chi-square distribution on f degrees of freedom.

(ii) Let $P'\beta = w$ be the null hypothesis to be tested. The hypothesis is consistent iff

(2.10) $GG^-u = u, \ u = P'\hat{\beta} - w.$

If the hypothesis is consistent, then

$$F = \frac{u'G^-u}{h} \div \frac{R_0^2}{f}, \qquad h = R(G)$$

has central F distribution on h and f degrees of freedom when the null hypothesis is true.

The approach to linear estimation and tests of linear hypotheses as outlined in Theorems 2.1 and 2.2 is called the IPM method. The matrix (2.2) is like the *Pandora Box* which provides all that is necessary for drawing inferences on the unknown parameters. Computer programs exist at several computer centres in the U.S.A. for obtaining g-inverses.

The proofs of Theorems 2.1 and 2.2 are contained in [12], [14], [16] and explicit algebraic expressions for C_1, C_2, C_3 C_4 are given in [13]. A satifactory algorithm for the computation of C_1, C_2, C_3 and C_4 has recently been developed by Björck [28].

Note that the consistency test (2.10) reveals any internal contradictions in the formulation of the hypothesis $P'\beta = w$ as well as contradictions with the sure information $K'X\beta = C$ where K and C are as defined in (1.3). The F statistic (2.11) tests only that part of the hypothesis $P'\beta = w$ where the linear functions are estimable subject to error. The degrees of freedom h correspond to the number of such independent linear functions in $P'\beta$.

3. Unified theory of least squares

In Section 2, we have given a complete treatment of inference on unknown parameters in the GGM model (1.1) through the *Pandora Box* (2.2), which is different from the usual least squares theory. Note that in the IPM approach no assumption was made on $R(V)$, whereas in the usual least squares theory V is assumed to be non-singular. In the present section we shall develop an analogue of least squares theory which is applicable whether V is singular or not, thus providing a unified theory of least squares (and a generalization of Aitken's theorem on least squares [1]).

We raise the following questions. Does there exist a symmetric matrix M such that the following hold?

(R_1) A stationary value $\hat{\beta}$ (i.e., at which the derivative vanishes) of

$$(3.1) \qquad (Y - X\beta)'M(Y - X\beta)$$

provides the BLUE of an estimable function $p'\beta$ as $p'\hat{\beta}$.

(R_2) An unbiased estimator of σ^2 is given by R_0^2/f where

$$(3.2) \qquad \begin{aligned} R_0^2 &= (Y - X\beta)'M(Y - X\beta), \\ f &= R(V : X) - R(X). \end{aligned}$$

(R_3) Let $P'\beta = w$ be a given null hypothesis and R_1^2 be the value of (3.1) at its stationary value when β is subject to the condition $P'\beta = w$. Then

$$(3.3) \qquad F = \frac{R_1^2 - R_0^2}{h} \div \frac{R_0^2}{f}$$

has an F distribution on h and f degrees of freedom, with h as defined in (2.11).

(R_1), (R_2) and (R_3) constitute the basic results in the theory of least squares when $|V| \neq 0$, by choosing $M = V^{-1}$. In the general case the answer is provided by Theorems 3.1–3.6.

Theorem 3.1.   A necessary and sufficient condition for (R_1) to hold is that M is of the form

$$(3.4) \qquad M = (V + XUX')^- + K$$

where U and K are any symmetric matrices such that

$$(3.5) \qquad R(V : X) = R(V + XUX'),$$

$$(3.6) \qquad X'KX = 0, \qquad VKX = 0$$

and $(V + XUX')^-$ is any g-inverse.

Theorem 3.2.   A necessary and sufficient condition for (R_1) and (R_2) to hold is that

$$(3.7) \qquad M = (V + XUX')^-$$

for any choice of g-inverse, where U is any symmetric matrix such that

(3.8) $$R(V + XUX') = R(V:X).$$

Theorem 3.3.   Let M be as in (3.7), $p'\beta$, $q'\beta$ be estimable parametric functions and $\hat{\beta}$ a stationary value of (3.1). Then

(3.9) $$V(p'\hat{\beta}) = \sigma^2 p'[(X'MX)^- - U]p,$$

(3.10) $$\mathrm{Cov}(p'\hat{\beta}, q'\hat{\beta}) = \sigma^2 p'[(X'MX)^- - U]q.$$

Note that the corresponding expressions for variances and covariances in the usual least squares theory do not contain the extra term involving the U matrix. For this reason the following theorem holds.

Theorem 3.4.   There exists no choice of M if (R_3) were to hold for all testable hypotheses in addition to (R_1) and (R_2) unless $M(X) \subset M(V)$.

Note 1.   The proofs of Theorems 3.1–3.3 are given in [12], [15], [16]. The result of Theorem 3.4 is mentioned in [14], [16], and [29].

Note 2.   A simple choice of U is I, the identity matrix which is valid in all situations whether V is singular or not, as mentioned by Rao and Mitra in [22].

Note 3.   The choice of M as in (3.4) for (R_1) to hold or as in (3.7) for (R_1) and (R_2) to hold need not be a g-inverse of V, although the class (3.4) contains g-inverses of V. For instance the simple choice of $M = (V + XX')^-$ need not be a g-inverse of X. However U can be chosen such that $(V + XUX')^-$ is a g-inverse of V. For this, a necessary and sufficient condition is that $\mathcal{M}(V)$ and $\mathcal{M}(XUX')$ are disjoint. The computations involved in such a choice of U are not simple.

The following theorems show that an analogue of least squares theory is possible by slightly altering the condition (R_3).

Theorem 3.5.   Let U be a symmetric matrix such that

(3.11) $\mathcal{M}(V + XUX') = \mathcal{M}(V:X)$ and $\mathcal{M}(V) \cap \mathcal{M}(XUX') = \{\varnothing\}$

where $\{\varnothing\}$ is the null set, in which case $(V + XUX')^-$ is a g-inverse of V. Further let $K = V^{\perp}$. With the choice of M as in (3.11), (R_1) and (R_2) hold. Further if R_1^2 is redefined as the value of $(Y - X\beta)' M(Y - X\beta)$ at a stationary point β subject to the conditions $P'\beta = w$ and $K'X\beta = K'Y$ (instead of the single condition $P'\beta = w$), then (R_3) also holds.

The proof is essentially given in [14]; however, in the paper cited an attempt was made to combine the two conditions $P'\beta = w$ and $K'X\beta = K'Y$ into a single condition $Q'\beta = v$ which serves the same purpose. Note that the hypotheses $P'\beta = w$ and $Q'\beta = v$ are equivalent.

Theorem 3.5 is a better formulation of the corresponding Theorem 5.4 in [14] in two ways. First, we do not insist on $V + XUX'$ being an n.n.d. matrix. Second, the computation of the single condition $Q'\beta = v$ is avoided by using directly the two conditions $P'\beta = w$ and $K'X\beta = K'Y$.

Now we consider a problem posed in [19]. Does there exist a symmetric matrix M such that:

(Q_1) A stationary value β^* of $(Y - X\beta)'M (Y - X\beta)$, subject to the restriction $K'X\beta = K'Y$ where $K = V^\perp$, provides the BLUE of any estimable parametric function $p'\beta$ as $p'\beta^*$.

(Q_2) An unbiased estimator of σ^2 is R_0^2/f where $R_0^2 = (Y - X\beta)'M (Y - X\beta)$, $f = R(V : X) - R(X)$, and has the same value as in (3.2).

(Q_3) Let $P'\beta = \omega$ be any given restriction consistent with $K'X\beta = K'Y$ and $P'\beta$ be estimable. Then $R_1^2 - R_0^2$ and R_0^2 are independently distributed; further

$$R_1^2 - R_0^2 \sim \sigma^2 \chi_h^2,$$

$$R_0^2 \sim \sigma^2 \chi_j^2,$$

where R_1^2 is the value of $(Y - X\beta)'M (Y - X\beta)$ at a stationary value β subject to the conditions $K'X\beta = K'Y$ and $P'\beta = \omega$, and $h = R(P : X'K) - R(X'K)$.

Mitra and Rao [6] have shown that (Q_1), (Q_2) and (Q_3) are satisfied when $M \in \{V^-\}$. Goldman and Zelen [4] gave a similar solution. We show that the condition $M \in \{V^-\}$ is not necessary if only (Q_1) and (Q_2) are satisfied but necessary if (Q_1), (Q_2) and (Q_3) are satisfied.

Theorem 3.6.   Let $A = (X'K)^\perp$. If (Q_1) holds then it is necessary and sufficient that

(3.12) $$\mathcal{M}(X'MXA) \cup \mathcal{M}(X'K) = \mathcal{M}(X')$$

and M is of the form

(3.13) $$M = (V + XAWA'X')^- + B$$

for any choice of symmetric g-inverse where W is a symmetric matrix such that

(3.14) $$R(V + XAWA'X') = R(V : XA)$$

and B is such that

$$(3.15) \qquad A'X'BXA = 0, \qquad A'X'BV = 0.$$

Proof of necessity. The equations for finding a stationary value of $(Y - X\beta)' M(Y - X\beta)$ subject to the restriction $K'Y = K'X\beta$ are

$$X'MX\beta + X'K\lambda = X'MY,$$
$$(3.16)$$
$$K'X\beta = K'Y,$$

where λ is a Lagrangian multiplier. If (3.16) admits a solution then β satisfies the equations

$$(3.17) \qquad A'X'MX\beta = A'X'MY, \; K'X\beta = K'Y.$$

A solution is

$$(3.18) \qquad \beta^* = \begin{pmatrix} A'X'MX \\ K'X \end{pmatrix}^- \begin{pmatrix} A'X'MY \\ K'Y \end{pmatrix}.$$

Then $X\beta^*$ is unbiased for $X\beta$ if

$$(3.19) \qquad X \begin{pmatrix} A'X'MX \\ K'X \end{pmatrix}^- \begin{pmatrix} A'X'MX \\ K'X \end{pmatrix} = X \Leftrightarrow (3.12).$$

For $X\beta^*$ to be BLUE we need only ensure that $A'X'MY$ are BLUE's of their expectations. Using the familiar argument that BLUE's are uncorrelated with linear functions unbiased for zero we obtain

$$(3.20) \qquad A'X'MV(Z: K) = 0, \; Z = X^\perp.$$

Now we apply Theorem 2.1 of [15] to deduce the form (3.13) of M, with the conditions (3.14) and (3.15), by observing that $(Z: K) = (XA)^\perp$.

Sufficiency is easily established.

Theorem 3.7.   If (Q_1) and (Q_2) hold, then it is necessary and sufficient that

$$(3.21) \qquad M \in \{(V + XAWA'X')^-\}$$

where W is a symmetric matrix such that $R(V + XAWA'X') = R(V: XA)$.

The proof follows on the same lines as Theorem 2.2 of [15].

Theorem 3.8.   If in addition to (Q_1) and (Q_2), the result (Q_3) holds for all estimable functions $P'\beta$, then it is necessary and sufficient that $M \in \{V^-\}$.

In order to prove the proposition we need only consider a consistent hypothesis of the form $X\beta = w$, leading to

$$(3.22) \qquad R_1^2 = (Y - w)'M(Y - w).$$

If (3.22) has the same distribution as $(Y - w)' \, V^-(Y - w)$ then it follows that $M \in \{V^-\}$.

Note that in Theorem 3.8 any choice of g-inverse was used. But in Theorem 3.5 'a carefully chosen g-inverse' in the class $(V + XUX')^-$ is used. The latter choice does not seem to have any particular advantage since, if the matrix K were available, the results of Theorem 3.8 provide all the formulae.

4. Use of projection operators

It is well known that when V is non-singular the BLUE of $X\beta$ is obtained by the orthogonal projection of Y on $\mathcal{M}(X)$ using the norm $\|x\| = (x'V^{-1}x)^{\frac{1}{2}}$, which is the same as the projection of Y on $\mathcal{M}(X)$ along $\mathcal{M}(VZ)$, where $Z = X^\perp$. We consider similar results when V is not necessarily non-singular. Naturally the results have to be stated in a different way when V^{-1} does not exist (so that the inner product cannot be properly defined) and $\mathcal{M}(X)$ and $\mathcal{M}(VZ)$, although disjoint, may not span E^n the entire Euclidean space where n is the number of rows of X (so that the projection on $\mathcal{M}(X)$ along $\mathcal{M}(VZ)$ is not properly defined).

We give two definitions of projection operators.

Definition 1. Let D be an n.n.d. matrix of order n and consider D-norm as $\|x\| = (x'Dx)^{\frac{1}{2}}$. Further let A be an $n \times m$ matrix. Then P_{AD} is called a projector into $\mathcal{M}(A)$ under the D-norm iff

$$(4.1) \qquad \mathcal{M}(P_{AD}) \subset \mathcal{M}(A),$$

$$(4.2) \qquad \|y - P_{AD}y\| \leq \|y - A\lambda\| \qquad \forall y \in E^n, \lambda \in E^m.$$

Definition 1 was introduced in [21] and further examined in detail in [8].

It is easy to see that the condition (4.2) is equivalent to

$$(4.3) \qquad P_{AD}'DA = DA.$$

Note that P_{AD} need not be idempotent if $|D| = 0$, but

$$(4.4) \qquad P_{AD}'D = DP_{AD}$$

and one representation of P_{AD} is

$$(4.5) \qquad P_{AD} = A(A'DA)^-A'D.$$

Definition 2.   Let the columns of A and B span disjoint subspaces. Any vector $y \in \mathcal{M}(A : B)$ has the unique resolution:

$$(4.6) \qquad y = y_1 + y_2, \quad y_1 \in \mathcal{M}(A), \quad y_2 \in \mathcal{M}(B).$$

Then $P_{A|B}$ is said to be a projector onto $\mathcal{M}(A)$ parallel to (or along) $\mathcal{M}(B)$ iff

$$(4.7) \qquad\qquad P_{A|B}y = y_1 \qquad \forall y \in \mathcal{M}(A : B).$$

If $P_{A|B}$ is a projector in the sense of (4.7), then

$$(4.8) \qquad\qquad P_{A|B}A = A \quad \text{and} \quad P_{A|B}B = 0.$$

One representation of $P_{A|B}$ is

$$(4.9) \qquad\qquad P_{A|B} = A(C'A)^- C' \quad \text{where} \quad C = B^\perp.$$

$P_{A|B}$ is idempotent and unique if $\mathcal{M}(A)$ and $\mathcal{M}(B)$ span E^n.

The following theorems use projection operators in the computation of the BLUE's.

Theorem 4.1.   Consider the GGM model (1.1). Let L_0 be any given vector such that $L_0 X = p'$, i.e., $L_0 Y$ is an unbiased estimator of $p'\beta$. Then $L'_* Y$ is the BLUE of $p'\beta$ where

$$(4.10) \qquad\qquad L_* = (I - P_{ZV})L_0 = (I - P'_{VZ|X})L_0.$$

Theorem 4.2.   The BLUE of $X\beta$ can be expressed in the alternative forms

$$(4.11) \qquad (i) \quad (I - P'_{ZV})Y,$$

$$(4.12) \qquad (ii) \quad P_{X|VZ}Y = (I - P_{VZ|X})Y,$$

$$(4.13) \qquad (iii) \quad P_{XT^-}Y,$$

where T^- is an n.n.d. g-inverse of $T = (V + XUX')$ for any symmetric U such that T is n.n.d. and $R(T) = R(V:X)$.

Theorem 4.3.   An unbiased estimator of σ^2 can be expressed in the alternative forms

$$(4.14) \qquad (i) \quad f^{-1}Y'Z(Z'VZ)^- ZY,$$

$$(4.15) \qquad (ii) \quad f^{-1}Y'P'_{VZ|X}V^- P_{VZ|X}Y,$$

$$(4.16) \qquad (iii) \quad f^{-1}Y'T^-(I - P_{XT^-})Y,$$

where $f = R(V:X) - R(X)$ and T is as defined in Theorem 4.2.

The proofs are given in [20].

5. Representations of BLUE's and BLUE(W)'s

It is well known that if T_1 and T_2 are two minimum variance unbiased estimators (MVUE) of a parameter then $T_1 - T_2 = 0$ with probability 1, i.e., the MVUE is essentially unique. Suppose $L_1'Y$ and $L_2'Y$ are BLUE's or BLUE(W)'s of a given parametric function $p'\beta$, (see Definitions 1 and 2 of Section 1), then $L_1'Y - L_2'Y = 0$, but this may not imply that $L_1 - L_2 = 0$. In this section we find the set of L such that $L'Y$ is a BLUE or BLUE(W) of $p'\beta$ and also give conditions under which L is unique.

We consider the GGM model $(Y, X\beta, \sigma^2 V)$. Let

(5.1) $\qquad \mathscr{L}_p^V = \{L : L'Y \text{ is BLUE of } p'\beta\}$,

(5.2) $\qquad \mathscr{L}^V = \{L : L'Y \text{ is BLUE of some } p'\beta\}$,

(5.3) $\qquad \mathscr{L}_p^V(W) = \{L : L'Y \text{ is BLUE(W) of } p'\beta\}$,

(5.4) $\qquad \mathscr{L}^V(W) = \{L : L'Y \text{ is BLUE(W) of some } p'\beta\}$.

Let us recall that $Z = X^\perp$, $K = V^\perp$, $N = K(K^\perp Y)^\perp$ and $S = (X'N)^\perp$ giving the restrictions $K'Y = C$, $N'Y = 0$ (on Y) and $K'X\beta = C$, $N'X\beta = 0$ (on β). We denote $T = (V + XUX')$ where U is a symmetric matrix such that $R(T) = R(V : X)$.

Theorem 5.1.

(5.5) (i) $\quad \mathscr{L}^V(W) = \mathscr{M}[(VZ)^\perp] = \mathscr{M}(T^- X : I - T^- T)$.

(5.6) (ii) $\quad \mathscr{L}_p^V = \{L : X'L = p, \ Z'VL = 0\}$.

(5.7) (iii) $\quad \mathscr{L}_p^V(W) = \{L : S'X'L = S'p, \ Z'VL = 0\}$.

(iv) Let $L_1'Y$ and $L_2'Y$ be two representations of the BLUE of a given parametric function. Then $L_1 - L_2 = 0$ iff $R(V : X) = n$.

(v) Let $L_1'Y$ and $L_2'Y$ be two representations of the BLUE(W) of a given parametric function. Then $L_1 - L_2 = 0$ iff $R(V : X) = n$ and $X'N = 0$.

Theorem 5.1 provides a complete answer to the questions raised about the representations of BLUE's and BLUE(W)'s and the conditions under which they are unique. Note that non-singularity of V is sufficient but not necessary for the results (iv) and (v) of Theorem 5.1 to hold. Theorem 5.2 gives explicit representations of the classes (5.5), (5.6) and (5.7).

Theorem 5.2.

(5.8) (i) $\quad L \in \mathscr{L}_p^V \Leftrightarrow L = L_0 + Z(Z'V)^\perp \lambda$

where L_0 is a particular member of $\cdot \mathcal{L}_p^V$ and λ is some vector.

(5.9)   (ii) $L \in \mathcal{L}_p^V \Leftrightarrow L = T^- X (X' T^- X)^- p + (I - T^- T)\lambda$

where T is as defined above, T^- is any g-inverse of T and λ is some vector.

(5.10)   (iii) $L \in \mathcal{L}_p^V(W) \Leftrightarrow L_0 + L_1 + N\mu$

where L_0 is the first term in (5.8) or (5.9), L_1 is the second term in (5.8) or (5.9) and μ is a vector.

Theorem 5.3.   If $C'Y$ is the BLUE of $X\beta$, then C has the following forms.

(5.11)   (i) $C = I + Z\Lambda$

where Λ is a solution of $- Z'V = Z'VZ\Lambda$.

(5.12)   (ii) $C = C_0 + Z(Z'V)^{\perp}M$

where C_0 is a particular matrix for which $C_0'Y$ is the BLUE of $X\beta$ and M is some matrix.

(5.13)   (iii) $C = T^- X(X'T^-X)^- X' + (I - T^- T)F$

where F is some matrix.

Theorem 5.4.   If $C'Y$ is the BLUE(W) of $X\beta$, then

(5.14) $C = C_1 + NB$

where C_1 has any one of the forms (5.11)–(5.13) and B is some matrix.

The proofs of Theorems 5.1–5.3 are contained in [17].

6. Representation of V for given BLUE's and BLUE(W)'s

In the previous sections we have considered the computations and representations of BLUE's and BLUE(W)'s for given V. In this section we consider the converse problem of finding the class of V's for given representations of BLUE's and BLUE(W)'s. First we establish a basic theorem.

Theorem 6.1.   Let V be an n.n.d. matrix satisfying the conditions

(6.1) $C'VB = 0, \quad VK = 0$

where C, B, K are given. If $D = (C: K)^{\perp}$ and $B^{\perp}$ are disjoint, i.e., the intersection of $\mathscr{M}(D)$ and $\mathscr{M}(B^\perp)$ is the null space, then a general n.n.d. solution of (6.1) is of the form

(6.2) $$V = DU_1U_1'D' + XFU_2U_2'F'X$$

where $F = (X'K)^\perp$ and U_1, U_2 are arbitrary.

The result of Theorem 6.1 proved in [17] provides answers to a number of questions raised in the following theorems.

Theorem 6.2.   Let $(Y, X\beta, \sigma^2 V)$ be a GGM model where V is subject to the condition $VK = 0$ for a given matrix K. Further let $C'Y$ be the BLUE of $P'\beta$ where $R(P) = R(X)$. Then it is necessary and sufficient that V is of the form

(6.3) $$V = DG_1D' + XFG_2F'X'$$

where $D = (C : K)^\perp$, $F = (X'K)^\perp$ and G_1, G_2 are n.n.d. matrices.

The result (6.3) follows from Theorem 6.1 by choosing $B = X^\perp$ and showing that D and X are disjoint.

Note 1.   If in particular $K = 0$ in Theorem 6.2 then (6.3) becomes

(6.4) $$V = DG_2D' + XG_2X'$$

where $D = C^\perp$, which is established in [9] using a different argument.

Note 2.   If $K = 0$ and $C = X$, then (6.3) becomes

(6.5) $$V = ZG_1Z' + XG_2X'$$

where G_1 and G_2 are n.n.d. matrices.

The basic representation (6.5) was established in complete generality by the author in [10], presented at the Fifth Berkeley Symposium in 1965, as an answer to the question: What is the class of dispersion matrices V for which the simple least squares estimators (i.e., assuming $V = I$) are BLUE's? Subsequent writers, Kruskal [5], Watson [25] and Zyskind [26], gave some characterizations of V all of which seem to follow from the basic representation (6.5) or the result, $\mathscr{M}(VZ) \subset \mathscr{M}(Z)$, from which (6.5) is deduced as shown in [11] and [21]. Other papers of interest in this connection are due to Anderson [2], Cleveland [3], Seely and Zyskind [23] and Styan [24]. The work on representations of V was continued and extended to more general cases by the author [12], Mitra and Rao [7], Rao and Mitra [21] and Mitra and Moore [9]. Some of these more general results are contained in Theorems 6.3–6.7.

Theorem 6.3.   Let V_1 and V_2 be two alternative choices of V in the GGM model $(Y, X\beta, \sigma^2 V)$. If every representation $C'Y$ of the BLUE of $X\beta$ under V_1 is also the BLUE under V_2 then the following necessary and sufficient conditions are equivalent:

(6.6)   (i) $\mathcal{M}(V_2 Z) \subset \mathcal{M}(V_1 Z)$,

(6.7)   (ii) $V_2 = XG_2 X' + V_1 ZG_1 Z' V_1$,

where $Z = X^\perp$ and G_1, G_2 are n.n.d. matrices.

The condition (6.6) is obtained in [12] but its equivalent consequence (6.7) is established under an additional assumption which is not necessary. The representation (6.7) is given in [9] through a different argument without establishing (6.7). Alternative versions of Theorem 6.3 are as follows.

Theorem 6.4.   If every linear function of Y which is BLUE under V_1 is also BLUE under V_2 then the conditions in Theorem 6.3 are necessary and sufficient.

Theorem 6.5.   If $\mathcal{L}^{V_1}$ and $\mathcal{L}^{V_2}$ are complete classes of BLUE's under V_1 and V_2 respectively and $\mathcal{L}^{V_1} \subset \mathcal{L}^{V_2}$, then the conditions of Theorem 6.3 are necessary and sufficient.

Note that Theorem 6.6 only demands that $L \in \mathcal{L}^{V_1} \Rightarrow L \in \mathcal{L}^{V_2}$ without requiring that $\mathcal{P}_L^{V_1} \subset \mathcal{P}_L^{V_2}$ where

$$\mathcal{P}_L^V = \{p : E(L'Y) = p'\beta \text{ under } V\}.$$

Theorem 6.6 takes this into account.

Theorem 6.6.   Let N be a matrix of maximum rank such that $N'Y = 0$ with probability 1 under V_1 as defined in (1.5). Further let

(6.8) $L \in \mathcal{L}^{V_1} \Rightarrow L \in \mathcal{L}^{V_2}$,

(6.9) $\mathcal{P}_L^{V_1} \subset \mathcal{P}_L^{V_2}$.

(i) If $N'X = 0$, then (6.8) $\Rightarrow$ (6.9) in which case V has representation (6.7).

(ii) If $N'X \neq 0$, then it is necessary that

(6.10) $V = DG_1 D' + XFG_2 F'X'$

where $D = V_1 Z$, $F = (N'X)^\perp$ and G_1, G_2 are n.n.d. matrices.

Finally we establish the condition under which common BLUE's exist under V_1 and V_2.

Theorem 6.7.   Let $C'Y$ be BLUE of $X\beta$ under V_1 and also under V_2. Then:

(i) C satisfies the equations

(6.11) $$X'C = X', \quad Z'V_1C = 0, \quad Z'V_2C = 0.$$

(ii) V_2 admits the representation

(6.12) $$V_2 = XU_1X' + (S:V_1Z)\,U_2(S:V_1Z)'$$

where S is any matrix such that $(S:V_1Z)$ and X are disjoint and U_1, U_2 are n.n.d. matrices.

The proofs of Theorems 6.3–6.7 are given in [17].

References

[1] AITKEN, A. C. (1934) On least squares and linear combination of observations. *Proc. Roy. Soc. Edinburgh* A55, 42–47.

[2] ANDERSON, T. W. (1972) Efficient estimation of regression coefficients in time series. *Proc. Sixth Berkeley Symp. Math. Statist. Prob.* 1, 471–482.

[3] CLEVELAND, W. S. (1970) Projection with wrong inner product and its application to regression with correlated errors and linear filtering of time series. *Ann. Math. Statist.* 42, 616–624.

[4] GOLDMAN, A. J. AND ZELEN, M. (1964) Weak generalized inverses and minimum variance linear unbiased estimation. *J. Research Nat. Bureau of Standards* 68 B, 151–172.

[5] KRUSKAL, W. (1968) When are Gauss-Markoff and least squares estimators identical? A coordinate free approach. *Ann. Math. Statist.* 39, 70–75.

[6] MITRA, S. K. AND RAO, C. R. (1968) Some results in estimation and tests of linear hypotheses under the Gauss-Markoff model. *Sankhyā* A 30, 281–290.

[7] MITRA, S. K. AND RAO, C. R. (1969) Conditions for optimality and validity of least squares theory. *Ann. Math. Statist.* 40, 1617–1624.

[8] MITRA, S. K. AND RAO, C. R. (1973) Projections under semi-norms and generalized inverse of matrices. *Tech. Report*, Indiana University, Bloomington.

[9] MITRA, S. K. AND MOORE, J. B. (1973) Gauss-Markoff estimation with an incorrect dispersion matrix. *Sankhyā* A 35, 139–152.

[10] RAO, C. R. (1967) Least squares theory using an estimated dispersion matrix and its application to measurement of signals. *Proc. Fifth Berkeley Symp. Math. Statist. Prob.* 1, 355–372.

[11] RAO, C. R. (1968) A note on a previous lemma in the theory of least squares and some further results. *Sankhyā* A 30, 259–266.

[12] RAO, C. R. (1971) Unified theory of linear estimation. *Sankhyā* A 33, 371–394.

[13] RAO, C. R. (1972a) A note on the IPM method in the unified theory of linear estimation. *Sankhyā* A 34, 285–288.

[14] RAO, C. R. (1972b) Some recent results in linear estimation. *Sankhyā* B 34, 369–378.

[15] RAO, C. R. (1973a) Unified theory of least squares. *Communications in Statistics* **1,** 1–8.

[16] RAO, C. R. (1973b) *Linear Statistical Inference and its Applications.* Second Edition. Wiley, New York.

[17] RAO, C. R. (1973c) Representations of best linear unbiased estimators in the Gauss-Markoff model with a singular dispersion matrix. *J. Multivariate Anal.* **3,** 276–292.

[18] RAO, C. R. (1973d) On a unified theory of estimation in linear models. Mimeograph series 319, Department of Statistics, Purdue University, U.S.A.

[19] RAO, C. R. (1973e) Theory of estimation in the general Gauss-Markoff model. Paper presented at the International Symposium on Statistical Design and Linear Models, Fort Collins.

[20] RAO, C. R. (1974) Projectors, generalized inverses and the BLUE's. To appear.

[21] RAO, C. R. AND MITRA, S. K. (1971a) *Generalized Inverse of Matrices and its Applications.* Wiley, New York.

[22] RAO, C. R. AND MITRA, S. K. (1971b) Further contributions to the theory of generalized inverse of matrices and its applications. *Sankhyā* A **33,** 289–300.

[23] SEELY, J. AND ZYSKIND, G. (1971) Linear spaces and minimum variance unbiased estimation. *Ann. Math. Statist.* **42,** 691–703.

[24] STYAN, G. P. H. (Personal communication mentioned in the reference [9]).

[25] WATSON, G. S. (1967) Linear least squares regression. *Ann. Math. Statist.* **38,** 1679–1699.

[26] ZYSKIND, G. (1967) On canonical forms, negative covariance matrices and best and simple least squares linear estimator in linear models. *Ann. Math. Statist.* **38,** 1092–1110.

[27] ZYSKIND, G. AND MARTIN, F. B. (1969) On best linear estimation and a general Gauss-Markoff theorem in linear models with arbitrary negative co-variance structure. *SIAM J. Appl. Math.* **17,** 1190–1202.

[28] BJÖRCK, Å. (1974) A uniform numerical method for linear estimation from general Gauss-Markoff model. To appear.

[29] MITRA, S. K. (1973) Unified least squares approach to linear estimation in a general Gauss-Markoff model. *SIAM J. Appl. Math.* **25,** 671–680.

The Power of Some Tests of Correlation

E. J. WILLIAMS

Abstract

The coefficient of correlation between suitably defined statistics provides a means of testing various parametric hypotheses. The distribution of such coefficients, when the null hypothesis is not true, takes various forms in different applications. In particular, the correlation coefficients used to test hypotheses about the structural parameters in linear functional relations have doubly non-central distributions.

For tests of correlation in some typical situations, the curvature of the function defining the power in terms of the parameter in the neighbourhood of the null hypothesis is determined. This curvature is shown to be simply related to that of the function defining the squared correlation coefficient in terms of the parameter, in the neighbourhood of its minimum.

1. Introduction

Various tests of parametric hypotheses may be framed as tests of independence of suitably defined statistics (see, for example, Williams [8]), and the outcomes of these tests can be used to set confidence regions for the parameters. In previous studies of these tests, estimation of the parameters of interest was the primary purpose; as well as outlining methods for the finding of confidence regions (e.g., intervals), methods for the determination of point estimates and their standard errors were described. In accordance with these objectives, no attention was given to the performance of the tests against a specific hypothesis. For the purpose then in mind, there was no preferred hypothesis whose testing and possible rejection was of interest. In particular, then, the power of the tests was not considered.

The use of significance tests for setting confidence regions for parameters (or, in general, for families of distributions) has the technical advantage that only the null distribution of the test statistic is required. Since no specific null hypothesis engages our attention, the power of the test of that hypothesis, when it is not true, is not of interest.

However, there are two reasons why it appeared worth while to study the power of these tests of correlation. First, although the distribution of the correlation coefficient (or equivalent test statistic) is of a familiar form when the null hypothesis is true, its distribution when alternative hypotheses prevail takes different forms in different applications. This fact was noted by Fisher [3], who studied two of the most important examples (which would be now described as 'fixed effects' and 'random effects' models) as early as 1928. In the present paper we give some other examples, and compare the power curves in the neighbourhood of the null hypothesis.

The second reason for this study is that the variance of the parametric estimate has been based on the curvature of the graph of the (squared) correlation coefficient plotted against the parameter. It was considered to be of interest to compare this curvature with the curvature of the power curve in the neighbourhood of the null hypothesis.

Because the main reason for studying power is not so much to evaluate probabilities as to determine the effectiveness of the significance test (Pitman's [6] asymptotic relative efficiency), only its behaviour in the neighbourhood of the null hypothesis has been studied. Further, to simplify discussion and avoid troublesome technical details, as well as to provide results comparable with those for the standard errors of parametric estimates, only two-tailed tests (i.e., tests of r^2 rather than of r) have been considered.

It should also be noted that, although the set of hypotheses under consideration involves in general an arbitrary set of parameter values, the correlation test is so framed and involves the specific value of the parameter in such a way that the test is always one of the null hypothesis of zero correlation (more generally, independence). This point has been discussed, and examples given, in [8]. Accordingly the power considered is always that in the neighbourhood of $\rho = 0$, where ρ is the population correlation of the defined statistics.

2. Curvature of the power functions for classical statistics

We first briefly summarize the results given by Tang [7], and then give the first adjustment term in the expansions of the power function as a series in ρ^2 (bivariate correlation) or λ (fixed effects).

2.1. Bivariate correlation

The distribution of $u = r^2$, the squared correlation coefficient, for a sample of n from a bivariate normal population, is

(1)
$$
(1 - \rho^2)^{\frac{1}{2}(n-1)} \sum_{k=0}^{\infty} \frac{\Gamma(\frac{1}{2}(n-1)+k)}{\Gamma(\frac{1}{2}(n-1))k!} \, \rho^{2k} \, \frac{u^{k-\frac{1}{2}}(1-u)^{\frac{1}{2}(n-4)}}{B(k+\frac{1}{2}, \frac{1}{2}(n-2))} \, .
$$

This is readily seen to be a negative binomial mixture of beta distributions, the mixing distribution being defined by

$$
\Pr(K = k) = (1 - \rho^2)^{\frac{1}{2}(n-1)} \frac{\Gamma(\frac{1}{2}(n-1)+k)}{\Gamma(\frac{1}{2}(n-1))k!} \, \rho^{2k}
$$

(see also [3]). As will be seen, this mixture of distributions may itself be derived from the mixture defining the distribution for the fixed-effects model (Fisher's C distribution), by making the effect a random variable with a χ^2 distribution rather than a fixed quantity. In this way the relation between the random-effects model and the fixed-effects model may be shown in a manner alternative to that used by Fisher.

In order to encompass various cases within the same analysis, we define a more general negative binomial mixture of beta distributions as follows:

(2)
$$
f(u, n; \rho^2, m) = (1 - \rho^2)^{\frac{1}{2}m} \sum_{k=0}^{\infty} \frac{\Gamma(\frac{1}{2}m+k)}{\Gamma(\frac{1}{2}m)k!} \, \rho^{2k} \, \frac{u^{k-\frac{1}{2}}(1-u)^{\frac{1}{2}(n-4)}}{B(k+\frac{1}{2}, \frac{1}{2}(n-2))} \, .
$$

The coefficient of $m\rho^2$ in the density (2) is

$$
\frac{1}{2} \left[\frac{u^{\frac{1}{2}}(1-u)^{\frac{1}{2}(n-4)}}{B(\frac{3}{2}, \frac{1}{2}(n-2))} - \frac{u^{-\frac{1}{2}}(1-u)^{\frac{1}{2}(n-4)}}{B(\frac{1}{2}, \frac{1}{2}(n-2))} \right]
$$

$$
= -\frac{d}{du} \frac{u^{\frac{1}{2}}(1-u)^{\frac{1}{2}(n-2)}}{B(\frac{1}{2}, \frac{1}{2}(n-2))} \, .
$$

Hence, if u_α is the upper α-point of the null distribution of u, the coefficient of $m\rho^2$ in the power, given by the integral of (2), is

(3)
$$
\frac{u_\alpha^{\frac{1}{2}} (1-u_\alpha)^{\frac{1}{2}(n-2)}}{B(\frac{1}{2}, \frac{1}{2}(n-2))} \, .
$$

For the non-central distribution (1), $m = n - 1$; values of Expression (3) for typical values of n and α are given in Table I.

TABLE I

Values of Expression (3)

$n - 2$	$\alpha = 0.05$		$\alpha = 0.01$	
	u_α	(3)	u_α	(3)
1	0.9938	0.02490	0.9998	0.00500
2	0.9025	0.04631	0.9801	0.00985
5	0.5693	0.07799	0.7648	0.01992
10	0.3318	0.09444	0.5011	0.02692
15	0.2325	0.10073	0.3666	0.02994
20	0.1787	0.10402	0.2882	0.03160
∞	—	0.11454	—	0.03725

2.2. Fixed effects (Fisher's C distribution)

This distribution is simply a variant of non-central F, and is accordingly expressible as a Poisson mixture of central distributions. One way of arriving at the distribution is to take the limit of (2) as $m \to \infty$, $\rho^2 \to 0$, $m\rho^2 \to \lambda$. Then λ is the non-centrality parameter, and the coefficient of λ in the power is given by (3).

The bivariate correlation distribution can be recovered from the fixed-effects distribution by noting that, in the former, the 'effect' is proportional to a random variable distributed as χ^2 with $n - 1$ degrees of freedom. Indeed, if X_1 and X_2 are standardized normal variates with correlation ρ, the partition of the sum of squares of one of them into regression and residual sums of squares may be expressed in the following way:

$$[\rho\chi_{n-1} + (1 - \rho^2)^{\frac{1}{2}}\chi_1]^2 + (1 - \rho^2)\chi_{n-2}^2,$$

where the three χ variates are independently distributed with the designated degrees of freedom, and the first term in the bracket represents the correlation, or non-centrality.

For the bivariate case, therefore, the Poisson distribution is replaced by a χ_{n-1}^2 mixture of Poissons which, as is well known, is a negative binomial distribution:

$$\left(\frac{1-\rho^2}{\rho^2}\right)^{\frac{1}{2}(n-1)} \int_0^\infty \frac{e^{-\frac{1}{2}\lambda}(\frac{1}{2}\lambda)^k}{k!} \exp\{-[\frac{1}{2}(1-\rho^2)/\rho^2]\} \frac{(\frac{1}{2}\lambda)^{\frac{1}{2}(n-3)}}{\Gamma(\frac{1}{2}(n-1))} d(\frac{1}{2}\lambda)$$

$$= (1-\rho^2)^{\frac{1}{2}(n-1)} \rho^{2k} \frac{\Gamma(\frac{1}{2}(n-1)+k)}{\Gamma(\frac{1}{2}(n-1))k!}.$$

2.3. *Correlation with equal variances*

If X_1 and X_2 are bivariate normal with the same variance and correlation ρ, the maximum-likelihood estimator of ρ for a sample of n observations (X_{1j}, X_{2j}) is

$$r_A = \frac{2t_{12}}{t_{11}+t_{22}},$$

where

$$t_{hi} = \sum_{j=1}^n (x_{hj} - \bar{x}_h)(x_{ij} - \bar{x}_i).$$

The notation r_A refers to the fact that the arithmetic mean, rather than the geometric mean, of the sums of squares appears in the denominator. Consequently $|r_A| \leq |r|$; however, the distributions of the two squared coefficients are similar.

Putting $u_A = r_A^2$, we find that the null distribution of u_A has density

$$\frac{u_A^{-\frac{1}{2}}(1-u_A)^{\frac{1}{2}(n-3)}}{B(\frac{1}{2}, \frac{1}{2}(n-1))},$$

which is the same as that of u for a sample of $n + 1$ observations. When ρ is not zero, the density of r_A has the relatively simple form (DeLury [1])

(4)
$$\frac{(1-\rho^2)^{\frac{1}{2}(n-1)}}{(1-\rho r_A)^{n-1}} \frac{(1-r_A^2)^{\frac{1}{2}(n-3)}}{B(\frac{1}{2}, \frac{1}{2}(n-1))}.$$

Although this differs substantially in form from the non-central distribution of r, it is at once apparent that the non-central distribution of u_A is, like that of u, a negative binomial mixture of beta distributions. In fact, the density is

$$f(u_A, n+1; \rho^2, n-1)$$

$$= (1-\rho^2)^{\frac{1}{2}(n-1)} \sum_{k=0}^\infty \frac{\Gamma(\frac{1}{2}(n-1)+k)}{\Gamma(\frac{1}{2}(n-1))k!} \rho^{2k} \frac{u_A^{k-\frac{1}{2}}(1-u_A)^{\frac{1}{2}(n-3)}}{B(k+\frac{1}{2}, \frac{1}{2}(n-1))}.$$

The coefficient of ρ^2 in the power is

$$(n - 1) \frac{u_\alpha^{\frac{1}{2}} (1 - u_\alpha)^{\frac{1}{2}(n-1)}}{B(\frac{1}{2}, \frac{1}{2}(n - 1))},$$

where it must now be noted that u_α is the upper α-point of the null distribution of u_A, with $n - 1$ degrees of freedom.

It should be noted here that the distribution of the intraclass correlation coefficient, for a bivariate population in which the expectations as well as the variances are equal, is somewhat more complicated, and has not been considered here. Its distribution was given by Fisher [2]; Pitman [5] showed that a rational function of r and ρ is distributed as a beta variate.

3. The linear functional relation

The usual specification of a linear functional relation between random variables X_1 and X_2 is

$$E(X_{1j}) = \mu_j, \ E(X_{2j}) = \alpha + \beta\mu_j,$$

the subscript j referring to the jth pair. We here assume that the X_{1j} and X_{2j} are independently normally distributed with the same variance σ^2.

It is convenient for the present discussion to take $\alpha = 0$ and to redefine the other parameters in terms of polar coordinates, so that $\beta = \tan \theta$,

$$E(X_{1j}) = \mu_j \cos \theta, \ E(X_{2j}) = \mu_j \sin \theta.$$

Then, for any prescribed value θ_0 of θ, the variates

$$Y_1 = X_1 \cos \theta_0 + X_2 \sin \theta_0$$

and

$$Y_2 = X_1 \sin \theta_0 - X_2 \cos \theta_0$$

are also independently normally distributed with variance σ^2, and if

$$\delta = \theta_0 - \theta,$$
$$E(Y_{1j}) = \mu_j \cos \delta,$$

and

$$E(Y_{2j}) = \mu_j \sin \delta.$$

When $\delta = 0$, the Y_{1j} and Y_{2j} are respectively the sufficient statistics and ancillary statistics for the μ_j; for this value of δ, the sample correlation between Y_1 and Y_2 will be centrally distributed, being independent of the values of the μ_j. In general, the sample correlation will be inflated by the variation among the μ_j.

It will also be observed that, if δ is replaced by $\delta + \frac{1}{2}\pi$, Y_1 is replaced by $-Y_2$ and Y_2 by Y_1. Accordingly, the squared sample correlation, and consequently the power of the correlation test, will be a periodic function of δ with period $\frac{1}{2}\pi$. The correlation test does not distinguish between values of θ_0 differing by $\frac{1}{2}\pi$. However, the value of θ_0 chosen as an estimate of θ is that giving the smaller sum of squares of Y_2; in fact, θ is often estimated by the minimization of this sum of squares.

For general values of δ, the sums of squares and products of Y_1 and Y_2 for a sample of n observations may be expressed as follows:

$$s_{11} = (\Phi \cos \delta + f_1)^2 \qquad\qquad + h_{11}$$

$$s_{12} = (\Phi \cos \delta + f_1)(\Phi \sin \delta + f_2) + h_{12}$$

$$s_{22} = (\Phi \sin \delta + f_2)^2 \qquad\qquad + h_{22},$$

where

$$\Phi^2 = \Sigma(\mu_j - \bar{\mu})^2,$$

f_1, f_2 are independent normal deviates with variance σ^2, and h_{11}, h_{12} and h_{22} are sums of squares and products of independent normal deviates with $n - 2$ degrees of freedom, independent of f_1 and f_2.

This representation shows that, for example, s_{22} is distributed as χ^2 with $n - 1$ degrees of freedom, scale parameter σ^2 and non-centrality $\Phi^2 \sin^2 \delta / \sigma^2$.

Rather than examine the distribution of the correlation coefficient, which turns out to be doubly non-central, we begin with the equivalent F-statistic for testing the significance of the regression of Y_2 on Y_1.

Conditionally on the Y_1 being fixed, we have

$$E(s_{12}) = (\Phi \cos \delta + f_1)\Phi \sin \delta$$

and

$$V(s_{12}) = [(\Phi \cos \delta + f_1)^2 + h_{11}]\sigma^2$$

$$= s_{11}\sigma^2.$$

Consequently the regression sum of squares, s_{12}^2/s_{11}, is distributed with non-centrality

$$\frac{\Phi^2 \sin^2 \delta}{\sigma^2} \cdot \frac{(\Phi \cos \delta + f_1)^2}{(\Phi \cos \delta + f_1)^2 + h_{11}}.$$

We accordingly have the following partition of degrees of freedom and non-centrality:

TABLE II

	D.F.	Non-centrality
Regression	1	$\psi^2 \dfrac{(\Phi \cos \delta + f_1)^2}{(\Phi \cos \delta + f_1)^2 + h_{11}}$
Residual	$n-2$	$\psi^2 \dfrac{h_{11}}{(\Phi \cos \delta + f_1)^2 + h_{11}}$
Total	$n-1$	$\psi^2 (= \Phi^2 \sin^2 \delta / \sigma_0^2).$

Now in 'standard' regression analysis the conditional distribution of the regression coefficient and the sums of squares provide tests that are independent of any nuisance parameters in the (possibly unknown) distribution of the regression variables. In this application, however, the conditional distributions are inadequate, for two reasons. First, as has been shown, these distributions depend on the unknown parameter Φ^2. Secondly, since Y_1 and Y_2 enter symmetrically into the problem, so that either one of them, or neither, may be distributed independently of the incidental parameters μ_j, it is plausible that an appropriate analysis will involve both variates in the same way.

If a formal F test were carried out to test the significance of the regression, it would be relevant to determine the expectation of each of the mean squares above. Fortunately each of the coefficients of ψ^2 in the non-centrality parameters is the ratio of one of two χ^2 variates to their sum. Therefore the expectation of each ratio equals the ratio of the expectations (even though one of the χ^2 variates is non-centrally distributed) by a well-known result for gamma variates; the expectations are:

Effect	Expectation of Mean Square
Regression	$\Phi^2 \sin^2 \delta \dfrac{(\Phi^2 \cos^2 \delta + \sigma^2)}{\Phi^2 \cos^2 \delta + (n-1)\sigma^2} + \sigma^2$
Residual	$\Phi^2 \sin^2 \delta \dfrac{\sigma^2}{\Phi^2 \cos^2 \delta + (n-1)\sigma^2} + \sigma^2$

The difference of these expected values is

$$\frac{\Phi^4 \sin^2 \delta \cos^2 \delta}{\Phi^2 \cos^2 \delta + (n-1)\sigma^2},$$

which has the satisfactory property that it vanishes when $\delta = 0$ or $\frac{1}{2}\pi$ (as well as in the trivial case $\Phi^2 = 0$, when the test has constant power against any alternative). Hence, apart from questions of finding the distribution, and in particular the significance points, of the doubly non-central F-ratio, the formal test appears to have some merit.

To determine the unconditional power of the test, one may determine the power conditional on fixed Y_1 and then find its expectation with respect to the distribution of the Y_1 (see, for example, Lehmann [4], p. 140). The first terms in the adjustment to the power, which are relevant in the neighbourhood of the null hypothesis, are linear in the non-centrality parameters, so that their expectations may be used directly.

The doubly non-central F distribution is a double Poisson mixture of central F distributions (Tang [7]). Denoting the non-centrality parameters by λ_1 and λ_2, and the ratio of two non-central χ^2 variates by v, we have for the density function of v

$$e^{-\frac{1}{2}(\lambda_1+\lambda_2)} \sum_{k_1=0}^{\infty} \sum_{k_2=0}^{\infty} \frac{(\frac{1}{2}\lambda_1)^{k_1}}{k_1!} \frac{(\frac{1}{2}\lambda_2)^{k_2}}{k_2!} \frac{v^{k_1-\frac{1}{2}}}{B(k_1+\frac{1}{2}, \frac{1}{2}(n-2)+k_2)(1+v)^{\frac{1}{2}(n-1)+k_1+k_2}}.$$

For comparison with previous results, we transform to the doubly non-central squared correlation coefficient, u, whose density is

$$e^{-\frac{1}{2}(\lambda_1+\lambda_2)} \sum_{k_1=0}^{\infty} \sum_{k_2=0}^{\infty} \frac{(\frac{1}{2}\lambda_1)^{k_1}}{k_1!} \frac{(\frac{1}{2}\lambda_2)^{k_2}}{k_2!} \frac{u^{k_1-\frac{1}{2}}(1-u)^{\frac{1}{2}(n-4)+k_2}}{B(k_1+\frac{1}{2}, \frac{1}{2}(n-2)+k_2)}.$$

The coefficients of λ_1 and λ_2 in the power of a test of size α are found in the same way as Expression (3). Accordingly we find the linear contribution to the power to be

$$\left(\lambda_1 - \frac{\lambda_2}{n-2}\right) \frac{u_\alpha^{\frac{1}{2}}(1-u_\alpha)^{\frac{1}{2}(n-2)}}{B(\frac{1}{2}, \frac{1}{2}(n-2))}.$$

It will be noted that the non-centrality of the residual mean square has the effect of reducing the power. Substituting the conditional non-centrality parameters given in Table 2, we have

$$\lambda_1 - \frac{\lambda_2}{n-2} = \psi^2 \frac{[(\Phi \cos \delta + f_1)^2 - h_{11}/(n-2)]}{(\Phi \cos \delta + f_1)^2 + h_{11}}.$$

Hence in the unconditional power, this factor becomes

$$\psi^2 \frac{E[(\Phi\cos\delta + f_1)^2 - h_{11}/(n-2)]}{E[(\Phi\cos\delta + f_1)^2 + h_{11}]} = \frac{\Phi^4 \sin^2\delta \cos^2\delta}{\sigma^2[\Phi^2\cos^2\delta + (n-1)\sigma^2]} \cdot$$

The coefficient of $\sin^2\delta$ in the power is therefore

$$\frac{\Phi^4}{\sigma^2(\Phi^2 + (n-1)\sigma^2)} \frac{u_\alpha^{\frac{1}{2}}(1 - u_\alpha)^{\frac{1}{2}(n-2)}}{B(\frac{1}{2}, \frac{1}{2}(n-2))} \cdot$$

As might have been expected, the linear term in the power vanishes when $\delta = 0$ or $\frac{1}{2}\pi$.

The power itself, and not only the linear term, is periodic in δ with period $\frac{1}{2}\pi$. One interesting deduction from this fact is that the power will attain a maximum, less than unity, when $\delta = \frac{1}{4}\pi$. The actual determination of this power, which is a function of Φ^2/σ^2, has not been attempted here.

4. Instrumental variables

The estimation of linear functional relations is facilitated by the availability of auxiliary variables that are closely related to the incidental parameters. These instrumental variables are most effective when their regression on the incidental parameters is linear, but are useful in general provided their correlation with the incidental parameters is non-zero.

We consider the use of a single instrumental variable X_3 in the estimation of a linear functional relation between X_1 and X_2, and confine attention to the simplest case, where the expectation of X_{3j} is linear in μ_j; without loss of generality we assume that

$$X_{3j} = \mu_j + g_j,$$

where the g_j are 'errors' with variance σ_3^2, uncorrelated with the X_{1j} or X_{2j}. Here we assume that X_1 and X_2 are independently normally distributed with variances σ_1^2 and σ_2^2, not necessarily equal.

Much of the development and notation follows that of Section 3, but there are some important differences of detail. The variate

$$Y_2 = X_1 \sin\theta_0 - X_2 \cos\theta_0$$

will be distributed independently of the incidental parameters μ_j provided $\theta_0 = \theta$. Under this condition, the sample correlation coefficient of Y_2 and X_3 will be centrally distributed. We accordingly seek the power of the test of this correlation.

The sums of squares and products of Y_2 and X_3 for a sample of n observations may be expressed as follows:

$$s_{22} = (\Phi \sin \delta + f_2)^2 + h_{22}$$
$$s_{23} = (\Phi \sin \delta + f_2)(\Phi + f_3) + h_{23}$$
$$s_{33} = (\Phi + f_3)^2 + h_{33},$$

where f_2, f_3 are independent normal deviates with variances

$$\sigma_0^2 = \sigma_1^2 \sin^2 \theta_0 + \sigma_2^2 \cos^2 \theta_0$$

and σ_3^2 respectively, and h_{22}, h_{23} and h_{33} are sums of squares and products of independent normal deviates with $n - 2$ degrees of freedom, independent of f_2 and f_3.

Following the analysis given in Section 3, we find that, conditionally on fixed X_3, the sums of squares for regression of Y_2 on X_3 and for residuals are distributed with the following parameters:

TABLE III

	D.F.	Non-centrality
Regression	1	$\psi^2 \dfrac{(\Phi + f_3)^2}{(\Phi + f_3)^2 + h_{33}}$
Residual	$n - 2$	$\psi^2 \dfrac{h_{33}}{(\Phi + f_3)^2 + h_{33}}$
Total	$n - 1$	$\psi^2 (= \Phi^2 \sin^2 \delta / \sigma_0^2)$.

In a manner similar to that of the previous treatment, we finally obtain the linear term in the power as

$$\frac{\Phi^4 \sin^2 \delta}{\sigma_0^2 [\Phi^2 + (n-1)\sigma_3^2]} \frac{u_\alpha^{\frac{1}{2}} (1 - u_\alpha)^{\frac{1}{2}(n-2)}}{B(\frac{1}{2}, \frac{1}{2}(n-2))} .$$

Recalling that $\sigma_0^2 = \sigma_1^2 \sin^2 \theta_0 + \sigma_2^2 \cos^2 \theta_0$, and so is periodic in δ with period π, we see that this term in the power has period π.

The coefficient of $\sin^2 \delta$ in the power is

$$\frac{\Phi^4}{(\sigma_1^2 \sin^2 \theta + \sigma_2^2 \cos^2 \theta)(\Phi^2 + (n-1)\sigma_3^2)} \frac{u_\alpha (1 - u_\alpha)^{\frac{1}{2}(n-2)}}{B(\frac{1}{2}, \frac{1}{2}(n-2))} .$$

The power attains a maximum, but this is not located at $\delta = \frac{1}{2}\pi$ unless $\sigma_1^2 = \sigma_2^2$; its location can be readily found if the ratio σ_1^2 / σ_2^2 is known.

5. Discussion

The examples presented above show some of the ways in which various correlation coefficients, following a common distribution when the relevant null hypothesis is true, are distributed when the hypothesis is not true. The result least expected was the occurrence of the doubly non-central distribution for the correlation coefficient used to test linear functional relations; before obtaining this result we had regarded the study of doubly non-central distributions as somewhat academic.

A second point of interest is the relation between the curvatures, at their minima, of the power function of the correlation test and the function defining the squared correlation coefficient, in terms of a particular structural parameter. Results for the latter have been given in Williams [8], to provide approximate variances of estimators of structural parameters. Comparison of the results show that the ratio of the curvature of the power curve to that of the squared correlation curve is in each case equal to Expression (3). Any apparent discrepancies are the result of the parameters' having been defined differently in that paper and the present paper.

Acknowledgement

The assistance of Mr. Than Pe of the University of Melbourne in the preparation of material for this paper is acknowledged.

References

[1] DeLury, D. B. (1938) Note on correlations. Ann. Math. Statist. 9, 149–151.

[2] Fisher, R. A. (1921) On the "probable error" of a coefficient of correlation deduced from a small sample. Metron 1, 3–32.

[3] Fisher, R. A. (1928) The general sampling distribution of the multiple correlation coefficient. Proc. Roy. Soc. A 121, 654–673.

[4] Lehmann, E. L. (1959) Testing Statistical Hypotheses. Wiley, New York.

[5] Pitman, E. J. G. (1939) A note on normal correlation. Biometrika 31, 9–12.

[6] Pitman, E. J. G. (1949) Non-Parametric Statistical Inference. Columbia University Press.

[7] Tang, P. C. (1938) The power function of the analysis of variance tests with tables and illustrations of their use. Statist. Res. Memoirs 2, 126–149.

[8] Williams, E. J. (1973) Tests of correlation in multivariate analysis. Bull. Int. Statist. Inst. 45, 219–232.

Soft Modelling by Latent Variables: The Non-Linear Iterative Partial Least Squares (NIPALS) Approach

HERMAN WOLD

Abstract

The NIPALS approach is applied to the 'soft' type of model that has come to the fore in sociology and other social sciences in the last five or ten years, namely path models that involve latent variables which serve as proxies for blocks of directly observed variables. Such models are seen as hybrids of the 'hard' models of econometrics where all variables are directly observed (path models in the form of simultaneous equations systems) and the 'soft' models of psychology where the human mind is described in terms of latent variables and their directly observed indicators. For hybrid models that involve one or two latent variables the NIPALS approach has been developed in [38], [41] and [42]. The present paper extends the NIPALS approach to path models with three or more latent variables. Each new latent variable brings a rapid increase in the pluralism of possible model designs, and new problems arise in the parameter estimation of the models. Iterative procedures are given for the point estimation of the parameters. With a view to cases when the iterative estimation does not converge, a device of range estimation is developed, where high profile versus low profile estimates give ranges for the parameter estimates.

1. Introduction: Path models with latent variables

1.1. *Two cases of soft modelling*: *Coleman's and Hauser's models.* Coleman's educational model, Chart 1, exemplifies several aspects of hard versus soft model building, including

   (i)   experimental versus non-experimental data;
   (ii) hard versus soft data;
   (iii) directly observed (manifest) variables versus indirectly observed (latent) variables.

117

Coleman's model is of a type that has forcefully come to the foreground
in sociology and other social sciences in the last five or ten years, namely,
path models that involve latent variables.[1] At the gateway of this broad
and important field of model building is the simple model in Chart 2a, first
launched by Hauser ((1968); (1969)) and remodelled in several ways by
Hauser and Goldberger (1971), using an MGLS (Modified Generalized
Least Squares) approach; by Jöreskog and Goldberger (1973), using the
ML (Maximum Likelihood) method; and by H. Wold ((1973 a,b); (1974
a–c)), using NIPALS modelling (see also (1966a)).

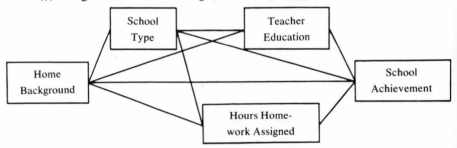

Chart 1.   Coleman's educational model, quoted from Coleman (1973).

The present paper continues to develop the NIPALS approach in soft
modelling by latent variables, with special regard to complex situations
where the latent variables serve as proxies for large blocks of observables.

1.2. *Path models with one or two latent variables: various NIPALS
models.*

1.2.1.   The studies we shall refer to set forth (a) two NIPALS versions
of Hauser's model, denoted by A_1 and A_2, and involving one and two
latent variables (see Chart 2 b,c), and (b) four NIPALS models, denoted
by B_1, B_2, C_1, C_2, and obtained by reversing the inferential directions in
Models A_1, A_2 (see Chart 3 a–d). Two of these six models were known
earlier, Models C_1 and B_2 being equivalent to the NIPALS models for the
(first) principal component and the (first) canonical correlation, respectively [36]. Further we restate that Model B_1 is equivalent to Model B_2
[40], [42].

---

[1] The line of evolution referred to is in focus in the comprehensive volumes edited by
Blalock (1971b) and Costner (1971). For applied work of soft modelling that is of special
interest from the point of view of the present paper, see Adelman and Morris ((1967),
(1973)).

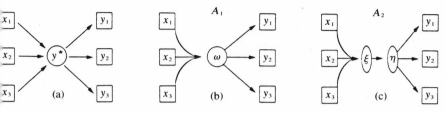

Chart 2. (a) Hauser's model; (b)–(c) NIPALS versions A_1 and A_2.

These earlier studies develop the six models $A_i - C_i$ ($i = 1, 2$) by the general methods of NIPALS modelling. To specify, the analysis includes:

(i) Specification of the model's structural relations as predictors (conditional expectations).

(ii) Model estimation by iterative OLS (Ordinary Least Squares).

(iii) Algebraic estimation of the model.

(iv) Applications to theoretical populations and to real-world data.

(v) Comparison with the ML approach.

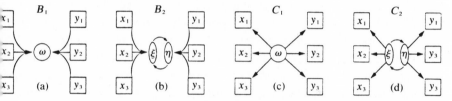

Chart 3 a–d. The NIPALS models B_1, B_2, C_1, C_2.

1.2.2. The six models $A_i - C_i$ link up with earlier reports on NIPALS modelling to give evidence of the advantages of the NIPALS approach.[2] The predictor specification 1.2.1 (i) is at a premium in several respects:

(i) Flexibility in the adaptation of the model to its intended use for purposes of predictive and/or causal inference.

(ii) Interpretation of the rationale of the model in terms of ordinary regression analysis.

(iii) Economy of assumptions, due to the predictor specification of NIPALS models, which entails that the basic assumptions refer to the systematic parts of the structural relations, whereas the basic assumptions of ML modelling refer to the properties of the residuals.

As an example under (iii), for a Hauser model with p variables x_i and q

---

[2] Reference is made to reports on applied work in three areas where NIPALS modelling is gaining momentum: (a) principal components [11], [45]; (b) econometric macro-models [3], [6], [9]; (c) linear cluster analysis [46]. To venture a broad appraisal, NIPALS has its forte in modelling where the unknown parameters increase in number, or tend to increase, with the size of the sample.

variables y_j, the ML approach involves $p \times q$ assumptions of zero correlation between the residuals and the variables x_i, while the NIPALS version only involves $p + q$ zero correlations between the residuals and the manifest or latent variables (cf. [18], [38]).

In NIPALS modelling with latent variables it is characteristic, but not so in the ML approach, that the latent variables are explicitly defined in terms of the manifest variables, usually as a linear aggregate of the observables, [40]. While the ML approach is thus more general in this respect, the explicit definition of latent variables in NIPALS modelling adds to the advantages under (i)–(iii). We note that:

(iv) In the NIPALS approach, the sample items of the latent variables can be numerically assessed, providing consistent information that can be used for further development of the model, including hypothesis testing, checking for outliers, and exploring the interrelations between latent variables and endogenous or exogenous variables.

(v) Likewise, the NIPALS approach allows the numerical assessment of sample items of residuals that involve latent variables, and again this information can be used for further development of the model.

(vi) In line with (iii), it is typical for ML modelling to impose assumptions of zero intercorrelation between residuals of different relations, but not so for the NIPALS approach.

For one thing, under (vi), the ML approach sometimes encounters identification problems that do not occur in the corresponding NIPALS model. As an example, considering a model C_2 (see Chart 3d) with two variables x_i and two variables y_j, suppose that the residuals are intercorrelated for the variables x_1, x_2 and for y_1, y_2, but not for x_1, y_2 or for x_2, y_1. Then the model cannot be identified by the ML approach [19] whereas its identification and estimation is straightforward in NIPALS modelling.

1.2.3. Background reference is made to GLS (Generalized Least Squares) estimation [31]. While GLS minimizes the total sum of squared residuals in a multirelational model, NIPALS minimizes the residual square sum in each structural relation of the model, under the ancillary condition that the explanatory variables in that same relation are known. As typical cases of GLS modelling we note (a) Merritt Brown's estimation of interdependent systems by minimizing the total sum of residual squares in the reduced form of the system [10]; and (b) the extension of canonical correlation to three blocks of observables, [21]. At first sight

NIPALS is conceptually closer to GLS than to ML modelling. There is the distinct difference, however, that GLS as a rule is not compatible with predictor specification; hence in GLS modelling the causal and predictive inference from the structural relations will in general be more or less biased.

1.2.4. The features outlined in 1.2.2 (iii)–(vi) mark a parting of the ways between NIPALS and ML approaches in path models with latent variables. Broadly speaking,it is a parting of the ways between soft and hard modelling. According to this view, NIPALS and ML modelling are complementary rather than competitive. Each approach has a wide domain of applications.[3] In the awakening area of soft modelling, the path models A_1, A_2, open up a new avenue of NIPALS modelling.

We shall next elaborate these broad statements by way of a general discussion of modelling with latent variables.

1.3. *Ends and means of modelling with latent variables.*   Reference is made to four broad fields of application for models that involve latent variables, and to some typical cases of the models at issue.

1.3.1. In physics we are often concerned with variables and relationships subject to observational error. A typical and well-known model is

(1a–b) $x = \xi + \epsilon_1$ $y = \eta + \epsilon_2$

(2a–b) $\alpha\xi + \beta\eta = \lambda$ with $\alpha^2 + \beta^2 = 1$.

In verbal terms, the true values ξ, η of the manifest variables x, y are subject to observational errors ϵ_1, ϵ_2. The true values ξ, η are in the nature of latent variables, and are assumed to be linearly related by (2).

Model (1)–(2) with its non-stochastic relation (2) and its explicit treatment of the residuals is a case of hard modelling. We recall the classical theorem that Relation (2) cannot be assessed without prior knowledge of the relative size of the variances of the observational errors, [15]. More on the soft side of errors-in-variables models is the estimation of linear relations by orthogonal regression, [30] or, equivalently, by principal components, [31].

1.3.2. In psychology we deal with the unobservables of the human mind. The classical models of factor analysis (FA) and principal compo-

---

[3] See note 2.

nents (PC) have much in common, and yet they are typical cases of hard versus soft modelling. For example, we refer to Rao's work [31] in the general context of multivariate analysis. For reviews with special regard to NIPALS modelling, the reader is referred to [24], [36]–[38]. In the present briefing of FA versus PC models, we ignore the immaterial differences that exist in the normalization of loadings and factors-components. Given a data-matrix, say

(3) x_{it} $(i = 1, \cdots, m;\quad t = 1, \cdots, n)$

the one-factor and one-component models take the same form, in current symbols

(4) $x_{it} = \lambda_i \xi_t + \psi_i + \epsilon_{it}$

except that the specific factor ψ_i is absent in the PC model. The FA and PC models have numerically the same loadings λ_i, whereas the factors-components ξ_t differ. Key differences are: (a) the principal component is a linear form of the observables,

(5) $\xi_t = \sum_i \lambda_i x_{it} \qquad (t = 1, \cdots, n),$

whereas the factor ξ_t does not allow an explicit representation, cf. 1.2.2 (iv); and (b) the residuals $\epsilon_{it}, \epsilon_{jt}$ $(i \neq j)$ are assumed to be uncorrelated in FA, but not in PC analysis (cf. 1.2.2 (vi)).

The NIPALS version of PC analysis is numerically equivalent to the classical analysis. Based on the predictor specifications

(6a) $\lambda_i \xi_t = E(x_{it} | \xi_t) \qquad (t = 1, \cdots, n),$

(6b) $= E(x_{it} | \lambda_i) \qquad (i = 1, \cdots, m),$

the NIPALS estimation alternates between (6a) and (6b) to compute an iterative sequence of OLS regressions.

1.3.3. In econometrics, we shall refer to two models that involve latent variables:

(i) Milton Friedman's classical hypothesis of permanent income over time t, [14]. In symbols,

(7) $x_t = \xi_t + \omega_t.$

In words, manifest income x_t in the period t is the sum total of permanent income ξ_t and transitory income ω_t. A current approach is to estimate ξ_t as a lagged distribution of manifest income x_t.

(ii) NIPALS remodelling of classical interdependent (ID) systems by REID (Reformulated ID) and GEID (General ID) systems, [29], [36]. In classical ID systems the interdependence between the current endogenous variables $y_i (i = 1, \cdots, n)$ makes it impossible to specify the structural relations as predictors. REID systems remodel the structural form of classical ID systems by replacing each explanatory y_i by a latent variable y_i^* defined as its systematic part, that is, as its conditional expectation. The estimation of REID systems is a non-linear problem. The NIPALS approach to this problem, called the Fix-Point (FP) method, is an iterative sequence of OLS regressions based on the predictor specification of the structural form. While the residuals in Classical ID and REID systems are subject to stringent correlation assumptions, the FP method extends to a broader class of models, called GEID (General ID) systems (cf. 1.2.2 (iii)).

The development of the FP approach has given rise to several improvements and generalizations, [27]. The nomenclature falls short of lucidity, since it uses a multitude of abbreviations for the various FP methods. The following code,

$$C_1 FP(C_2, C_3), \text{ or briefly } C_1 FP$$

is an attempt to systematize these; to specify:

Code C_1: P for Parametric FP estimation, [26]; may be combined with F for Fractional FP estimation, [3], and/or with R for Recursive FP estimation, [9].

Code C_2: S or R, according as the consecutive proxies for y_i^* are computed from the structural or the reduced form.

Code C_3: Indicates the starting point for the proxies of y_i^*, usually 0 which is the zero start; or Y which is the start with the vector of the variables y_i; or TSLS which is the same start as in Theil-Basmann's Two-Stage Least Squares method [5], [32].

For example, PFFP indicates Parametric Fractional Fix-Point estimation, and PFFP(S, 0) indicates that the iterative procedure in each step gives a proxy for y_i^* from the structural form, starting with the zero vector.

1.3.4. Fourth and last, we consider path models with latent variables as proxies for blocks of observables. To repeat from 1.1, such models have come strongly to the fore in recent years. With regard to model designs and statistical methods this line of evolution is a merger of 1.3.2 and 1.3.3. Across this merger, however, there is the same watershed between hard and soft modelling that we have noted in 1.2.4. On the one hand, ML and other methods from factor analysis make for hard modelling, oriented towards microanalysis based on data from controlled experiments. On the other hand, least squares and other methods of principal component analysis are more in the nature of soft modelling, oriented towards macroanalysis based on non-experimental or operations analysis data. It is this last-mentioned aspect that has given the incentive for the present paper.

2. Path models with three blocks of manifest variables

Chart 4 shows three path models, each of which has three blocks of observables, say

$$(1a\text{--}c) \quad x_{it} \ (i = 1, \cdots, p); \quad y_{jt} \ (j = 1, \cdots, q); \quad z_{kt} \ (k = 1, \cdots, r)$$

with $t = 1, \cdots, n$ indicating the sample items. For graphic simplicity, each block is drawn with two observables; $p = q = r = 2$. In path models with two blocks of manifest variables, the NIPALS models A_i–C_i $(i = 1, 2)$ mark a considerable pluralism in the designs; see Charts 2b and 3. Turning from two to three blocks of observables, the pluralism multiplies, as we shall now indicate in some detail.

2.1. *Sources of pluralism in the design of path models with latent variables.*

2.1.1.   We first consider the number of latent variables. The three models in Chart 4 will be denoted A_{31}, A_{32}, A_{33}, letting the first subscript indicate the number of blocks of observables, the second subscript the number of latent variables. We note the analogy between models A_{31} and A_1 where the designs involve just one latent variable, and also between models A_{33} and A_2, inasmuch as these designs have one latent variable for

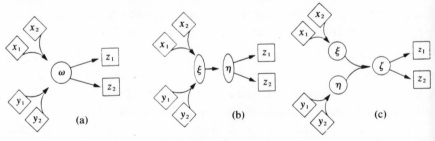

Chart 4a–c. Path models with three blocks of observables, and one, two or three latent variables.

each block of observables. With regard to this aspect of the models, there is just one design of type A_{31} and one design of type A_{33}, but there are three designs of type A_{32}, since there are three ways in which two of the three blocks of observables can be combined to generate one latent variable.

2.1.2. Let us now examine inward versus outward indicators. For each design under 2.1.1, an inferential arrow between manifest and latent variable may point either from manifest to latent variable, or conversely. Hence for each block of observables in a design under 2.1.1 the inferential arrows can be specified in two ways. Thus if the model has three blocks, as in Chart 4, there are $2^3 = 8$ different versions for each of the three graphs, each with a specific design of the inferential directions between manifest and latent variables.

As to terminology, the manifest variables are called *inward indicators* or *outward indicators* depending upon whether the inferential arrows point from manifest to latent variable, or conversely (Wold (1974 a–c)). For the same distinction, Blalock (1971a) uses the terms *cause indicator* and *effect indicator.* These causal terms may sometimes be confusing, however, for they may be mixed up with the causal directions between the latent variables, directions which need not necessarily combine with the indicator arrows into a uni-directional path system. We shall revert to this last feature in 2.1.3. Other and shorter terms that come to mind for inward versus outward indicators are *generators* versus *indicators*, the term generator reflecting that the latent variable serves as a proxy aggregate for the block observables. This again may be somewhat confusing since in NIPALS modelling both the inward and outward indicators are formed as linear aggregates of manifest variables.

2.1.3. We proceed to study inner versus outer relations. This distinction refers to the relations between latent variables on the one hand, and the inferential relations that specify inward and outward indicators on the other. The inner relations are a source of pluralism that enters as a new distinctive feature when passing from two to three latent variables in the model. In NIPALS modelling the latent variables are normalized to unit variance, and so in models with two latent variables and one inner relation (Models A_2, B_2 and C_2; see Charts 2a and 3 b, d) the regression coefficient between the two variables is the same for the two possible directions of the inner relation; hence with regard to parameter estimation there is no need to distinguish between the two directions. So much the richer as a source of pluralism are the inner relations in models with three or more latent variables. Some few of the designs with three variables are shown in Chart 5. The model in Chart 5a is uni-relational, while the models in Charts 5 b,c have two and three inner relations respectively. We see that the models in Chart 5 will generate 11 different designs of inner relations if we include the various versions that are obtained by permutation of the three blocks.

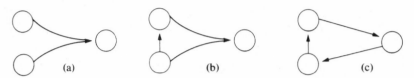

Chart 5a–c.   The inner relations in path models with three latent variables and one, two or three inner relations.

2.1.4.   We can now sum up the position. Taking into account the various sources of pluralism under 2.1.1–2.1.3, thére are 160 or more different designs of path models with three blocks of manifest variables.[4] Many of these are of potential relevance for applied work. We proceed to develop the NIPALS modelling of one of these designs. We choose Model A_{33} (see Chart 4c), which is interesting both with regard to potential applications and to new features that enter in the passage from two to three latent variables.

3.   The NIPALS Model A_{33}: Structure and estimation

We shall keep the notation (2.1) for the three blocks of observables, and write ξ_t, η_t and ζ_t for the corresponding latent variables. All variables are assumed to have zero mean, a formal simplification that can readily be recovered.

3.1.   *Formal specification.*   The structural relations of Model A_{33} are one multiple regression,

$$(1) \qquad \zeta_t = \sum_i \alpha_i x_{it} + \sum_j \beta_j y_{jt} + \epsilon_t$$

and for each k a regression of z_{kt} on the two latent variables ξ_t and η_t,

---

[4] This count is not exhaustive. For one thing, it does not include designs with partial or complete symmetry between the latent variables, such as the extension of canonical correlation to three blocks of observables, [21], or cases of interdependence between two latent variables in the various designs in Chart 5.

(2) $$z_{kt} = \gamma_{k1}\xi_t + \gamma_{k2}\eta_t + \epsilon_{kt} \qquad (k = 1, \cdots, r).$$

The latent variables are defined as linear aggregates of the corresponding blocks of observables, namely

(3a) $$\xi_t = \kappa_1 \sum_i \alpha_i x_{it} \,;$$

(3b) $$\eta_t = \kappa_2 \sum_j \beta_j y_{jt} \,;$$

(3c) $$\zeta_t = \kappa_3 \sum_k \gamma_k z_{kt}$$

with

(4) $$\gamma_k = \tfrac{1}{2}(\gamma_{k1} + \gamma_{k2}), \qquad (k = 1, \cdots, r),$$

and with normalization factors κ_1, κ_2, κ_3 that give the latent variables unit variance,

(5a–c) $$E(\xi_t^2) = E(\eta_t^2) = E(\zeta_t^2) = 1.$$

Furthermore, each of the regressions (1)–(2) is specified as a predictor; that is,

(6a) $$E(\zeta_t | x_{it}, i = 1, \cdots, p \,; y_{jt}, j = 1, \cdots, q) = \sum_j \alpha_i x_{it} + \sum_j \beta_j y_{jt}$$

(6b) $$E(z_{kt} | \xi_t, \eta_t) = \gamma_{k1}\xi_t + \gamma_{k2}\eta_t.$$

Relations (1)–(6) specify Model A_{33} in terms of the latent variables ξ_t, η_t, ζ_t and the parameters α_i, β_j, γ_k of its outer relations. Model A_{33} further involves the inner relation

(7a) $$\zeta_t = \pi_1\xi_t + \pi_2\eta_t + v_t$$

subject to the predictor specification

(7b) $$E(\zeta_t | \xi_t, \eta_t) = \pi_1\xi_t + \pi_2\eta_t.$$

3.1.1. We can now make some relevant comments.

(i) Model A_{33} reduces to A_2 if the second block of observables y_{jt} is absent, and $\gamma_k = \gamma_{k1}$ $(k = 1, \cdots, r)$. The inner relation of Model A_2 reduces to the simple regression

(8a–b) $$\zeta_t = \pi\xi_t + v_t \quad \text{with} \quad E(\zeta_t | \xi_t) = \pi\xi_t$$

where

(9) $$\pi = r(\xi_t, \eta_t).$$

(ii)   In NIPALS modelling, the inner relations are implications of the latent variables, and thereby of the outer relations. Relation (9) is a simple case in point. In (7a) the coefficients π_1, π_2 are the partial regression coefficients of ζ_t and ξ_t, η_t.

(iii)   In (3c) the coefficients γ_k are overidentified, in the sense that the regressions (6b) give two parameters γ_{k1}, γ_{k2} for each k. This ambiguity is settled by the simple device (4). As to the rationale of this device we note that (4) is in order in the special case where the latent variables ξ_t, η_t are identically the same (cf. also Comment (i)). More refined devices than (4) are at hand, but we leave it at that to proceed to the estimation of Model A_{33}. (See note added in proof, p. 140.)

3.2.   *NIPALS point estimation.*   The following procedure for the point estimation of Model A_{33} is in formal and computational respects a straightforward extension of the NIPALS estimation of Model A_2 (see [38]). The procedure is iterative, $s = 1, 2, \cdots$. At each step, OLS regression is applied alternately to (6a) and (6b), and new proxies for the latent variables are computed in accordance with (3 a–c). The NIPALS estimates for the unknowns are obtained in the limit as $s \to \infty$, giving

(10a) $$a_i = \lim_{s \to \infty} a_i^{(s)}, \qquad (i = 1, \cdots, p);$$

(10b) $$x_t = \lim_{s \to \infty} x_t^{(s)}, \qquad (t = 1, \cdots, n)$$

as estimates for α_i and ξ_t, and similarly for β_j, η_t and γ_k, ζ_t.

We shall spell out the start of the estimation and the general step from s to $s + 1$. The resulting estimates of the latent variables provide the material for estimating the inner relation (7a) of A_{33}.

3.2.1.   We start with $s = 1$. Make $a_i^{(1)} = b_j^{(1)} = 1$ for $i = 1, \cdots, p$ and $j = 1, \cdots, q$. Next calculate the sample items of the first proxy of ξ_t as

(11) $$x_t^{(1)} = k_1^{(1)} \sum_i x_{it}, \qquad (t = 1, \cdots, n)$$

where $k_1^{(1)}$ is determined so as to give $x_t^{(1)}$ unit variance, in accordance with (5a). The sample items $y_t^{(1)}$ of the first proxy of η_t are computed in the same manner.

3.2.2. We now proceed with the step from s to $s + 1$. First, using the proxies $x_t^{(s)}$, $y_t^{(s)}$ computed in step s, the proxies $g_{k1}^{(s+1)}$, $g_{k2}^{(s+1)}$ for the parameters γ_{k1}, γ_{k2} are for each fixed $k = 1, \cdots, r$, computed from the OLS regression

$$(12) \qquad z_{kt} = g_{k1}^{(s+1)} x_t^{(s)} + g_{k2}^{(s+1)} y_t^{(s)} + e_{kt}^{(s+1)}$$

formed in accordance with (2). Second, (4) gives

$$(13) \qquad g_k^{(s+1)} = \tfrac{1}{2}(g_{k1}^{(s+1)} + g_{k2}^{(s+1)}) \quad (k = 1, \cdots, r),$$

and these parameter proxies are used to compute

$$(14) \qquad z_t^{(s+1)} = k_3^{(s+1)} \sum_k g_k^{(s+1)} z_{kt} \qquad (t = 1, \cdots, n),$$

where $k_3^{(s+1)}$ is calculated so as to give $z_t^{(s+1)}$ unit variance. Third, the parameter proxies $a_i^{(s+1)}$ with $i = 1, \cdots, p$ and $b_j^{(s+1)}$ with $j = 1, \cdots, q$ are computed from the multiple OLS regression

$$(15) \qquad z_t^{(s+1)} = \sum_i a_i^{(s+1)} x_{it} + \sum_j b_j^{(s+1)} y_{jt} + e_t^{(s+1)}$$

formed in accordance with (1), and the resulting proxies give

$$(16) \qquad x_t^{(s+1)} = k_1^{(s+1)} \sum_i a_i^{(s+1)} x_{it} \qquad (t = 1, \cdots, n),$$

where $k_1^{(s+1)}$ is computed in accordance with the normalizing condition (5a), and similarly for $y_t^{(s+1)}$. Step $s + 1$ is now completed, and the iteration continues with step $s + 2$.

3.2.3. Let us consider the inner relation (7a). After the limit passage $s \to \infty$ is completed, (7a) is estimated from the OLS regression

$$(17) \qquad z_t = p_1 x_t + p_2 y_t + u_t$$

where the predictor specification (7b) gives the normal equations

$$(18a) \qquad p_1 \quad + p_2 r_{xy} = r_{xz}$$

$$(18b) \qquad p_1 r_{xy} + p_2 \quad = r_{zy}$$

in obvious symbols. The parameter estimates p_1, p_2 fall out as the partial regressions of z_t with respect to x_t and y_t,

$$(19a) \qquad p_1 = \frac{r_{xz} - r_{xy} r_{yz}}{1 - r_{xy}^2};$$

(19b)
$$p_2 = \frac{r_{yz} - r_{xy}r_{xz}}{1 - r_{xy}^2}.$$

3.3. *Computer programs.* The estimation procedure 3.2 has been programmed for the computer by Björn Areskoug, who has earlier programmed the NIPALS estimation procedures for the six models $A_i - C_i$
($i = 1, 2$) with one or two latent variables, [4]. Computer programs for an
array of other models with three or more latent variables are being
developed. Completed programs are available on request from the
Statistics Department, University of Göteborg, at nominal cost.

3.4. *The theoretical estimator.* We shall next write down the theoretical estimator for the NIPALS estimation procedure 3.2, following the
general theory of NIPALS modelling, [3], [38]. The theoretical estimator
is obtained from a system of algebraic equations formed by the normal
equations for the predictor relations (6) of the model, and by the
normalizing equations (5) for the latent variables.

3.4.1. Minimizing the least squares criterion $E(\epsilon_i^2)$ as formed for
Relation (1) gives the following normal equation for any fixed $a = 1, \cdots, p$,

(20) $$\kappa_3 \sum_k \gamma_k E(z_k x_a) = \sum_i \alpha_i E(x_i x_a) + \sum_j \beta_j E(y_j x_a)$$

where in the left-hand member $E(\zeta_t x_{at})$ has been expanded, using (3c).
For Relation (2) with any fixed k the least squares criterion $E(\epsilon_{kt}^2)$ gives
the following normal equation when minimizing with respect to γ_{k1},

(21) $$\kappa_1 \sum_i \alpha_i E(z_k x_i) = \gamma_{k1} + \gamma_{k2} E(\xi_t \eta_t)   (k = 1, \cdots, r)$$

where the left-hand member expands $E(z_{kt} \xi_t)$, using (3a). The normalizing
Equation (5a) gives

(22) $$\kappa_1^2 \sum_{h=1}^{p} \sum_{i=1}^{p} \alpha_h \alpha_i E(x_{ht} x_{it}) = 1.$$

3.4.2. We shall write the resulting system of algebraic equations in
vector and matrix notation, using current symbols, such as R_{xz} for the
covariance matrix of the blocks $x_{it} (i = 1, \cdots, p)$ and $z_{kt} (k = 1, \cdots, q)$ of
directly observed variables.

Equation (21) and the corresponding relation obtained when minimizing
with respect to γ_{k2} give

(23a) $\qquad \kappa_1 \alpha R_{xz} = \gamma_1 I_p \qquad\qquad + \gamma_2 \kappa_1 \kappa_2 \alpha R_{xy} \beta'$

(23b) $\qquad \kappa_2 \beta R_{yz} = \gamma_1 \kappa_1 \kappa_2 \beta R_{yx} \alpha' \quad + \gamma_2 I_q.$

Equation (20) and the corresponding equation obtained when minimizing with respect to y_{bt} $(b = 1, \cdots, q)$ give

(24a) $\qquad\qquad\qquad \kappa_3 \gamma R_{zx} = \alpha R_{xx} + \beta R_{yx}$

(24b) $\qquad\qquad\qquad \kappa_3 \gamma R_{zy} = \alpha R_{xy} + \beta R_{yy}.$

Equation (22) and the analogous normalizing equations for η_t and ζ_t give

(25a) $\qquad\qquad\qquad \alpha R_{xx} \alpha' = 1/\kappa_1^2;$

(25b) $\qquad\qquad\qquad \beta R_{yy} \beta' = 1/\kappa_2^2;$

(25c) $\qquad\qquad\qquad \gamma R_{zz} \gamma' = 1/\kappa_3^2.$

Finally, Equations (4) belong to the system without change, giving

(26) $\qquad\qquad\qquad \gamma = \tfrac{1}{2}(\gamma_1 + \gamma_2).$

3.5. Performance of NIPALS modelling.

3.5.1. Given the path model (1)–(7), its parameters will satisfy the algebraic system (23)–(26). System (23)–(26) and its analogues for other path models with latent variables provide theoretical information on the performance of the iterative procedure 3.2 of NIPALS estimation, notably its convergence and consistency. For the six NIPALS models $A_i - C_i$ $(i = 1, 2)$ with one or two latent variables (see 1.2), the iterative estimation will almost always converge and give estimates that are consistent in the large sample sense, [44]. System (23)–(26) is, however, much more complicated than the algebraic systems for the six models $A_i - C_i$. Specifically, the factors $\gamma_2 \kappa_1 \kappa_2 \alpha$ and $\gamma_1 \kappa_1 \kappa_2 \beta$ in (23 a,b) are non-linearities of an unwieldy type that belong to the new problems arising in path models when passing from two to three latent variables.

3.5.2. To explore the performance of procedure 3.2 and other NI-PALS estimation we can always fall back on the elementary and pedestrian approach of simulation. When dealing with models with many variables, it is well known that simulation is very laborious and time-consuming.[5] This is particularly so for path models with three or more

---

[5] For simulation experiments in NIPALS modelling, see [29], and the comprehensive bibliography in [27].

variables, owing to the heavy pluralism in the model design (see 2.1.4). An array of simulation experiments has been carried out on procedure (11)–(19) and NIPALS estimation of related models. The results are encouraging, and more experiments are under way. The problem area is, however, extensive, and more experience is needed before results of any scope can be reported.

3.6. *Range estimation.* The NIPALS estimation procedure 3.2 is a case of point estimation, and is thereby on the hard side relative to the soft approach of interval estimates. While the current methods for interval estimation are based on intervals in the nature of confidence intervals, we shall now set forth a somewhat different type of device, to be called *range estimation.* The simple idea is to form on the one hand what we shall call *low profile* estimates; that is, estimates that as a rule will be on the low side (numerically) of the parameters to be estimated. On the other hand we also form *high profile* estimates which are designed to be numerically larger than these same parameters, and obtain the range estimates as the difference between the high profile and low profile estimates. We note in advance that the distinction between inner and outer relations (see 2.1.3) is important in the approach of range estimation.

3.6.1. Let us first consider the low profile (l.p.) estimation. As before, we consider Model A_{33}. First, the l.p. estimate $\breve{x}_t$ of the latent variable ξ_t is computed as the first principal component of the block (2.1a) of observables x_{it}; in symbols, after normalizing $\breve{x}_t$ to unit variance,

$$(27) \qquad\qquad x_{it} = l_i \breve{x}_t + d_{it}.$$

In the same manner the l.p. estimate $\breve{y}_t$ of the latent variable η_t is computed, and similarly for $\breve{z}_t$. Second, the l.p. estimate $\breve{r}_{xy}$ of the correlation ρ_{xy} between the latent variables ξ_t and η_t is computed as

$$(28) \qquad\qquad \breve{r}_{xy} = r(\breve{x}_t, \breve{y}_t)$$

and similarly for $\breve{r}_{xz}$ and $\breve{r}_{yz}$. Third and last, the l.p. estimates $\breve{p}_1, \breve{p}_2$ of the parameters π_1, π_2 of the inner relation (7a) are obtained by substitution in Formulas (19 a,b); this gives

$$(29) \qquad\qquad \breve{p}_1 = (\breve{r}_{xz} - \breve{r}_{xy} \breve{r}_{yz})/(1 - \breve{r}_{xy}^2)$$

and similarly for $\breve{p}_2$.

3.6.2. We now continue with high profile (h.p.) estimation. First, Model A_2 is applied to the two blocks of variables $x_{it} (i = 1, \cdots, p)$,

$z_{kt}(k = 1, \cdots, q)$. The resulting estimates x_t, z_t of the latent variables ξ_t, ζ_t in Model A_2 are taken as the h.p. estimate $\hat{x}_t$ of the latent variable ξ_t in A_{33} and as a provisional h.p. estimate $\tilde{z}_t$ of the latent variable ζ_t in A_{33}. Similarly, Model A_2 is applied to the blocks y_{jt}, z_{kt} to compute the h.p. estimate $\hat{y}_t$ of η_t and a second provisional item $\tilde{z}'_t$ for the h.p. estimate of ζ_t. Second, the h.p. estimate of ζ_t is computed as the average of its two provisional estimates,

(30) $$\hat{z}_t = \tfrac{1}{2}(\tilde{z}_t + \tilde{z}'_t).$$

Finally, the h.p. estimates of the parameters of the inner relation (7a) are obtained by substitution in (19 a–b); as in (29), we write out the first coefficient,

(31) $$\hat{p}_1 = (\hat{r}_{xz} - \hat{r}_{xy}\hat{r}_{yz})/(1 - \hat{r}_{xy}^2).$$

4. Generalization aspects

The NIPALS methods of soft modelling in Section 3 can be modified and extended in several ways, sometimes in a straightforward manner, sometimes after suitable adaptations. We shall now focus on the generalization to models with four or five latent variables and with two or three inner relations.

4.1. *One inner relation with three or more latent variables.* We specify Model A_{44} as a straightforward extension of Model A_{33}, augmenting formulas (3.1)–(3.7) by a fourth block of directly observed variables $w_{ht}(h = 1, \cdots, m)$ and a corresponding latent variable

(1) $$\omega_t = \kappa_4 \sum_n \phi_h w_{ht}.$$

In the inner relation (3.7), ω_t joins ξ_t and η_t to explain ζ_t. The point estimation 3.2 of A_{33} carries over to A_{44} if in the $(s + 1)$th step a third term $g_{k3}^{(s+1)} w_t^{(s)}$ is included in the multiple regression (3.12), and the average (3.13) is changed to involve three items. Similarly, the extensions to Model A_{44} of the theoretical estimator 3.4 and the range estimation 3.6 are immediate.

4.1.1. As to low profile estimation 3.6.1 it will be noted that the l.p. estimation by (3.27) of the latent variable ξ_t can be based on several principal components of the block $x_{it}(i = 1, \cdots, p)$. Thus if X_{at} denotes the ath principal component and θ_a its variance, and if we base $\check{x}_t$ on two components,

(2) $$\check{x}_t = (X_{1t} + X_{2t})/(\theta_1 + \theta_2)^{\frac{1}{2}}.$$

4.2. *A model with two inner relations.* Let us consider the model, say A_{332}, which is obtained by including in Model A_{33} (see 3.1) a second inner relation that explains η_t in terms of ξ_t, say

(3a) $$\eta_t = \pi_{21}\xi_t + \Delta_t$$

subject to the predictor specification

(3b) $$E(\eta_t|\xi_t) = \pi_{21}\xi_t.$$

4.2.1. We now look into the point estimation of Model A_{332}. If (3) and the outer relations of the blocks x_{it} ($i = 1, \cdots, p$), y_{jt} ($j = 1, \cdots, q$) are taken from A_{332} to make a separate NIPALS model, this will be of type B_2, inasmuch as Chart 4c specifies the blocks x_{it} and y_{jt} as generators or inward indicators in the sense of 2.1.2. Hence for the point estimation of A_{332} we shall combine the estimation 3.2 of A_{33} with an estimation of (3) that is conceptually in line with Model B_2. This approach provides two estimates for each of the latent variables ξ_t and η_t, with the result that the parameters α_i and β_j in (3.3 a–b) become overidentified. To remove this dualism we use the same device as in (3.4).

To spell out the procedure in some detail, we change the notations in (3.1) to $\Sigma_i\alpha_{i1}x_{it} + \Sigma_j\beta_{j1}y_{jt}$, and similarly in 3.2. In the $(s + 1)$th round of the procedure 3.2 we use the sth round of proxies to compute the parameter proxies $a_{i2}^{(s+1)}$ and $b_{j2}^{(s+1)}$ from the two OLS regressions

(4a) $$y_t^{(s)} = \sum_i a_{i2}^{(s+1)} x_{it} + d_{1t}^{(s+1)};$$

(4b) $$x_t^{(s)} = \sum_j b_{j2}^{(s+1)} y_{jt} + d_{2t}^{(s+1)}.$$

The proxies $a_i^{(s+1)}$ to be used in (3.16) are computed from

(5) $$a_i^{(s+1)} = \tfrac{1}{2}(a_{i1}^{(s+1)} + a_{i2}^{(s+1)})$$

and similarly for $b_j^{(s+1)}$. After the limit passage $s \to \infty$, the resulting point estimates x_t, y_t for the latent variables ξ_t, η_t are used to estimate (3a) by the OLS regression

(6) $$y_t = p_{21}x_t + d_t.$$

4.2.2.   At this stage we examine the range estimation of Model A_{332}. As to l.p. estimation, this carries over without change from 3.6.1 (with or without the modification 4.1.1). To specify, the l.p. estimates $\breve{p}_1$ and $\breve{p}_2$ remain the same, and in accordance with (3a,b) and (3.28) the l.p. estimate of π_{21} is computed from

(7) $$\breve{p}_{21} = r(\breve{x}_t, \breve{y}_t) = \breve{r}_{xy}.$$

For the h.p. estimation of Model A_{332} we supplement the h.p. estimation 3.6.2 of Model A_{33} by a separate h.p. estimation of the model B_2 dealt with in 4.2.1. This gives us two h.p. estimates for the latent variable ξ_t, say $\hat{x}_t$ and $\hat{x}'_t$, and their average gives $\hat{x}_t$, just as in (3.30) for $\hat{z}_t$. The h.p. estimate $\hat{y}_t$ is computed in the same manner as $\hat{x}_t$. Using the h.p. estimates $\hat{x}_t, \hat{y}_t, \hat{z}_t$ for ξ_t, η_t, ζ_t thus obtained, Formulas (3.19) and (3.9) give the h.p. estimates $\hat{p}_1, \hat{p}_2$ and $\hat{p}_{21}$.

4.3.   *A more complex model*: A_{443}.   The soft approaches of path modelling set forth in 4.1–4.2 are of wider scope, and go some way to estimate path models with several latent variables and several structural (inner) relations. It will suffice for our purpose to illustrate the method by the model A_{443} shown in Chart 6, an educational macro-model with four blocks of variables, four latent variables and three structural relations. With little or no change, the notations carry over from Models A_{44} in 4.1. and A_{332} in 4.2.2.

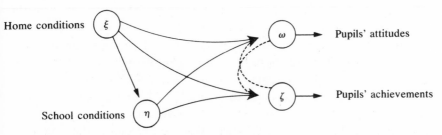

Home conditions ξ

Pupils' attitudes

Pupils' achievements

School conditions η

Chart 6.   The educational macro-model A_{443}.

4.3.1.   We first examine the data.   The four blocks of manifest variables in Model A_{443} refer to the home (x_{it}), the school (y_{jt}), the individual attitudes (w_{ht}) and the individual achievements (z_{kt}).

4.3.2.   Let us specify the outer relations.   In the sense of 2.1.2, the home and school variables are generators or inward indicators, while the individual attitude and achievement variables are indicators or outward indicators.

4.3.3.   Consider now the inner relations.   As seen from Chart 6, Model A_{443} has three inner relations, namely:
School conditions are explained by home conditions,

(8a–b) $\eta_t = \pi_{21}\xi_t + \delta_{1t} ; \quad E(\eta_t | \xi_t) = \pi_{21}\xi_t.$

Individual attitudes are explained by home and school conditions,

(9) $\omega_t = \pi_{31}\xi_t + \pi_{32}\eta_t + \delta_{2t}.$

Individual achievements are explained by home and school conditions,

(10) $\zeta_t = \pi_{41}\xi_t + \pi_{42}\eta_t + \delta_{3t}.$

The three relations are specified as predictors; for (8a) this is spelled out in (8b).

4.3.4.   We are now in a position to discuss interdependence between attitudes and achievements.   Again with reference to Chart 6, Relations (8)–(10) ignore the two broken arrows, which indicate interdependence between achievements and attitudes. Taking this interdependence into account, a term $\pi_{34}\zeta_t$ enters in (9) and a term $\pi_{43}\omega_t$ in (10). The resulting model will be denoted A^*_{443}.

Models A_{443} and A^*_{443} mark a sharp parting of the ways. In A_{443} Relations (8a), (9), (10) make a causal chain (CCh) system, in A^*_{443} the same relations make an interdependent (ID) system; in both cases the system is in structural form. According to the theory of multi-relational models, the structural relations of CCh systems allow predictor specification, but not so in ID systems. (For the theory of CCh and ID systems with regard to predictor specification and NIPALS modelling, the reader is referred to [29], [35], [36].) Hence CCh systems can be consistently estimated by OLS regression, while ID systems require other methods (see 1.3.3,(ii)).

4.3.5.   Let us consider the range estimation.   In l.p. estimation of Model A_{443} we take the first principal component for each of the four data blocks 4.3.1 as the l.p. estimate of the corresponding latent variable, or we may try the device 4.1.1. Using the resulting estimates to compute the requisite product moments of latent variables, l.p. estimates of the parameters in the CCh system (8)–(10) are obtained by applying OLS regression to each relation of the system separately.

In h.p. estimation of Model A_{443}, we first apply Model A_{332} to the three blocks x_{it}, y_{jt}, w_{ht} to compute h.p. estimates of the latent variables ξ_t, η_t, ω_t and then to the blocks x_{it}, y_{jt}, z_{kt} to compute an h.p. estimate for ζ_t and a second h.p. estimate for each of the variables ξ_t, η_t. The final h.p. estimate $\hat{x}_t$ of the latent variable ξ_t is obtained by averaging, as in (3.30), and similarly for $\hat{y}_t$. The h.p. estimates of the parameters in the inner system (8)–(10) are then computed in the same manner as the l.p. estimates, applying OLS regression to each separate relation.

The range estimation of Model A_{443} carries over to Model A^{*}_{443}, with the difference that the inner system (8)–(10) now is an ID system (see 4.3.4), which we transform to a GEID (General ID) system and estimate by the Fix-Point method; see 1.3.3, (ii).

5. Discussion: Why soft modelling?

Again with reference to Chart 1, Coleman's model illustrates the main incentives behind the present paper. His macro-model sums up the broad causal structure of a complex situation, and in Coleman's words ([12], p. 11) 'all analyses of school effect I know suggest this kind of scheme...' but the actual statistical analysis of the huge body of data at issue is fragmentary and primitive.[6] This is usually a matter of stepwise regression where the material has been drastically reduced by screening off explanatory variables on broad preparatory criteria, and is nowhere near an integrated approach to the situation; it may be added that Coleman himself does not offer a clue for an integrated statistical analysis. My plea is for soft statistical modelling in such situations, maintaining that hard versus soft methods of analysis are complementary rather than competitive, and recognizing that fargoing concessions from the current mainstream of hard modelling are needed in complex situations, at least in the present stage of the crafts, to bridge the gap between a plausible macro-model and a corresponding integrated analysis of the data.

Part of the story is that the methods of hard modelling usually have an array of technical limitations that bar the road into the domain of soft modelling. This is particularly so for the ML (Maximum Likelihood)

---

[6] Paraphrasing Coleman's appraisal [12], the statement refers to the 22-countries survey of The International Association for the Evaluation of Educational Achievement (I.E.A.) and the seven volumes of analysis of this body of data thus far published by I.E.A.

approach. For one thing, in soft modelling the number of unknowns usually increases with the size of the sample under analysis, a feature that sometimes endangers the ML approach. One may refer to van der Waerden's famous case, where the unknowns increase in number with sample size, and where ML estimation is shown to involve a large-sample bias, namely under-estimation amounting to 50%, [34]. (Cf. footnote 2.) One apprehends even more the fact that the basic assumptions of ML modelling refer to the distributional and correlational properties of the residuals in the model, assumptions that are to the point in experimental micro-analysis but usually have no basis and often are bluntly unrealistic when it comes to macro-models and complex non-experimental situations.

For a case in point, the forceful emphasis on ML methods in macro-economic model building in the 1950's has slackened or disappeared, partly by the impact of the Theil-Basmann Two-Stage Least Squares method, [5], [32]. Similarly, the stringent assumptions of zero residual intercorrelations in ML factor analysis are often unrealistic in macro-economic and other non-experimental applications. This last feature is aggravated when it comes to latent variables, for in ML modelling it is typical that no assumptions are made about the structure of the latent variables, and the basic assumptions are so much the more pinned to the residual properties of the model.

NIPALS modelling, like ML, is flexible and of general scope. In soft modelling, NIPALS comes to the fore thanks to the predictor specification of the structural relations of the model. This feature brings advantages on several scores. Conceptually, and with regard to the prior experience and information on which the model is founded, the predictor specification meets the intended use of the model for causal and/or predictive inference, and in soft modelling the intended use of the model is sometimes a main source of prior information. Technically, the predictor specification refers to the systematic part of each structural relation, not to the residual properties of the relation. This type of specification brings economy in the basic assumptions (see 1.2.1(iii)) and will in general suffice to yield consistent parameter estimates. Supplementary assumptions on the residuals are needed to obtain standard errors, confidence intervals and other instruments of hard modelling.[7]

---

[7] See references in [26], including the formulas for standard errors in fix-point estimation reported by Lyttkens (1970), and in principal components reported by Christoffersson (1970).

When the structural relations involve latent variables as explanatory, it is a necessity for the NIPALS approach to define the latent variables in terms of the observables, for otherwise the requisite regressions could not be computed. This necessity becomes a virtue, however, since it enables the model builder to obtain consistent estimates of the sample values of the latent variables, posterior information that can be used for testing and further development of the model (see 1.2.2, (iv), (v)). Similarly, the sample values of the residuals can be consistently estimated, adding to the posterior material for testing and development of the model.

Broadly speaking, soft modelling works with lower aspiration levels than comparable hard models. In the six NIPALS models $A_i - C_i$, with one or two latent variables, the aspiration levels of hard modelling are on the whole maintained. This is particularly so with regard to point estimation. Extending the NIPALS approach to path models that involve three or more latent variables, the methods of the present paper make two concessions relative to hard modelling. To specify: (a) In a first phase the parameter estimation is limited to the outer relations of the model and the sample values of the latent variables; the parameters of the inner relations are then estimated using the estimates of the latent variables; (b) Range estimation by way of low profile versus high profile estimation. Note that the NIPALS estimation of canonical correlations (Model B_2) is a case under (a) that involves only two latent variables. Along with the implementation of devices (a) and (b) for path models with several latent variables, applications are spelled out in Sections 3 and 4 for some few path models with three or four latent variables, including an educational macro-model which is in line with Coleman's conceptual model in Chart 1.

The limited scope of this paper must be emphasized. The report draws from a research project that is in an early stage of development. Applied work on real-world models and data are in the making, and plenty of experience is needed to judge the reach and limitation of the new methods. The project further includes other aspects of soft modelling, including cluster analysis and hypothesis testing. Under this last heading, John Tukey's jack-knife for exploring the stability of parameter estimates is conceptually in line with soft modelling.[8] Or to mention a split-plot device: will the estimates for the parameters of the inner relations of a NIPALS model remain stable if the outer relations are estimated by splitting the blocks of observables and using alternately the items with

---

[8] See Miller (1974) for a recent review.

odd and even numbers? As to cluster analysis, the recent method of linear clustering of cases (see [46]) is being developed into an approach for simultaneous clustering of cases and variables.

Acknowledgements

The research in this paper has received support from the Tercentenary Fund of the Bank of Sweden and from the Scientific Council of the Swedish Central Bureau of Statistics. Part of the research was carried out when, for several months in 1973 and 1974, the author had the privilege of visiting the Department of Statistics, Bell Laboratories, Murray Hill, N.J., with its prospering research in hard and soft data analysis.

This paper is partly a program of the NIPALS research group that I am conducting in Göteborg, partly a research contribution under this program. The group has the active collaboration of Dr. Richard Noonan, who worked previously on the IEA project, and the active consultation of Professor Irma Adelman, who collected and analysed the econometric data used in the study. I wish to express my pleasure in and appreciation of this cooperation.

A preliminary version of the paper has been read and commented upon by Professors Irma Adelman, Karl-Gustav Jöreskog, Ejnar Lyttkens, Sydney May and Werner Meissner. I of course take full responsibility for any remaining errors.

Note added in proof: While only one parameter γ_k is needed for each k in (3.3c) to form the latent variable ζ_t, the averaging in (3.4) serves to avoid the overidentification embodied in the double set of parameters γ_{k1}, γ_{k2}. The fixed average in (3.4) being a weak point in the design of Model A_{33}, a flexible and more adequate approach is to define

$$(*) \qquad \gamma_{kh} = \lambda_h \gamma_k \qquad (k = 1, r; h = 1, 2).$$

The NIPALS point estimation 3.2 allows straightforward adaptation to the model A_{33} thus amended. The device (*) and the NIPALS point estimation extend to the more complex models A_{443} etc. considered in this paper.

References

[1] ADELMAN, I. AND MORRIS, C. T. (1967) *Society, Politics, and Economic Development.* The Johns Hopkins Press, Baltimore. (Revised ed. 1971.)

[2] ———— (1973) *Economic Growth and Social Equity in Developing Countries.* Stanford University Press, California.

[3] ÅGREN, A. (1972) *Extensions of the Fix-Point Method. Theory and Applications.* Doctoral Thesis, University of Uppsala, Sweden.

[4] ARESKOUG, B. (1974) *Computer program MIMIC.* Department of Statistics, University of Göteborg, Sweden.

[5] BASMANN, R. L. (1957) A generalized classical method of linear estimation of coefficients in a structural equation. *Econometrica* **25**, 77–83.

[6] BERGSTRÖM, R. (1974) *Studies in the Estimation of Interdependent Systems, Especially the Fix-Point and Iterative Instrumental Variables Methods.* Doctoral Thesis, University of Uppsala, Sweden.

[7] BLALOCK, H. M., JR. (1971a) Causal models involving unmeasured variables in stimulus-response situations. In *Causal Models in the Social Sciences*, pp. 335–347. Aldine, Atherton, Chicago.

[8] ————, ed. (1971b) *Causal Models in the Social Sciences.* Aldine, Atherton, Chicago.

[9] BODIN, L. (1974) *Recursive Fix-Point Estimation. Theory and Applications.* Doctoral Thesis, University of Uppsala, Sweden.

[10] BROWN, T. M. (1959) Simplified full maximum likelihood and comparative structural estimates. *Econometrica* **27**, 638–653.

[11] CHRISTOFFERSSON, A. (1970) *The One Component Model with Incomplete Data.* Doctoral Thesis, University of Uppsala, Sweden.

[12] COLEMAN, J. S. (1973) Effects of school learning: The IEA findings. Harvard-IEA Conference, Teachers College, Harvard University, 12–17 November 1973.

[13] COSTNER, H. L., ed. (1971) *Sociological Methodology 1971.* Jossey-Bass, San Francisco.

[14] FRIEDMAN, M. (1957) *A Theory of the Consumption Function.* Princeton University Press, Princeton, New Jersey.

[15] GINI, C. (1921) Sull'interpolazione di una retta quando i valori della variabile indipendente sono affetti da errori accidentali. *Metron* **1**, 63–82.

[16] HAUSER, R. M. (1968) *Family, School and Neighborhood Factors in Educational Performances in a Metropolitan School System.* Unpublished Doctoral Dissertation, University of Michigan.

[17] ———— (1969) On 'social participation and social status'. *American Sociological Review* **34**, 587–611.

[18] HAUSER, R. M. AND GOLDBERGER, A. S. (1971) The treatment of unobservable variables in path analysis. In *Sociological Methodology 1971*, pp. 87–117. Jossey-Bass, San Francisco.

[19] JÖRESKOG, K. G. (1973) Analysis of covariance structures. In *Multivariate Analysis III*, pp. 263–285. Academic Press, New York.

[20] JÖRESKOG, K. G. AND GOLDBERGER, A. S. (1973) Estimation of a model with multiple indicators and multiple causes of a single latent variable. *Research Report* 73–14, Department of Statistics, Uppsala University, Sweden.

[21] KETTENRING, J. R. (1971) Canonical analysis of several sets of variables. *Biometrika* **58**, 443–451.

[22] KRISHNAIAH, P. R., ed. (1966) *Multivariate Analysis.* Academic Press, New York.

[23] ————, ed. (1973) *Multivariate Analysis III.* Academic Press, New York.

[24] LYTTKENS, E. (1966) On the fix-point property of Wold's iterative estimation method for principal components. In *Multivariate Analysis*, pp. 335–350. Academic Press, New York.

142   HERMAN WOLD

[25] ———— (1970) Some asymptotic formulas for standard errors and small-sample bias of FP estimates. In *Interdependent Systems. Structure and Estimation,* Chapter 3.9. North-Holland Publishers, Amsterdam.

[26] ———— (1973) The fix-point method for estimating interdependent systems with the underlying model specification. *J. R. Statist. Soc.* B **136**, 353–394.

[27] LYTTKENS, E. AND WOLD, H., eds. (1973) FP (Fix-Point), IIV (Iterative Instrumental Variables) and related approaches to ID (Interdependent) systems. Theory and applications. European Meeting of the Econometric Society, Oslo, August 28–31, 1973.

[28] MILLER, R. G. (1974) The jack-knife—a review. *Biometrika* **61**, 1–15.

[29] MOSBAEK, E. J. AND WOLD, H. with contributions by E. Lyttkens, A. Ågren and L. Bodin (1970) *Interdependent Systems. Structure and Estimation.* North-Holland Publishers, Amsterdam.

[30] PEARSON, K. (1901) On lines and planes of closest fit to systems of points in space. *Philosophical Magazine* (6) **2**,559–572.

[31] RAO, C. R. (1964) The use and interpretation of principal component analysis in applied research. *Sankhyā* A **26**, 329–358.

[32] THEIL, H. (1953) Estimation and simultaneous correlation in complete equation systems. Central Planning Bureau, The Hague.

[33] TUKEY, J. (1958) Bias and confidence in not-quite large samples. Abstract. *Ann. Math. Statist.* **29**, p. 614.

[34] VAN DER WAERDEN, B. L. (1957) *Mathematische Statistik.* Springer, Berlin.

[35] WOLD, H. (1965) Toward a verdict on macroeconomic simultaneous equations. *Scripta Varia* **28**, 115–166. Pontifical Academy of Sciences, Vatican City.

[36] ———— (1966a) Non-linear estimation by iterative least squares procedures. In *Research Papers in Statistics,* pp. 411–444. Festschrift for J. Neyman, ed. F. N. David. Wiley, New York.

[37] ———— (1966b) Estimation of principal components and related models by iterative least squares. In *Multivariate Analysis,* pp. 391–420. Academic Press, New York.

[38] ———— (1973a) Non-linear iterative partial least squares (NIPALS) modelling. Some current developments. In *Multivariate Analysis III,* pp. 383–407. Academic Press, New York.

[39] ———— (1973b) A panorama of OLS and NIPALS modelling. See [27], Chapter 2.

[40] ———— (1974a) Path models with latent variables that have several indicators. To be published in *Quantitative Sociology,* ed. H. M. Blalock, Jr. Seminar Press, San Francisco.

[41] ———— (1974b) Causal flows with latent variables. Partings of the ways in the light of NIPALS modelling. *European Economic Review* **5**, 67–86.

[42] ———— (1974c) Path models with one or two latent variate aggregates. *Research Report* 1974, 6, Department of Statistics, University of Göteborg, Sweden.

[43] WOLD, H. AND LYTTKENS, E. eds. (1969) Non-linear iterative partial least squares (NIPALS) estimation procedures. *Bull. Internat. Statist. Inst.* **43**, 29–51.

[44] WOLD, H., LYTTKENS, E. AND ARESKOUG, B. (1974) The convergence of NIPALS estimation procedures for six path models with one or two latent variables. Manuscript in preparation.

[45] WOLD, S. (1974a) A theoretical foundation of extrathermodynamic relationships (linear free energy relationships). *Chemica Scripta* **5**, 97–106.

[46] ———— (1974b) Pattern cognition and recognition (cluster analysis) based on disjoint principal components models. Technical Report No. 357, Department of Statistics, University of Wisconsin.

PART IV

MATHEMATICAL METHODS IN
PROBABILITY AND STATISTICS

The Wiener-Hopf Technique in Applied Probability

J. W. COHEN

Abstract

In this study some of the basic ideas needed for the application of the Wiener-Hopf Technique in solving problems occurring in applied probability theory are discussed; the paper aims to give a short introduction. The method is illustrated by applying it to two problems; one, although basic in probability theory, is rather simple to handle by this method. The second is much more intricate, but shows clearly the power of the method.

1. Introduction

The application of the Wiener-Hopf Technique (W.H.T.) in probability theory is not unknown; particularly in [2], its possibilities are extremely well demonstrated. However, the power of the W.H.T. in solving problems concerning random walks still seems to be underestimated, presumably owing to the unpopularity of complex variable analysis among applied probabilists and statisticians.

The W.H.T. stems from mathematical physics. Many problems in elasticity theory, aero- and hydrodynamics and electro-magnetic field theory lead to integral equations of the Wiener-Hopf type. By applying Fourier transforms, the integral equation is transferred into a form suitable for the application of the W.H.T. Frequently, however, it is possible to avoid the description of the problem by integral equations by formulating it in such a way that the W.H.T. is directly applicable; this approach is advocated by Noble ([1], Preface) and is extremely useful in probability theory, since here characteristic functions and Laplace-Stieltjes transforms are a natural concept.

The aim of the present study is to describe briefly a class of problems to which the W.H.T. has been applied very successfully, to discuss some of its basic features and to illustrate its application by treating a few characteristic examples. These examples, although it is not explicitly stated, concern non-lattice stochastic variables. The use of the W.H.T. in the case of lattice variables is quite similar, although it then relates to analytic properties of generating functions instead of Laplace-Stieltjes transforms.

2. Types of problems

Let $\{\sigma_n, n = 1, 2, \cdots\}$ and $\{\tau_n, n = 1, 2, \cdots\}$ be independent families, each sequence consisting of i.i.d. positive variables.

For x real put

$$[x]^+ \overset{def}{=} \max(0, x), \qquad [x]^- \overset{def}{=} \min(0, x);$$

and let k and K be positive constants.

With

(2.1)
$$w_1 \overset{def}{=} 0,$$

each of the following formulae defines a recurrence relation for a sequence $\{w_n, n = 1, 2, \cdots\}$ of stochastic variables.

i. $w_{n+1} = [w_n + \tau_n - \sigma_n]^+;$ ([5], p. 142).

ii. $w_{n+1} = [w_n + \tau_n - \sigma_n]^+$ if $w_n < K$,
        $= [w_n - \sigma_n]^+$ if $w_n \geq K$;   ([6]).

iii. $w_{n+1} = [w_n + \tau_n - \sigma_n]^+$ if $w_n + \tau_n < K$,
         $= [w_n - \sigma_n]^+$ if $w_n + \tau_n \geq K$;   ([6]).

iv. $w_{n+1} = [w_n + \tau_n - \sigma_n]^+$ if $w_n + \tau_n < K$,
         $= [K - \sigma_n]^+$ if $w_n + \tau_n \geq K$;   ([5], p. 496).

v. $w_{n+1} = [K - \sigma_n + [w_n + \tau_n - K]^-]^+;$ equivalent with iv.

vi. $w_{n+1} = w_n + \tau_n - \sigma_n$ if $w_n < K$,
        $= w_n - \sigma_n$ if $w_n \geq K$;   ([3], p. 238).

vii. $w_{n+1} = w_n - \sigma_n$ if $w_n \geqq K$,

          $= w_n - \sigma_n + \tau_n$ if $k \leqq w_n < K$,

          $= K - \sigma_n + \tau_n$ if $w_n < k$;   ([4], p. 258).

viii. $w_{n+1} = [\min(w_n + \tau_n, K) - k]^+$, $k < K$;   ([7], p. 192).

ix. $w_{n+1} = [w_n + \tau_n - \sigma_n]^+$ if $w_n < u_n$,

          $= [w_n - \sigma_n]^+$ if $w_n \geqq u_n$,   ([6]).

$\{u_n, n = 1, 2, \cdots\}$ is a sequence of i.i.d. positive variables, independent of the σ- and τ-sequences mentioned above.

These recurrence relations are only a few examples of those encountered in inventory theory, queueing and congestion theory and dam theory (see [3], [4], [5], [6], [7]). The description of the stochastic properties of the sequence $\{w_n, \ n = 1, 2, \cdots\}$ determined by such a recurrence relation provides the basic information for the study of the inventory, queueing or dam process involved.

Obviously, w_n, τ_n and σ_n are independent, and $\{w_n, \ n = 1, 2, \cdots\}$ is a discrete time parameter Markov process, in fact a random walk.

Of the types of recurrence relations described above the simplest and most fundamental one is

$$(2.2) \qquad\qquad w_{n+1} = w_n + \tau_n - \sigma_n;$$

it determines the basic random walk in R_1.

With

$$(2.3) \qquad s_n \overset{\text{def}}{=} \sum_{k=1}^{n} \tau_k - \sigma_k, \quad n = 1, 2, \cdots; \qquad s_0 \overset{\text{def}}{=} 0,$$

and ρ any real or complex number, it follows from (2.2) that

$$e^{-\rho w_{n+1}} = e^{-\rho w_n} e^{-\rho(s_n - s_{n-1})}.$$

Taking expectations conditionally with respect to $w_1 = 0$, (cf. (2.1)), we have, since w_n and $s_n - s_{n-1}$ are independent, for $\text{Re } \rho = 0$, $n = 1, 2, \cdots$,

$$E\{e^{-\rho w_{n+1}} | w_1 = 0\} = E\{e^{-\rho(s_n - s_{n-1})}\} \ E\{e^{-\rho w_n} | w_1 = 0\},$$

$$(2.4)$$

Define

$$= E\{e^{-\rho s_n}\}.$$

$$(2.5) \qquad \Phi(r, \rho) \overset{\text{def}}{=} \sum_{n=1}^{\infty} r^n E\{e^{-\rho w_n} | w_1 = 0\}, \qquad \text{Re } \rho = 0, \ |r| < 1,$$

then, since $\tau_n - \sigma_n$, $n = 1, 2, \cdots$, are i.i.d. variables, it follows easily from (2.4) that

(2.6) $\Phi(r,\rho) = r/[1 - rE\{e^{-\rho s_i}\}] = r/[1 - r\alpha(-\rho)\beta(\rho)],$ $|r| < 1, \operatorname{Re}\rho = 0,$

with

(2.7) $\alpha(\rho) \overset{\text{def}}{=} E\{e^{-\rho\sigma_i}\}, \quad \beta(\rho) \overset{\text{def}}{=} E\{e^{-\rho\tau_i}\}, \quad \operatorname{Re}\rho \geqq 0, \quad i = 1,2,3,\cdots.$

Obviously, $\Phi(r,\rho)$ as given by (2.6) is an analytic function of r for $|r| < 1$ and fixed ρ with Re $\rho = 0$, so that the coefficients of the series expansion of $\Phi(r,\rho)$ with respect to r are uniquely determined, and, as can easily be verified, they satisfy a recurrence relation of the same type as (2.4). Since (2.4) has a unique solution, which for $\rho = -iu, -\infty < u < \infty$, is a characteristic function of a probability distribution, and since such a distribution is uniquely determined by its characteristic function if the distribution function is defined to be continuous from the left, it is seen that $\Phi(r,\rho)$ as given by (2.6) uniquely determines the distribution of every element of the sequence w_n, recursively defined by (2.2).

The derivation of (2.6) from (2.2) is characteristic for the investigation of recurrence relations of the type $i,\cdots,ix$ mentioned above; however, the construction of the explicit expression for $\Phi(r,\rho)$ is never so simple as in the example discussed here. In fact, it is always the essential difficulty of the problem, and it is at this point that the W.H.T. plays its role.

The function of ρ and r

(2.8) $\phi(r,\rho) \overset{\text{def}}{=} 1/[1 - rE\{e^{-\rho s_i}\}] \equiv 1/[1 - r\alpha(-\rho)\beta(\rho)],$ $|r| < 1, \operatorname{Re}\rho = 0,$

is of basic importance in the investigation of the problems mentioned above; therefore, we discuss here one of its main properties ([8], Chapter XIII).

If $\alpha(\rho)$ and $\beta(\rho)$ are both defined for a $\rho = \rho_0$ with $\rho_0 < 0$ then $\phi(r,\rho)$ is analytic in a strip containing the axis Re $\rho = 0$ in its interior. A basic problem in this case is to represent $\phi(r,\rho)$ as a product of two functions of ρ, one analytic and non-zero for Re $\rho > \rho_0$, the other analytic and non-zero for Re $\rho < -\rho_0$. The W.H.T. provides methods for solving such a problem ([1]). In the case where $\alpha(\rho)$ and $\beta(\rho)$ are both rational functions of ρ, the solution is simple, viz., one of the functions has the same poles as $\phi(r,\rho)$ in the right semi-plane, the other has the same poles as $\phi(r,\rho)$ in the left semi-plane, and, apart from a factor independent of ρ, the factorisation is unique, since $\phi(r,\rho), |r| < 1$, has no poles with $|\operatorname{Re}\rho| < |\rho_0|$, and the denominators of $\alpha(-\rho)$ and $\beta(\rho)$ have no zeros with Re $\rho < -\rho_0$ and Re $\rho > \rho_0$, respectively.

For general $\alpha(\rho)$ and $\beta(\rho)$ the factorisation of $\phi(r,\rho)$ is formally possible and known as Spitzer's identity. This famous identity reads for $|r| < 1$,

$$(2.9) \qquad \phi(r,\rho) = \phi_-(r,\rho)\phi_0(r)\phi_+(r,\rho), \qquad \text{Re } \rho = 0,$$

with

$$\phi_-(r,\rho) \overset{\text{def}}{=} \exp\left[\sum_{n=1}^{\infty} \frac{r^n}{n} E\{e^{-\rho s_n}(s_n < 0)\}\right], \qquad \text{Re } \rho \leqq 0,$$

$$(2.10) \qquad \phi_0(r) \overset{\text{def}}{=} \exp\left[\sum_{n=1}^{\infty} \frac{r^n}{n} E\{(s_n = 0)\}\right],$$

$$\phi_+(r,\rho) \overset{\text{def}}{=} \exp\left[\sum_{n=1}^{\infty} \frac{r^n}{n} E\{e^{-\rho s_n}(s_n > 0)\}\right], \qquad \text{Re } \rho \geqq 0.$$

Obviously, for $|r| < 1$, $\phi_+(r,\rho)$ $(\phi_-(r,\rho))$ is analytic for Re $\rho > 0$ (Re $\rho < 0$), continuous, bounded and non-zero for Re $\rho \geqq 0$ (Re $\rho \leqq 0$); for these conditions the factorisation (2.9) is unique apart from a factor independent of ρ ([1], [8]).*

3. A simple example

In this section we shall discuss the distribution of w_n where this is defined by

$$w_{n+1} = [w_n + \tau_n - \sigma_n]^+, \qquad n = 1, 2, \cdots,$$
$$(3.1)$$
$$w_1 = 0.$$

Starting from the identity

$$(3.2) \qquad e^{-\rho x} + 1 = e^{-\rho[x]^+} + e^{-\rho[x]^-},$$

with x real and ρ a complex number, it follows from (3.1) and (3.2) that for $n = 1, 2, \cdots$,

$$e^{-\rho w_{n+1}} = e^{-\rho[w_n + \tau_n - \sigma_n]^+}$$
$$(3.3)$$
$$= e^{-\rho w_n} e^{-\rho(\tau_n - \sigma_n)} - e^{-\rho[w_n + \tau_n - \sigma_n]^-} + 1.$$

From (3.1) it is seen that w_n is non-negative, and $[w_n + \tau_n - \sigma_n]^-$ is non-positive, so we can define for $|r| < 1$,

---

* In (2.10) $(s_n > 0)$ stands for the indicator function of the event '$s_n > 0$'.

$$\Phi(r,\rho) \overset{\text{def}}{=} \sum_{n=1}^{\infty} r^n E\{e^{-\rho w_n} | w_1 = 0\}, \qquad \text{Re } \rho \geq 0,$$

(3.4)

$$\psi(r,\rho) \overset{\text{def}}{=} \sum_{n=1}^{\infty} r^n E\{e^{-\rho\{w_n + \tau_n - \sigma_n\}^-} | w_1 = 0\}, \quad \text{Re } \rho \leq 0.$$

Taking conditional expectations with respect to $w_1 = 0$ in (3.3), multiplying by r^n, summing over $n = 1, 2, \cdots$, and noting that w_n and $\tau_n - \sigma_n$ are independent, it is readily found that

$$(3.5) \quad \{1 - r\alpha(-\rho)\beta(\rho)\}\Phi(r,\rho) = \frac{r}{1-r} - r\psi(r,\rho), \ |r| < 1, \quad \text{Re } \rho = 0.$$

For the derivation of (3.5) the same scheme has been used as in the derivation of (2.6). In the present case, however, (3.5) does not provide the expression for $\Phi(r,\rho)$ by pure algebraic arguments. It is at this point that the special features of the W.H.T. are applied.

The actual problem is to construct two functions $\Phi(r,\rho)$ and $\psi(r,\rho)$ such that:

  i. $\Phi(r,\rho)$ and $\psi(r,\rho)$ satisfy (3.5) for $|r| < 1$, Re $\rho = 0$,

  ii. $\Phi(r,\rho)$ is analytic for Re $\rho > 0$, continuous and bounded (by $r/(1-r)$) for Re $\rho \geq 0$,

  iii. $\psi(r,\rho)$ is analytic for Re $\rho < 0$, continuous and bounded (by $r/(1-r)$) for Re $\rho \leq 0$,

as follows from the definition (3.4) and from

$$|E\{e^{-\rho w_n} | w_1 = 0\}| \leq 1, \text{Re } \rho \geq 0;$$

$$|E\{e^{-\rho\{w_n + \tau_n - \sigma_n\}^-} | w_1 = 0\}| \leq 1, \quad \text{Re } \rho \leq 0,$$

and by noting that the series in (3.4) converge uniformly in ρ for Re $\rho \geq 0$ and Re $\rho \leq 0$, respectively.

Using (2.9) we rewrite (3.5),

$$(3.6) \quad \Phi(r,\rho)/\phi_+(r,\rho) = \left\{\frac{1}{1-r} - \psi(r,\rho)\right\}r\phi_0(r)\phi_-(r,\rho), |r| < 1, \text{Re } \rho = 0.$$

From the properties of ϕ_+, ϕ_0 and ϕ_- (see (2.10)) it is seen that the left (right) hand side of (3.6) is analytic for Re $\rho > 0$ (Re $\rho < 0$) and continuous for Re $\rho \geq 0$ (Re $\rho \leq 0$).

Consequently, the left hand side of (3.6) with Re $\rho \geq 0$ and the right hand side of (3.6) for Re $\rho \leq 0$ are each other's analytic continuation. Introducing the function $Z(r,\rho)$, by definition equal to the left hand side of (3.6) for Re $\rho \geq 0$ and to the right hand side for Re $\rho \leq 0$, it is seen that for

$|r| < 1$, $Z(r, \rho)$ is analytic in the whole ρ-plane. However, as is seen from the boundedness of Φ, ψ, ϕ_+, ϕ_0 and ϕ_-, $Z(r, \rho)$ is also bounded in the whole ρ-plane and hence by Liouville's theorem [9] it is, as a function of ρ, a constant. Therefore

(3.7) $\qquad \Phi(r, \rho)/\phi_+(r, \rho) = C(r), \qquad |r| < 1, \quad \text{Re } \rho \geqq 0.$

Taking $\rho = 0$ in (3.7) it follows from (2.10) and (3.4)

(3.8) $\qquad C(r) = \dfrac{r}{1-r} \Big/ \phi_+(r, 0), \qquad |r| < 1;$

so that for $|r| < 1$,

$$\Phi(r, \rho) = \frac{r}{1-r} \frac{\phi_+(r, \rho)}{\phi_+(r, 0)}, \qquad \text{Re } \rho \geqq 0;$$

(3.9)

$$\psi(r, \rho) = \frac{1}{1-r} - \frac{\phi_-(r, 0)}{\phi_-(r, \rho)}, \qquad \text{Re } \rho \leqq 0.$$

Since the analytic continuation and the factorisation of $\phi(r, \rho)$, apart from a constant factor, are both unique (cf. (2.9)), it is seen that the solution of (3.5), satisfying ii. and iii. above, is unique and given by (3.9). Similarly, as in the preceding section, it follows that $\Phi(r, \rho)$ determines the distribution of every element of the sequence $\{w_n, n = 1, 2, \cdots\}$ defined by (3.1).

The solution obtained above is a rather formal one; we therefore illustrate the derivation of the solution of (3.5) by the W.H.T. for the case where

(3.10) $\qquad \alpha(\rho) = 1/(1 + \alpha \rho), \qquad \text{Re } \rho > -1/\alpha, \quad \alpha > 0.$

In this case, for $|r| < 1$, Re $\rho = 0$, (3.5) becomes

(3.11) $\qquad \{1 - \alpha\rho - r\beta(\rho)\} \ \Phi(r, \rho) = (1 - \alpha\rho) \left\{\dfrac{r}{1-r} - r\psi(r, \rho)\right\}.$

It is readily proved by applying Rouché's theorem·([9]) that for fixed $|r| < 1$ the function $1 - \alpha\rho - r\beta(\rho)$, Re $\rho \geqq 0$, has exactly one zero $\delta(r)$. Hence by taking for $|r| < 1$,

$$\Phi(r, \rho) = \frac{\rho - \delta(r)}{1 - \alpha\rho - r\beta(\rho)} \ f(r, \rho), \qquad \text{Re } \rho \geqq 0,$$

(3.12)

$$\psi(r, \rho) = \frac{1}{1-r} - \frac{1}{r} \frac{\rho - \delta(r)}{1 - \alpha\rho} \ f(r, \rho), \qquad \text{Re } \rho \leqq 0,$$

with $f(r, \rho)$ an entire function of ρ, (3.11) is satisfied and Φ and ψ satisfy the conditions ii. and iii. above if $f(r, \rho)$ is bounded for all ρ, i.e., as a result of Liouville's theorem, $f(r, \rho)$ is independent of ρ. Since $\Phi(r, 0) = r/(1 - r)$ it follows that

(3.13) $f(r, \rho) = - r/\delta(r)$ for $|r| < 1$,

and

$$\Phi(r, \rho) = \frac{r}{\delta(r)} \frac{\rho - \delta(r)}{r\beta(\rho) + \alpha\rho - 1}, \qquad |r| < 1, \text{ Re } \rho \geqq 0,$$

(3.14)

$$\psi(r, \rho) = \frac{1}{1 - r} + \frac{1}{\delta(r)} \frac{\rho - \delta(r)}{1 - \alpha\rho}, \qquad |r| < 1, \text{ Re } \rho \leqq 0,$$

which for the present case (3.10) gives the solution of (3.5).

4. A more complicated example

To illustrate the W.H.T. for a more difficult problem we shall consider

$$w_{n+1} = [w_n + \tau_n - \sigma_n]^+ \quad \text{if} \quad w_n < K,$$

(4.1) $$= [w_n - \sigma_n]^+ \quad \text{if} \quad w_n \geqq K,$$

$$w_1 = 0.$$

From (4.1) we have for Re $\rho \geqq 0$, $n = 1, 2, \cdots$,

$$E\{e^{-\rho w_{n+1}} | w_1 = 0\} =$$

(4.2)

$$E\{e^{-\rho[w_n + \tau_n - \sigma_n]^+} (w_n < K) | w_1 = 0\} + E\{e^{-\rho[w_n - \sigma_n]^+} (w_n \geqq K) | w_1 = 0\}.$$

By writing

$$\int_{C_\eta} \cdots d\eta = \lim_{\delta \to \infty} \int_{\epsilon - i\delta}^{\epsilon + i\delta} \cdots d\eta, \qquad \text{Re } \eta = \epsilon,$$

we have for x real

(4.3) $$e^{-\rho[x]^+} = \frac{1}{2\pi i} \int_{C_\eta} \left(\frac{1}{\rho - \eta} + \frac{1}{\eta} \right) e^{-\eta x} d\eta, \qquad \text{Re } \rho > \text{Re } \eta > 0,$$

since Jordan's lemma ([10]) applies to the integrand, so that by Cauchy's theorem the right hand side of (4.3) is equal to the residue of the integrand at $\eta = \rho$ if $x > 0$, and to that at $\eta = 0$ if $x \leqq 0$.

In order not to complicate the analysis too much, it will be assumed that $\alpha(\rho)$ and $\beta(\rho)$ (cf.(2.7)) are rational functions of ρ.

(4.4) $\qquad \alpha(\rho) = \alpha_1(\rho)/\alpha_2(\rho), \qquad \beta(\rho) = \beta_1(\rho)/\beta_2(\rho),$

with α_1, α_2, β_1 and β_2 polynomials in ρ, m and n being the degree of α_2 and β_2 respectively, and the degree of α_1 and β_1 being at most $m - 1$ and $n - 1$ respectively.

From (4.3) it follows for Re $\rho > 0$, that

$$E\{e^{-\rho[w_n - \sigma_n]^+}(w_n \geq K)|w_1 = 0\}$$

$$= \frac{1}{2\pi i} E\left\{\int_{C_\eta} \left(\frac{1}{\rho - \eta} + \frac{1}{\eta}\right) e^{-\eta(w_n - \sigma_n)}(w_n \geq K)d\eta \,\middle|\, w_1 = 0\right\}$$

(4.5)

$$= \frac{1}{2\pi i} \int_{C_\eta} \left(\frac{1}{\rho - \eta} + \frac{1}{\eta}\right) \alpha(-\eta) E\{e^{-\eta w_n}(w_n \geq K)|w_1 = 0\}d\eta,$$

$$\text{Re } \eta = 0+ ;$$

since w_n and σ_n are independent, $\alpha(-\eta)$ exists for Re $\eta = 0+$, because $\alpha(\eta)$ is rational, and expectation and integral can be interchanged by noting that

$$\int_{C_\eta} \left|\frac{1}{\rho - \eta} + \frac{1}{\eta}\right| |d\eta| < \infty \quad \text{for} \quad \text{Re } \rho > \text{Re } \eta = 0+.$$

| In the same way we treat the first term on the right hand side of (4.2); then multiplying (4.2) by r^n and summing over $n = 1,2,\cdots$, it is found that for Re $\rho > \text{Re } \eta = 0+$,

$$r = \frac{1}{2\pi i} \int_{C_\eta} \left(\frac{1}{\rho - \eta} + \frac{1}{\eta}\right) \{1 - r\alpha(-\eta)\beta(\eta)\} \Phi_1(r, \eta)d\eta$$

(4.6)

$$+ \frac{1}{2\pi i} \int_{C_\eta} \left(\frac{1}{\rho - \eta} + \frac{1}{\eta}\right) \{1 - r\alpha(-\eta)\} \Phi_2(r, \eta)d\eta,$$

where for $|r| < 1$,

(4.7) $\qquad \Phi_1(r, \rho) = \displaystyle\sum_{n=1}^{\infty} r^n E\{e^{-\rho w_n}(w_n < K)|w_1 = 0\},$

(4.8) $\qquad \Phi_2(r, \rho) = \displaystyle\sum_{n=1}^{\infty} r^n E\{e^{-\rho w_n}(w_n \geq K)|w_1 = 0\}, \qquad \text{Re } \rho \geq 0.$

From (4.7) it is seen, since $w_n \geq 0$, that for $|r| < 1$:

i. $\Phi_1(r,\rho)$ is an entire function of ρ,

ii. $\Phi_1(r,\rho)$ is bounded and continuous for Re $\rho \geqq 0$,

iii. $e^{\rho K}\Phi_1(r,\rho)$ is bounded and continuous for Re $\rho \leqq 0$,

iv. $\Phi_2(r,\rho)$ is analytic for Re $\rho > 0$, continuous for Re $\rho \geqq 0$,

v. $e^{\rho K}\Phi_2(r,\rho)$ is bounded for Re $\rho \geqq 0$,

vi. $\Phi_1(r,\rho)$ and $\Phi_2(r,\rho)$ should satisfy (4.6).

The problem described by the conditions i–vi is again characteristic for the application of the W.H.T. The derivation of its solution, however, is not so simple and straightforward as in the preceding sections. Some 'trial and error' is involved; however, the assumption that $\alpha(\rho)$ and $\beta(\rho)$ are rational functions of ρ (cf.(4.4)) leads to an insight in the structure of $\Phi_1(r,\rho)$ and $\Phi_2(r,\rho)$ since the integrals in (4.6) can be evaluated by contour integration in the right semi-plane as a result of this assumption; and it is seen that $\Phi_1(r,\rho)$ and $\Phi_2(r,\rho)$ consist of terms with factors which are rational functions of ρ. Moreover, from iv. and v. it follows that the expression for $\Phi_2(r,\rho)$ should contain the factor $e^{-\rho K}$, and hence as a result of (4.6) $\Phi_1(r,\rho)$ should contain a term with the factor $e^{-\rho K}$. It follows also from the contour integration just mentioned that the factor $1 - r\alpha(-\rho)\beta(\rho)$ should occur in the denominator of the expression for $\Phi_1(r,\rho)$.

From (4.4) and Rouché's theorem it follows that the function $1 - r\alpha(-\rho)\beta(\rho)$ with $|r| < 1$ has $m + n$ zeros, when counted according to their multiplicity, of which m, say $\delta_j(r)$, $j = 1,\cdots,m$, lie in the positive semi-plane and n, say $\epsilon_i(r)$, $i = 1,\cdots,n$, lie in the negative semi-plane, since $|r| < 1$;

(4.9)   Re $\epsilon_i(r) < 0$, $i = 1,\cdots,n$,   Re $\delta_j(r) > 0$, $j = 1,\cdots,m$.

For $|r| < 1$, let $f(r,\rho)$ and $g(r,\rho)$ be two polynomials in ρ of degree $m - 1$ and $n - 1$ respectively, and such that

(4.10) $\dfrac{\rho f(r,\rho)}{\alpha_2(-\rho)} + \{\alpha_2(-\rho) - r\alpha_1(-\rho)\}\dfrac{g(r,\rho)}{\beta_2(r,\rho)}\, e^{-\rho K} + r = 0,$

for $\rho = \epsilon_i(r)$, $i = 1,\cdots,n$ and for $\rho = \delta_j(r)$, $j = 1,\cdots,m$. Obviously, $f(r,\rho)$ and $g(r,\rho)$ are uniquely determined by these conditions.

We now prove that, for $|r| < 1$, $\Phi_1(r,\rho)$ and $\Phi_2(r,\rho)$ are given by

$$\Phi_1(r,\rho) =$$

(4.11)

$$\frac{1}{1-r\alpha(-\rho)\beta(\rho)}\left\{\frac{\rho f(r,\rho)}{\alpha_2(-\rho)}+\{\alpha_2(-\rho)-r\alpha_1(-\rho)\}\frac{g(r,\rho)}{\beta_2(\rho)}e^{-\rho K}+r\right\},$$

(4.12) $\qquad \Phi_2(r,\rho) = -\alpha_2(-\rho)\dfrac{g(r,\rho)}{\beta_2(\rho)}e^{-\rho K}, \qquad \mathrm{Re}\,\rho \geqq 0.$

Proof. From the definition of $f(r,\rho)$ and $g(r,\rho)$ and from (4.4) it is seen that $\Phi_1(r,\rho)$ is an entire function of ρ, satisfying the conditions ii. and iii. above; also $\Phi_2(r,\rho)$ satisfies iv. and v. For $|r|<1$, $\mathrm{Re}\,\rho > \mathrm{Re}\,\eta = 0+$,

$$\frac{1}{2\pi i}\int_{C_\eta}\left(\frac{1}{\rho-\eta}+\frac{1}{\eta}\right)\frac{\eta f(r,\eta)}{\alpha_2(-\eta)}d\eta = 0,$$

as is seen by contour integration in the left semi-plane, noting that $\alpha_2(-\rho)$ has no zeros for $\mathrm{Re}\,\rho < 0$; further, since integration in the right semi-plane yields for $\mathrm{Re}\,\rho > \mathrm{Re}\,\eta = 0+$,

$$\frac{1}{2\pi i}\int_{C_\eta}\left(\frac{1}{\rho-\eta}+\frac{1}{\eta}\right)\left[\{\alpha_2(-\eta)-r\alpha_1(-\eta)\}\frac{g(r,\eta)}{\beta_2(\eta)}e^{-\eta K}+r\right]d\eta$$

$$=\{\alpha_2(-\rho)-r\alpha_1(-\rho)\}\frac{g(r,\rho)}{\beta_2(\rho)}e^{-\rho K}+r$$

$$=-\frac{1}{2\pi i}\int_{C_\eta}\left(\frac{1}{\rho-\eta}+\frac{1}{\eta}\right)\{1-r\alpha(-\eta)\}\Phi_2(r,\eta)d\eta + r,$$

it is seen that (4.11) and (4.12) satisfy (4.6).

It remains to show that $\Phi_1(r,\rho)$ and $\Phi_2(r,\rho)$ as given by (4.11) and (4.12) indeed represent the functions defined by (4.1) and the right hand sides of (4.7) and (4.8). From the definition of $\epsilon_i(r)$ and $\delta_i(r)$ it is seen that these zeros are analytic functions of r for $|r|<1$, and hence Φ_1 and Φ_2 as given by (4.11) and (4.12) are analytic functions of r for $|r|<1$, thus possessing a series expansion in powers of r. Inserting these series expansions in (4.6) and equating the coefficients of the powers of r^n, $n = 1,2,\cdots$, to zero yields a set of recurrence relations, which is identical with that for $E\{e^{-\rho w_n}(w_n < K)|w_1 = 0\}$ and $E\{e^{-\rho w_n}(w_n \geqq K)|w_1 = 0\}$, obtained from (4.1), this set has a unique solution, and the proof is complete.

From the considerations above about the structure of the solution and from the meaning of the various steps in the proof just given, a feeling about the application of the W.H.T. is developed; such a feeling is needed to solve problems of the types described in Section 2. In this respect it is of some interest to compare the expressions for $\Phi(r,\rho)$ given in (2.6), (3.14) and (4.11). The relation (2.6) refers to a random walk without boundaries, whereas (3.14) and (4.11) refer to random walks with one and two boundaries, respectively. The extra terms in (3.14) and (4.11), when compared to (2.6), are needed to compensate the effect of the boundaries on the unbounded random walk; a phenomenon on which the Green's function method of Keilson is based ([11]).

Of course the solution provided by the W.H.T. is just a starting point for the analysis of the stochastic problem involved, and for further details the reader may consult [5] and [6], particularly for the method to be used to avoid, partly or completely, the assumption of rationality of $\alpha(\rho)$ and $\beta(\rho)$ (cf. (4.4)).

Finally, it should be mentioned that the literature on applied stochastic processes still contains a large number of interesting and unsolved problems which seem apt for a fruitful application of the W.H.T.

References

[1] NOBLE, B. (1958) *The Wiener-Hopf Technique*. Pergamon Press, London.

[2] KEMPERMAN, J. H. B. (1961) *The Passage Problem for a Stationary Markov Chain*. The University of Chicago Press, Chicago.

[3] ARROW, K. J., KARLIN, S. AND SCARF, H. (1958) *Studies in the Mathematical Theory of Inventory and Production*. Stanford University Press, Stanford.

[4] ARROW, K. J., KARLIN, S. AND SCARF, H. (1962) *Studies in Applied Probability and Management Science*. Stanford University Press, Stanford.

[5] COHEN, J. W. (1969) *The Single Server Queue*. North-Holland Publ. Co., Amsterdam.

[6] COHEN, J. W. (1969) Single server queues with restricted accessibility. *J. Engin. Math.* **3**, 265–284.

[7] PRABHU, N. U. (1965) *Queues and Inventories*. Wiley, New York.

[8] FELLER, W. (1966) *An Introduction to Probability Theory and its Applications*. Vol. II. Wiley, New York.

[9] TITCHMARSH, E. C. (1952) *Theory of Functions*. Oxford University Press, London.

[10] WHITTAKER, E. T. AND WATSON, G. N. (1946) *A Course of Modern Analysis*. Cambridge University Press, London.

[11] KEILSON, J. (1965) *Green's Function Method in Probability Theory*. Griffin, London.

Iteration Near a Fixed Point

CEDRIC A. B. SMITH

Abstract

An exposition is given of the properties of the iterates of complex functions near a fixed point, with explicit expressions for their power series in certain cases. The relevance to problems in genetics and statistics is pointed out.

1. Introduction

The following paper is dedicated to Professor M. S. Bartlett with great affection. He was my original research supervisor; as such always most friendly and helpful. His teaching inspired a love of the subject of statistics, as a theoretical discipline, and a practical tool. Later, when I joined a genetical department, I found that he too was much interested in statistical genetics and biology, and has indeed contributed many important ideas and results to mathematical biology.

After thought, I have chosen for this contribution a topic not in itself either statistical or genetical, but which has considerable relevance to both statistics (especially certain stochastic processes) and population genetics, namely the theory of iteration of functions. This occupied various mathematicians especially during the period 1870–1920. Since then, interest has rather declined, and some of the previous work may be forgotten. Hence the paper which follows is largely expository, putting together in an orderly way a number of results of various authors. But I have been interested in the subject for almost 40 years, and some of the results given here are to the best of my knowledge new (including the explicit formulas (5.15), (5.18). (5.23), except in so far as they were included in my Ph.D. thesis, Smith (1942)). A résumé of the subject, including most of the earlier results of importance, is to be found in Picard ((1928), Chapter 4).

Before considering the main topic I make a few remarks about notation. A great deal of the power of matrix theory lies in the brevity and simplicity of the notation, which uses a single symbol for a whole array of numbers. Thus a relation written in the form $a = 2b + cd$ is easier to comprehend and manipulate than the same written in full as

$$\forall i(1 \leqq i \leqq m), \ \forall j(1 \leqq j \leqq n) \qquad a_{ij} = 2b_{ij} + \sum_{\lambda=1}^{p} c_{i\lambda}d_{\lambda j}.$$

Professor Karl Menger (1953) has remarked that much the same simplification can be applied to functions, which indeed are closely related to matrices (both can be thought of as mappings). For example, it is well known that $(\forall x)\cos^2 + \sin^2 x = 1$ (where we usually leave out the qualification 'for all x' as understood). This is effectively a relation between the cosine and sine functions, and could be written without ambiguity $\cos^2 + \sin^2 = 1$. There is no more need to bring in the argument x in every equation concerning functions than there is to insert the row and column indices a_{ij} in a matrix a every time it is used. The rule for differentiation $d(\sin x)/dx = \cos x$ can be written more briefly $\sin' = \cos$. Similarly $\tan = \sin/\cos$. In order to make the notation work we require a notation for the identity function, say $I[x] = x$ for all x. Then the square function can be written as I^2, that is, $I^2[x] = x^2$, and so on. Thus we have $\ln' = 1/I$. A Taylor series will be written, e.g., as $\exp = 1 + I + I^2/2 + \cdots$. In general, F^2 will denote the square of $F = F \times F$, and so on. This notation is, of course, a little unfamiliar, but it is simple, elegant and concise, and should quickly become readily understood. (It will only be used for functions of a single variable here.) In order to make formulas unambiguous, I will be consistent in what follows in using square brackets to denote a function of a argument, e.g., $F[2]$ means 'the function of F of 2', and other shapes of brackets for other purposes, e.g., to distinguish $(a + b)^2$ from $a + b^2$. Thus 'ln [sin]' will mean 'the natural logarithm of the sine', to make the meaning clear, a dot will be inserted in 'ln $\cdot$ sin' = logarithm times sine. Of course, like most notations, this is to be read with common sense; it would be pedantic to write $\cos[0] = 1$, instead of $\cos 0 = 1$. Also, in strict logic, the symbol '1' in the equation $\cos^2 + \sin^2 = 1$ means not the number 1 itself but 'that function which takes the value 1 for all values of the argument'. But in practice the symbol '1' covers both meanings without ambiguity, just as in matrix algebra we write *I* for the unit matrix and **0** for a zero matrix without usually having to specify the number of rows and columns.

Consider a function *F*. We discuss later more exactly what kind of function *F* we are most interested in. For the present we proceed in a simple non-rigorous way. Such a function *F* can equally well be thought of as a mapping $x_1 = F[x_0]$ from a point x_0 to a point x_1. This mapping can be repeated, to give $x_2 = F[x_1] = F[F[x_0]]$. The mapping from x_0 to x_2 is then the *second iterate* of *F*, say $^2F = F[F]$. Similarly we can define the third iterate $^3F = F[F[F]]$, and so on. (This notation, ^nF, is not necessarily proposed for general use; but it is very convenient here.) It is also an obvious generalization to take ^0F to mean the identity function *I*, ^{-1}F to mean the inverse function, ^{-2}F to mean $^{-1}F[^{-1}F]$, and so on. Thus (arguing at present naively) the set of iterates will obey the relations

$$(1.1) \qquad\qquad ^mF[^nF] = {}^{m+n}F = {}^nF[^mF],$$

$$(1.2) \qquad\qquad ^1F = F,$$

$$(1.3) \qquad\qquad ^m(^nF) = {}^{mn}F = {}^n(^mF),$$

analogous to the relations for powers, $a^m a^n = a^{m+n}$ etc. For this reason, the iterates are sometimes called 'functional powers'.

2. Genetical and statistical applications of iteration

Such iterates arise in statistical and genetical theory in three main ways. In the first place, if we are studying the behaviour of a large population (so large that random fluctuations may be neglected) then its state in one generation will be some specifiable function of its state in the previous generation. For example, suppose we have a random-mating population carrying two alleles, *G*, *g*, with respective frequencies p_n, q_n in the *n*th generation. Suppose that the homozygote *gg* dies between birth and adult life. Then the frequency q_{n+1} of the allele at the birth of generation $(n + 1)$ is equal to its frequency in adults of generation *n*, that is (see any standard work on statistical genetics)

$$(2.1) \qquad\qquad q_{n+1} = \frac{p_n q_n}{1 - q_n^2} = \frac{q_n}{1 + q_n} = \dot{F}[q_n]$$

where $F = I/(1 + I)$. Thus, if the frequency is initially q_0, in successive generations it becomes $q_1 = F[q_0]$, $q_2 = F[q_1] = {}^2F[q_0]$, and so on. In fact, in this simple case we have explicitly $q_n = q_0/(1 + nq_0)$, showing that the frequency decreases asymptotically like $1/n$. However, if we suppose that GG, Gg, gg have respective chances w_{11}, w_{12} and w_{22} of survival, the relation becomes

$$(2.2) \qquad q_{n+1} = \frac{q_n(w_{12}p_n + w_{22}q_n)}{w_{11}p_n^2 + 2w_{12}p_nq_n + w_{22}q_n^2} = F[q_n]$$

(where, of course, $p_n = 1 - q_n$). The frequency in generation n is again $^nF[q_0]$, but, in general, this is much more difficult to express in any useful explicit form, although its general behaviour for large n is understood.

The second important use of functional iteration is in connection with the Galton-Watson process. Let a_{nr} denote the probability that a population A contains exactly r individuals in generation n. This can be usefully expressed in terms of the probability generating function

$$(2.3) \qquad \alpha_n = a_{n0} + a_{n1}I + a_{n2}I^2 + \cdots$$

Each individual in generation n is supposed to give rise to a (possibly empty) set of individuals in generation $n + 1$; different individuals behave independently, and there is a probability f_r that any one individual has exactly r children in the next generation. We can represent the set of f_r conveniently by the corresponding generating function $F = \Sigma_{\lambda=0}^{\infty} f_\lambda I^\lambda$. It is a well-known result, derivable from the addition and multiplication laws of probability, that

$$(2.4) \qquad \alpha_{n+1} = F[\alpha_n].$$

This equation effectively gives the probabilities $a_{(n+1)r}$ of different sizes r of the population in generation $(n + 1)$ expressed in terms of the corresponding probability in generation n. From it we obtain

$$(2.5) \qquad \alpha_n = {}^nF[\alpha_0].$$

From this it is possible to study the behaviour of the population in successive generations. In particular, if r_n denotes the population size in generation n, and $\alpha_n^{(i)} = D^i[\alpha_n]$ denotes the ith derivative of α_n, then it is easy to see (by direct differentiation) that the factorial moments are given by

$$(2.6) \qquad \mathscr{E}[r_n(r_n - 1)(r_n - 2) \cdots (r_n - j + 1)] = \alpha_n^{(i)}[1].$$

Hence, in particular, the expected size of the population in generation n is $\mu_n = \alpha_n'[1]$, and the variance is

$$(2.7) \qquad v_n = \alpha_n''[1] + \mu_n - \mu_n^2.$$

A third use of iteration occurs of course in the numerical solution of equations. For example, the maximum likelihood equation $L'[\hat{\theta}] = 0$ is usually solved as follows. Take a provisional value, θ_0 say. Define

$$(2.8) \qquad \theta_1 = \theta_0 - L'[\theta_0]/L''[\theta_0] = F[\theta_0], \text{ say.}$$

This is usually closer to the required root $\hat{\theta}$. Indeed the sequence θ_0, θ_1, $\theta_2 = F[\theta_1]$, $\theta_3 = F[\theta_2], \cdots$ usually converges very rapidly to $\hat{\theta}$.

3. Fixed points

Because of these applications to statistical and genetical problems as well as other fields of application it would seem worth while to develop a general theory of iteration. What follows is an account of a few aspects, although concentrating on the pure mathematical theory, rather than any necessary applicability to the problems considered above.

The theory follows different courses according to the kind of functions considered. Thus we could take F to be a continuous monotone real function. The theory has then been explored in detail by Walker (1946) and Walker and Batty (1946). But it does not lend itself to convenient algebraic forms for ^nF or related expressions. We might take F to be a (complete) analytic function of a complex variable. Difficulties arise in trying to treat this in full generality; for example, $^2F = F[F]$ is not necessarily a single analytic function: it may not be defined, or may break up into more than one analytic function. Thus, if $F = \sqrt{(1 - I^2)}$ then $^2F = \pm I$ and I and $-I$ are distinct analytic functions. However, if there is a fixed point ξ, i.e., $F[\xi] = \xi$, and F is regular (holomorphic) at ξ, the theory is much simplified. For then, by restricting ourselves to the neighbourhood of ξ, we can take F to be single-valued. Furthermore,

$^n F[\xi] = \xi$ for all positive integers n, and $^n F$ is also regular near ξ. In addition, if $F'[\xi] \neq 0$, the inverse function ^{-1}F and all negative iterations ^{-n}F have ξ as a fixed point and are regular at ξ.

The fixed point plays an important role in all three applications already discussed. In the genetical case, if $F[q] = q$, q corresponds to an equilibrium point in the population. In the Galton-Watson process, 1 is necessarily a fixed point, since $F[1] = \Sigma_\lambda f_\lambda = 1$. In iterative maximum likelihood estimation, the fixed point is $\hat\theta$, the maximum likelihood estimate or evaluate itself. Further investigation (which we will not elaborate on here) shows that the derivative $\mu = F'[\xi]$ at the fixed point also plays an important role. Thus, in the Galton-Watson process, μ is the mean number of offspring of an individual.

4. Function matrices

If F is regular at 0, then so is F^j for any non-negative integer j, and we can expand it in a Taylor series

(4.1) $$F^j = f_{j0} + f_{j1}I + f_{j2}I^2 + \cdots.$$

The coefficients (f_{jk}) form an infinite matrix f, the 'function-matrix' associated with the function F. They are polynomials in the coefficients f_{1k} of the Taylor series for F; thus $f_{21} = 2f_{10}f_{11}$, $f_{22} = f_{11}^2 + f_{10}f_{12}$, etc. Put in another way, let x denote the vector $(1, x, x^2, x^3, \cdots)^T$ and y the vector $(1, y, y^2, y^3, \cdots)^T$. Then the mapping $y = F[x]$ can be written in matrix form $y = fx$. If we have a second mapping $z = G[y]$, then $z = gy$ with obvious notation. But $z = G[F[x]] = H[x]$ say, and correspondingly $z = gy = gfx$, so that corresponding to the relation $H = G[F]$ between functions, we have the ordinary matrix product $h = fg$. Similarly, corresponding to the nth iterate ^nF of the function F we have the nth power f^n of the matrix f. The problem of iteration becomes formally reduced to the problem of finding the nth power of a matrix. It should be added that, because f is an infinite matrix, this may not be at all simple, and convergence and existence problems may arise. These function-matrices have already been studied by various authors; for example Turnbull (1934) gives an explicit expression for some determinant minors. Particular values of the function F lead to well-known coefficients f_{jk}. Thus, if $F = I$, then $f = I$ and f_{jk} is the Kronecker δ_{jk}. If $F = cI$, then $f_{jk} = c^j\delta_{jk}$, and we write $f = \Delta[c]$. If $F = 1 + I$, f_{jk} is the binomial coefficient $\binom{j}{k}$. If $V = \exp - 1$, $\Lambda = \ln[1 + I]$, so that V, Λ are in verse functions, then $\lambda_{jk} = S_k^j j!/k!$, and $\nu_{jk} = \sigma_k^j j!/k!$, where S_k^j and σ_k^j are respectively the Stirling numbers of the first and second kind (Abramowitz and Stegun (1965)).

Problems of convergence and existence largely disappear when $F[0] = 0$. Now we have said above that we are interested in functions with a fixed point ξ. There is no effective loss of generality by taking $\xi = 0$. For suppose $\Phi[\xi] = \xi$, and set $F = \Phi[\xi + I] - \xi$. Then $F[0] = 0$. And there is a one-one correspondence between the iterates of F and those of Φ given by

$$(4.2) \qquad {}^n F = {}^n \Phi[\xi + I] - \xi.$$

Hence, if we can find the iterates of F, we can find those of Φ. Also we have

$$(4.3) \qquad F'[0] = \Phi'[\xi] = \mu.$$

In particular, if Φ (rather than F) denotes the generating function of the offspring distribution in a Galton-Watson process, $\xi = 1$ and $\mu = \Phi'[1] = F'[0]$ is the average family size. The coefficients f_{1k} are the reduced factorial moments.

When zero is a fixed point, the function-matrix is upper-triangular, with $f_{jk} = 0$ when $j > k$, and $f_{jj} = \mu^j$. Its latent roots are therefore the powers μ^j of μ. By using Laurent series the matrix can be extended to negative values of j, k. The well-known Lagrange-Jacobi theorem for inversion of a power series (Bromwich (1931), p. 160) takes the form that if $G = {}^{-1}F$, then

$$(4.4) \qquad kg_{(-j)k} = -jf_{(-k)j},$$

thus explicitly defining the g matrix (except for column $k = 0$) in terms of the f matrix. Also, one definition of the Bernoulli numbers can be written $B_n = n! v_{(-1)(n-1)}$ (Abramowitz and Stegun (1965)).

5. Koenigs families of functions

(5a) *Simple attractive points.* The solution of the problem of finding the iterates ${}^n F$ depends on the value of $\mu = F'[0]$. The simplest case is that $0 < |\mu| < 1$, when we call zero a 'simple attractive point' for F. Such an 'attractive point' often has implications in applications of the theory. For example, in the discussion in Section 2, it corresponds to a stable genetic equilibrium, a contracting Galton-Watson population, or a series of iterates tending towards the required solution of the equation. That is so because for any c such that $|\mu| < c < 1$, we have $|F[x]| < cx$ sufficiently near 0, and hence $|{}^nF[x_0]| = |x_n| < c^n|x_0|$, i.e., x_n tends geometrically to zero as $n \to \infty$. Now by the function-of-a-function rule for differentiation,

$$(5.1) \qquad\qquad ({}^nF)' = \prod_{r=0}^{n-1} F'[{}^rF].$$

Hence

$$(5.2) \qquad\qquad \lim_{n \to \infty} \frac{({}^nF)'}{\mu^n} = \prod_{r=0}^{\infty} \frac{F'[{}^rF]}{\mu} = \psi \qquad \text{(say)},$$

where the infinite product converges uniformly (near to 0), so that ψ is a regular function near 0. Now integrate ψ, with lower limit 0, to get a 'Schröder function' $S = \int_0 \psi$ (i.e., more explicitly $S[x] = \int_o^x \psi[x]\,dx$). The Schröder function is accordingly regular near 0, and satisfies

$$(5.3) \qquad\qquad S[0] = 0, \qquad S'[0] = \psi[0] = 1,$$

$$(5.4) \qquad\qquad S = \lim_{n \to \infty} [\mu^{-n} \cdot {}^nF].$$

From this last equation we readily get

$$(5.5) \qquad\qquad S[F] = \mu S,$$

which is known as 'Schröder's equation'. The formal proof of the existence of the function S regular at the fixed point 0 is due to Koenigs (1884). Any non-zero multiple of S also satisfies (5.5), and can be called a Schröder function; the relation $S'[0] = 1$ merely picks one out for definiteness. The inverse function $Z = {}^{-1}S$ for the particular function defined by (5.4) accordingly satisfies

$$(5.6) \qquad\qquad Z = \lim_{n \to \infty} [{}^{-n}F[\mu^n I]],$$

whence

(5.7) $$Z[0] = 0, \qquad Z'[0] = 1,$$

and in general whenever Schröder's equation (5.5) holds,

(5.8) $$F[Z] = Z[\mu I].$$

(5b) *Koenigs families.* Now let us suppose that we have a function S satisfying Schröder's equation (5.5), whether or not zero is an attractive point for F, and that S is regular at zero, $S[0] = 0$, and $S'[0] \neq 0$. Then (5.5) can be written

(5.9) $$F = Z[\mu S]$$

where $Z = {}^{-1}S$. Consider the 'Koenigs family' of functions

(5.10) $$F_{(\lambda)} = Z[\lambda S]$$

with parameter λ. It is easily verified that $F_{(\lambda)}$ is regular near 0, which is a fixed point, $F'_{(\lambda)}[0] = \lambda$, and $F_{(\mu)} = F$, and $F_{(1)} = I$, and that

(5.11) $$F_{(\lambda)}[F_{(\kappa)}] = F_{(\lambda\kappa)} = F_{(\kappa)}[F_{(\lambda)}]$$

so that any two functions of the family commute. It also follows from (5.11) that ${}^2F = F_{(\mu)}[F_{(\mu)}] = F_{(\mu^2)}$, ${}^3F = F_{(\mu)}[F_{(\mu^2)}] = F_{(\mu^3)}$, and in general, for any integral n,

(5.12) $$^nF = F_{(\mu^n)}.$$

This may be taken as a *definition* of ^nF for arbitrary complex n; note that $^nF[x]$ so defined is an analytic function of the two variables n and x.

Section (5a) above proves the existence of such a Koenigs family if $0 < |\mu| < 1$. If $|\mu| > 1$ we have a 'simple repulsive point', which is often unfavourable in applications—e.g., giving an unstable genetic equilibrium, an expanding population or a series of iterates not tending to a solution of the equation. If x_0 is near the fixed point, the sequence $x_0, x_1, x_2, \cdots$ will, at least for a time, tend to move further and further away from the fixed point. Hence it is difficult to predict the behaviour of x_n for large n. However, if $G = {}^{-1}F$, then $G[0] = 0$ and

$$|G'[0]| = |F'[0]|^{-1} = |\mu|^{-1} < 1$$

so that 0 is attractive for G. We can then construct a Schröder function S for G, as in Section (5a), so that $S[G] = \mu^{-1}S$, and therefore

$$S[F] = \mu\mu^{-1}S[F] = \mu S[G[F]]$$

$$= \mu S[I] = \mu S$$

and S is also a Schröder function for F. Hence F belongs to a Koenigs family (5.10), and this gives at least an explicit formula (5.12) for ^nF in the neighbourhood of the fixed point.

If $|\mu| = 1$, zero is a neutral point, and the proof given above breaks down. But Siegel (1942) has shown that there is still almost always a regular Schröder function S satisfying (5.3) and (5.4), in the sense that those values of u for which such an S may (possibly) not exist form a set of measure zero. We return to considering some of these exceptional values later.

(5c) μ *not a root of unity.* The formula (5.12) for ^nF is of most practical or theoretical use if we can find the value of the Schröder function S, at any rate in a more explicit form than is provided by the limit definition (5.4). In a limited number of cases we can find a simple closed form for S; for example, Schröder (1870) showed that if $F = \mu I/(1 + aI)$, then $S = (1 - \mu)I/(1 - \mu + aI)$ and

$$(5.13) \qquad\qquad F_{(\lambda)} = \frac{\lambda(1 - \mu)I}{1 - \mu + a(1 - \lambda)I}.$$

But such closed forms are exceptional.

However, we can find the function-matrix s of the Schröder function S in terms of the function-matrix f of F provided that μ is not a root of unity, i.e., provided that $\mu^N \neq 1$ for any integer N. For the Schröder equation (5.5) gives the matrix equation

$$(5.14) \qquad\qquad sf = \Delta[\mu]s$$

where $\Delta_{jk}[\mu] = \mu^j\delta_{jk}$, as above. This is a set of linear equations in the elements s_{jk} of the matrix s, which can either be solved consecutively to give $s_{jj} = 1$ and

(5.15) $\quad s_{jk} = (\mu^{j} - \mu^{k})^{-1} \displaystyle\sum_{\alpha=j}^{k-1} s_{j\alpha} f_{\alpha k} \qquad (k = j+1,\ j+2,\cdots);$

or alternatively the solution can be put in determinant form

$$
S_{jk} = \frac{\begin{vmatrix}
f_{j(j+1)} & \mu^{j+i} - \mu^{j} & 0 & \cdots & 0 \\[4pt]
f_{j(j+2)} & f_{(j+1)(j+2)} & \mu^{j+2} - \mu^{j} & \cdots & 0 \\[4pt]
\cdots & \cdots & \cdots & \cdots & \cdots \\[4pt]
f_{j(k-1)} & f_{(j+1)(k-1)} & f_{(j+2)(k-1)} & \cdots & \mu^{k-1} - \mu^{j} \\[4pt]
f_{jk} & f_{(j+1)k} & f_{(j+2)k} & \cdots & f_{(k-1)k}
\end{vmatrix}}{(\mu^{j} - \mu^{j+1})(\mu^{j} - \mu^{j+2}) \ \cdots \ (\mu^{j} - \mu^{k})}
$$

with, of course, $s_{jk} = 0$ for $j < k$. (This is a development of an observation due to W. T. Tutte.) Thus, for example, we find

$$
S^{2} = I^{2} + \frac{f_{23}}{\mu^{2} - \mu^{3}}\, I^{3}
$$

(5.16)

$$
+ \left(\frac{f_{24}}{\mu^{2} - \mu^{4}} + \frac{f_{23} f_{34}}{(\mu^{2} - \mu^{3})(\mu^{2} - \mu^{4})} \right) I^{4} + \cdots .
$$

Similarly, the function-matrix z for the inverse Schröder function satisfies $fz = z\Delta[\mu]$, again a set of linear equations for the elements z_{jk}. These can either be solved consecutively as $z_{kk} = 1$ and

(5.17) $\quad z_{jk} = (\mu^{k} - \mu^{j})^{-1} \displaystyle\sum_{\alpha=j+1}^{k} f_{j\alpha} z_{\alpha k}, \qquad (j = k-1, k-2, \cdots)$

or in determinant form as

$$
(5.18)\ z_{jk} = \frac{\begin{vmatrix}
f_{j(j+1)} & f_{j(j+2)} & \cdots & f_{j(k-1)} & f_{jk} \\[4pt]
\mu^{j} - \mu^{k} & f_{(j+1)(j+2)} & \cdots & f_{(j+1)(k-1)} & f_{(j+1)k} \\[4pt]
0 & \mu^{j+1} - \mu^{k} & \cdots & f_{(j+2)(k-1)} & f_{(j+2)k} \\[4pt]
\cdots & \cdots & \cdots & \cdots & \cdots \\[4pt]
0 & 0 & \cdots & \mu^{k-1} - \mu^{k} & f_{(k-1)k}
\end{vmatrix}}{(\mu^{k} - \mu^{j})(\mu^{k} - \mu^{j+1}) \cdots (\mu^{k} - \mu^{k-1})}
$$

The function-matrix $f_{(\lambda)}$ for the function $F_{(\lambda)}$ can also be found without use of the Schröder function using the property that $F_{(\lambda)}$ commutes with F, and hence

$$(5.19) \qquad\qquad f_{(\lambda)}f = ff_{(\lambda)}.$$

Together with the properties that $f_{(\lambda)}$ is upper-triangular, and that $f_{(\lambda)jj} = \lambda^j$, this gives a set of linear equations which can be solved to give the element $f_{(\lambda)jk}$. Alternatively, there is an explicit formula, obtained as follows. For any non-empty set $\{p, q, \cdots, u, v\}$ of distinct integers define

$$(5.20) \qquad \Omega[\lambda\; ; p, q, \cdots, u, v] = \sum_{\alpha}\left(\lambda^{\alpha}\Big/ \prod_{\beta \neq \alpha}(\mu^{\alpha} - \mu^{\beta})\right),$$

where α ranges over all members of the set $\{p, q, \cdots, u, v\}$, and β over all members of the set other than α. When there is only one parameter p, we take this definition to mean $\Omega[\lambda\; ; p] = \lambda^p$. By taking the contour integral of the function $(I - \mu^p)^{-1}(I - \mu^q)^{-1}\cdots(I - \mu^v)^{-1}$ round a large circle we find

$$(5.21) \qquad\qquad \Omega[1; p, q, \cdots, u, v] = 0,$$

except that when there is only one parameter $p, \Omega[1; p] = 1$. Then Ω satisfies the recurrence relation

$$(5.22) \qquad \Omega[\mu\lambda\; ; p, \cdots, u, v] = \Omega[\lambda\; ; p, \cdots, u] \;\; + \mu^v\,\Omega[\lambda\; ; p, \cdots, u, v].$$

Let us now define, for $j < k$,

$$(5.23) \qquad f^{*}_{\lambda jk} = \sum (f_{jp}f_{pq} \cdots f_{uv}f_{vk}\,\Omega[\lambda\; ; j, u, \cdots, v, k]),$$

where the summation is over all (possibly empty) sequences of integers $p, q, \cdots, v$ such that $j < p < q < \cdots < v$. Also set $f^{*}_{\lambda jj} = \lambda^j$, and $f^{*}_{\lambda jk} = 0$ when $j > k$, and $f^{*}_{\lambda} = $ the matrix with elements $f^{*}_{\lambda jk}$. Then we assert that $f^{*}_{\lambda} = f_{(\lambda)}$ (and hence, putting $\lambda = \mu^n$, we have an explicit formula for the Taylor series for $(^nF)^j$). To prove this, we first note that by (5.20) and (5.21), $f^{*} = I = f_{(1)}$. Also, a direct matrix multiplication and use of the recurrence relation (5.22) shows that $f^{*}_{\lambda} = f^{*}_{\lambda}\mu$, and we know that $f_{(\lambda)}f = f_{(\lambda)}f_{(\mu)} = f_{(\lambda\mu)}$. Hence, starting from $f^{*}_1 = f_{(1)}$ and multiplying repeatedly on the right by f we get $f^{*}_{\lambda} = f_{(\lambda)}$ wherever $\lambda = \mu^m$. But $f^{*}_{\lambda jk}$ is a polynomial in λ by its definition, and $f_{\lambda jk}$ is a polynomial in λ because $f_{(\lambda)} = z\,\Delta[\lambda]s$, so the equation $f^{*}_{\lambda} = f_{(\lambda)}$ is an identity.

Note that these formulas imply that if μ is not a root of unity, then the Schröder function S (with slope $S'[0] = 1$) and the functions $F_{(\lambda)}$ are unique, provided that they exist. In that case a function F with fixed point 0 belongs to at most one Koenigs family defined with respect to this fixed point. It does not follow that if there is another fixed point ξ, the Koenigs family defined around ξ would coincide with the family defined around 0; one could only expect that to happen in particular cases.

(5d) μ *a root of unity*. Suppose that $\mu^N = 1$. If F belongs to a Koenigs family $F_{(\lambda)}$, defined around the fixed point 0, then we must have $^NF = F_{(1)} = I$. Conversely, if $^NF = I$, then

$$S = \sum_{\alpha=1}^{N} (\mu^{-\alpha} \cdot {}^{\alpha}F)/N$$

is a Schröder function satisfying (5.3), (5.4), (5.5). It is no longer unique, and the formulas (5.15) and (5.16) for the coefficients break down. For let

$$\psi = I \cdot (1 + \sum_{1}^{\infty} a_{\alpha} I^{M\alpha})$$

for arbitrary a_{α}. Then, since $\mu^M = 1$, we have $\psi[\mu I] = \mu\psi$, so that $\psi[S[F]] = \psi[\mu S] = \mu\psi[S]$, so that $\psi[S]$ is also a Schröder function.

Note that, in this case, the sequence of iterates $x_0, x_1, x_2, \cdots$ is periodic with period N.

6. Slope 1 at a fixed point

A case of major theoretical importance is that in which $\mu = 1$. For example, this corresponds to a branching process in which the expected size of the population is stationary. Apart from the trivial case $F = I$, F cannot then belong to any Koenigs family. Despite its apparent simplicity, this is one of the most difficult and troublesome cases mathematically. However Schröder gave an explicit formula for the function-matrix f^n corresponding to the iterate ^nF for integral n, easily demonstrated by matrix methods. For, if $\mu = 1$, we can write $f = I + J$, where $J = f - I$ is zero on and below the principal diagonal. Hence by the binomial theorem

(6.1) $$f^n = I + nJ + \binom{n}{2} J^2 + \cdots$$

or, in terms of the matrix elements,

(6.2) $$(f^n)_{jk} = \sum_{p=0}^{n} \left\{ \binom{n}{p} \sum_{u_0 \cdots u_p} f_{u_0 u_1} f_{u_1 u_2} \cdots f_{u_{p-1} u_p} \right\}$$

where the summation is over all sets of integers such that $j = u_0 < u_1 < \cdots < u_p = k$.

One might conjecture, in view of the simplicity of the series (6.2), that it would hold for non-integral n. Unfortunately it seems probable that in general this is not so, and that the series is divergent. Smith (1942) gave a construction for a function A, regular within a sector of a circle around the origin, such that Abel's (1881) equation holds:

(6.3) $$A[F] = A + 1$$

from which we may deduce that, under suitable conditions,

(6.4) $$^nF = {}^{-1}A[A + n].$$

But although this is in principle an explicit formula for ^nF, it does not seem practically useful.

7. The hyperattractive fixed point

If $\mu = 0$, we could call zero a 'hyperattractive fixed point'. F then has a Taylor series beginning with the term in I^M, where $M > 1$. We can write

(7.1) $$F = c^{M-1}I^M \cdot R,$$

where c is a non-zero constant and R a function regular at zero, and $R[0] = 1$. If x_0 is near enough to 0, it is then easy to see that the sequence of iterates $x_0, x_1, x_2, \cdots$ converges to 0 uniformly faster than any geometric series. Let us write

(7.2) $$Q = \sum_{p=0}^{\infty} M^{-p} \ln[R[^pF]].$$

Then near 0, Q is the sum of a uniformly convergent series of regular functions, and hence regular at 0. Also

(7.3) $$Q[0] = 0,$$

(7.4) $$Q = \ln[R] + M^{-1}Q[F].$$

Now set $T = cI \cdot \exp[M^{-1}Q]$, then by (7.4) and (7.1)

$$T[F] = c \cdot F \cdot \exp[Q - \ln[R]]$$

(7.5) $$= c \cdot F \cdot \exp^M[M^{-1}Q]/R$$

$$= T^M.$$

By iteration,

$$T[^2F] = T^M[F] = I^M[T[F]] = (T^M)^M = T^{M^2},$$

and in general $T[^nF] = T^{M^n}$, or

(7.6) $$^nF = {}^{-1}T[T^{M^n}].$$

This defines ^nF explicitly in terms of the function T, which has rather the same role in the case of a hyperattractive point as the Schröder function S has for a simple attractive point (see Picard (1928)). T is regular at the origin, $T[0] = 0$ and $T'[0] \neq 0$. We could define a function $F_{\{\lambda\}} = {}^{-1}T[T^\lambda]$: so that

$$F_{\{\lambda\}}[F_{\{\kappa\}}] = F_{\{\lambda\kappa\}} = F_{\{\kappa\}}[F_{\{\lambda\}}].$$

Then $F_{\{\lambda\}}$ is regular at the origin when λ is a positive integer, and then has Taylor series with leading term $t_{11}^{\lambda-1}I^{M\lambda}$. If $\lambda = M^n$, then $F_{\{\lambda\}} = {}^nF$.

The function-matrix t of T can be found from the relation $tf = i_M t$ where i_M is the function-matrix of I^M. This is a set of linear equations which can be solved consecutively to find the elements of t. Similarly the function-matrix u of $U = {}^{-1}T$ can be found from $fu = ui_M$.

8. Iteration in many variables

The obvious generalization to many variables is a mapping $x_1 = F[x_0]$ of a vector x_0 onto a vector x_1 of the same dimensionality. On iteration, this gives $x_2 = F[x_1]$, $x_3 = F[x_2]$ and so on. The two simplest non-trivial examples are linear ones; $x_{r+1} = x_r + a$, with constant a, with the solution

172   C. A. B. SMITH

$x_n = x_0 + na$; and $x_{r+1} = bx_r$, giving $x_n = b^n x_0$, where an explicit expression for b^n in terms of the latent roots and vectors of b can be obtained by standard methods.

Such a mapping F has a fixed point ξ if $F[\xi] = \xi$; as in the one-variable case, we can take $\xi = 0$ without loss of generality. It would be natural to call it an attractive point if the absolute value of every latent root is less than 1. One might then suppose that the theory for the one variable case would carry over straightforwardly. However, this case has been considered by Leau (1897) and Bennett (1915), and Leau showed that it is by no means easy, not even if all latent roots are distinct and non-zero. Apart from the work of these authors, our knowledge of multidimensional iteration is virtually zero, apart from a few isolated special cases, and apart from the fairly obvious result that if all latent roots of the jacobian at a fixed point ξ are less than 1 in absolute value, there is a neighbourhood of ξ within which the sequence of iterates $^nF[x_0]$ tends geometrically to ξ.

In addition to the works quoted in the discussion above, I have included in the bibliography some references to particularly important and relevant papers concerning iteration by Abel, Babbage, Bennett, Boole, Domb and Fisher, Fatou, Grévy, Haldane, Julia, Lémeray, and Szekeres; this list is still far from complete.

References

ABEL, N. H. (1881) Détermination d'une fonction au moyen d'une équation qui ne contient qu'une seule variable. *Oeuvres Complètes* **2**, 36–39.

ABRAMOWITZ, M. AND STEGUN, I. A. (1965) *Handbook of Mathematical Functions.* Dover, New York.

BABBAGE, C. (1815) An essay towards a calculus of functions. *Phil. Trans. R. Soc.* **105**, 389–423.

BENNETT, A. A. (1915a) The iteration of functions of one variable. *Ann. of Math.* **17**, 23–60.

BENNETT, A. A. (1915b) A case of iteration in several variables. *Ann. of Math.* **17**, 188–196.

BOOLE, G. (1860) *A Treatise on the Calculus of Finite Differences.* Macmillan, London.

BROMWICH, T. J. I'A. (1931) *An Introduction to the Theory of Infinite Series.* Macmillan, London.

DOMB, C. AND FISHER, M. E. (1956) On iterative processes and functional equations. *Proc. Camb. Phil. Soc.* **52**, 652–662.

FATOU, P. (1919, 1920a, 1920b) Sur les équations fonctionelles, I, II, III. *Bull. Soc. Math. France* **47**, 161–271; **48**, 33–94; **48**, 208–314.

GRÉVY, A. (1894) Études sur les équations fonctionelles. *Ann. Sci. École Norm. Sup.* Série 3, **11**, 249–323.

HALDANE, J. B. S. (1932) On the non-linear functional equation $\Delta x_n = k\phi(x_n)$. *Proc. Camb. Phil. Soc.* **28**, 234–243.

HARRIS, T. E. (1963) *The Theory of Branching Processes*. Springer, Berlin.

JULIA, G. (1924) Sur quelques applications de la représentation conforme à la résolution d'équations fonctionelles. *Bull. Soc. Math. France* **52**, 279–315.

KOENIGS, G. (1884) Recherches sur les intégrales de certaines équations fonctionelles. *Ann. Sci. École Norm. Sup.* Série 3, **1**, Supplément S1–S45.

KOENIGS, G. (1885) Nouvelles recherches sur les équations fonctionelles. *Ann. Sci. École Norm. Sup.* Série 3, **2**, 385–404.

LEAU, L. (1897) Études sur les équations fonctionelles à une ou a plusieurs variables. *Ann. Fac. Sci. Univ. Toulouse* **11**, E1–E110.

LÉMERAY, E. M. (1898) Sur quelques algorithmes généraux et sur l'itération. *Bull. Soc. Math. France* **27**, 10–15.

MENGER, K. (1953) *Calculus: A Modern Approach*. Illinois Institute of Technology, Chicago.

PICARD, E. (1928) *Leçons sur quelques Équations Fonctionelles*. Gauthier-Villars, Paris.

RAUSENBERGER, O. (1881) Theorie der allgemeinen Periodicität. *Math. Ann.* **18**, 379–409.

SCHRÖDER, E. (1870) Über iterierte Functionen. *Math. Ann.* **3**, 296–322.

SIEGEL, C. L. (1942) Iterations of Analytic Functions. *Ann. of Math.* **43**, 607–612.

SMITH, C. A. B. (1942) *On Tests of Significance*. Ph. D. Thesis, University of Cambridge.

SZEKERES, G. (1958) Regular iteration of real and complex functions. *Acta Math.* **100**, 203–258.

TURNBULL, H. W. (1934) Power vectors. *Proc. London Math. Soc.* (2) **37**, 106–146.

WALKER, A. G. (1946) Commutative functions (I and II). *Quart. J. Math. Oxford Ser.* **17**, 65–92.

WALKER, A. G. AND BATTY, J. S. (1946) Non-integral function powers. *Quart. J. Math. Oxford Ser.* **17**, 145–152.

WATSON, H. W. AND GALTON, F. (1874) On the probability of the extinction of families. *J. Anthropol. Inst. Great Britain and Ireland* **4**, 138–144.

PART V

STOCHASTIC PROCESSES

Fonctions Certaines Admettant des Répartitions Asymptotiques et Fonctions Aléatoires Stationnaires

A. BLANC-LAPIERRE

Abstract

In the article below, we consider sets of non-random functions of time t admitting certain asymptotic distributions. Purely temporal and deterministic considerations lead us to associate to a set $\mathcal{H}$, say, of functions $H(t)$ of this type, a space Ω of samples ω.

To each function $H(t) \subset \mathcal{H}$, there corresponds a random variable $h(\omega)$. To the set of translated functions $H(t + \lambda)$ of a function $H(t) \subset \mathcal{H}$, there corresponds a stationary random function of the translation parameter λ, say, $h(\lambda, \omega)$. We study the transposition to the set $\mathcal{H}$ of non-random functions $H(t)$ of such properties as moments, gaussian character, independence, harmonic analysis, and others, of the random variables $h(\omega)$ and of the random functions $h(\lambda, \omega)$.

Some remarks are made concerning the links between ergodicity and the above problems.

1. Introduction

1.1. *Point de vue physique*

Un expérimentateur étudiant un phénomène 'fluctuant' $X(t)$ procède, souvent, à son *enregistrement*. Pour lui, les grandeurs macroscopiques associées à ce phénomène s'identifient à des *moyennes temporelles* prises pendant des temps 'assez longs' et l'idée de *stationnarité* traduit *une certaine stabilité* de ces moyennes. Tout ceci ne sort pas du cadre des *fonctions certaines*. L'introduction d'une *fonction aléatoire* (f.a.) *stationnaire* $X(t, \omega)$ $(\omega \in \Omega)$ intervient généralement par référence à un modèle théorique. Si l'on part d'une telle f.a. stationnaire $X(t, \omega)$ se révélant à un observateur particulier par une de ses réalisations, soit $X(t, \omega_1)$, l'exigence de *reproductibilité macroscopique*, qui veut que les divers

177

expérimentateurs possibles (correspondant à—presque—tous les ω)
mesurent les mêmes valeurs moyennes, à la précision des expériences
près, pose le problème des *propriétés ergodiques* de $X(t, \omega)$. Nous
adoptons ici un cheminement en quelque sorte inverse: nous resterons
dans le cadre d'un ensemble de *fonctions certaines présentant des
caractères de permanence* que nous préciserons, et nous montrerons
comment des considérations *purement temporelles et déterministes* con-
duisent à introduire des fonctions aléatoires stationnaires associées,
*permettant ainsi l'utilisation, dans ce cadre de fonctions certaines, de tout
le formalisme des fonctions aléatoires stationnaires et de toutes les notions
et propriétés correspondantes.* Le point de vue développé ici présente des
liens ou des convergences avec les travaux de Kac et Steinhaus [1] sur
les *fonctions (certaines) indépendantes (au sens stochastique)*, de
Wiener [2] sur l'*analyse harmonique généralisée* et de Bass et Bertrandias
[3] sur les *fonctions pseudo-aléatoires.* Les résultats de cet article ont été
rassemblés à propos d'un problème d'automatique lié à la stabilité d'un
système bouclé posé par Lefèvre. Ils sont, par ailleurs, résumés dans [4].

1.2. *Notations et hypothèses*

Soit $\mathcal{H}$ un espace vectoriel de fonctions $H(t)$ mesurables, à valeurs
complexes ($H(t) \in C$ = plan complexe) telles que:

a) si $H(t) \in \mathcal{H}$, il en est de même de $H(t + \tau)$ ($\forall \tau$);

b) toute combinaison linéaire, soit $G(t)$, d'un nombre fini d'éléments de
$\mathcal{H}$, a une répartition asymptotique au sens suivant: pour toute fonction ϕ,
continue et bornée sur C, la moyenne temporelle suivante existe:

$$(1.2.1) \qquad \lim_{T \to \infty} \frac{1}{T} \int_0^T \phi[G(t)]dt = \overline{\phi[G(t)]}.$$

Pour la possibilité de l'existence et les propriétés de tels ensembles $\mathcal{H}$,
voir [5]. L'existence de la limite (1.2.1) pour tout ϕ entraine automatique-
ment celle d'une mesure μ_G sur C telle que l'on ait:

$$(1.2.2) \qquad \overline{\phi[G(t)]} = \int_C \phi(x)d\mu_G(x).$$

Par ailleurs, l'hypothèse b) entraîne qu'une fonction vectorielle quel-
conque $K(t) = [H_1(t), \cdots, H_k(t)]$ admet une répartition asymptotique sur
C^k en ce sens que, pour toute fonction complexe Φ, continue et bornée
sur C^k, on a, de façon analogue à (1.2.1) et (1.2.2):

$$\lim_{T \to \infty} \frac{1}{T} \int_0^T \Phi[H_1(t), \cdots, H_k(t)]dt = \overline{\Phi[K(t)]}$$

(1.2.3)

$$= \int_{C^k} \cdots \int \Phi[x_1, \cdots, x_k] d\mu_k(x_1, \cdots, x_k),$$

où μ_k est une mesure de probabilité sur C^k.

2. Variables aléatoires associées aux $H \in \mathcal{H}$

Sous les hypothèses énoncées ci-dessus, la loi P_T, image (pour l'application $t(0 \le t \le T) \to \Pi_{\mathcal{H}} H(t)$ de $[0, T]$ dans $C^{\mathcal{H}}$) de la mesure $[dt/T]$, converge cylindriquement, pour $T \to \infty$, vers une probabilité P dans $C^{\mathcal{H}}$. Par ce procédé, un ensemble de K fonctions: $H_j \in \mathcal{H}$ $(j = 1, 2, \cdots, K)$ définit une *multivariable aléatoire* $h_j(\omega)$ $(\omega \in \Omega = C^{\mathcal{H}})$ $(j = 1, 2, \cdots, K)$ dont la loi est conforme à P.

Naturellement, la correspondance $H \to h$ est linéaire.

A ce stade, toutes les propriétés des variables aléatoires (v.a.) sont transposables à l'ensemble $\mathcal{H}$:

Indépendance. Si les $\{h_j(\omega)\}$ $(j = 1, 2, \cdots, J)$ sont des v.a. indépendantes, on dira que les fonctions certaines $\{H_j(t)\}$ le sont aussi. Alors, si $\eta[\cdots, H_j(t) < a_j, \cdots; T]$ représente le temps relatif, sur $[0, T]$, correspondant aux t pour lesquels on a $H_j(t) < a_j (\forall j = 1, \cdots, J)$, on a:

(2.1.1) $\quad \lim_{T \to \infty} \eta[H_1(t) < a_1, \cdots, H_J(t) < a_J; T] = \prod_1^J \lim_{T \to \infty} \eta[H_j(t) < a_j; T].$

Les moyennes temporelles se factorisent dans le cas de l'indépendance. Si g_j sont J nouvelles fonctions du temps et si les $h_j(\omega)(j = 1, 2, \cdots, J)$ sont indépendantes, on a, sous réserve de l'existence des grandeurs introduites:

(2.1.2) $\qquad \overline{\prod_1^J g_j[H_j(t)]} = \prod_1^J \overline{g_j[H_j(t)]}.$

Caractère gaussien. Si les $h_j(\omega)$ $(j = 1, 2, \cdots, J)$ sont gaussiens dans leur ensemble, in dira qu'il en est de même des $H_j(t)$ $(j = 1, 2, \cdots, J)$.

Moments — Second ordre. Les relations (1.2.1), (1.2.2) et (1.2.3) identifient, pour les ϕ continues *bornées*, l'espérance mathématique (dans P) $E_{(P)}\{\phi[g(\omega)]\}$ avec la moyenne temporelle $\overline{\phi\{G(t)\}}$. Dans beaucoup d'applications, cette propriété subsistera pour des ϕ *non bornées* et (notamment) pour certaines puissances entières des x (moments). Il faudra faire, à ce sujet, des hypothèses adaptées à chaque problème particulier. Dans ce qui suit, nous admettrons que, quelles que soient les deux fonctions H et H' de $\mathcal{H}$, $\overline{H(t)H'^*(t)}$ existe et vaut

$E_{(P)}\{h(\omega)h'^*(\omega)\}$. Dans $\mathcal{H}$, nous introduirons alors la norme $\|H\|$ définie par $\|H\|^2 = E_{(P)}\{|h(\omega)|^2\} = \overline{|H(t)|^2}$ et nous supposerons $\mathcal{H}$ complet pour cette norme.

Convergences des suites de v.a., etc.

3. Fonctions aléatoires stationnaires associées aux $H(t)$

3.1. *Introduction de la f.a. stationnaire $h(\lambda, H; \omega)$ associée à $H(t)$*

Soient $H \in \mathcal{H}$, K valeurs réelles quelconques $\lambda_j (j = 1, 2, \cdots, K)$, les K translatées de H, $H(t + \lambda_j)$, et $h(\lambda_j, H; \omega)$ les v.a. associées. L'ensemble des $h(\lambda_j, H; \omega)$ $(\omega \subset C^*)$ définit une multivariable aléatoire de loi P. Si λ varie de $-\infty$ à $+\infty$, on introduit ainsi f.a. de $\lambda : h(\lambda, H; \omega)$, correspondant à H, à valeurs dans C, et définie sur $\lambda \times C^*)$. Evidemment, $h(\lambda, H; \omega)$ est *stationnaire en λ* (strictement); de même, $\{h(\lambda, H_m; \omega)\}$ $(m = 1, 2, \cdots, M)$ définit une *f.a. vectorielle stationnaire*.

3.2. *Propriétés du second ordre des $h(\lambda, H; \omega)$*

Les propriétés des f.a. stationnaires du second ordre s'appliquent aux $h(\lambda, H; \omega)$. Elles induisent des propriétés corrélatives pour les $H(t + \lambda)$. Il en est ainsi pour tout ce qui touche au filtrage linéaire, à la corrélation, aux spectres, à l'analyse harmonique (cf. [6] pp. 464–489 et [7] pp. 342–470). On notera que la filtrée $\mathcal{F}[h(\lambda, H; \omega)]$ de la f.a. $h(\lambda, H; \omega)$ est la f.a. de λ $h(\lambda, \mathcal{F}[H]; \omega)$ associée à la filtrée $\mathcal{F}[H(t)]$ de $H(t)$.

Pour introduire les propriétés harmoniques, on fait intervenir la f.a. $l(\lambda, \nu, H; \omega)$ résultant du filtrage de la f.a. $h(\lambda, H; \omega)$ dans le filtre $\mathcal{F}_{-\infty, \nu}$ [ ] de gain 1 sur $[-\infty, \nu[$ et zéro ailleurs ($\mathcal{F}_{-\infty, \nu}$ transmet sans déformation la bande de fréquences $[-\infty, \nu[$ et coupe le reste du spectre). On peut alors écrire:

$$h(\lambda, H; \omega) = \int_{-\infty}^{+\infty} e^{2\pi i \nu \lambda} d_\nu \eta(\nu, H; \omega) \text{ avec } \eta(\nu, H; \omega)$$

(3.2.1)

$$= l(0, \nu, H; \omega).$$

Si $\mathcal{F}_1$ et $\mathcal{F}_2$ sont des filtres disjoints $(G_1(\nu)G_2(\nu) \equiv 0)$, on a, $\forall \tau$:

$$\overline{\mathcal{F}_1[H(t)] \cdot [\mathcal{F}_2[H(t + \tau)]]^*} = E\{h(\lambda, \mathcal{F}_1[H]; \omega) \cdot h^*(\lambda + \tau, \mathcal{F}_2[H]; \omega)\}$$

(3.2.2)

$$= E\{\mathcal{F}_1[h(\lambda, H; \omega)] \cdot [\mathcal{F}_2[h(\lambda + \tau, H; \omega)]]^*\}$$

$$= 0.$$

Les $d_\nu \eta(\nu, \dot{H}; \omega)$ sont, naturellement, orthogonaux. Les passages à la limite intervenant dans la définition des filtres linéaires, ou dans celle de l'intégrale (3.2.1), sont entendus en moyenne quadratique au sens de $[\omega, P]$. D'après ce qui précède, ces moyennes quadratiques peuvent, si on se réfère aux $H(t)$ eux-mêmes, être interprétées comme des moyennes temporelles.

N.B. On notera que, dans la correspondance $H(t + \lambda) \to h(\lambda, H; \omega)$, t et λ, quoique, l'un et l'autre, homogènes à un temps, jouent des rôles très différents. λ est le paramètre de la f.a. $h(\lambda, H; \omega)$, tandis que t sert à prendre les moyennes temporelles qui, par hypothèse, s'identifient aux $E_{(P)}\{\cdot\}$ correspondants.

3.3. *Propriétés d'ordres supérieurs*

Ensemble $\mathcal{H}_{(\infty)}$. Par analogie avec la classe $\Phi(\infty)$ de la théorie des f.a. (cf. [7] p. 365 et p. 419), nous introduirons ici des ensembles $\mathcal{H}_{(\infty)}$. Un ensemble $\mathcal{H}$ sera dit du type $\mathcal{H}_{(\infty)}$, si, en plus des hypothèses de définition de $\mathcal{H}$, les $H(t)$ satisfont, encore, aux suivantes.

Quels que soient: l'entier $K > 0$, les $H_j(t)$ (distincts ou non), les $\epsilon_j = \pm 1$ et les $\tau_j (j = 1, 2, \cdots, K)$, on a:

a) (3.3.1) $\qquad \overline{H_{\epsilon_1}(t + \tau_1) \cdots H_{\epsilon_K}(t + \tau_K)}$ existe et vaut

$$E_{(P)}\{h_{\epsilon_1}(\tau_1, H_1; \omega) \cdots h_{\epsilon_k}(\tau_k, H_K; \omega)\}$$

où $a_\epsilon = a$ si $\epsilon = +1$ et $a_\epsilon = a^*$ (imaginaire conjugué) si $\epsilon = -1$;

b) (3.3.2) $\displaystyle\int_{-\infty}^{+\infty} \cdots \int_{-\infty}^{+\infty} |E_{(P)}\{d_{\nu_1}\eta_{\epsilon_1}(\nu_1, H_1; \omega) \cdots d_{\nu_K}\eta_{\epsilon_K}(\nu_K, H_K; \omega)\}| < +\infty,$

les $\eta(\nu, H_j, \omega)$ étant conformes à la définition de (3.2.1).

Théorème. Pour tout ensemble $\{\nu_j, \epsilon_j, H_j\} (j = 1, 2, \cdots, K)$ *ne satisfaisant pas à*:

(3.3.3) $\qquad\qquad \epsilon_1 \nu_1 + \epsilon_2 \nu_2 + \cdots + \epsilon_K \nu_K = 0$

on a, si $\mathcal{H}$ *est un* $\mathcal{H}_{(\infty)}$:

$$E_{(P)}\{d_{\nu_1}\eta_{\epsilon_1}(\nu_1, H_1; \omega) \cdots d_{\nu_K}\eta_{\epsilon_K}(\nu_K, H_K; \omega)\}$$

(3.3.4) $\qquad = \overline{[\mathcal{F}_{d\nu_1}[H_1(t)]]_{\epsilon_1} \cdots [\mathcal{F}_{d\nu_K}[H_K(t)]]_{\epsilon_K}}$

$$= 0$$

où $\mathcal{F}_{d\nu_j}$ est le filtre laissant passer la bande $[\nu_j, \ \nu_j + d_{\nu_j}]$.

Seuls peuvent différer de zéro les éléments du type (3.3.4) qui sont distribués sur les multiplicités définies par (3.3.3) qu'on peut appeler *multiplicités 'stationnaires'*.

4. Fonctions indépendantes ainsi que leurs translatées

Nous avons (cf. *paragraphe* 2) *défini l'indépendance des fonctions* $H_j(t)$ *par celle des variables aléatoires associées* $h_j(\omega)$. Nous introduisons ici une notion plus stricte: *l'indépendance des fonctions* $H_j(t)$ *et de leurs translatées* caractérisée par celle des *fonctions aléatoires* $h(\lambda, H_j; \omega)$ ou, de façon équivalente, par celle des *fonctions* $H_j(t + \lambda_j)$ (∀ *les* λ_j).

Si deux ensembles $H_j(t)$ $(j = 1, 2, \cdots)$ et $H'_l(t)$ $(l = 1, 2, \cdots)$. sont indépendants, l'un par rapport à l'autre, au sens des fonctions et de leurs translatées, les moyennes temporelles et les espérances mathématiques se scindent en deux facteurs et, ∀ les τ_j et les τ'_j, on a:

$$\overline{H_{1_{\epsilon_1}}(t + \tau_1) \cdots H'_{1_{\epsilon'_1}}(t + \tau'_1) \cdots}$$

(4.1.1)
$$= E_{(P)}\{h_{\epsilon_1}(\tau_1, H_1; \omega) \cdots h_{\epsilon'_1}(\tau'_1, H'_1; \omega) \cdots\}$$

$$= \overline{H_{1_{\epsilon_1}}(t + \tau_1) \cdots} \quad \cdot \quad \overline{H'_{1_{\epsilon'_1}}(t + \tau'_1) \cdots}$$

$$= E_{(P)}\{h_{\epsilon_1}(\tau_1, H_1; \omega) \cdots\} E_{(P)}\{h_{\epsilon'_1}(\tau'_1, H'_1; \omega) \cdots\}.$$

Remarques

a) Soient les deux fonctions

(4.1.2)
$$H(t) = \sum_{\text{m.q.}} A_n e^{2\pi i \nu_n t} \quad \text{et} \quad H'(t) = \sum_{\text{m.q.}} A'_n e^{2\pi i \nu_n t},$$

soient, d'autre part, ν et ν' les ensembles constitués, le premier, soit ν, par les combinaisons linéaires d'un nombre fini d'éléments ν_n à coefficients entiers $\gtreqless 0$ et le second, soit ν', de la même façon du côté des ν'_n. *Si ν et ν' n'ont d'autre élément commun que $\nu = 0$, alors $H(t)$ et $H'(t)$ sont deux fonctions indépendantes ainsi que leurs translatées.*

b) On rencontre souvent, en automatique, des transformations $x(t) \rightarrow s(t)$ du type:

(4.1.3)
$$s(t) = M\{x(t)\} = \mathscr{F}\{f(t)x(t)\},$$

où $\mathcal{F}$ est un filtre linéaire et $x(t)$ une fonction contenue dans un certain ensemble X. Supposons que $f(t)$ et X fassent partie d'un $\mathcal{H}_{(\infty)}$. L'indépendance, pour les fonctions et leurs translatées, de $f(t)$ et de l'ensemble X, qui peut être imposée par des raisons physiques (par exemple, si le signal $x(t)$ provient de phénomènes n'ayant aucun couplage avec l'appareil qui produit $f(t)$), introduit de grandes simplifications dans le calcul des moments de s à partir des propriétés respectives de f et des $x \in X$. En particulier, cette indépendance assure que M conserve l'orthogonalité des fonctions et leurs translatées. On trouvera dans [8] des applications de ces considérations à l'étude de la stabilité du système bouclé:

(4.1.4) $\mathcal{F}\{f(t)[e(t) - s(t)]\} = s(t)(e(t)$: signal d'entrée; $s(t)$: réponse).

5. Fonctions de Laplace-Gauss

Pour simplifier, supposons les H réels. Soit $\mathcal{H}_1 \subset \mathcal{H}$. Nous dirons que tous les $H \in \mathcal{H}_1$ sont, *dans leur ensemble,* de Laplace-Gauss, *ainsi que leurs translatées,* si, $\forall$ K et L, $\forall$ les $H_k \in \mathcal{H}_1$ ($k = 1, \cdots, K$) et $\forall$ les λ_l ($l = 1, \cdots, L$), les LK v.a. $h(\lambda_1, H_K ; \omega)$ correspondant aux $H_k(t + \lambda_l)$ sont gaussiennes dans leur ensemble au sens de P. S'il en est ainsi, les fonctions aléatoires $h(\lambda, H_k ; \omega)$ constituent un ensemble de f.a. de Laplace-Gauss. Toutes les propriétés de ces f.a. induisent alors des propriétés corrélatives pour les fonctions certaines $H \in \mathcal{H}_1$.

6. Fonctions à répartitions asymptotiques et ergodisme

Nous sommes partis d'un ensemble de fonctions certaines $H \in \mathcal{H}$, essentiellement caractérisé par une invariance vis-à-vis des translations et par l'existence des répartitions asymptotiques. A cet ensemble, nous avons associé un ensemble de f.a. stationnaires $h(\lambda, H ; \omega)$

(6.1.1) $\mathcal{H} \rightarrow h(\lambda, H ; \omega)$.

On peut chercher à faire le cheminement inverse. Partons d'un ensemble ϵ' de f.a. $X_j(t, \omega') \in \epsilon'$, *strictement stationnaires dans leur ensemble,* définies sur les épreuves $\omega' \in \Omega'$. Considérons une épreuve particulière ω_0'. Les $X_j(t, \omega_0')$ correspondants constituent-ils–ou non–un ensemble $\mathcal{H}$? *Est-il possible que la réponse soit affirmative avec une probabilité* 1? Suggérons, dans ses grandes lignes, la construction d'un exemple où il en est ainsi. Nous partons d'une f.a. à accroissements *indépendants* et *stationnaires*, soit $\mathcal{N}(\theta, \omega')$ et nous considérons les fonctions aléatoires

$$(6.1.2) \qquad X_{R_j}(t, \omega') = \int_{-\infty}^{+\infty} R_j(t - \theta)\, d\mathcal{N}(\theta, \omega').$$

Par généralisation du raisonnement donné en [7], à la page 368, on peut montrer que, sous réserve d'astreindre $R(t)$ à des conditions très larges de régularité, d'intégrabilité et de décroissance pour les grands $|t|$, il est possible d'imposer à l'ensemble des $X_j(t, \omega')$, d'une part, de faire partie d'un ensemble $\phi(\infty)$ et, d'autre part, de posséder un *ergodisme suffisant* (conséquence de la décroissance des R pour $|t| \to \infty$ et de théorèmes du type de celui donné en [7] p. 467) pour que la réponse à la question posée soit affirmative.

Soit, alors, P' la loi temporelle de l'ensemble des $X_j(t, \omega')$. Presque sûrement, on peut affirmer ce qui suit. Considérons les réalisations $X_j'(t, \omega_0')$ correspondant à une épreuve particulière ω_0'. Procédons sur cet ensemble comme nous l'avons fait sur $\mathcal{H}$ aux paragraphes 1 et 2. Nous obtenons alors une loi asymptotique $P(\omega_0')$. *Cette loi n'est autre que P'* (p.s.).

Il y a plus. On peut construire des ensembles ϵ'' de f.a. $X_j(t, \omega'') \subset \epsilon''$ *non stationnaires* mais *ergodiques au sens suivant*:

F étant une fonction de $[X_{j_1}(t_1), \cdots, X_{j_M}(t_M)]$, on a:

$$(6.1.3) \qquad \begin{aligned} &\lim_{T \to \infty} \frac{1}{T} \int_0^T F[X_{j_1}(t + \tau_1) \cdots X_{j_M}(t + \tau_M)]\, dt \\ &\overset{\text{p.s.}}{=} \lim_{T \to \infty} \frac{1}{T} \int_0^T E\{F[X_{j_1}(t + \tau_1) \cdots X_{j_M}(t + \tau_M)]\}\, dt \end{aligned}$$

(ces moyennes temporelles étant supposées exister).

Alors, sur presque tous les ω'', on définira une loi asymptotique $P''(\omega'')$ qui sera indépendante de ω'', soit $P''(\omega'') = P$. Naturellement, P différera de la loi temporelle P'' des $\{X_j(t, \omega'')\}$. De toute évidence, P est stationnaire (par construction), alors que P'' ne l'est pas. On montre aussi que, si P'' présente le caractère markovien, en général il n'en sera pas de même de P.

Bibliographie

[1] KAC, M. (1936) Sur les fonctions indépendantes I. *Studia Math.* **6**, 45–58.
— ET STEINHAUS, H. (1936) Sur les fonctions indépendantes II. *Studia Math.* **6**, 59–66.
STEINHAUS, H. (1938) La théorie et les applications des fonctions indépendantes au sens stochastique. *Actualités Sci. Indust.* **738**, 57–73.

[2] WIENER, N. (1930) Generalized harmonic analysis. *Acta Math.* **55**, 117, 258.

[3] BERTRANDIAS, J. P. (1964) *Espaces de fonctions bornées et continues en moyenne asymptotique d'ordre p*. Thèse, Université de Paris.

[4] BLANC-LAPIERRE, A. ET LEFÈVRE, C. (1972) Analyse harmonique généralisée et fonctions aléatoires stationnaires. *C. R. Acad. Sci. Paris Sér. A* **274**, 257–261.

[5] PHAM, P. H. (1968) Fonctions admettant une répartition asymptotique des valeurs. *C. R. Acad. Sci. Paris Sér. A* **267**, 803.

— (1969) Deux théorèmes sur les mesures asymptotiques. *C. R. Acad. Sci. Paris Sér. A* **268**, 448.

— (1972) *Mesures asymptotiques*. Thèse, Université de Paris.

[6] LOEVE, M. (1962) *Probability Theory*. 3ème edition. D. Van Nostrand Company, New York.

[7] BLANC-LAPIERRE, A. ET FORTET, R. (1953) *Théorie des fonctions aléatoires*. Masson et Cie, Paris.

[8] BLANC-LAPIERRE, A. ET LEFÈVRE, C. (1972) Sur quelques propriétés de moments d'ordres supérieurs intervenant dans l'étude de la stabilité de certains systèmes bouclés. *C. R. Acad. Sci. Paris Sér. A* **274**, 1266–1270.

On the Multiplicity of a Stochastic Vector Process

HARALD CRAMÉR

Abstract

This note deals with a q-dimensional stochastic vector process $x(t) = \{x_1(t), \cdots, x_q(t)\}$, satisfying certain stated general conditions. For such a process, there is a representation (1) in terms of stochastic innovations acting throughout the past of the process. The number N of terms in this representation is called the multiplicity of the $x(t)$ process, and is uniquely determined by the process. For a one-dimensional process ($q = 1$) it is known that under certain conditions we have $N = 1$. For an arbitrary value of q, this note gives conditions under which we have $N \leq q$.

1. Introduction

Let $x(t) = \{x_1(t), \cdots, x_q(t)\}$ be a q-dimensional stochastic vector process, where the $x_i(t)$ are real-valued random variables on some fixed probability space, defined in the interval $A \leq t \leq B$. Here A may be finite or $-\infty$, while B may be finite or $+\infty$. All $x_i(t)$ will be supposed to have zero mean values and finite variances. The Hilbert spaces $H(x)$ and $H(x, t)$ are spanned in the customary way by the random variables $x_i(u)$ according to the relations

$$H(x) = S\{x_i(u), \ i = 1, \cdots, q, \ A \leq u \leq B\},$$

$$H(x, t) = S\{x_i(u), \ i = 1, \cdots, q, \ A \leq u \leq t \ \}.$$

We shall suppose that the mean square (m.s.) limits $x_i(t \pm 0)$ exist for all i and t, and that there is always m.s. continuity to the left, so that $x_i(t - 0) = x_i(t)$. The Hilbert space $H(x)$ will then be separable. We shall

187

further suppose that in the case of a finite A we have $x_i(A) = 0$, while if $A = -\infty$ we have $H(x, -\infty) = 0$, so that the $x(t)$ process is purely non-deterministic. For the literature on multiplicity theory, we refer to the recent publication, [1].

If z is any element of $H(x)$, we denote by $z(t)$ the projection of z on the subspace $H(x, t)$. Then $z(t)$ determines a stochastic process with zero mean values and orthogonal increments. By $H(z)$ we denote the cyclic subspace of $H(x)$ spanned by all the $z(t)$. We then have $Ez^2(t) = F(t)$, where $F(t)$ is a non-decreasing function of t in (A, B), which is always continuous to the left, and such that $F(A) = 0$, $F(B) = Ez^2$.

It is then known that there is a number N uniquely defined by the $x(t)$ process and called the *multiplicity* of the process. N may be a finite positive integer or $+\infty$, and has the following properties.

There exists a sequence of random variables $z_1, \cdots, z_N$ in $H(x)$ such that

$$(1) \qquad\qquad x_i(t) = \sum_{n=1}^{N} \int_A^t g_{in}(t, u) dz_n(u)$$

for $i = 1, \cdots, q$ and all t in (A, B). The g_{in} are real-valued non-random functions, and the integrals are m.s. integrals. We have

$$Ex_i^2(t) = \sum_{n=1}^{N} \int_A^t |g_{in}(t,u)|^2 dF_n(u),$$

where $F_n(u) = Ez_n^2(u)$. The cyclic subspaces $H(z_n)$ are mutually orthogonal, and the space $H(x)$ is identical with the vector sum of all the $H(z_n)$, so that we have in the usual Hilbert space notation

$$(2) \qquad\qquad H(x) = H(z_1) \oplus \cdots \oplus H(z_N).$$

Finally, every F_n is absolutely continuous with respect to the preceding F_{n-1}.

The representation (1) shows how the random variables $x_i(t)$ are additively built up by the N-dimensional *innovation elements* $\{dz_1(u), \cdots, dz_N(u)\}$ acting throughout the past of the process, $A \leq u \leq t$. This is a canonical representation of the $x(t)$ process in the sense that any two representations satisfying the above conditions must have the same number N of terms. Moreover, if $F_n^{(1)}$ and $F_n^{(2)}$ are the corresponding functions occurring in the two representations, then $F_n^{(1)}$ and $F_n^{(2)}$ are mutually absolutely continuous for every n.

2. The multiplicity problem

It would be very desirable to be able to determine the multiplicity N of a given $x(t)$ process. This problem is largely unsolved, and the object of the present note is to make a modest contribution to the study of the problem.

For a one-dimensional process ($q = 1$) it is known (cf. [1], p. 319) that, if it is assumed that the functions $g_n(t, u)$ and $F_n(u)$ occurring in a canonical representation (1) of the process satisfy certain simple regularity conditions, the multiplicity of the process will have the simplest possible value $N = 1$.

For the case of a number $q > 1$ of dimensions, it seems obvious that it is only under rather special conditions that we may expect to have a multiplicity $N < q$. It will, however, be proved below that under somewhat more complicated regularity conditions we shall have $N \leq q$. The conclusion seems to be that, in a case where it is only known that our general regularity conditions are satisfied, we should expect to have $N = q$.

For the proof we shall use the following remark (cf. [1], p. 318). Suppose that (1) is a canonical representation of the $x(t)$ process. The Hilbert spaces occurring in the two members of the relation (2) will then be identical. It follows, in particular, that the vector sum of the mutually orthogonal $H(z_n)$ spaces does not contain any element orthogonal to the space $H(x)$. Now any non-zero element of the vector sum of the $H(z_n)$ is a random variable y of the form

$$(3) \qquad y = \sum_{n=1}^{N} \int_{A}^{B} h_n(u)dz_n(u),$$

where

$$(4) \qquad 0 < Ey^2 = \sum_{n=1}^{N} \int_{A}^{B} h_n^2(u)dF_n(u) < \infty.$$

If y is orthogonal to $H(x)$, it will be orthogonal to all $x_i(t)$ for $A \leq t \leq B$, so that

$$(5) \qquad Eyx_i(t) = \sum_{n=1}^{N} \int_{A}^{t} h_n(u)g_{in}(t, u)dF_n(u) = 0$$

for $i = 1, \cdots, q$ and $A \leq t \leq B$. It thus follows that, if we are able to find functions $h_1(u), \cdots, h_N(u)$ satisfying the conditions (3)–(5), the representation (1) cannot be canonical, and we have a contradiction.

3. A lemma on Volterra integral equations

Let $R = \{\alpha_{in}(t)\}$, where $i = 1, \cdots, q$ and $n = 1, \cdots, q + 1$, be a matrix the elements of which are functions of a real variable t defined in the interval (A, B) and having at most a finite number of zeros in (A, B). We shall say that the matrix R satisfies the *condition* Q if the following properties hold:

(1) Any second order minor of the form

$$D_{in} = \alpha_{in}\alpha_{q,q+1} - \alpha_{i,q+1}\alpha_{qn}$$

with $i < q$, $n < q + 1$, has at most a finite number of zeros in (A, B).

(2) The matrix $R^{(1)}$ with elements D_{in}, where $i = 1, \cdots, q - 1$, $n = 1, \cdots, q$, has second order minors of the form

$$D_{in}^{(1)} = D_{in}D_{q-1,q} - D_{iq}D_{q-1,n},$$

with $i < q - 1$, $n < q$, all of which have at most a finite number of zeros in (A, B).

(3) The corresponding properties hold for the matrix $R^{(2)}$ with elements $D_{in}^{(1)}$, where $i = 1, \cdots, q - 2$, $n = 1, \cdots, q - 1$, and so on, until we finally arrive at a matrix with a single row of two elements, each of which has at most a finite number of zeros in (A, B).

It will be seen that the condition Q implies that the elements $\alpha_{in}(t)$ of the matrix R are not related by certain simple algebraic identities.

Consider now a system of q integral equations with $q + 1$ unknown functions

$$(6) \qquad \sum_{n=1}^{q+1} \left[\alpha_{in}(t)\phi_n(t) + \int_A^t \beta_{in}(t, u)\phi_n(u)du \right] = 0$$

where $i = 1, \cdots, q$ and $A \leqq t \leqq B$. The $\phi_n(t)$ are unknown functions, while the $\alpha_{in}(t)$ and $\beta_{in}(t, u)$ are known. We shall suppose that the α_{in} and β_{in} are bounded and continuous in (A, B), that the α_{in} have at most a finite number of zeros in (A, B), and that the matrix $R = \{\alpha_{in}(t)\}$ with q rows and $q + 1$ columns satisfies the condition Q.

Under these conditions it is possible to find functions $\phi_1(t), \cdots, \phi_{q+1}(t)$ *which are bounded in* (A, B), *have at most a finite number of discontinuities and are not all identically zero, so that the system* (6) *is satisfied.*

This lemma will be proved by induction. For $q = 1$ the system (6) reduces to the single equation

(7) $$\sum_{n=1}^{2} \left[\alpha_{1n}(t)\phi_n(t) + \int_A^t \beta_{1n}(t,u)\phi_n(u)du \right] = 0.$$

From the assumptions made with respect to the α_{1n} and β_{1n} it follows that it is possible to find in the interior of (A, B) an interval, say (a, b), such that α_{11} and α_{12} are both bounded away from zero in (a, b). We now take $\phi_1(t) = \phi_2(t) = 0$ outside (a, b), while for $a \leq t \leq b$ we determine ϕ_1 and ϕ_2 from the Volterra integral equations

$$\alpha_{1n}(t)\phi_n(t) + \int_a^t \beta_{1n}(t,u)\phi_n(u)du = (-1)^n$$

for $n = 1$ and 2. According to the classical theory, these equations have solutions which are bounded and continuous in (a, b) and are not identically zero. The functions ϕ_1 and ϕ_2 so determined in (A, B) will satisfy the equation (7), so that the lemma has been proved for $q = 1$.

We now suppose that the lemma has been proved up to the case of a system of $q - 1$ equations with q unknown functions, and consider the system (6) of q equations with $q + 1$ unknown functions. By our assumptions there will be an interval (a, b) inside (A, B) such that all the $\alpha_{in}(t)$, as well as all the minors of the $\{\alpha_{in}(t)\}$ matrix occurring in the conditions of the lemma, will be bounded away from zero in (a, b). The system (6) will be satisfied if we take $\phi_1(t) = \cdots = \phi_{q+1}(t) = 0$ outside (a, b), while for $a \leq t \leq b$ we determine the ϕ_n so as to satisfy the system (6) after replacing the lower limit A of the integral by a. In order to show that this is possible, we write

(8) $$\alpha_{in}(t)\phi_n(t) + \int_a^t \beta_{in}(t,u)\phi_n(u)du = \alpha_{in}(t)\psi_{in}(t),$$

so that the system (6) becomes

(9) $$\sum_{n=1}^{q+1} \alpha_{in}(t)\psi_{in}(t) = 0$$

for $i = 1, \cdots, q$. We then have to show that the $\psi_{in}(t)$ can be determined for $a \leq t \leq b$ so that the equations (9) will be satisfied.

Regarding (8) as a Volterra integral equation with $\phi_n(t)$ as the unknown function, we have the solution

$$\phi_n(t) = \psi_{in}(t) + \int_a^t K_{in}(t,u)\psi_{in}(u)du,$$

where $K_{in}(t, u)$ is the resolvent corresponding to the kernel

$$J_{in}(t,u) = -\beta_{in}(t,u)/\alpha_{in}(t).$$

J_{in} and K_{in} are both bounded and continuous for $a \leq u \leq t \leq b$. We thus obtain

(10)
$$\psi_{in}(t) + \int_a^t K_{in}(t, u)\psi_{in}(u)du = \phi_n(t)$$
$$= \psi_{qn}(t) + \int_a^t K_{qn}(t, u)\psi_{qn}(u)du$$

for $i = 1, \cdots, q - 1$ and $n = 1, \cdots, q + 1$. Now regarding this as an integral equation with the unknown function $\psi_{in}(t)$, we obtain after some calculation the following solution expressing ψ_{in} in terms of ψ_{qn}

$$\psi_{in}(t) = \psi_{qn}(t) + \int_a^t L_{in}(t, u)\psi_{qn}(u)du$$

with

$$L_{in}(t, u) = K_{qn}(t, u) - J_{in}(t, u) - \int_u^t J_{in}(t, s)K_{qn}(s, u)ds.$$

L_{in} is bounded and continuous for $a \leq u \leq t \leq b$.

The system (9) is then equivalent to

(9a)
$$\sum_{n=1}^{q+1} \alpha_{in}(t) \left[\psi_{qn}(t) + \int_a^t L_{in}(t, u)\psi_{qn}(u)du \right] = 0$$

for $i = 1, \cdots, q - 1$, and

(9b)
$$\sum_{n=1}^{q+1} \alpha_{qn}(t)\psi_{qn}(t) = 0.$$

Solving (9b) with respect to $\psi_{q,q+1}$ and inserting the solution in (9a), we have

(11)
$$\sum_{n=1}^{q} \left[D_{in}(t)\psi_{qn}(t) + \int_a^t M_{in}(t, u)\psi_{qn}(u)du \right] = 0$$

for $i = 1, \cdots, q - 1$, with

$$D_{in}(t) = \alpha_{in}(t)\alpha_{q,q+1}(t) - \alpha_{i,q+1}(t)\alpha_{q,n}(t),$$

and a $M_{in}(t, u)$ which is bounded and continuous for $a \leq u \leq t \leq b$, while by hypothesis, $D_{in}(t)$ is continuous and bounded away from zero in (a, b).

Thus (11) constitutes a system of $q - 1$ equations for the q unknown functions $\psi_{qn}(t)$ with $n = 1, \cdots, q$. The system (10) is of the same form as (6), and by hypothesis has a solution with the desired properties. As has been shown, the ψ_{qn} will determine all the ψ_{in} so as to satisfy (9). By (8) and (10), the corresponding ϕ_n will form a solution of the system (6). This completes the proof of the lemma.

4. A theorem on multiplicity

Let $x(t) = (x_1(t), \cdots, x_q(t))$ be a q-dimensional stochastic vector process of the kind specified in the Introduction. Suppose that $x(t)$ has a canonical representation of the form (1), such that the following regularity conditions are satisfied:

(R_1) The $g_{in}(t, u)$ and $\partial g_{in}(t, u)/\partial t$ are bounded and continuous for $A \leqq u \leqq t \leqq B$.

(R_2) If $N > q$, the matrix $\{g_{in}(t, t)\}$ of order $q \cdot N$ contains at least one submatrix of order $q \cdot (q + 1)$ satisfying the condition Q in (A, B).

(R_3) The functions $F_n(u)$ defined in the Introduction are absolutely continuous, with derivatives $f_n(u) = F_n'(u)$ having at most a finite number of discontinuities in (A, B).

Then the multiplicity N of the $x(t)$ process is at most equal to q.

Suppose, in fact, that we have a canonical representation of the form (1) with $N > q$. In order to prove that this is not possible, we have to show that functions $h_n(u)$ satisfying (3)–(5) can be found. By hypothesis, (5) can be differentiated and yields a system of equations

$$(12) \qquad \sum_{n=1}^{N} \left[g_{in}(t, t) h_n(t) f_n(t) + \int_A^t \frac{\partial g_{in}}{\partial t} h_n(u) f_n(u) du \right] = 0.$$

Without restricting the generality we may evidently assume that the matrix of the 'instantaneous response functions' $g_{in}(t, t)$ occurring in condition (R_2) consists of the $g_{in}(t, t)$ with $i = 1, \cdots, q$ and $n = 1, \cdots, q + 1$. Then there must be an interval, say (a, b), in the interior of (A, B) such that the $f_n(t)$ and all the minors of the $g_{in}(t, t)$ matrix occurring in condition Q are bounded away from zero in (a, b). If $N > q + 1$, we then take $h_n(t) = 0$ for all t and $n > q + 1$, while for $n \leqq q + 1$, we take $h_n(t) = 0$ outside (a, b). The system (12) then reduces to a system of equations of the form (6), satisfying conditions corresponding to those stated in Section 3. It thus follows that $h_n(u)$ can be determined so as to satisfy the relations (3)–(5). Consequently our assumption $N > q$ must be false, and we have $N \leqq q$, as was to be proved.

Reference

[1] EPHREMIDES, A. AND THOMAS, J. B. (Editors) (1973) *Random Processes, Multiplicity Theory and Canonical Decompositions.* Dawden, Hutchinson and Ross. Distributed by Wiley, London.

Rumination on Infinite Markov Systems

J. M. HAMMERSLEY

Abstract

Recent work by Moussouris [10] has clarified our present knowledge of finite Markov fields. The present note examines, in a loose and general fashion, whether one can extend the treatment to infinite fields.

1. Introduction

A volume in honour of Maurice Bartlett should contain something on Markov systems because he has contributed so much to our knowledge of interacting phenomena. References [1] to [4] represent a selection of his work on spatial interaction. There is a sharp distinction between one-dimensional interaction (Markov chains and processes) and spatial interaction in several dimensions (Markov fields). The latter are mathematically more formidable and have received much less attention from probabilists. Most of the progress has hitherto come from the physicists, starting from Willard Gibbs on statistical mechanics around 1900. However, within the last decade a number of probabilists (see [5] for a bibliography) have shown that there is a formal equivalence between Gibbsian ensembles and Markov fields on a finite space *provided* that all probabilities are assumed strictly positive. This assumption simplified the mathematics (indeed that was exactly its pure mathematical *raison d'être*) but it robbed the theory of a good deal of its applicability because many of the interesting physical situations involve constraints and entail zero probabilities. Thus it was a welcome breakthrough when Moussouris [10] first managed to handle zero probabilities in a Markov field on an arbitrary finite graph, thus producing examples of fields which were *not* representable in terms of Gibbsian potentials.

The present position, then, is that we are beginning to understand finite Markov fields (i.e., ones on a finite space); but our knowledge of infinite Markov fields (i.e., ones on an infinite space) is largely undeveloped. In the present paper I shall try to formulate the general problem of infinite Markov fields. This formulation is tentative, and may well require recasting or adjustment before it can become a satisfactory basis for the analysis or classification of fields. So it is best to describe this paper as a mere rumination and nothing more.

2. Infinite Markov fields

We consider an arbitrary set Z composed of elements z called *sites*. Each site z carries an *elementary state* from a given *repertoire* Ω_z. Given any subset $A \subseteq Z$, we write $\Omega_A = \Pi_{z \in A} \Omega_z$ for the Cartesian product of the repertoires of the sites in A. A list of elementary states $\alpha \in \Omega_A$ is called a *substate with domain* A, and a complete list $\omega \in \Omega_Z$ is called a *state* of the whole system. In effect the substate α is the restriction to the subset A of some state ω. We use lower case Greek letters $\alpha, \beta, \gamma, \cdots$ for substates and the corresponding upper case Roman letters $A, B, C, \cdots$ for their domains. Different substates on the same domain A can be distinguished by $\alpha, \alpha', $ etc. When Z is partitioned into disjoint subsets A, $B, C, \cdots$ we write $\omega = \alpha\beta\gamma \cdots$ for the state which agrees with α on A, with β on B, etc. The states and substates constitute the possible events of our theory; and, just as in the theory of probability we run into pathological difficulties unless we restrict attention to some subclass of events (say 'measurable events'), so here we shall need to restrict ω to some specified subset Ω of Ω_Z. Clearly, we want to make Ω as comprehensive as we can, subject to the tractability of the resulting theory; but we leave open the question of just how this is to be done. Similarly, we should restrict the domains to some specified class J. We shall suppose that J is an algebra:

(i) $A \in J, B \in J$ imply $A + B \in J$,

(ii) $A \in J$ implies $Z - A \in J$.

Here and later we use the following notation: given two subsets A and B, we write $A + B$ for their union, AB for their intersection, $A - B$ for all elements of A not in B; and 0 denotes the empty set.

We also suppose that we are given a prescribed symmetric hereditary subclass Δ of disjoint pairs in $J \times J$: thus

(iii) $(A, B) \in \Delta$ implies $A \in J$, $B \in J$, $AB = 0$,

(iv) $(A, B) \in \Delta$ implies $(B, A) \in \Delta$,

(v) $(A, B) \in \Delta$, $A \supseteq C \in J$ imply $(C, B) \in \Delta$.

If $(A, B) \in \Delta$, we say that A and B are *detached* domains. Otherwise, two domains are attached when not detached. As an illustration of these definitions, we could take Z to be the Euclidean plane, J for its Borel subsets, and we could say that two Borel subsets were detached if and only if every point of one were more than unit distance away from every point of the other.

Given any pair $(A, B) \in \Delta$, we define $S = Z - (A + B)$ to be the *separator* of A and B. Let $\alpha \sigma \beta$ and $\alpha' \sigma \beta'$ be two states which agree on S. These two states generate two *cross-over states*, namely $\alpha \sigma \beta'$ and $\alpha' \sigma \beta$. We postulate that, if $\alpha \sigma \beta$ and $\alpha' \sigma \beta'$ both belong to Ω for any detached pair $(A, B) \in \Delta$, then their two cross-over states also belong to Ω.

Next we introduce the *probability* of a state, written $P(\omega)$. We tacitly suppose that such a probability is a non-negative real number; but otherwise place no restrictions on it.(In applications it might,for example, be a likelihood ratio, or a relative probability, etc.) We can now formulate a *Markov field* as any quintuple $(Z, J, \Delta, \Omega, P)$ such that the *Markov condition*

(1) $$P(\alpha \sigma \beta)P(\alpha' \sigma \beta') = P(\alpha \sigma \beta')P(\alpha' \sigma \beta)$$

holds for all detached pairs $(A, B) \in \Delta$ and all pairs of states $\alpha \sigma \beta$, $\alpha' \sigma \beta'$ which belong to Ω and agree on the separator of A and B. We write $[Z, J, \Delta, \Omega]$ for the family of all non-negative real solutions $P(\cdot)$ of (1). The *Markov problem* is to determine and classify $[Z, J, \Delta, \Omega]$ in terms of its four arguments.

3. The Markov problem

It is clear that $[Z, J, \Delta_1, \Omega] \subseteq [Z, J, \Delta_2, \Omega]$ whenever $\Delta_1 \supseteq \Delta_2$. Thus the simplest possible case of the Markov problem will arise when Δ is as large as possible, namely $\Delta = \Delta_0$, where Δ_0 is simply the class of disjoint pairs in $J \times J$. Even this simplest case can be quite elaborate. For example, consider the special case when there are just two available elementary states at each site $z = Z$, a passive elementary state and an active elementary state. Then we can specify any state $\omega \in \Omega$ by specifying the subset L consisting of all sites with active elementary states; and P will be a set function of L, say $P(\omega) = Q(L)$. Then (1) becomes

(2) $Q(M + N)Q(MN) = Q(M)Q(N)$

for all $M, N \in J$; and a possible solution of (2) is

(3) $Q(M) = ce^{\mu(M)}$

where $\mu(M)$ is any signed measure on J and c is a constant. More generally, if we do not confine ourselves to Δ_0, we find that (2) holds subject to the condition $(M - N, N - M) \in \Delta$. So a possible solution of the illustration given above (the Borel subset of the plane, detached when more than unit distance apart) would be

(4) $$Q(M) = c \exp \int \int_{x \in M, |x - y| \leq 1/2} \mu(dx, dy)$$

where $\mu(\cdot, \cdot)$ is a signed measure on $Z \times Z$. This is far from being the only possible type of solution: for instance, there are similar solutions involving triple or higher integrals.

In the finite case, a distinguished role is played by the *active clans* of the system. A clan K is defined to be a subset $K \in J$ such that K does not contain any pair of non-empty detached subsets: that is to say, the conditions

(5) $0 \neq A \subseteq K, 0 \neq B \subseteq K, (A, B) \in \Delta$

are incompatible. To define the notion of *activity*, we choose a particular reference state $o \in \Omega$ called the *passive state*. We use the same symbol o for substates of o, relying on the context to reveal the domain of the substate. As a special case of (1) we obtain

(6) $P(\alpha\sigma\beta)P(o\sigma o) = P(\alpha\sigma o)P(o\sigma\beta)$.

If it should happen that $P(o\sigma o) > 0$, then (6) is actually equivalent to (1). We say that a clan K is *active with respect to a state* ω if ω disagrees with o throughout K. In the finite case, it (usually) turns out that the solutions of the Markov problem have the form that $\log P(\omega)$ is an arbitrary linear functional on the space of clans which are active with respect to ω. (The qualification 'usually' is required to deal with situations in which $P(\omega)$ may be zero and so has no logarithm.) By analogy, we might expect something similar in the infinite case; and we might hope to classify the solutions with the help of linear functionals, Daniell integrals, and that sort of thing (perhaps with appeals to the Hahn-Banach extension theorem). However, the space of all active clans in the infinite case is uninvitingly large: at least it frightens me off, and I fancy that a more profitable plan of campaign would be to approach the infinite case via an increasing sequence of finite algebras $J_1, J_2, \cdots$ converging to J.

4. Approach through finite algebras

Thus consider the finite algebras

(7) $J_1 \subseteq J_2 \subseteq \cdots$ such that $J_n \to J$

with associated finite state spaces and detachment classes

$$\Omega_1 \subseteq \Omega_2 \subseteq \cdots \text{ such that } \Omega_n \to \Omega,$$
(8)
$$\Delta_1 \subseteq \Delta_2 \subseteq \cdots \text{ such that } \Delta_n \to \Delta.$$

The solution set $[Z, J_n, \Delta_n, \Omega_n]$ is now the solution set of a finite Markov system, and so is expressible in terms of linear functionals on the active clans. We should like to have

(9) $[Z, J_n, \Delta_n, \Omega_n] \to [Z, J, \Delta, \Omega].$

Can we define convergence suitably in (7), (8), (9) to make this true? This seems to me to be a more promising line of attack than the alternative method via Möbius inversion [11], where we might find it constricting to have to work throughout with *locally finite* partial orderings.

The foregoing approach also seems closer to the physical realities of applications of the theory. The extent to which physical systems are not discrete or finite is largely a philosophical question. We cannot, for example, envisage any experiment to test whether or not space-time is a continuum. A large but finite set of rational numbers suffices for the quantitative description of Nature; and many fundamental concepts, such as the structure of matter, are particulate. We only introduce infinity into the theory in the hope of spotting asymptotic simplicity; so it is self-defeating to introduce it in such a way that it generates some pathological measure-theoretic jungle. The main reason for infinite spaces in statistical mechanics is the study of phase changes: for phase changes do not arise in finite systems. The way in which they arise in Nature is through the presence of long-range order transmitted from distant boundaries. It is therefore natural to construct the sequence of algebras $\{J_n\}$ in such a way that the domain which contains the remote horizons of Z retreats to infinity as $n \to \infty$. And we can certainly arrange that.

In conclusion we remark on the difficulties encountered by Lévy [6], [7], [8] and Moran [9] in their formulation of Markov fields. Their source of trouble arose from attempts to use separators S which were merely surfaces having no thickness. That trouble would evaporate in a Euclidean space Z if J_n were generated by a finite number of disjoint *non-degenerate* intervals.

References

[1] BARTLETT, M. S. (1968) A further note on nearest-neighbour models. *J. R. Statist. Soc.* A **131**, 579–580.

[2] BARTLETT, M. S. (1971) Physical nearest-neighbour models and non-linear time series. *J. Appl. Prob.* **8**, 222–232.

[3] BARTLETT, M. S. (1971) Two-dimensional nearest-neighbour systems and their ecological applications. *Statistical Ecology* **1**, 179–194.

[4] BARTLETT, M. S. (1974) The statistical analysis of spatial pattern. *Adv. Appl. Prob.* **6**, 336–358.

[5] BESAG, J. E. (1974) Spatial interaction and the statistical analysis of lattice systems. *J. R. Statist. Soc.* B. **36**, 192–236.

[6] LÉVY, P. (1948) Chaînes doubles de Markoff et fonctions aléatoires de deux variables. *C. R. Acad. Sci. Paris* **226**, 53–55.

[7] LÉVY, P. (1948) Exemples de processus doubles de Markoff. *C. R. Acad. Sci. Paris* **226**, 307–308.

[8] LÉVY, P. (1949) Processus doubles de Markoff. *Colloques Internat. du Centre National de la Recherche Scientifique, Paris* **13**, 53–59.

[9] MORAN, P. A. P. (1973) A Gaussian-Markovian process on a square lattice. *J. Appl. Prob.* **10**, 54–62.

[10] MOUSSOURIS, J. (1974) Gibbs and Markov random systems with constraints. *J. Statist. Phys.* **10**, 11–33.

[11] ROTA, G. C. (1964) On the foundations of combinatorial theory. *Z. Wahrscheinlichkeitsth.* **2**, 340–368.

Anticipation Processes

J. F. C. KINGMAN

Abstract

An anticipation process is a continuous-time Markov process, having an element of deterministic drift in its transition structure. The theory of such processes, developed here from an elementary (Chapman-Kolmogorov) point of view, draws together a number of threads of theoretical and applied probability.

1. Definition and examples

An *anticipation process* on a set I is a bivariate stochastic process

$$(1.1) \qquad \mathscr{X}(t) = (X(t), \xi(t)), \qquad (t \geq 0),$$

where $X(t)$ takes its values in the positive[1] half-line $R^+ = [0, \infty)$ and $\xi(t)$ takes its values in I, such that $\mathscr{X}$ is a Markov process (with stationary transition probabilities, and perhaps with finite lifetime) on the space $\mathscr{I} = R^+ \times I$, and such that

$$(1.2) \qquad \mathscr{X}(0) = (x, i) \Rightarrow \mathscr{X}(t) = (x - t, i) \quad \text{for } 0 < t \leq x.$$

Although parts of the theory may be developed for quite general sets I (and the beginnings of such a general account from a quite different point of view may be found in [16] and [17]) the most important case is that in which I is finite. Throughout this paper, therefore, it will be supposed that, for some integer $N \geq 1$,

$$(1.3) \qquad I = \{1, 2, \cdots, N\}.$$

---

[1] Words like 'positive' and 'increasing' are here used in the weak sense unless qualified by the adverb 'strictly'.

Thus the state space $\mathcal{S}$ consists of N copies of the half-line R^+, and (1.2) requires that $\mathcal{X}$ should drift at constant rate towards the origin of the half-line on which it finds itself, only jumping to a different half-line on reaching the origin. Anticipation processes arise in a number of different contexts, and the following general examples will illustrate the scope of the theory.

Example 1. If Y is a right-continuous strong Markov process on an arbitrary state space, and $H = \{y_1, y_2, \cdots, y_N\}$ any finite set of states, define

(1.4) $X(t) = \inf\{x \geqq 0; Y(t + x) \in H\}$,

so that there is a unique $\xi(t) \in I$ with

(1.5) $y_{\xi(t)} = Y[t + X(t)]$.

Then $\mathcal{X} = (X, \xi)$ is a Markov process which manifestly satisfies (1.2). Notice that $Y(t) = y_j$ if and only if $\mathcal{X}(t) = (0, j)$, so that the process $\mathcal{X}$ summarises the random sets $\{t; Y(t) = y_j\}$ for $j = 1, 2, \cdots, N$.

When $N = 1$ this construction is a familiar one, and anticipation processes with $N = 1$ (sometimes called 'semilinear') form the basis of the theory of Markov random sets ([14], [8], [9]). Their structure relates them closely with the theory of subordinators ([22]). In one sense the present analysis merely generalises the known theory to higher values of N.

Example 2. A *semi-Markov process* ([15], [21], [19], [20], [7]) on I is a process $Z(t)$ which takes the values in I in random order according to a Markov chain, but has a sojourn time in each state of I which, given the chain, is independent of all other sojourn times, and has a distribution depending on the state and its successor. If $t + X(t)$ is the instant of the next jump of Z after time t, and $\xi(t) = Z(t)$, then $\mathcal{X} = (X, \xi)$ is an anticipation process. Notice that, since $Z(t)$ is a function of $\mathcal{X}(t)$, no information is lost in passing from Z to $\mathcal{X}$.

Example 3. Some aspects of Chung's *boundary theory* for continuous-time Markov chains ([2], [3], [4]) are most naturally viewed in terms of anticipation processes. If a continuous-time Markov chain has a finite exit boundary $\{a_1, a_2, \cdots, a_N\}$, and if $t + X(t)$ is the first infinity of the chain after t, then this infinity is associated with exactly one of the boundary points $a_{\xi(t)}$. Chung shows that $\mathcal{X} = (X, \xi)$ is a Markov process, and (1.2) clearly holds. Thus the movement of the chain between its boundary points may be described by the anticipation process $\mathcal{X}$.

Example 4. The concept of a *subordinator* (a process with positive, stationary, independent increments) has been generalised by Neveu, who in an important paper ([18]) has considered Markov processes $\mathscr{Y}(t) = (Y(t), \eta(t))$ with state space $R \times I$ such that Y is increasing, and such that the transition function of $\mathscr{Y}$ is invariant under the shift $(y, i) \to (y + c, i)$ for any real c. He has shown that any such process may be described as follows: η follows a continuous-time Markov chain on I, conditional on which Y is a subordinator on each interval of constancy of η, and when η jumps from one state in I to another, Y also jumps by an amount whose distribution depends on the two states.

If $\mathscr{Y}$ is such a process, and is right-continuous, then

(1.6) $\qquad X(t) = \inf \{x \geqq 0; Y(s) = t + x \text{ for some } s\}, \quad \xi(t) = \eta(s),$

may be shown to define an anticipation process. When $N = 1$ it is the familiar *inverse local time process* ([1], [12]). One of the consequences of the present theory is that every anticipation process can be realised by (1.6) in terms of an appropriate Neveu process.

Example 5. A *quasi-Markov chain* ([10], [11]) is a process $Z(t)$ taking values in $\{0, 1, 2, \cdots, N\}$, which has the Markov property with respect to each of the states except perhaps 0. If Z is standard and right-continuous, then

$$X(t) = \inf \{x \geqq 0; Z(t + x) \neq 0\},$$

(1.7)

$$\xi(t) = Z[t + X(t)]$$

defines an anticipation process, and once more no information is lost in passing from Z to $\mathscr{X} = (X, \xi)$.

If in Example 1 the states y_j are all *heavy* (in the sense ([12]) that $Y(t) = y_j$ for a set of values of t having positive Lebesgue measure) a quasi-Markov chain can be defined by

$$Z(t) = j \quad \text{if} \quad Y(t) = y_j \qquad (j \in I)$$

(1.8)

$$= 0 \quad \text{otherwise.}$$

Then it is clear that (1.4) and (1.5) define the same anticipation process as does (1.7). In a sense the construction of Example 1 extends the technique, used in [10] for the study of finite sets of states in Markov chains, to more general situations where the process (1.8) may be trivial.

2. The fundamental integral equation and its solution

Suppose that $\mathscr{X}$ is an anticipation process on the finite set I. Since $\mathscr{X}$ is a Markov process with stationary transition probabilities, its stochastic structure (for given initial conditions) is described by its transition function[2]

(2.1) $\Pr\{\mathscr{X}(t)\in B\,|\,\mathscr{X}(0)=(x,i)\}$

for $t>0$, $x\geqq 0$, $i\in I$, $B\subseteq\mathscr{I}$. Because of (1.2) and the Markov property, this probability equals

$$\langle(x-t,i)\in B\rangle$$

when $t\leqq x$, and

$$\Pr\{\mathscr{X}(t-x)\in B\,|\,\mathscr{X}(0)=(0,i)\}$$

when $t>x$, so that (2.1) need only be specified when $x=0$. Hence the transition function of $\mathscr{X}$ is determined by the measures

(2.2) $P_{ij}(t,\cdot)\qquad(i,j\in I,t>0)$

defined on the Borel subsets A of R^+ by

(2.3) $P_{ij}(t,A)=\Pr\{X(t)\in A,\xi(t)=j\,|\,X(0)=0,\ \xi(0)=i\}.$

It is convenient to assemble these into a matrix

(2.4) $\boldsymbol{P}(t,A)=(P_{ij}(t,A);\ i,j=1,2,\cdots,N)$

which then summarises in a compact form the transition structure of $\mathscr{X}$.

The transition function (2.1) must of course satisfy the Chapman-Kolmogorov equation, and in particular, for $s,t>0$, $i,j\in I$, $A\subseteq R^+$,

$$P_{ij}(s+t,A)=\Pr\{X(s+t)\in A,\ \xi(s+t)=j\,|\,X(0)=0,\ \xi(0)=i\}$$

$$=\int_{R^+}\sum_{k=1}^{N}\Pr\{X(s)\in dy,\xi(s)=k\,|\,X(0)=0,\xi(0)=i\}$$

$$\times\Pr\{X(t)\in A,\xi(t)=j\,|\,X(0)=y,\ \xi(0)=k\}$$

$$=\int_{[0,t)}\sum_{k=1}^{N}P_{ik}(s,dy)\,P_{kj}(t-y,A)+P_{ij}(s,t+A),$$

---

[2]   Since the old-fashioned boldface notation will be needed for matrices and vectors, 'Pr' will denote probability. For any proposition $\mathscr{P}$, $\langle\mathscr{P}\rangle$ means 1 if $\mathscr{P}$ is true and 0 if $\mathscr{P}$ is false.

where $t + A = \{t + x ; x \in A\}$. Hence the function $P = P(\cdot, \cdot)$ must satisfy the integral equation

$$(2.5) \qquad P(s + t, A) = \int_{[0,t)} P(s, dy)P(t - y, A) + P(s, t + A).$$

To solve this equation, consider the Laplace-Stieltjes transform

$$(2.6) \qquad Q(t, \theta) = \int_{R^+} e^{-\theta x} P(t, dx),$$

which exists for all $\theta \geqq 0$ and, by (2.5), satisfies

$$Q(s + t, \theta) = \int_{[0,t)} P(s, dy) \, Q(t - y, \theta)$$

$$(2.7)$$

$$+ \int_{[t,\infty)} P(s, dy) e^{-\theta(y-t)}.$$

Writing

$$(2.8) \qquad R(\alpha, \theta) = \int_0^\infty e^{-\alpha t} \, Q(t, \theta) dt \qquad (\alpha > 0),$$

(2.7) shows that, for $\theta \geqq 0$, $\alpha, \beta > 0$, $\alpha \neq \beta \neq \theta$,

$$[R(\alpha, \theta) - R(\beta, \theta)]/(\beta - \alpha) = R(\alpha, \beta) \, R(\beta, \theta)$$
$$+ [R(\alpha, \beta) - R(\alpha, \theta)]/(\theta - \beta)$$

which can be cast into the form

$$(2.9) \quad I + (\theta - \alpha)R(\alpha, \theta) = \{I + (\beta - \alpha)R(\alpha, \beta)\} \, \{I + (\theta - \beta)R(\beta, \theta)\},$$

where I is the identity matrix of order N. By continuity, (2.9) holds for all $\theta \geqq 0$, $\alpha, \beta > 0$. If we write

$$(2.10) \qquad S(\beta) = I + (\beta - 1)R(1, \beta) \qquad (\beta \geqq 0),$$

then $\alpha = \theta = 1$ in (2.9) gives

$$I = S(\beta) \, \{I + (1 - \beta) \, R(\beta, 1)\}$$

when $\beta > 0$. Hence $S(\beta)$ is invertible for $\beta > 0$, with

$$(2.11) \qquad S(\beta)^{-1} = I + (1 - \beta)R(\beta, 1).$$

Now set $\theta = 1$ in (2.9) to obtain

$$S(\alpha)^{-1} = \{I + (\beta - \alpha) R(\alpha, \beta)\} S(\beta)^{-1},$$

whence

$$R(\alpha, \beta) = \int_0^\infty \int_{R^+} e^{-\alpha t - \beta x} P(t, dx) dt$$

(2.12)

$$= S(\alpha)^{-1}[S(\beta) - S(\alpha)]/(\beta - \alpha).$$

Hence we have proved the existence of the continuous matrix-valued function $S(\beta)$ in $\beta \geq 0$, which is invertible in $\beta > 0$, and satisfies the equation (2.12) for $\alpha > 0$ and $\beta \geq 0$. Since the double Laplace transform may be inverted uniquely (subject to an 'almost everywhere' qualification which may easily be removed using (2.7)) the structure of the Markov process $\mathscr{X}$ is determined by this function alone.

The converse is not quite true, since the right-hand side of (2.12) is unchanged if $S(\cdot)$ is replaced by $KS(\cdot)$ for any constant invertible matrix K. This, however, is the only ambiguity, since (2.12) determines $S(\alpha)^{-1}S(\beta)$ in terms of P for any $\alpha, \beta > 0$. We shall see in the next section that K may be chosen so that KS has certain desirable properties.

Suppose therefore that S is any function (not necessarily the one defined by (2.10)) which satisfies (2.12) for a given P. Repeated differentiation of (2.12) gives

$$S(\alpha)^{-1}\left\{\left(-\frac{\partial}{\partial\beta}\right)^n \frac{S(\beta) - S(\alpha)}{\beta - \alpha}\right\} = \int_0^\infty \int_{R^+} x^n e^{-\alpha t - \beta x} P(t, dx) \geq 0,$$

where inequalities between matrices (and vectors) are to be interpreted element by element. Expanding the left-hand side by Leibniz's formula, and letting $\beta \to \alpha$, we obtain

(2.13) $(-1)^n S(\alpha)^{-1} S^{(n+1)}(\alpha) \geq 0$ $(n \geq 0, \alpha > 0),$

(cf. [12], page 80). Hence, for $\alpha \geq \delta > 0$,

$$\left(-\frac{\partial}{\partial\alpha}\right)^n S(\delta)^{-1} S'(\alpha)$$

$$= \{I + (\alpha - \delta) R(\delta, \alpha)\} \{(-1)^n S(\alpha)^{-1} S^{(n+1)}(\alpha)\} \geq 0,$$

since $R \geq 0$. Thus each of the elements of the matrix

$$S(\delta)^{-1} S'(\cdot)$$

is a completely monotonic function in $[\delta, \infty)$. Bernstein's theorem therefore implies the existence of a positive matrix-valued measure σ_δ on R^+ such that

$$S(\delta)^{-1}S(\alpha) = \int_{R^+} e^{-\alpha x}\sigma_\delta(dx)$$

for all $\alpha \geqq \delta$. Integrating from $\alpha = \delta$ to $\alpha = \theta$, we have for $\theta \geqq \delta$,

$$(2.14) \qquad S(\theta) = S(\delta)\left\{I + (\theta - \delta)\sigma_\delta + \int_{(0,\infty)}(e^{-\delta x} - e^{-\theta x})\rho_\delta(dx)\right\},$$

where $\sigma_\delta = \sigma_\delta\{0\}$ and $\rho_\delta(dx) = x^{-1}\sigma_\delta(dx)$.

In (2.14) substitute successively $\delta = \alpha$ and $\delta = \beta$, and compare the resulting expressions for $S(\theta)$ ($\theta \geqq \max(\alpha, \beta)$). The unique inversion of the Laplace-Stieltjes transform then yields

$$(2.15) \qquad S(\alpha)\sigma_\alpha = S(\beta)\sigma_\beta, \ \ S(\alpha)\rho_\alpha(\cdot) = S(\beta)\rho_\beta(\cdot),$$

and

$$S(\beta) = S(\alpha)\left\{I + (\beta - \alpha)\sigma_\alpha + \int_{(0,\infty)}(e^{-\alpha x} - e^{-\beta x})\rho_\alpha(dx)\right\}$$

in $\alpha, \beta > 0$. Letting $\beta \to 0$,

$$S(0) = S(\alpha)\left\{I - \alpha\sigma_\alpha - \int_{(0,\infty)}(1 - e^{-\alpha x})\rho_\alpha(dx)\right\}.$$

Hence, if the constant matrix C and the matrix-valued measure μ are defined (unambiguously because of (2.15)) by

$$(2.16) \qquad C = S(\alpha)\sigma_\alpha, \ \ \mu(\cdot) = S(\alpha)\rho_\alpha(\cdot),$$

then

$$(2.17) \qquad S(\alpha) = S(0) + C\alpha + \int_{(0,\infty)}(1 - e^{-\alpha x})\mu(dx)$$

for all $\alpha \geqq 0$. Moreover, since $\sigma_\alpha(\cdot) \geqq 0$, we have

$$(2.18) \qquad S(\alpha)^{-1}C \geqq 0, \ \ S(\alpha)^{-1}\mu(\cdot) \geqq 0$$

for all $\alpha > 0$.

3. Properties of the function S

The conditions which (2.18) imposes on C and μ are inconveniently non-linear, since $S(\alpha)$ depends through (2.17) on C and μ, and this non-linearity is inherent in the fact that P determines S only up to constant left multiples. Both the non-linearity and, up to a point, the non-uniqueness, can be removed.

Consider the subset Δ_α of R^N defined for $\alpha > 0$ by

(3.1) $$\Delta_\alpha = \{x \in R^N ; S(\alpha)^{-1}x \geqq 0\}.$$

Thus Δ_α is the proper simplicial cone[3] spanned by the columns of the invertible matrix $S(\alpha)$. Moreover, if $\alpha < \beta$ and $x \geqq \Delta_\beta$, then

$$S(\alpha)^{-1}x = \{I + (\beta - \alpha) R(\alpha, \beta)\} S(\beta)^{-1}x \geqq 0,$$

so that $x \in \Delta_\alpha$. Hence

(3.2) $$\Delta_\alpha \supseteq \Delta_\beta \qquad (\alpha < \beta),$$

and it follows[4] that the intersection

(3.3) $$\Delta = \bigcap_{\alpha > 0} \Delta_\alpha = \{x \in R^N ; S(\alpha)^{-1}x \geqq 0 \text{ for all } \alpha > 0\}$$

is a simplicial cone.

There is the possibility that Δ might not be proper, which since $\Delta \subseteq \Delta_\alpha$ can only occur if Δ lies in a proper subspace of R^N. If this is so, there is a non-zero row vector γ with $\gamma x = 0$ for all $x \in \Delta$. In particular, since (2.18) implies that the columns of C and of $\mu(A)$ $(A \subseteq R^+)$ lie in Δ, we have $\gamma C = \gamma \mu(A) = 0$, and (2.17) then gives

$$\gamma S(\alpha) = c \qquad (\alpha > 0),$$

where $c = \gamma S(0)$. Since $S(\alpha)$ is non-singular, $c \neq 0$, and

---

[3] A *cone* is a subset $\mathscr{C}$ with $\alpha x + \beta y \in \mathscr{C}$ whenever $\alpha, \beta \geqq 0$, $x, y \in \mathscr{C}$, and it is proper if it is contained in no proper subspace, and if $x \in \mathscr{C}$, $-x \in \mathscr{C}$ implies $x = 0$. The cone $\mathscr{C}$ is *simplicial* if it is spanned by (is the smallest cone containing) a linearly independent set. Thus a proper simplicial cone is the cone spanned by the elements of a basis of R^N, and is exactly the set of points whose coordinates with respect to that basis are all positive.

[4] The clearest statement of this theorem, and of the extension of it which is needed later to prove (3.5), is to be found in the paper of Edwards [6]. The result is however inherent in the earlier literature; it follows for instance from Theorems 13 and 14 of [5]. I am greatly indebted to Dr. Edwards for discussion of this point.

$$cR(\alpha, \beta) = cS(\alpha)^{-1}[S(\beta) - S(\alpha)]/(\beta - \alpha)$$

$$= [\gamma S(\beta) - \gamma S(\alpha)]/(\beta - \alpha)$$

$$= 0.$$

Inverting the Laplace transforms, we have

(3.4) $$\sum_{i=1}^{N} c_i P_{ij}(t, A) = 0$$

for all j, t, A. This is clearly a degenerate situation, which will not be pursued further.

Suppose therefore that (3.4) does not hold for any constants c_i which are not all zero. Then Δ is a proper simplicial cone, and ([6]) the extreme rays of Δ_α can be labelled and normalised so that they converge to the extreme rays of Δ. The extreme rays of Δ_α are represented by the columns of $S(\alpha)$, and continuity in α requires that the labelling should ultimately be a fixed permutation of the order of the columns. Hence there are functions $s_j(\alpha)$ such that the limits

(3.5) $$\xi_{ij} = \lim_{\alpha \to \infty} S_{ij}(\alpha)/s_j(\alpha)$$

exist, and such that the vectors

(3.6) $$\boldsymbol{\xi}_j = (\xi_{1j}, \xi_{2j}, \cdots, \xi_{Nj})^T, \qquad (j = 1, 2, \cdots, N)$$

form a basis for R^N, and then Δ is the cone spanned by this basis.
The matrix (ξ_{ij}) is invertible, and if K denotes its inverse, then

(3.7) $$\Delta = \{x; Kx \geq 0\}.$$

Since the columns of C and of $\mu(A)$ belong to Δ, we have

(3.8) $$KC \geq 0, \quad K\mu(\cdot) \geq 0.$$

On the other hand, $\boldsymbol{\xi}_j \in \Delta \subseteq \Delta_\alpha$, so that $S(\alpha)^{-1}\boldsymbol{\xi}_j \geq 0$, and therefore

(3.9) $$S(\alpha)^{-1}K = (KS(\alpha))^{-1} \geq 0.$$

Now S may be replaced by KS without affecting the fundamental equation (2.12). If this is done, then C and μ are clearly replaced by KC and $K\mu$. Hence we have shown that, excluding the degenerate case (3.4), *S may be chosen to satisfy* (2.12) *and* (2.17) *in such a way that*

(3.10) $$C \geqq 0, \ \mu \geqq 0,$$

(3.11) $$S(\alpha)^{-1} \geqq 0 \quad (\alpha > 0),$$

and there are functions $s_j(\alpha)$ *such that*

(3.12) $$\lim_{\alpha \to \infty} S_{ij}(\alpha)/s_j(\alpha) = \delta_{ij}.$$

This last relation follows from (3.5) and the fact that $(\xi_{ij}) = K^{-1}$, and may also be expressed in the form

(3.13) $$\lim_{\alpha \to \infty} S_{ij}(\alpha)/S_{jj}(\alpha) = 0 \quad (i \neq j).$$

It will henceforth be supposed that S has indeed been chosen to satisfy these conditions. It is not difficult to see that they determine S uniquely (given P), except for multiples of the form $S \to DS$, where D is a constant diagonal matrix with strictly positive diagonal entries.

An immediate consequence of (3.11) is that the matrix $T(\alpha) = S(\alpha)^{-1}$ is completely monotonic as a function of α. To see this, differentiate the identity $S(\alpha)\, T(\alpha) = I, n$ times, to obtain

$$(-1)^n T^{(n)}(\alpha) = \sum_{r=1}^{n} \binom{n}{r} \{(-1)^{r-1} S(\alpha)^{-1} S^{(r)}(\alpha)\} \ \{(-1)^{n-r} T^{(n-r)}(\alpha)\},$$

whence (2.13) and (3.11) show by induction on n that

(3.14) $$(-1)^n T^{(n)}(\alpha) \geqq 0 \quad (n \geqq 0, \alpha > 0).$$

Bernstein's theorem shows that there is a positive matrix-valued measure Π on R^+ with

(3.15) $$S(\alpha)^{-1} = \int_{R^+} e^{-\alpha t} \, \Pi(dt) \quad (\alpha > 0).$$

If this and (2.17) are substituted into (2.12), we have

$$\int_0^\infty \int_{R^+} e^{-\alpha t - \beta x} P(t, dx)\, dt$$

(3.16)

$$= \int_{R^+} e^{-\alpha t} \, \Pi(dt) \left\{ C + \int_{(0,\infty)} \frac{e^{-\alpha x} - e^{-\beta x}}{\beta - \alpha} \, \mu(dx) \right\}.$$

The double Laplace transforms may be removed from (3.16); assuming for simplicity that μ has a density h and that Π has a density π,

$$(3.17) \qquad P(t, \{0\}) = \pi(t)C,$$

$$(3.18) \qquad P(t, dx) = \int_0^t \mu(u)h(t - u + x)\,du\,dx \qquad (x > 0).$$

If $\Sigma(\alpha)$ denotes the diagonal matrix with entries $S_{ii}(\alpha)$, (3.12) shows that

$$(3.19) \qquad \lim_{\alpha \to \infty} S(\alpha)\,\Sigma(\alpha)^{-1} = I,$$

so that

$$\lim_{\alpha \to \infty} \Sigma(\alpha)\,T(\alpha) = I,$$

or

$$(3.20) \qquad \lim_{\alpha \to \infty} S_{ii}(\alpha)\,T_{ij}(\alpha) = \delta_{ij}.$$

Taking $i = j$ and using (3.11), we have

$$(3.21) \qquad S_{ii}(\alpha) > 0$$

for all sufficiently large $\alpha > 0$.

Now take $i \neq j$, and use (3.10) and (3.11) to show that, if $\beta > \alpha \geq 0$, then

$$0 = \sum_{k=1}^N T_{ik}(\beta)\,S_{kj}(\beta) \geq \sum_{k=1}^N T_{ik}(\beta)\,S_{kj}(\alpha).$$

Hence

$$\sum_{k=1}^N \{S_{ii}(\beta)\,T_{ik}(\beta)\}\,S_{kj}(\alpha) \leq 0,$$

and letting $\beta \to \infty$, (3.20) shows that

$$(3.22) \qquad S_{ij}(\alpha) \leq 0 \qquad (i \neq j, \alpha \geq 0).$$

This is a crucial result, and it has the obvious consequences, proved by letting $\alpha \to \infty$ in (2.17), that

$$(3.23) \qquad C_{ij} = 0 \qquad (i \neq j)$$

and

$$(3.24) \qquad \mu_{ij}(0, \infty) \leq -S_{ij}(0) < \infty \qquad (i \neq j).$$

In particular, C is a positive diagonal matrix. Since the transformation $S(\cdot) \to DS(\cdot)$ is still at our disposal, we can choose S so that

$$(3.25) \qquad\qquad C = \mathrm{diag}\,(\epsilon_1, \epsilon_2, \cdots, \epsilon_N),$$

where each ϵ_j is equal to 0 or 1. If this is added to (3.10), (3.11) and (3.12), then S is almost uniquely determined; the only freedom is multiplication by the constant diagonal matrix D, where $D_{ii} > 0$ for all i, and $D_{ii} = 1$ whenever $\epsilon_i = 1$.

In all the analysis so far, we have not used the fact[5] that the transition function of a Markov process is substochastic, so that

$$(3.26) \qquad\qquad \sum_{j=1}^{N} P_{ij}(t, R^+) \leqq 1$$

for all i, t. This implies that

$$R(\alpha, 0)\mathbf{1} = \int_0^\infty e^{-\alpha t} P(t, R^+)\mathbf{1}\, dt \leqq \alpha^{-1}\mathbf{1}$$

(where $\mathbf{1} = (1, 1, \cdots, 1)^T$) and (2.12) shows that

$$S(\alpha)^{-1} S(0)\, \mathbf{1} \geqq \mathbf{0} \qquad (\alpha > 0).$$

Hence the vector $S(0)\mathbf{1}$ lies in Δ, so that

$$(3.27) \qquad\qquad \sum_{j=1}^{N} S_{ij}(0) \geqq 0.$$

If the transition function happens to be stochastic, so that the anticipation process has infinite lifetime, then the inequality (3.27) is replaced by equality.

4. Probabilistic meaning of the results

To summarise the outcome of the purely analytical arguments of the last section, any anticipation process has its transition function described by (2.12) in terms of a matrix-valued function S on R^+, whose elements are of the form

---

[5] Indeed, much of the argument will go through if the underlying 'probability' measure has infinite total mass, except that caution is needed in the use of Laplace transforms (cf. [13]).

(4.1) $$S_{ij}(\alpha) = S_{ij}(0) + \epsilon_i \delta_{ij}\alpha + \int_{(0,\infty)} (1 - e^{-\alpha x})\mu_{ij}(dx),$$

where

(i) $S_{ij}(0) \leqq 0 \ (i \neq j), \Sigma_{j=1}^N S_{ij}(0) \geqq 0,$
(ii) $\epsilon_i = 0$ or $1,$
(iii) for $i \neq j$, μ_{ij} is a positive measure on $(0, \infty)$ with total mass not exceeding $-S_{ij}(0),$
(iv) μ_{ii} is a positive measure on $(0, \infty)$, perhaps of infinite total mass, but satisfying

(4.2) $$\int_{(0,\infty)} (1 - e^{-x})\mu_{ii}(dx) < \infty.$$

If these facts are compared with the theorems of Neveu [18], a converse appears. If $S_{ij}(0)$, ϵ_i, μ_{ij} satisfy (i)–(iv), then it is not difficult to see that there is a Neveu process which can be treated in the manner described in Section 1 to yield an anticipation process satisfying (2.12) and (4.1). Moreover, Neveu's description of the sample functions of his process makes it possible to interpret these quantities in terms of the behaviour of $\mathcal{X}$. We shall assert these quite baldly, leaving their verification to the reader.

(I) The successive values taken by ξ follow a discrete-time Markov chain with transition probabilities

(4.3) $$p_{ij} = -S_{ij}(0)/S_{ii}(0) \qquad (i \neq j).$$

(II) During an interval in which $\xi(t) = i$, $X(t)$ behaves as the 'semilinear' process

(4.4) $$X_i(t) = \inf\{x \geqq 0; \ Y_i(s) = t + x \text{ for some } s\}$$

corresponding to a subordinator Y_i with Lévy exponent

(4.5) $$\psi_i(\alpha) = S_{ii}(0) + \epsilon_i\alpha + \int_{(0,\infty)} (1 - e^{-\alpha x})\mu_{ii}(dx).$$

In particular, we may classify $(0, i) \in \mathscr{I}$ as a state of $\mathscr{X}$ in the way described in [12]:

(a) if $\epsilon_i = 1$, then $(0, i)$ is *heavy*, and $\mathscr{X}$ is in it for a set of t-values of positive measure; if $\varepsilon_i = 0, (0, i)$ is *light*, and $\mathscr{H}(t) \neq (0, i)$ for almost all t;

(b) if $\mu_{ii}(0, \infty) < \infty$, then $(0, i)$ is *stable*, and there are only finitely many excursions from it in any time interval; if $\mu_{ii}(0, \infty) = \infty$, $(0, i)$ is *unstable*, and there may be infinitely many such excursions.

214   J. F. C. KINGMAN

(III) When ξ jumps from i to j at τ (say), X jumps to a point $X(\tau +)$ of R^+ whose distribution is described by

(4.6) $\Pr\{X(\tau +) \geqq x\} = \mu_{ij}[x, \infty)/ - S_{ij}(0).$

Like Example 4, Example 1 is capable of generating any anticipation process. The other examples of Section 1 are more special. Example 2 describes a general anticipation process with $\epsilon_i = 0$ and $\mu_{ii}(0, \infty) < \infty$ for all i. Example 3 also has $\epsilon_i = 0$, but μ_{ii} may have infinite or finite total mass (this is the distinction between a sticky and a non-sticky boundary point). In this example the measures μ_{ij} are subject to other restrictions [12]. Finally, Example 5 is another way of looking at the general anticipation process with $\epsilon_i = 1$ for all i.

References

[1] BLUMENTHAL, R. M. AND GETOOR, R. K. (1964) Local times for Markov processes. *Z. Wahrscheinlichkeitsth.* **3**, 50–74.

[2] CHUNG, K. L. (1963) On the boundary theory for Markov chains. *Acta Math.* **110**, 19–77.

[3] CHUNG, K. L. (1966) On the boundary theory for Markov chains II. sActa *Acta Math.* **115**, 111–163.

[4] CHUNG, K. L. (1970) *Lectures on Boundary Theory for Markov Chains.* Princeton University Press.

[5] DAVIES, E. B. AND VINCENT-SMITH, G. F. (1968) Tensor products, infinite products, and projective limits of Choquet simplexes. *Math. Scand.* **22**, 145–164.

[6] EDWARDS, D. A. (1974) On descending sequences of Choquet simplexes. *Bull. Soc. Math. France* (To appear).

[7] FELLER, W. (1964) On semi-Markov processes. *Proc. Nat. Acad. Sci.* **51**, 653–659.

[8] HOFFMAN-JØRGENSEN, J. (1969) Markov sets. *Math. Scand.* **24**, 145–166.

[9] HOROWITZ, J. (1972) Semilinear Markov processes, subordinators and renewal theory. *Z. Wahrscheinlichkeitsth.* **24**, 167–193.

[10] KINGMAN, J. F. C. (1965) Linked systems of regenerative events. *Proc. London Math. Soc.* **15**, 125–150.

[11] KINGMAN, J. F. C. (1972) *Regenerative Phenomena.* Wiley, London.

[12] KINGMAN, J. F. C. (1973) Homecomings of Markov processes. *Adv. Appl. Prob.* **5**, 66–102.

[13] KINGMAN, J. F. C. (1974) On the Chapman-Kolmogorov equation. *Phil. Trans. Roy. Soc.* A. **276**, 341–369.

[14] KRYLOV, N. V. AND YUSKEVITCH, A. A. (1964) Markov random sets. *Teor. Veroyatnost. i Primenen*, **9**, 738–743.

[15] LÉVY, P. (1954) Processus semi-Markoviens. *Proc. Int. Cong. Math. Amsterdam* **3**, 416–426.

[16] MAISONNEUVE, B. (1972) *Systèmes Régénératifs.* Doctoral Thesis, University of Strasbourg.

[17] MEYER, P. A. (1974) Ensembles aléatoires markoviens homogènes. *Sém. Prob. Univ. Strasbourg* (To appear).

[18] NEVEU, J. (1961) Une généralisation des processus à accroissements positifs indépendants. *Abh. Math. Sem. Hamburg* **25**, 36–61.

[19] PYKE, R. (1961) Markov renewal processes; definitions and preliminary properties. *Ann. Math. Statist.* **32**, 1231–1242.

[20] PYKE, R. (1961) Markov renewal processes with finitely many states. *Ann. Math. Statist.* **32**, 1243–1259.

[21] SMITH, W. L. (1955) Regenerative stochastic processes. *Proc. Roy. Soc.* A **232**, 6–31.

[22] TAYLOR, S. J. (1973) Sample path properties of processes with stationary independent increments. *Stochastic Analysis*, eds. D. G. Kendall and E. F. Harding. Wiley, London, 387–414.

Reversibility and Acyclicity

P. WHITTLE

Abstract

It is well-known that the transition matrix of a reversible Markov process can have only real eigenvalues. An example is constructed which shows that the converse assertion does not hold. A generalised notion of reversibility is proposed, 'dynamic reversibility', which has many of the implications for the form of the transition matrix of the classical definition, but which does not exclude 'circulation in state-space' or, indeed, periodicity.

Festschrift contributors seem often to feel that delicacy demands that any reference to the object of their homage should be in the obliquest possible terms. In the case of Maurice Bartlett, such a convention is impossible; for too many of us is respect warmed by gratitude and friendship.

When I began research, in the late nineteen forties, Maurice Bartlett had already created his reputation, based on his unique blend of statistical/probabilistic/physical thinking and instinct for the fundamental. Time series analysis, factor analysis, stochastic population models, spatial processes — wherever one looked he had made pioneering contributions, and one could scarcely determine whether, in trying these areas oneself, one was merely following his lead, or rather finding one's instinct for the significant constantly anticipated.

Despite this closeness of interest, I did not meet Maurice until 1953, at a conference on factor analysis in Uppsala. I recall plainly my first glimpse of him on a drizzly railway platform: an unexpectedly bulky, ruddy and cheery figure, almost farmer-like, with a hat whose floppy brim was etched by the several chromatograms of successive seasons.

217

A King Charles' head in both Maurice's writings and my own has been the question of statistical reversibility. This first manifested itself in my own case in a paper [3] which Maurice kindly communicated for publication on my behalf, but which met with a referee, alas, less kindly and less percipient. However, that the paper indeed contained something is supported by the indubitable facts, that some of its material has slowly surfaced in the literature over subsequent years, and that some of it has not. At all events, the theme of that paper has recurred in my mind frequently, and this is an appropriate moment to develop it further.

A temporal process is *reversible* if its statistics are invariant under a time-reversal about an arbitrary time origin. By considering two consecutive reversals about two arbitrary origins, one sees then immediately that reversibility implies stationarity. Suppose for simplicity that the process is in discrete time and that the variable, x_t, takes a finite set of values labelled by $j = 1,2,3, \cdots$. Then reversibility will imply that (x_t, x_{t+1}) will take the pairs of values (j, k) or (k, j) with equal probability, so that

(1) $$P_j p_{jk} = P_k p_{kj}$$

in an obvious notation.

If the process is Markov then the p_{jk} are just the transition probabilities defining the process, and Relation(1) (known in this case as the 'detailed balance' condition) implies a condition on these, which is necessary, and very nearly sufficient, for reversibility. Suppose that all the states of the process are recurrent, and of a single ergodic class, so that the equilibrium probabilities P_j are unique and strictly positive. (The more general case is dealt with easily enough, at the expense of a more careful argument.) Relation (1) then implies the representation for the transition probabilities

(2) $$p_{jk} = \alpha_{jk} / P_j$$

where $\alpha_{jk} = \alpha_{kj}$. A Markov process with such transition probabilities is readily found to be reversible, with P_j indeed identifiable as proportional to the equilibrium distribution over states.

So Condition (2) is both necessary and sufficient for reversibility as Kolmogorov established already in 1936, see [2]. I observed in [3] that representation (2) could always be achieved for a one-species birth-and-death process (and so, formally, for a one-dimensional diffusion with the right boundary conditions). This has been seen since as explaining certain properties of such processes.

Condition (2) implies the *Kolmogorov conditions*

(3) $$p_{j_1 j_2} p_{j_2 j_3} \cdots p_{j_{n-1} j_n} = p_{j_n j_{n-1}} p_{j_{n-1} j_{n-2}} \cdots p_{j_2 j_1}$$

for any sequence of states $j_1, j_2, \cdots, j_n$ $(n = 1, 2, 3, \cdots)$.These in fact imply (2), and so also reversibility as noted in [2]. The conditions hold trivially for $n = 1, 2$; it was shown in [3] that if all the p_{jk} are strictly positive, then it is sufficient for reversibility if (3) holds only for $n = 3$ and for some fixed value of j_1. If some of the p_{jk} are zero, as will more usually be the case, then the situation is more complicated, and the *minimal* sufficient condition of type (3) has not yet been determined.

Condition (3) is of great interest in itself in the light it throws on the qualitative implications of reversibility. It states that, given a starting point j_1 in state-space, the probability of any sequence of steps which ultimately returns to j_1 must have the same probability, whether this cycle is traced in one direction or the other. This could be expressed: *a reversible Markov process shows no net circulation in state-space.*

This acyclicity manifests itself in another way, noted in [3]. The transition matrix (2) will have the same eigenvalues as the matrix P^* with elements $\alpha_{jk}/\sqrt{(P_j P_k)}$, obtained from (2) by a similarity transformation by a diagonal matrix $(\delta_{jk}\sqrt{P_j})$. Since P^* is symmetric, it must have real eigenvalues, as will then the original transition matrix (p_{jk}). This absence of complex eigenvalues is another indication of the absence of any periodic behaviour on the part of the process (with the exception of 'periods' of two time units in discrete time, which are not inconsistent with reversibility).

One can ask the converse question: whether a process whose transition matrix P has only real eigenvalues is necessarily reversible. This is certainly not so: consider the case

$$P = \begin{bmatrix} \cdot & 1 & \cdot \\ \frac{3}{4} & \cdot & \frac{1}{4} \\ 1 & \cdot & \cdot \end{bmatrix}$$

for which P has all real eigenvalues; $\lambda = 1, -\frac{1}{2}, -\frac{1}{2}$. Yet this process is not reversible, for the sequence 1231 has positive probability, and the sequence 1321 zero probability.

For a more general version of this same example, consider the case

$$
(4) \qquad P =
\begin{bmatrix}
a_1 & b_1 & \cdot & \cdot & \cdots & \cdot \\
a_2 & \cdot & b_2 & \cdot & \cdots & \cdot \\
a_3 \cdot & \vdots & \cdot & b_3 & \cdots & \cdot \\
\cdot \, \cdot \, \cdot & \cdot \, \cdot \, \cdot \, \cdot \, \cdot \, \cdot & & & \cdots & \cdot \\
a_{n-1} & \cdot & \cdot & \cdot & \cdots & b_{n-1} \\
1 & \cdot & \cdot & \cdot & \cdots & \cdot
\end{bmatrix}.
$$

If we define

$$
\pi_j = b_1 b_2 \cdots b_{j-1} a_j \qquad (j = 1,2,\cdots,n)
$$

with the convention $a_n = 1$, then $(\pi_1, \pi_2, \cdots, \pi_n)$ is a distribution; the distribution of the time of first return to state 1 ('return' including 'non-departure'). The eigenvalues λ of P are found to be determined by

$$
\lambda^n = \sum_1^n \pi_j \lambda^{n-j}
$$

or

$$
(5) \qquad\qquad\qquad \Pi(\lambda^{-1}) = 1
$$

where $\Pi(z)$ is the p.g.f. $\Sigma \pi_j z^j$. Equation (5) has a single root at $\lambda = 1$, the other $n-1$ roots are at the zeros of

$$
\frac{1 - \Pi(\lambda^{-1})}{1 - \lambda^{-1}} = 1 + b_1 \lambda^{-1} + b_1 b_2 \lambda^{-2} + \cdots + b_1 b_2 \cdots b_{n-1} \lambda^{1-n}.
$$

If real, these are necessarily non-positive; suppose them at $-\alpha_1$, $-\alpha_2, \cdots, -\alpha_{n-1}$, so that this last expression can be written

$$
\sum_{j=0}^{n-1} \lambda^{-j} \left(\prod_1^j b_k \right) = \prod_1^{n-1} (1 + \alpha_j \lambda^{-1}) = \sum_0^{n-1} S_j \lambda^{-j}
$$

where S_j is the jth symmetric function of the α's (sum of all products of j distinct α-values). Thus

$$
(6) \qquad\qquad b_j = S_j / S_{j-1} \qquad (j = 1,2,\cdots,n-1)
$$

with the convention $S_0 = 1$. Since $b_1 \leqq 1$, it is necessary that $S_1 \leqq 1$, or

$$
(7) \qquad\qquad\qquad \sum_1^{n-1} \alpha_j \leqq 1.
$$

In fact, one can find b_0, b_1, b_2, $\cdots$, b_{n-1} in $[0, 1]$ such that the α_j can take *any* set of real non-negative values consistent with (7). For, if the α_j are so chosen, then the b_j of (6) are plainly positive, and also plainly do not exceed unity, for

$$(8) \qquad\qquad S_j \leqq S_1 S_{j-1} \leqq S_{j-1}.$$

As a particular and extreme case, choose the α_j all equal with equality in (7), so that $\alpha_j = 1/(n - 1)$. Then

$$(9) \qquad\qquad b_j = (n - j)/(n - 1)j \qquad (j = 1, 2, \cdots, n - 1)$$

and the transition matrix specified by (4) and (9), which clearly specifies an irreversible process, has all its eigenvalues real: a simple value at $\lambda = 1$, and an $(n - 1)$-fold one at $-1/(n - 1)$.

One can see from this example how a process can be irreversible, and yet not exhibit what one might term 'quasi-periodic' behaviour. There is certainly a net circulation in state-space: the state passes up from the value 1, then progresses through 2,3, $\cdots$, finally to drop back to 1 and start all over again. However, the time expiring from leaving state 1 until returning there is so diffusely distributed that there is nothing like a periodicity and P has only real eigenvalues.

It might seem remarkable that reversibility, which is often regarded as a natural property of physical systems, should preclude periodic behaviour, which is so frequently exhibited by physical systems. However, to get a notion of reversibility appropriate to, say, Newtonian dynamics, one must modify the definition above. The state-variable of a Newtonian dynamic system would specify a number of co-ordinates and velocities, denoted by q and v say. The reversibility demand one would make would be that the statistics of the reversed (q, v) process should be identical with those of the $(q, -v)$ process.

So, suppose that to each state j of the Markov process there corresponds another state j', conjugate to j, and such that $(j')' = j$. This notion of conjugate states j, j', introduced in [3], generalises the idea of state-pairs (q, v) and $(q, -v)$, which differ only in the sign of the velocities.

We say then that a process is *dynamically reversible* if its statistics are unchanged by application of the double operation: time reversal about an arbitrary origin and state conjugation.(The order is immaterial; the two operations commute.)

For a dynamically reversible process one deduces, in analogy to (1), that

(10) $$P_j p_{jk} = P_k \cdot p_{k'j'}$$

so that, if $P_j > 0$,

(11) $$p_{jk} = \alpha_{jk}/P_j$$

where

(12) $$\alpha_{jk} = \alpha_{k'j'}.$$

For a Markov process with all states persistent and in the same ergodic class, conditions (11), (12) are readily found to be sufficient for dynamic reversibility, and to imply that P_j is indeed proportional to the equilibrium distribution, and that also

(13) $$P_j = P_{j'}.$$

The Kolmogorov relations (3) will now hold with all states in the right-hand member conjugated; circulation around a given path must now equal the circulation around the reversed *and* conjugated path. Something like periodicity would appear to be no longer precluded, and this is in fact the case. Suppose we assume no state self-conjugate (i.e., 'velocity is never zero') so that the states are necessarily even in number. Divide the states into two mutually conjugate sets $(1,2,\cdots,n)$ $(1',2',\cdots,n')$. It follows thus from (11)–(13) that we can write the transition matrix in the form

(14) $$P = \begin{bmatrix} \varpi^{-1}A & \varpi^{-1}B \\ \varpi^{-1}C & \varpi^{-1}A' \end{bmatrix}$$

where ϖ is the diagonal matrix $(\delta_{jk}P_j)$, and B, C are symmetric. Such a matrix can certainly have complex eigenvalues.

Consider, for example, the case where a particle can move step-wise through n positions on the circumference of a circle, with a velocity which changes randomly between the two values ± 1. States j, j' correspond to 'position j' and 'velocity $+1$, -1' respectively. Thus

$$p_{j,j-1} = \alpha, \quad p_{jj'} = \beta = 1 - \alpha, \quad p_{j',(j-1)'} = \alpha, \quad p_{j'j} = \beta,$$

where $j = n + 1$ and $j' = 0'$ are identified with $j = 1$ and $j' = n'$ respectively. Matrix (14) then has the form

(15) $$P = \begin{bmatrix} \alpha W & \beta I \\ \beta I & \alpha W^{-1} \end{bmatrix}$$

where W is the circulant matrix for which $w_{jk} = 1$ if $j - k = 1$ (mod n), $w_{jk} = 0$ otherwise. Matrix (15) indeed has the form of (14), with $\varpi \propto I$, so that the process is dynamically reversible with all states equiprobable in equilibrium. The eigenvalues λ of P are at the roots of

$$|(\alpha W - \lambda I)(\alpha W^{-1} - \lambda I) - \beta^2 I| = 0$$

or of any of

$$\lambda^2 - 2\alpha\lambda \cos(2\pi r/n) + \alpha^2 - \beta^2 = 0 \qquad (r = 1, 2, \cdots, n)$$

and so can be written as

(16) $$\lambda = \rho e^{\pm i\theta_r} \qquad (r = 1, 2, \cdots, n)$$

where

$$\rho = \sqrt{(\alpha^2 - \beta^2)}, \qquad \theta_r = \cos^{-1}(\alpha\rho^{-1}\cos(2\pi r/n)).$$

None of the roots (16) is actually complex if $\beta > \frac{1}{2}$, but the number of complex roots increases as β decreases, until for β small enough the only real roots are those corresponding to r equal to n or $\frac{1}{2}n$. We can thus certainly construct dynamically reversible processes with behaviour as close to periodic as desired. This last example would indeed be exactly periodic in the limit case $\beta = 0$, but one then has a process needing more careful discussion, for which the states j, j' are in different ergodic classes.

There is so much more one could say about reversibility; in [4], [5], for example, one can see how the property can occur naturally, and make a seemingly intractable problem amenable. I shall merely note, however, its potentialities as an instrument of low guile: to provide problems for a solution. Given a distribution P_j, one can very well construct via (2) a Markov process having P_j as equilibrium distribution. The same is true for the dynamically reversible case, if one observes conditions (11)–(12).

As an example, consider a Markov population process in continuous time with m_j individuals in the jth population and *total* birth and death intensities for this population equal to

(17)
$$\lambda_j(m) = \nu_j(m_j + 1),$$

$$\mu_j(m) = \nu_j m_j \exp\left[c_j + \sum_k h_{jk} m_k\right].$$

The terms $\Sigma_k h_{jk} m_k$ represent the effect of competition, although their occurrence in an exponent may represent competition as excessively fierce. At all events, the process is reversible, with equilibrium distribution

(18) $$P(m) \propto \exp[-\tfrac{1}{2}\Sigma\Sigma h_{jk}m_j(m_k - \delta_{jk}) - \Sigma c_j m_j].$$

I freely confess that the specification (17) was deduced from the solution (18), rather than conversely. However, the rates (17) do incorporate genuine competition effects, and the solution (18) can imply a wide variety of coexistence or non-coexistence phenomena. This is due to the fact that, since the distribution is restricted to $m \geqq 0$, the quadratic form $\Sigma\Sigma h_{jk}m_j m_k$ need not be positive definite, and $P(m)$ can have multiple maxima in the positive orthant.

References

[1] BARTLETT, M. S. (1955) *An Introduction to Stochastic Processes*. Cambridge University Press.

[2] KOLMOGOROV, A.N. (1936) Zur Theorie der Markoffschen Ketten. *Math. Ann.* 112, 155–160.

[3] WHITTLE, P. (1955) Reversibility in Markov processes. Unpublished manuscript.

[4] WHITTLE, P. (1965) Statistical processes of aggregation and polymerisation. *Proc. Camb. Phil. Soc.* 61, 475–495.

[5] WHITTLE, P. (1965) The equilibrium statistics of a clustering process in the uncondensed phase. *Proc. Roy. Soc.* A 285, 501–519.

PART VI

STATISTICAL INFERENCE ON
STOCHASTIC PROCESSES

Measuring the Velocity of a Signal

E. J. HANNAN

Abstract

The problem considered is that of measuring the velocity of a signal, constituted by a plane wave, from measurements at a number of recorders receiving noise as well as signal. The asymptotic properties of the estimates are considered under rather general conditions on the noise and signal processes.

1. Introduction

We consider a situation where we have p recorders in two-dimensional space, the ath being at a point with coordinates given by the vector $\xi(a)$. This recorder receives a signal $z(t,a)$ together with noise $x(t,a)$. We put $y(t,a) = z(t,a) + x(t,a)$ for the output of the ath recorder. We shall take $z(t,a)$, $x(t,a)$, $a = 1, \cdots, p$ to be generated by stationary processes with absolutely continuous spectra but shall be more explicit later.

We initially consider the situation where $z(t,a)$ is constituted by a plane wave propagating in the direction ϕ with speed c. Thus we take ϕ to be a unit length vector, i.e., $\langle \phi, \phi \rangle = 1$. Then

$$z(t,a) = \int_{-\infty}^{\infty} \exp - i\{\omega t - \theta(\omega,a)\}d\zeta(\omega),$$

(1)

$$E\{d\zeta(\omega)d\zeta(\omega')\} = \delta_{\omega\omega'} \cdot f_z(\omega)d\omega.$$

Here $\theta(\omega,a) = \omega\langle\xi(a),\phi\rangle/c$. We call $z(t)$ the expression (1) when $\theta(\omega,a)$ is replaced by zero. This case just introduced we speak of as the

227

non-dispersive case since c is independent of ω. More generally we may consider the model

$$\theta(\omega,a) \equiv \theta(\omega,a,\tau) = \sum_{j=1}^{s} \beta_j(a,\tau)\omega^j, \qquad \omega \geq 0$$

(2)

$$\theta(-\omega,a,\tau) = -\theta(\omega,a,\tau).$$

Here τ is a vector of q parameters. Of course θ must be an odd function of ω since the speed is the same for ω and $-\omega$. To illustrate, consider the case where $p > 2$ and there is no dispersion. Then $s = 1$ and τ may be taken to be $c^{-1}\phi$. If $p = 2$ we cannot estimate both speed and direction and τ may be taken to be $\langle \xi(1) - \xi(2), \phi \rangle / c$. If $c(\omega) = c\omega^{-1}$ and $p > 2$ we again take $\tau = c^{-1}\phi$ and so on. One does not need to be so special as (2) implies but this seems sufficiently general and simplifies the discussion. We have assumed that τ can be, globally, represented as a vector in p-dimensional Euclidean space, as is true for our examples. The theory would not be affected if, say, τ was required to be in an open submanifold of a twice differentiable manifold. This would allow, say, for the possibility of non-linear constraints. We assume that the $\beta_j(a, \tau)$ are twice, continuously, differentiable in the elements of τ.

We shall assume that observations are made at N equidistant time points and we take the time unit as the interval between successive observations. We also assume that observations are taken sufficiently close together in time for there to be no aliasing of frequencies for $z(t)$ with frequencies in the set $\mathcal{B} \subset (-\pi, \pi]$, $0 \notin \mathcal{B}$, that we shall use. Here $\mathcal{B}$ is to be composed of a finite number of intervals and is to be symmetric with respect to the origin. We shall use $\mathcal{B}_+$ for the part of $\mathcal{B}$ in $(0, \pi]$. Thus we are assuming that the spectrum for $z(t)$ is contained in $[-\pi - \delta, \pi + \delta]$, $0 \leq \delta < \pi$. This will not be strictly true but in many applications should be sufficiently near to true for the effect of aliasing to be negligible. Of course the problem is not peculiar to the methods of this paper. We assume $f_z(\omega) \neq 0$, $\omega \in \mathcal{B}$. This is a relatively harmless assumption. Finally we assume that the $z(t)$, $x(t,a)$ $a = 1, \cdots, p$, processes are mutually independent. For some purposes incoherence will suffice but for a central limit theorem some condition equivalent to independence at least up to moments of the fourth order is needed for a useful result. All of the assumptions of this section will be maintained throughout the remainder of the paper and we shall refer to them collectively as Conditions A.

The model discussed, or elaborations of it, has occurred in various applications. Thus Munk *et al.* [10] deal with oceanographic data as also do Hamon and Hannan [3]. Fedor [2] deals with ionospheric drift and Krause, Steadman and Williams [9] with the speed of propagation of a signal along a nerve fibre. In the first of these references a situation is met where a number of interfering wave forms are simultaneously received. The statistical treatment is then rather complicated unless the recorders are arranged in a symmetrical fashion and there is a large number of them. This type of situation is considered in Hinich and Shaman [7], under rather restrictive assumptions, and these writers also give a number of references. For lack of space we shall not consider such a situation here but merely mention that the methods of the present paper may be extended to deal with this problem.

2. The estimation of the wave velocity

We shall now use τ_0 for the true vector τ so as to distinguish it from a trial value. Our purpose is to construct an estimate of τ_0 and to discuss its asymptotic properties. Some of the results of this section have been discussed, without proof, and the methods used in [3]. Special cases of the model are close to ones discussed in [5] and [6] but the present treatment is more relevant and more general. We introduce the discrete Fourier transforms

$$Y_a(\omega) = \frac{1}{\sqrt{N}} \sum_1^N y(n, a) e^{in\omega}, \; I_{a,b}(\omega) = Y_a(\omega)\overline{Y_b(\omega)},$$

which we compute for $\omega_s = 2\pi s/N$, $-\frac{1}{2}N < s \leqq \frac{1}{2}N$. The results proved below will continue to hold for methods of estimating spectra other than those we here study but for simplicity we confine ourselves to the one method. We introduce a weight function $W(\omega)$ that is to be an even, non-negative, symmetric, matrix-valued function of ω for $\omega \in \mathcal{B}$. One obvious choice is $W_{ab}(\omega) \equiv 1$, $a, b = 1, \cdots, p$. Quasi maximum likelihood procedures (i.e., maximum likelihood procedures on Gaussian assumptions that we do not maintain) produce, via a certain amount of 'sleight of hand', the weight function

$$W_0(\omega) = \{f_z(\omega)1_p 1_p' + f_x(\omega)\}^{-1},$$

where $f_x(\omega)$ is diagonal with $f_j(\omega)$ in the jth place and 1_p is the p-rowed vector of units. We shall later discuss the estimation of W_0. We form

$$q_N(\tau) = \frac{1}{N} \sum_{\mathcal{B}} \sum_{a \neq b} W_{ab}(\omega_s) I_{ab}(\omega_s) \exp i\{\theta(\omega_s, b, \tau) - \theta(\omega_s, a, \tau)\}.$$

It will be convenient to write $\theta_{ab}(\omega,\tau) = \theta(\omega,a,\tau) - \theta(\omega,b,\tau)$. We omit the terms for $a = b$ since they do not depend on τ. We may rewrite $q_N(\tau)$ as

$$\frac{4}{N} \sum_{\mathscr{B}_+} \sum\sum_{a<b} W_{ab}(\omega_s)\mathscr{R}[I_{ab}(\omega_s)\exp\{-i\theta_{ab}(\omega,\tau)\}].$$

We call $\hat{\tau}$ the value of the vector τ that maximises $q_N(\tau)$. Now if $y(n)$ is ergodic $q_N(\tau)$ converges almost surely to

$$(3) \qquad q(\tau) = \sum\sum_{a\neq b} \int_{\mathscr{B}} W_{ab}(\omega)f_z(\omega)\exp i\{\theta_{ab}(\omega,\tau_0) - \theta_{ab}(\omega,\tau)\}d\omega,$$

and the convergence is uniform in τ for τ confined to any compact set. The proof is essentially the same as that contained in the lemma in [5] and will not be repeated. Moreover the uniformity of convergence will hold for all τ if $y(n)$ is also purely non-deterministic (see immediately below) as follows from Theorem 2 in [4]. By pure non-determinism we mean the following. Let the $y(n,a)$ be defined over a probability space $(\mathscr{U},\mathscr{A},P)$, $\mathscr{M}_n$ be the σ-algebra of events determined by $y(m,a)$, $m \leqq n$, $a = 1,\cdots,p$ and $\mathscr{M}_{-\infty} = \cap \mathscr{M}_n$, $\mathscr{M}_\infty = \cup \mathscr{M}_n$. Let $H_n = H(\mathscr{M}_n)$ be the Hilbert space of random variables measurable $\mathscr{M}_n$ and of finite mean square and put $S_n = H_n \ominus H_{n-1}$. Then if $u(n,a,j)$ is the projection of $y(n,a)$ on S_j and $u(n,a,-\infty)$ is its projection on $H_{-\infty}$ we have

$$y(n,a) = \sum_0^\infty u(n,a,n-j) + u(n,a,-\infty)$$

where the series converges in mean square. If $u(n,a,-\infty)$ is null we say that $y(n,a)$ is purely non-deterministic. This seems to be a very non-restrictive requirement. We call $u(n,a,j)$ the innovation for $y(n,a)$ at time j.

If $W = W_0$ then

$$W_{ab}(\omega) = f_a^{-1}(\omega)\delta_{ab} - \frac{f_z(\omega)}{\{1 + \sum_a f_z(\omega)/f_a(\omega)\}}\frac{1}{f_a(\omega)f_b(\omega)}.$$

Let us add back to (3) the terms for $a = b$, which do not depend on τ, and replace $f_z(\omega)$ by $f_z(\omega) + f_a(\omega)$ for those terms. Then (3) becomes

$$\int_{\mathscr{B}} \left| \sum_a \exp i\{\theta(\omega,a\tau) - \theta(\omega,a,\tau_0)\} \right|^2 d\omega$$

which is maximised when and only when $\theta(\omega,a,\tau) \equiv \theta(\omega,a,\tau_0)$, mod 2π,

$a = 1, \cdots, p$. However if $W_{ab}(\omega) \equiv w(\omega) > 0$ the same is evidently again true since adding back terms for $a = b$ we obtain for (3)

$$\int_{\mathscr{B}} w(\omega) f_z(\omega) \left| \sum_a \exp i\{\theta(\omega, a, \tau) - \theta(\omega, a, \tau_0)\} \right|^2 d\omega.$$

We finally assume

(4) $\qquad\qquad \theta(\omega, a, \tau) \not\equiv \theta(\omega, a, \tau_0), \bmod 2\pi, \; \tau \neq \tau_0.$

This is the same as saying that $\beta_j(a, \tau_0) \not\equiv \beta_j(a, \tau)$, $\tau \neq \tau_0$. Clearly (5) is a necessary condition for the estimation of τ for if it did not hold for $\tau' \neq \tau_0$ then we could not distinguish τ' from τ_0 from our observations. Now the following theorem holds.

Theorem 1. Let $y(n)$ be ergodic. If Conditions A hold, as well as (4) and $W(\omega) = W_0(\omega)$ or $W_{ab}(\omega) \equiv w(\omega) \geqq 0$ then $\hat{\tau}$ converges almost surely to τ_0 if either τ_0 is *a priori* restricted to lie in a compact set or $y(n)$ is purely non-deterministic.

Proof. The proof of the theorem follows immediately from (4) via the following relations, which hold, almost surely, for N sufficiently large and any $\epsilon > 0$,

$$q(\tau_0) - \epsilon \leqq q_N(\tau_0) \leqq q_N(\hat{\tau}) \leqq q(\hat{\tau}) + \epsilon \leqq q(\tau_0) + \epsilon.$$

Now let us assume that $\beta_j(a, \tau)$ is twice continuously differentiable. Then

(5) $\quad N^{\frac{1}{2}} \partial q_N(\tau_0)/\partial \tau_j = -N^{\frac{1}{2}} \Sigma(\hat{\tau}_k - \tau_{0,k}) \partial^2 q_N(\bar{\tau})/\partial \tau_j \partial \tau_k, |\bar{\tau} - \tau_o| \leqq |\hat{\tau} - \tau_0|.$

Here we use $\partial q_N(\tau_0)/\partial \tau_j$ to mean the derivative of $q_N(\tau)$ evaluated at τ_0 and similarly for higher derivations while $|\cdot|$ is the Euclidean length of the indicated vector. Now, under the conditions of Theorem 1,

$$\lim_{N \to \infty} \partial^2 q_N(\bar{\tau})/\partial \tau_j \partial \tau_k =$$

$$-\sum_{a \neq b} \sum \int_{\mathscr{B}} W_{ab}(\omega) f_z(\omega)(\partial \theta_{ab}(\omega, \tau_0)/\partial \tau_j)(\partial \theta_{ab}(\omega, \tau_0)/\partial \tau_k) d\omega, \text{ a.s.}$$

Indeed the proof is the same as in Hannan and Robinson (1973), the only point needing attention being the vanishing from the limiting expression of the second derivatives. However $W_{ab}(\omega) = W_{ab}(-\omega) = W_{ba}(\omega)$ while $\partial^2\theta_{ab}(\omega, \tau_0)/\partial\tau_j\partial\tau_k$ is an odd function of ω (that changes sign when a and b are interchanged) and $f_z(\omega)$ also is even. To establish a central limit theorem we therefore need only to consider the left side of (5). This expression can be broken into four terms deriving from the decomposition $y(n,a) = z(n,a) + x(n,a)$ and involving the four possibilities x with x, z with x, x with z and z with z. To obtain a useful result it is necessary to eliminate the fourth type of term for it alone will introduce fourth moments and the occurrence of these will lead to very complicated expressions for the limiting variance. We assume that the fourth moments for $z(t)$ are finite. We can therefore define the fourth cumulant function $\beta(t_1,t_2,t_3,t_4)$ between the $z(t_j)$, $j = 1,\cdots,4$. (We must consider $z(t)$ as a process in continuous time, since it occurs with non-integral relative lags at the various recorders.) The function β is not necessarily the Fourier transform of an ordinary function (or of a signed measure) but it is, of course, a Fourier transform in the sense of the theory of generalised functions. (See [8], pp. 146–154, for example.) As such the generalised function $\hat{\beta}$, that is its Fourier transform, has support on the plane $\omega_1 + \omega_2 + \omega_3 + \omega_4 = 0$, but our assumption concerning the spectrum of $z(t)$ ensures that the support is a compact planar subset. We assume that in some neighbourhood of $\omega_1 + \omega_2 = \omega_3 + \omega_4 = 0$ the generalised function $\hat{\beta}$ may be identified with a continuous function. We shall speak of the conditions of this paragraph as the fourth cumulant condition for $z(t)$.

The contribution to $N^{\frac{1}{2}}\partial q_N(\tau_0)/\partial\tau_j$ from $z(t)$ is

$$(6) \qquad N^{-\frac{1}{2}}\sum_{\mathcal{B}}\sum\sum_{a\neq b} W_{ab}(\omega)\partial \exp\{-i\theta_{ab}(\omega_s, \tau_0)\}/\partial\tau_j\bar{I}_{ab}(\omega_s)$$

where $\bar{I}_{ab}(\omega_s)$ is formed from $z(n,a),z(n,b)$ as was I_{ab} from $y(n,a)$, $y(n,b)$. Let us put $\phi_{ab}^{(j)}(\omega) = iW_{ab}(\omega)\partial\theta_{ab}(\omega,\tau_0)/\partial\tau_j$. Then from Theorem 3 in Hannan (1973) the variance of (6) is

$$
\sum_{a\neq b}\sum \sum_{c\neq d}\sum 2\pi\left[\int_{\mathcal{B}} \{\phi_{ab}^{(j)}(\omega)\overline{\phi_{cd}^{(j)}(\omega)} + \phi_{ab}^{(j)}(\omega)\phi_{cd}^{(j)}(\omega)\}f_z(\omega)^2d\omega\right.
$$
$$(7)$$
$$
\left. + \int_{\mathcal{B}}\int \phi_{ab}^{(j)}(\omega)\overline{\phi_{cd}^{(j)}(\omega')}\hat{\beta}(\omega, -\omega, \omega', -\omega')d\omega d\omega'\right].
$$

In deriving this formula from the cited reference we have used the fact that the cross spectrum between $z(t,a)$, $z(t,b)$ is $f_z(\omega) \exp i\theta_{ab}(\omega,\tau_0)$ and that there is no aliasing of frequencies for $z(t)$ with frequencies in $\mathcal{B}$. Now (7) is null for W_{ab} of the form required in Theorem 1 for, then

$$\sum\sum_{a \neq b} \sum\sum_{c \neq d} \{\phi_{ab}^{(j)}(\omega)\overline{\phi_{cd}^{(j)}(\omega)} + \phi_{ab}^{(j)}(\omega)\phi_{cd}^{(j)}(\omega)\} \equiv 0,$$

since $\phi_{ab}^{(j)}(-\omega) = \overline{\phi_{ab}(\omega)} = \phi_{ba}(\omega)$ (using the properties of $W_{ab}(\omega)$ cited earlier) while

$$\sum\sum_{a \neq b} \sum\sum_{c \neq d} \phi_{ab}(\omega)\phi_{cd}(\omega')$$

is an odd function of ω and ω' and $\hat{\beta}$ is even in these two variables so that the fourth cumulant term vanishes also. The mean of the expression (6) also converges to zero (see [5]) so that the contribution from (6) to $N^{-\frac{1}{2}}\partial q_N(\tau_0)/\partial \tau_i$ may be neglected. Thus introducing the DFT, $Z_a(\omega)$, $X_a(\omega)$, defined as for $y(n,a)$ but with $z(n,a)$, $x(n,a)$ replacing $y(n,a)$, we have to consider

$$b_j = N^{-\frac{1}{2}} \sum_{\mathcal{B}} \sum\sum_{a \neq b} \phi_{ab}^{(j)}(\omega_s) \exp\{-i\theta_{ab}(\omega_s, \tau_0)\}\{X_a(\omega_s)\overline{Z_b(\omega_s)}$$

(8)

$$+ Z_a(\omega_s)\overline{X_b(\omega_s)} + X_a(\omega_s)\overline{X_b(\omega_s)}\}.$$

Because of the symmetry properties of $\phi_{ab}^{(j)}, X_a, Z_b$ the first two terms within the last factor provide the same contribution, $\bar{b}_j$ let us say, to the whole expression. Putting $\hat{b}_j$ for the contribution from the last term we have $b_j = 2\bar{b}_j + \hat{b}_j$. We need a further condition on $x(n,a)$ to obtain a central limit theorem. We require in the first place that the $x(n,a)$ process should be weakly mixing (see [1], p. 12). In the second place we require it to be purely non-deterministic with innovation sequences, $v(n,a,j)$ let us say, satisfying

$$(9) \qquad \sum_{j=0}^{\infty} [E\{v^2(n,a,n-j)\}]^{\frac{1}{2}} < \infty.$$

Now it follows from Theorem 4 in [4] that the $\bar{b}_j, \hat{b}_k, j, k = 1, \cdots, p$, are jointly asymptotically normal with covariance matrix as follows. For $\bar{b}_j$ with $\hat{b}_k, j, k = 1, \cdots, p$ the covariance is zero. For $2\bar{b}_j$ with $2\bar{b}_k$ it is

$$8\pi \sum\sum_{a \neq b} \sum\sum_{c \neq d} \delta_{bd} \int_{\mathcal{B}} W_{ab}(\omega)W_{cd}(\omega)(\partial\theta_{ab}(\omega, \tau_0)/\partial \tau_j)$$

(10)

$$\times (\partial\theta_{ab}(\omega, \tau_0)/\partial \tau_k) f_z(\omega) f_b(\omega) d\omega$$

while for $\hat{b}_j$ with $\hat{b}_k$ it is

(11) $4\pi \sum\limits_{a \neq b} \sum \int_{\mathscr{B}} |W_{ab}(\omega)|^2 (\partial \theta_{ab}(\omega, \tau_0)/\partial \tau_j)(\partial \theta_{ab}(\omega, \tau_0)/\partial \tau_k) f_a(\omega) f_b(\omega) d\omega.$

Now we consider only the case $W = W_0$. Then on combining (10) and (11) and using the formula for $W_{ab}(\omega)$ for $W = W_0$ given above, we obtain for the covariances in the limiting distribution for (8), for b_j with b_k,

$$4\pi \sum\limits_{a \neq b} \sum \int_{\mathscr{B}} -W_{ab}(\omega) f_z(\omega)(\partial \theta_{ab}(\omega, \tau_0)/\partial \tau_j)(\partial \theta_{ab}(\omega, \tau_0)/\partial \tau_k) d\omega.$$

We observe that when $W = W_0$, $-W_{ab}(\omega) f_z(\omega) = \sigma^{ab}(\omega) \sigma_{ab}(\omega)$, $a \neq b$, where $\sigma_{ab}(\omega)$ is the coherence between $y(n,a)$, $y(n,b)$ while $\sigma^{ab}(\omega)$ is the typical element of the matrix inverse to that with entries $\sigma_{ab}(\omega)$. Thus for $W = W_0$, under the above conditions, we obtain a limiting normal distribution for $N^{\frac{1}{2}}(\hat{\tau} - \tau_0)$ with zero mean vector and covariance matrix

(12) $\left[\sum\limits_{a < b} \sum \dfrac{1}{\pi} \int_{\mathscr{B}_+} \sigma^{ab}(\omega) \sigma_{ab}(\omega)(\partial \theta_{ab}(\omega, \tau_0)/\partial \tau_j)(\partial \theta_{ab}(\omega, \tau_0)/\partial \tau_k) d\omega \right]^{-1}$

where the (j, k)th element of the matrix being inverted is shown. Thus we have the following theorem.

Theorem 2. Let Conditions A be satisfied and one of the two sets of conditions in Theorem 1. Let the fourth cumulant condition for $z(t)$ be satisfied and $x(n,a)$ be weakly mixing, purely non-deterministic and satisfy (9). Then if $W = W_0$ the vector $N^{\frac{1}{2}}(\hat{\tau} - \tau_0)$ has a limiting normal distribution with covariance matrix (12). This choice of W minimises the covariance matrix in the limiting distribution.

The last result follows from the quasi maximum likelihood principle discussed above, for the asymptotic variances we obtain are just those that would hold if the $Y(\omega_s, a)$ were complex Gaussian, and independent for different values of ω_s, and for any given ω_s have $W_0(\omega_s)^{-1}$ as covariance matrix.

It would not be easy to prove Theorem 2 under more general conditions, save possibly with respect to the fourth cumulant condition for $z(t)$. For $p = 2$ the variance becomes

$$\left\{ \dfrac{1}{\pi} \int_{\mathscr{B}_+} \dfrac{\sigma^2(\omega)}{1 - \sigma^2(\omega)} \dfrac{\partial \theta(\omega, \tau_0)}{\partial \tau_j} \dfrac{\partial \theta(\omega, \tau_0)}{\partial \tau_k} d\omega \right\}^{-1}$$

and for the non-dispersive case this becomes

$$\left\{ \frac{1}{\pi} \int_{\mathcal{B}_+} \frac{\sigma^2(\omega)}{1-\sigma^2(\omega)} \, \omega^2 d\omega \right\}^{-1}$$

It may be observed that (12) is not altered if the individual $y(n,a)$ series are filtered by any set of filters that do not alter the $\theta_{ab}(\omega,\tau_0)$. This is not unexpected but it will not hold, in general, if a non-optimal weight function is used.

3. The estimation of W_0

Let us decompose $\mathcal{B}$ into $2M$ narrow bands of approximately $m = N/2M$ frequencies each, centred at frequencies $\lambda_u = 2\pi u/M$. Over such a band the oscillation of $W_{ab}(\omega) \exp i\theta_{ab}(\omega,\tau)$ will be $O(m/N)$. Thus if we replace these functions by their mid-band values the asymptotic properties of $\hat{\tau}$ will not be affected. It follows therefore that the same will be true if m increases with N. Thus we consider

$$\bar{q}_N(\tau) = \frac{1}{2M} \sum_{\mathcal{B}} \sum\sum_{a \neq b} W_{ab}(\lambda_u)|\hat{f}_{ab}(\lambda_u)| \exp i\{\hat{\theta}_{ab}(\lambda_u) - \theta_{ab}(\lambda_u, \tau)\}$$

where $\hat{f}_{ab}(\lambda_u)$ is the average of the $I_{ab}(\omega_s)$ for ω_s belonging to the band centred at λ_μ, $\hat{f}_{ab}(\lambda_u) = |\hat{f}_{ab}(\lambda_u)| \exp i\hat{\theta}(\lambda_u)$ and the outer sum is over $\lambda_u \in \mathcal{B}$. It may be wise to allow m to vary from band to band. (See [3].) In that case we replace $(2M)^{-1}$ by $(2M_u)^{-1}$ where $2M_u m_u = N$. We shall deal only with the case of constant m, for simplicity. Now for $W = W_0$

$$W_{ab}(\lambda_u)|\hat{f}_{ab}(\lambda_u)| = -\sigma_{ab}(\lambda_u)\sigma^{ab}(\lambda_u).$$

This suggests that we replace the left side by $\hat{\sigma}_{ab}(\lambda_u)\hat{\sigma}^{ab}(\lambda_u)$ where $\hat{\sigma}_{ab}(\lambda_u)$ is the usual estimate of coherence. In precisely the same way as in [5] it follows that for m increasing sufficiently slowly with N the asymptotic theory is not affected. Thus we have to maximise

$$(13) \quad \hat{q}_N(\tau) = -\frac{4}{M} \sum_{\mathcal{B}_+} \sum\sum_{a<b} \hat{\sigma}^{ab}(\lambda_u)\hat{\sigma}_{ab}(\lambda_u) \cos\{\hat{\theta}_{ab}(\lambda_u) - \theta_{ab}(\lambda_u, \tau)\}.$$

We may consistently estimate the covariance matrix by

$$(14) \quad \left[\sum\sum_{a<b} \frac{1}{M} \sum_{\mathcal{B}_+} \hat{\sigma}^{ab}(\lambda_u)\hat{\sigma}_{ab}(\lambda_u)(\partial\theta_{ab}(\lambda_u,\hat{\tau})/\partial\tau_j)(\partial\theta_{ab}(\lambda_u,\hat{\tau})/\partial\tau_k) \right]^{-1}.$$

These formulae seem the easiest to use if p is not large. However for p large the inversion of the matrix with entries $\hat{\sigma}_{ab}(\lambda_u)$ for each u is a considerable task and an alternative procedure might profitably be used. This requires an iteration. We first take $W_{ab}(\omega) \equiv 1$ and obtain an estimate $\hat{\tau}^{(1)}$ that, by Theorem 1, is strongly consistent. We then form

(15) $$\hat{f}_z^{(1)}(\lambda_u) = \frac{1}{p(p-1)} \sum_{a \neq b} \sum \hat{f}_{ab}(\lambda_u) \exp\{i\theta_{ab}(\lambda_u, \hat{\tau}^{(1)})\},$$

(16) $$\hat{f}_a^{(1)}(\lambda_u) = \hat{f}_a(\lambda_u) - \hat{f}_z^{(1)}(\lambda_u),$$

and thence

$$\hat{W}_{ab}^{(1)}(\lambda_u) = -\hat{f}_z^{(1)}(\lambda_u) \Big/ \left[\hat{f}_a^{(1)}(\lambda_u)\hat{f}_b^{(1)}(\lambda_u)\left\{ 1 + \sum_a \hat{f}_z^{(1)}(\lambda_u)/\hat{f}_a^{(1)}(\lambda_u) \right\} \right], \quad a \neq b.$$

Then we form

$$\hat{q}_N^{(2)}(\tau) = \frac{4}{M} \sum_{\mathscr{B}_+} \sum_{a<b} \sum \hat{W}_{ab}^{(1)}(\lambda_u) |\hat{f}_{ab}(\lambda_u)| \cos\{\hat{\theta}_{ab}(\lambda_u) - \theta_{ab}(\lambda_u, \tau)\}$$

which is maximised to give an estimate $\hat{\tau}^{(2)}$. The procedure may then be iterated until $\hat{q}_N^{(j)}(\hat{\tau}^{(j)})$ ceases to change appreciably from iteration to iteration. We estimate (14) by means of

$$\{\sigma^{ab}(\lambda_u)\sigma_{ab}(\lambda_u)\}^{(j)} = \hat{W}_{ab}^{(j)}(\lambda_u) |\hat{f}_{ab}(\lambda_u)|, \qquad a < b.$$

There are other variations. In particular (15) and (16) are not asymptotically efficient estimators of f_z, f_a. The effect of this is, however, of the second order of magnitude. Again one might replace $|\hat{f}_{ab}(\lambda_u)|$, $a \neq b$, by $\hat{f}_z^{(j)}(\lambda_u)$. Finally we mention that iteration might possibly be needed even when (13) is used, because if $\theta_{ab}(\lambda_u, \tau_0)$ is large the estimate $\hat{\sigma}_{ab}(\lambda_u)$ will be affected. (See [6] and references cited therein.) We refer the reader to [3] for a further discussion of this problem.

In finding the estimate $\hat{\tau}$ we are led, as a first approximation, to replace, in (13), $\cos x$ by $1 - \frac{1}{2}x^2$. For example in case there is no dispersion, so that $\tau = c^{-1}\phi$, we thus obtain a first estimate of τ as

(17) $$\hat{\tau}^{(1)} = \left[\frac{1}{M} \sum_{\mathscr{B}_+} \sum_{a<b} \sum \lambda_u^2 \hat{\sigma}^{ab}(\lambda_u)\hat{\sigma}_{ab}(\lambda_u)\{\xi(a)-\xi(b)\}\{\xi(a)-\xi(b)\}' \right]^{-1}$$

$$\times \frac{1}{M} \sum_{\mathscr{B}_+} \sum_{a<b} \sum \hat{\sigma}^{ab}(\lambda_u)\hat{\sigma}_{ab}(\lambda_u)\lambda_u\hat{\theta}_{ab}(\lambda_u)\{\xi(a)-\xi(b)\},$$

in which the first factor is (14). This formula is just a weighted regression of the $\hat{\theta}_{ab}(\lambda_u)$, $a < b$, $\lambda_u \in \mathcal{B}_+$, on the vectors $\lambda_u\{\xi(a) - \xi(b)\}$ with weights $\hat{\sigma}_{ab}(\lambda_u)\hat{\sigma}^{ab}(\lambda_u)$. It is fairly evident that $\hat{\tau}^{(1)}$ will have the same asymptotic distribution as $\hat{\tau}$. The possibility of multiple determinations of $\hat{\theta}_{ab}(\lambda_u)$, does not affect (14), may be troublesome in (17) but of course the computations are much simpler in (17).

References

[1] BILLINGSLEY, P. (1965) *Ergodic Theory and Information.* John Wiley, New York.

[2] FEDOR, L. S. (1967) A statistical approach to the determination of three dimensional ionospheric drifts. *J. Geophys. Res.* **72**, 5401–5415.

[3] HAMON, B. V. AND HANNAN, E. J. (1974) Spectral estimation of time delay for dispersive and nondispersive systems. *Appl. Statist.* **23**, 134–142.

[4] HANNAN, E. J. (1973) Multivariate time series analysis. *J. Multivariate Anal.* 395–407.

[5] HANNAN, E. J. AND ROBINSON, P. M. (1973) Lagged regression with unknown lags. *J. Roy. Statist. Soc.* B **35**, 252–267.

[6] HANNAN, E. J. AND THOMSON, P. J. (1973) Estimating group delay. *Biometrika* **60**, 241–253.

[7] HINICH, M. J. AND SHAMAN, P. (1972) Parameter estimation from *R*-dimensional plane waves observed with additive independent Gaussian errors. *Ann. Math. Statist.* **43**, 153–169.

[8] KATZNELSON, Y. (1968) *Harmonic Analysis.* John Wiley, New York.

[9] KRAUSE, D. J., STEADMAN, J. W. AND WILLIAMS, T. W. (1972) Effect of record length on noise-induced error in the cross correlation estimate. *IEEE Trans. on Systems, Man and Cybernetics, SMC*-2, 255–261.

[10] MUNK, W. H., MILLER, G. R., SNODGRASS, F. E. AND BARBER, N. F. (1963) Directional recording of swell from dirt and storms. *Phil. Trans. Roy. Soc.* **255**, 505–584.

On Updating Algorithms and Inference for Stochastic Point Processes

D. VERE-JONES

Abstract

This paper is an attempt to interpret and extend, in a more statistical setting, techniques developed by D. L. Snyder and others for estimation and filtering for doubly stochastic point processes. The approach is similar to the Kalman-Bucy approach in that the updating algorithms can be derived from a Bayesian argument, and lead ultimately to equations which are similar to those occurring in stochastic approximation theory. In this paper the estimates are derived from a general updating formula valid for any point process. It is shown that almost identical formulae arise from updating the maximum likelihood estimates, and on this basis it is suggested that in practical situations the sequence of estimates will be consistent and asymptotically efficient. Specific algorithms are derived for estimating the parameters in a doubly stochastic process in which the rate alternates between two levels.

1. Introduction

This paper grew out of a seminar discussion which attempted to assess the value of updating techniques in the problem of estimating the parameters in a stationary point process. Such techniques have recently been developed in a series of papers by D. L. Snyder and co-authors (e.g., Snyder (1972a,b), (1973), Snyder and Rhodes (1972), Forrester and Snyder (1973)), in an engineering context related to the problems of signal detection and estimation. For a statistician not well versed in the engineering jargon, it is not easy to assess how widely applicable the techniques may be, nor how their statistical properties compare with those of other available techniques. These questions are the more important because no satisfactory approach to the problem of parameter estimation for point processes has yet emerged. Brillinger (1972) has shown that under reasonable conditions it is possible to obtain consistent estimates of the spectrum of counts, but this does not mean that an approach based on the spectrum of counts will necessarily give good parametric estimates in a parametric model. Unlike the situation for Gaussian processes, important information will usually be carried by other aspects of the process, such as the interval distributions, and it is not clear how this information should be combined with that from the spectrum. Different approaches lead to different estimates of the same parameter, and it is not clear which should be preferred nor how they should be combined.

Under these circumstances any method which offers a systematic approach to parameter estimation warrants serious consideration. The present paper should be regarded as only a preliminary skirmish with updating techniques. Some of the problems involved, such as rigorously establishing the consistency or asymptotic efficiency of the methods, are technically extremely difficult, and do not seem to have been resolved even in the simpler case of updating techniques applied to regression problems (e.g., Albert and Gardner (1967)). Throughout we shall be content with indicating the likely conditions under which a stated result may hold.

A brief synopsis of the paper is as follows. In Section 2, we derive a general updating formula of wide applicability, which appears to be a slight variant on the results given by Snyder. In the next section this general formula is used to derive explicit updating algorithms for the parameter estimates and their variance matrix. Again these appear to be slight variants on the forms used by Snyder, and in particular are not restricted to the case of a doubly stochastic process with Markovian rate function. In Section 4 the results are related to likelihood methods, and it is shown that essentially the same formulae are obtained by successively updating the maximum likelihood estimates as new information is received. On these grounds it is suggested that the updating techniques are likely to yield efficient parameter estimates under conditions similar to those for which the maximum likelihood estimates are themselves efficient. The main practical drawback to the method is the implicit requirement that the conditional rate function (the expected rate of events in $(t, t + dt)$, given the values of the parameters and observations on the process in an interval (t_0, t)), must be known as a function of the parameters and the past observations. This is very nearly tantamount to the requirement that the likelihood function itself should be known, and so restricts the immediate applicability of the techniques to situations which can in any case be handled by standard methods. Even in these cases, however, the updating approach may be computationally effective, and of course it will be the natural choice when real-time considerations are important.

This is not quite the complete story, however, as in particular cases it may be possible to suggest further approximations to the general results of Sections 2–3 which can be applied even when the conditional rates themselves cannot be obtained explicitly. This is the situation which occurs with the doubly stochastic processes discussed by Snyder. Under the assumption of a Markovian rate function, and with additional approximations, it is possible to update not only the parameter estimates but also a sufficient number of further variables to enable, in effect, the conditional rate function to be written down to an adequate degree of approximation. We illustrate these ideas by setting up the updating equations for estimating the parameters in a doubly stochastic process for which the rate function alternates between two values. So far as we know, this problem has not been treated in this way before, although closely related results are given in one of Snyder's (1973) most recent papers and in some recent work by Yashin (1970) and Rudemo (1973). It is a good example of a process which is not easily handled by standard methods, and for which the updating approach therefore represents a potential gain.

2. A general updating formula

Let $N(t)$ be a point process, stationary or non-stationary, and z a vector of random variables jointly distributed with $N(t)$; z may, for example, be a vector of parameters with a specified prior distribution in a Bayesian formulation of the problem, or the value at some specified time of a process jointly evolving with $N(t)$. Of the joint distributions we shall require that the conditional expectations

$$(1) \qquad \hat{n}(t,\tau;z) = E[N(t+\tau) - N(t)|z, \, dN(x), \, t_0 \leqq x \leqq t]$$

exist and are a.s. right differentiable at $\tau = 0$ for all t. We shall require also that the process is *orderly* (events occur singly); a suitable version of this condition in the present context would require $P[N(t+h) - N(t) \geqq 2|e] \to 0$ as $h \to 0$, uniformly for all t and all conditioning events e of the

type appearing in the right hand side of (1). Discussions of related
regularity conditions can be found in Daley (1974) and Papangelou ((1974),
Sections 2,7,5), but it is not our intention to develop a rigorous argument in
the present paper; at best we can hope to call attention to the kinds of
regularity condition which are likely to be needed.

The right derivative of (1) we shall term the *conditional intensity-
function* and denote by

$$(2) \qquad \hat{\lambda}(t, z) = \frac{\partial \hat{n}(t, \tau; z)}{\partial \tau} \bigg|_{\tau = 0}.$$

This notation is suggested by the case of a doubly stochastic process (see
below) and is conveniently brief; it should be noted, however, that it
suppresses the explicit dependence of the conditional rate on the time
instants $\{t_i, i = 1, \cdots, n, \ t_0 \leq t_1 \leq t_2 \cdots < t_n \leq t\}$ at which points of the
process are observed during the observation period (t_0, t). Where it is
desired, a more explicit notation can be formed in terms of the joint
probability $p_n(t_1, t_2, \cdots, t_n; t_0, t; z) dt_1 \cdots dt_n$ of finding exactly n points in
the interval (t_0, t), within the respective subinterval $(t_i, t_i + dt_i)$, $i =
1, \cdots, n$, given the value of z. We have then

$$(3) \qquad \hat{\lambda}(t, z) = -\frac{\partial}{\partial t} [\log p_n(t_1, t_2, \cdots, t_n; t_0, t; z)].$$

The appearance of the logarithm in this formula is an expression of the
fact that the conditional intensity can be interpreted as the hazard
function for the time interval from the last observed event to the next
event following it, all conditional on the earlier observations and the
parameter values. Thus (3) is an extension of the formula

$$h(t) = -\frac{d}{dt} \log [1 - F(t)]$$

giving the hazard function $h(t)$ in terms of the corresponding distribution
function $F(t)$; in fact (3) reduces to this form in the special case of a
renewal process.

Another special case of importance is that of a doubly stochastic
process; such a process may be regarded as a Poisson process with
time-dependent rate function $\lambda(t)$ which is itself a random process. To
introduce the dependence on the variables z, we suppose that $\lambda(t)$ can be
written in the form

$$\lambda(X(t), z) \equiv \lambda(t, z)$$

where $X(t)$ is the underlying random process governing the rate; then the value of z may affect the function $\lambda(t, z)$ governing the rate as a function of $X(t)$, as well as the evolution of $X(t)$ itself. The fundamental property of the Poisson process is that the occurrence of an event in a given time interval $(t, t + dt)$ is independent of the numbers and positions of events in preceding time intervals. The doubly stochastic process inherits this property to the extent that, given a realization of $X(t)$ and z, then the occurrence of events in disjoint intervals is independent. We can therefore write, using a differential notation for brevity, and for the same reason contracting the notation $E[\cdot|dN(x), 0 \le x \le t]$ to $E[\cdot|dN(x)]$,

$$\hat{\lambda}(t, z)dt = E[dN(t)|z, dN(x)]$$

(4)
$$= E\{E[dN(t)|z, \lambda(t), dN(z)]|dN(x)\}$$

$$= E\{E[dN(t)|z, X(t)]|dN(x)\}$$

$$= E[\lambda(t, z)|dN(x)].$$

(For a full discussion of the conditioning arguments, see Jowett (1974).) Thus, in the case of a doubly stochastic process, $\hat{\lambda}(t, z)$ can be written as an estimate of the rate $\lambda(t, z)$, given the observations in (t_0, t).

We turn now to a derivation of the updating formula referred to in the section heading. It is simply an application of Bayes' formula to obtain the increment in the posterior expectation of z, due to observing the process through a small time increment dt. Denoting by $\hat{z}(t)$ the posterior expectation $E[z|dN(x)]$, we have for the case that no event is observed in $(t, t + dt)$

$$\hat{z}(t + dt) = E\{z[1 - \chi(t, t + dt)]|dN(x)\}/[1 - \hat{\lambda}(t)dt]$$

$$= \hat{z}(t) - E[z\hat{\lambda}(t, z)|dN(x)]dt + \hat{z}(t)\hat{\lambda}(t)dt,$$

where $\chi(t, t + dt) = 1$ if $dN(t) = 1$ and is zero otherwise, $\hat{\lambda}(t)dt = E[\hat{\lambda}(t, z)dt|dN(x)] = E[dN(t)|dN(x)]$, and we have used the reduction

$$E[z\chi(t, t + dt)|dN(x)] = E\{E[z\chi(t, t + dt)|z, dN(x)]|dN(x)\}$$

$$= E[z\hat{\lambda}(t, z)|dN(x)]dt.$$

Simplifying further, we obtain

(5)
$$\frac{d\hat{z}(t)}{dt} = -\text{cov}[z, \hat{\lambda}(t, z)|dN(x)].$$

The case where $dN(t) = 1$ can be handled similarly, and yields the equation

$$\hat{z}(t+) = E[z\hat{\lambda}(t, z)|dN(x)]/\hat{\lambda}(t)$$

or

(6) $\Delta\hat{z}(t) \equiv \hat{z}(t+) - \hat{z}(t) = \text{cov}[z, \hat{\lambda}(t, z)|dN(x)]/\hat{\lambda}(t).$

Variant forms of these equations will prove useful for the special case of a doubly stochastic process. These variants can be derived in a similar way to (4), and are identical to (5) and (6) except that $\hat{\lambda}(t, z)$ is replaced by $\lambda(t, z)$ wherever the former appears on the right hand side of these equations. It is in this latter form that the equations are used in Snyder's original papers.

3. Evolution of the moments of parameter estimates

Equations (5) and (6) cannot be applied directly to the problem of finding updating formulae for parameter estimates, for if z is taken to be that vector of unknown parameters, the right hand sides of these equations will depend in general on aspects of the joint distribution of z and $N(t)$ going beyond the expectations which are updated on the left hand sides. To get over this difficulty it is necessary to take in place of the original z a family of random variables large enough to completely specify the evolution of the posterior distributions of z.

One method of achieving this might be to consider the evolution of the joint characteristic functional $E[\exp(is'z) + \int_{t_0}^t g(x)dN(x)]$. The left hand side of (5) would then be the rate of change of this functional with time, and the right hand side could also be expressed in terms of this functional.

A simpler approach is to supplement the equations for the evolution of $\hat{z}(t)$ itself by further equations describing the evolution of the moments of $\hat{z}(t)$. This is the approach we shall follow, since the resulting equations have a rather simple structural form, and lend themselves to meaningful approximation under assumptions of asymptotic normality.

To establish the form of the procedure, consider first the case when z is a scalar. We suppose that, for given past history $dN(x)$, the function $\hat{\lambda}(t, z)$ is an analytic function of z, thus admitting a Taylor series expansion

$$\hat{\lambda}(t, z) = \hat{\lambda}(t, \hat{z}(t)) + \sum_{r=1}^{\infty} \frac{1}{r!}[z - \hat{z}(t)]'D_{\lambda}^r,$$

where we have used the abbreviated notation

$$D_\lambda^r = \frac{\partial^r \hat{\lambda}(t, z)}{\partial z^r} \bigg|_{z = \hat{z}(t)}$$

Suppose also that the parameter z has conditional moments of all orders, say

$$\hat{\mu}_k(t) = E[(z - \hat{z}(t))^k | dN(x)].$$

Though drastic, these assumptions are not unreasonable if, for example, it can be asserted on prior grounds that the parameters lie in a bounded set. In fact weaker assumptions (existence of the first two moments and a continuous second derivative) should suffice to establish the approximate formulae which form the main target of this section.

Now inserting the Taylor expansion of $\hat{\lambda}(t, z)$ into (5), we obtain

(7)
$$\frac{d\hat{z}(t)}{dt} = -E[(z - \hat{z}(t))\hat{\lambda}(t, z) | dN(x)]$$

$$= -\sum_{r=1}^{\infty} \frac{1}{r!} \hat{\mu}_{r+1}(t) D_\lambda^r.$$

If we take $[z - \hat{z}(t)]^k$ in place of z in (5), similar equations can be derived for the evolution of the moments $\hat{\mu}_k(t)$. We have then

$$\frac{d\hat{\mu}_k(t)}{dt} = \frac{\partial \hat{\mu}_k(t)}{\partial \hat{z}(t)} \frac{d\hat{z}(t)}{dt} + \frac{\partial \hat{\mu}_k(t)}{\partial t},$$

where

$$\frac{\partial \hat{\mu}_k(t)}{\partial \hat{z}(t)} = -k\hat{\mu}_{k-1}(t),$$

and from (5),

$$\frac{\partial \hat{\mu}_k(t)}{\partial t} = -\sum_{r=1}^{\infty} \frac{1}{r!} [\hat{\mu}_{k+r}(t) - \hat{\mu}_k(t)\hat{\mu}_r(t)] D_\lambda^r.$$

Hence, for $k \geq 2$,

(8) $$\frac{d\hat{\mu}_k(t)}{dt} = -\sum_{r=1}^{\infty} \frac{1}{r!} [\hat{\mu}_{k+r}(t) - \hat{\mu}_k(t)\hat{\mu}_r(t) + \hat{\mu}_{k-1}(t)\hat{\mu}_{r+1}(t)] D_\lambda^r.$$

Equations (7) and (8) form a complete set of first order non-linear differential equations governing the evolution of the parameter estimates and their moments through an interval between points of the observed process. A similar set of equations can be obtained from (6) for the increments to the estimates which result when a new point is observed. In this way we find

(9) $\Delta \hat{z}(t) = \hat{\lambda}(t)^{-1} \sum_{r=1}^{\infty} \frac{1}{r!} \hat{\mu}_{r+1}(t) D_{\lambda}^{r}$

(10) $\Delta \hat{\mu}_k(t) = \Delta_0 \hat{\mu}_k(t) + \hat{\lambda}(t)^{-1} \sum_{l=1}^{k} \binom{k}{l} \hat{\mu}_{k-l}(t+) [-\Delta \hat{z}(t)]^l$

where for $k \geqq 2$

$$\Delta_0 \hat{\mu}_k(t) = \hat{\lambda}(t)^{-1} \sum_{r=1}^{\infty} \frac{1}{r!} [\hat{\mu}_{k+r}(t) - \hat{\mu}_k(t) \hat{\mu}_r(t)]$$

and in (10) we make the interpretations $\hat{\mu}_0(t+) = 1$, $\hat{\mu}_1(t+) = \Delta \hat{z}(1)$ and $\hat{\mu}_k(t+) = \hat{\mu}_k(t) + \Delta_0 \hat{\mu}_k(t)$.

The exact form of these equations is probably of academic interest, although they serve as the starting point of more useful approximations, and it is important in principle to know that they are available to provide higher order approximations if required.

The most important and natural approximations are analogous to those suggested by Snyder, based on the assumptions that only the largest order terms in the Taylor expansions need be retained, and that the estimates are approximately normally distributed, so that third and higher order cumulants may be neglected. Thus in (7) and (9) we neglect $\hat{\mu}_3(t)$, replace $\hat{\mu}_4(t)$ by $3\hat{\mu}_2(t)^2$, and neglect all higher order terms. The infinite systems (7)–(8) and (9)–(10) than reduce to the coupled pairs of equations

(11) $\dfrac{d\hat{z}(t)}{dt} = -\hat{\mu}_2(t) D_{\lambda}^{1}$ $\left.\rule{0pt}{40pt}\right\}$ if $dN(t) = 0$,

(12) $\dfrac{d\hat{\mu}_2(t)}{dt} = -\hat{\mu}_2(t)^2 D_{\lambda}^{2}$

(13) $\Delta \hat{z}(t) = \hat{\mu}_2(t) D_{\lambda}^{1}/\hat{\lambda}(t)$ $\left.\rule{0pt}{40pt}\right\}$ if $dN(t) = 1$.

(14) $\Delta \hat{\mu}_2(t) = [\hat{\mu}_2(t)]^2 \{-[D_{\lambda}^{1}/\hat{\lambda}(t)]^2 + D_{\lambda}^{2}/\hat{\lambda}(t)\}$

The last two equations can be simplified further, for it is consistent with the earlier approximations to replace $\hat{\lambda}(t)$ by $\hat{\lambda}(t, z(t))$, using $\hat{\lambda}(t) = E[dN(t)|dN(x)] = E[\hat{\lambda}(t, z)|dN(x)] = \hat{\lambda}(t, \hat{z}) + \text{small order terms}$. Then

(13) and (14) can be rewritten in the more suggestive forms

(15) $$\Delta \hat{z}(t) = \hat{\mu}_2(t) D^1_{\log \lambda}$$

(16) $$\Delta \hat{\mu}_2(t) = \hat{\mu}_2(t)^2 D^2_{\log \lambda}$$

where

$$D^k_{\log \lambda} = \frac{\partial^k \log \hat{\lambda}(t, z)}{\partial z^k}\Bigg|_{z = \hat{z}(t)}, \qquad k = 1, 2.$$

The equations are now in a form which can be extended readily to the vector case. Let $\hat{\Sigma}(t)$ be the variance matrix of the parameter estimates, say with elements $\hat{\sigma}_{ij}(t)$ where

$$\hat{\sigma}_{ij}(t) = E[(z_i - \hat{z}_i(t))(z_j - \hat{z}_j(t)) \,|\, dN(x)].$$

Also let $\boldsymbol{D}^1_\lambda$ and $\boldsymbol{D}^1_{\log \lambda}$ be the vectors of first order derivatives with elements

$$\partial \hat{\lambda}(t, z)/\partial z_i |_{z_i = \hat{z}_i(t)}, \ \partial \log \hat{\lambda}(t, z)/\partial z_i |_{z_i = \hat{z}_i(t)}$$

of second order derivatives. In place of Equations (11)–(12) and (15)–(16) we have then

(17) $$\frac{\partial \hat{z}(t)}{\partial t} = -\hat{\Sigma}(t) \boldsymbol{D}^1_\lambda$$
$$\left. \begin{array}{c} \\ \\ \end{array} \right\} \quad \text{if } dN(t) = 0$$

(18) $$\frac{\partial \hat{\Sigma}(t)}{\partial t} = -\hat{\Sigma}(t) \boldsymbol{D}^2_\lambda \hat{\Sigma}(t)$$

(19) $$\Delta \hat{z}(t) = \hat{\Sigma}(t) \boldsymbol{D}^1_{\log \lambda}$$
$$\left. \begin{array}{c} \\ \\ \end{array} \right\} \quad \text{if } dN(t) = 1 .$$

(20) $$\Delta \hat{\Sigma}(t) = \hat{\Sigma}(t) \boldsymbol{D}^2_{\log \lambda} \hat{\Sigma}(t)$$

4. The relation to likelihood procedures

We shall show in this section that Equations (17)–(20) closely resemble those which would result from updating the maximum likelihood estimates after observing the process over our additional interval $(t, t + \Delta)$. This resemblance is of importance in giving insight into the likely behaviour of the estimates.

We first recall some basic ideas from the asymptotic theory of likelihood estimates. If $L = L(t, z)$ denotes the log likelihood of the sample obtained from observations over the interval (t_0, t), the vector $\boldsymbol{S}(t, z) = \partial L / \partial z$ is called the vector of efficient scores for the parameters z. If the sample is thought of as a random vector ranging from realization to realization, but with t and z remaining fixed then the likelihood function itself, and also the vector of efficient scores, are *random variables*. In this sense it is easy to show that (under regularity conditions) $E(S|t, z) = 0$, and the variance matrix for S can be expressed in either of the two forms

$$E[SS'] = -E\left[\frac{\partial^2 L}{\partial z dz'}\right] = E\left[\frac{\partial L}{\partial z} \cdot \frac{\partial L}{\partial z'}\right].$$

This matrix is called the information matrix $I(t, z)$ for the experiment, and provides a measure of the effectiveness of the experiment in yielding information about the unknown parameters z. In the classical case of n independent observations on a single distribution, $I(n, z) = nI(z)$, where $I(z)$ provides a measure of the information per observation. For a stationary process, we may expect $I(t, z)$ to vary asymptotically linearly with t, say $I(t, z) \sim tI(z)$, where $I(z)$ represents the average information per unit time.

A maximum likelihood estimate is a solution $\hat{z}(t)$ to the equation

(21) $S(\hat{z}) = 0.$

Under further regularity conditions, it is known that, as the sample size n or the time t increases, the solutions to these equations provide estimates of the unknown parameters which are consistent, asymptotically normal, and asymptotically efficient. Moreover, the parameter estimates so obtained have a variance matrix which is asymptotically of the form $I(z, t)^{-1}$, the latter representing an asymptotic lower bound to the variance matrix of any consistent estimate of z based on observations over (t_0, t).

The likelihood equations (21) are rarely in a form which can be solved readily analytically, so that recourse is usually made to approximate numerical methods of solution. One such method, due to Fisher, makes use of the efficient scores. If z^* is an approximate solution to (21) then a Taylor series expansion about z^* yields for the maximum likelihood estimate $\hat{z}$

$$S(\hat{z}) = S(z^*) - D_L^2 \cdot (\hat{z} - z^*) + \cdots$$

where $-D_L^2$ is the matrix of second derivatives $\partial^2 L / \partial z_i \partial z_i$ evaluated at $z = z^*$. Since $\hat{z}$ is by definition a solution to (21), the left hand side vanishes and we obtain as a first approximation to the correction term

(22) $\hat{z} - z^* = (D_L^2)^{-1} \cdot S(z^*).$

If $I(z)$ is known explicitly, it may be convenient, and is likely to produce only a second order error, to replace D_L^2 by $I(z^*)$ in (22). More importantly, Le Cam (1960), (1969) has shown that this modification of (22) provides a general method for obtaining asymptotically efficient estimates. In brief, he has shown that if z^* is any 'reasonable' initial estimate of z(for example, one that converges to z at rate $n^{-\frac{1}{2}}$ where n is the sample size in the classical situation of identically distributed observations), then the improved estimate derived from the modified version of (22) is asymptotically efficient.

This technique could be applied directly to point processes, without any updating, along the lines of the discussion by Davies (1973) of inference on stationary, Gaussian, discrete-time series. To see the relevance to updating problems, a slight shift of viewpoint is needed. For this purpose we interpret $\hat{z}$ in (22) as $\hat{z}(t + \Delta)$, the maximum likelihood estimate of z based on observations over $(t_0, t + \Delta)$, and z^* as the preliminary estimate $\hat{z}(t)$ based on observations up to time t. Then $\hat{z} - z^*$ reduces to the increment $\hat{z}(t + \Delta) - \hat{z}(t)$ to the maximum likelihood estimates and $S(z^*)$ becomes the derivative $\partial L(t + \Delta)/\partial z$ evaluated at $z = \hat{z}(t)$. Because $\partial L(t)/\partial z$ vanishes when $z = \hat{z}(t)$, $\partial L(t + \Delta)/\partial z$ reduces to $\partial \Delta L/\partial z$ evaluated at $z = \hat{z}(t)$. Thus the relevant version of (22) for updating purposes is, at least to first order,

$$(23) \qquad \hat{z}(t + \Delta) - \hat{z}(t) = [D_L^2]^{-1} \frac{\partial \Delta L}{\partial z}$$

where D_L^2 is the matrix of second derivatives of $L(t)$ (strictly $L(t + \Delta)$ but the correction is again of second order) evaluated at $\hat{z}(t)$.

Now let us determine the particular form of (23) in the case of a point process. It is well-known (and follows by integrating (3) between points of the process) that the likelihood function for a point process can be written in the form

$$L(t, z) = - \int_{t_0}^{t} \hat{\lambda}(u, z)du + \int_{t_0}^{t} \log \hat{\lambda}(u, z)dN(u).$$

Hence $\Delta L = \hat{\lambda}(t, z)\Delta t$ if $\Delta N(t) = 0$ (no points in $(t, t + \Delta)$), and $\Delta L = \log \hat{\lambda}(t, z)$ if $\Delta N(t) = 1$. Introducing the notation D_λ^1, $D_{\log\lambda}^1$ etc., used in the preceding section we therefore obtain from (23) the pair of equations

$$(24) \qquad \frac{dz(t)}{dt} = - (D_L^2)^{-1}D_\lambda^1 \qquad \text{if} \quad dN(t) = 0,$$

(25) $$\Delta \hat{z}(t) = (\boldsymbol{D}_L^2)^{-1} \boldsymbol{D}_{\log\lambda}^1 \qquad \text{if } dN(t) = 1.$$

These equations are of similar form to (17), (19), if we can identify $\hat{\Sigma}(t)$ in those equations with $(\boldsymbol{D}_L^2)^{-1}$. The link between these two quantities is the result, to which we have already referred, that the inverse of the information matrix appears as the asymptotic form of the variance-covariance matrix for the maximum likelihood estimates. Thus we might expect $\hat{\Sigma}(t)$ to be an estimate of $\boldsymbol{I}(t, z)^{-1}$, while $\boldsymbol{D}_L^2$ is an estimate of $\boldsymbol{I}(t, z)$ itself. In fact there is a more precise relationship, for during an interval between points, the equation governing the growth of $\boldsymbol{D}_L^2$ is

$$\frac{d\boldsymbol{D}_L^2}{dt} = \left\{ \frac{\partial^2 \hat{\lambda}(t, z)}{\partial z_i \partial z_j} \right\}_{z = \hat{z}(t)} = \boldsymbol{D}_\lambda^2,$$

so that

$$\frac{d}{dt} [(\boldsymbol{D}_L^2)^{-1}] = -(\boldsymbol{D}_L^2)^{-1} \boldsymbol{D}_\lambda^2 (\boldsymbol{D}_L^2)^{-1},$$

which is identical in form to (18) if $(\boldsymbol{D}_L^2)^{-1}$ and $\hat{\Sigma}(t)$ are identical. Thus $\hat{\Sigma}(t)$ and $(\boldsymbol{D}_L^2)^{-1}$ evolve along the same trajectories in the intervals between points of the process, if they start from the same initial values. The corresponding result for passage past a point of the process is only approximately true, because the relationship

$$\Delta(A^{-1}) = A^{-1}(\Delta A) A^{-1}$$

is itself only approximate. Thus, although we have

$$\Delta(\boldsymbol{D}_L^2) = -\boldsymbol{D}_{\log\lambda}^2,$$

we can only write

$$\Delta(\boldsymbol{D}_L^2)^{-1} = (\boldsymbol{D}_L^2)^{-1} \boldsymbol{D}_{\log\lambda}^2 (\boldsymbol{D}_L^2)^{-1}$$

to first order.

Perhaps two morals can be drawn from this discussion. The first is that the equations derived in the preceding section are so close to the equations for approximately updating the maximum likelihood estimates that it is reasonable to expect the two sequences of estimates to behave in a similar way. Secondly, although none of the estimates so derived is *exactly* the maximum likelihood estimate, the general asymptotic theory of these estimates, and even more the work of LeCam, suggests that under reasonable conditions, (for example, conditions which would make the exact likelihood estimates themselves consistent and approximately efficient) the more approximate updating estimates will inherit the properties of consistency and asymptotic efficiency.

Example. It may be helpful, before proceeding further, to illustrate the forms of the various updating equations in the simplest case of a stationary Poisson process with unknown rate parameter α. In this case the log likelihood function is given by

$$L(t, \alpha) = -\alpha t + N(t)\log\alpha$$

where $N(t)$ denotes the total number of points observed over the observation period (t_0, t). Moreover $\hat{\lambda}(t, \alpha) = \alpha$ for all t. Hence

$$D_\lambda^1 = 1, \qquad D_{\log\lambda}^1 = \alpha^{-1},$$
$$D_\lambda^2 = 0, \qquad D_{\log\lambda}^2 = -\alpha^{-2}.$$

Then Equations (17)–(20) of the preceding section take the forms

$$\frac{d\hat{\alpha}(t)}{dt} = -v(t), \qquad \frac{dv(t)}{dt} = 0 \text{ if } dN(t) = 0,$$

$$\Delta\hat{\alpha}(t) = v(t)/\hat{\alpha}(t), \qquad \Delta v(t) = -[v(t)/\alpha(t)]^2 \text{ if } dN(t) = 1$$

where we have written $v(t)$ for $\hat{\sigma}^2(t)$.

The equations for approximately updating the maximum likelihood estimates discussed in the present section take the forms

$$\frac{d\hat{\alpha}(t)}{dt} = -1/j(t), \quad \frac{dj(t)}{dt} = 0 \qquad \text{if} \quad dN(t) = 0,$$

$$\Delta\hat{\alpha}(t) = [\hat{\alpha}(t)j(t)]^{-1}, \ \Delta j(t) = [\hat{\alpha}(t)]^{-2} \qquad \text{if} \quad dN(t) = 1,$$

where we have written $j(t)$ for D_λ^2, and $j(t)$ corresponds to $1/v(t)$ in the preceding pair of equations.

Even in such a simple case it is not altogether easy to discern the asymptotic behaviour of the estimates. However, some insight into their behaviour can be gained by considering the changes over a complete cycle, from just before the Nth observed point, past the point itself and over the following time interval (of length τ_N say) to the time instant just before the $(N + 1)$th observed point. Denoting by α_N, v_N the estimates of α and its variance at the beginning of the cycle, we find for both sets of estimates

(26) $$\alpha_{N+1} = \alpha_N + v_N(\alpha_N^{-1} - \tau_N v_{N+1}/v_N),$$

where

$$\frac{1}{v_{N+1}} = \frac{1}{v_N} + \frac{1}{\alpha_N^2}$$

for the approximate likelihood equations, and

$$\frac{1}{v_{N+1}} = \frac{1}{v_N} + \frac{v_N}{v_{N+1}} \cdot \frac{1}{\alpha_N^2}$$

for the equations derived from the previous section.

As we should anticipate, the difference between the two sets of estimates are of a trivial kind. As for the behaviour of the sequence $\{\alpha_N\}$ itself, Equation (26) is similar in character to recursive estimates for the mean, say μ_N, of the variables $\{\tau_N\}$. Such estimates, of the form

$$\hat{\mu}_{N+1} = \hat{\mu}_N + c_N(\tau_N - \mu_N),$$

are known to be consistent under wide conditions (see, for example, Albert and Gardner (1967)) and assuming that the same is true for (26), it follows from the equation after (26) that as $N \to \infty$,

$$\frac{1}{v_N} \sim \frac{N}{\alpha^2}.$$

Hence (26) approximates to the form

$$\alpha_{N+1} = \alpha_N + \frac{\alpha^2}{N}(\alpha_N^{-1} - \tau_N),$$

which can be compared with the updating equation for the optimal estimate $\alpha_N = N/\Sigma_1^n \tau_k$, namely

$$\alpha_{N+1} = \alpha_N + \frac{\alpha_N \alpha_{N+1}}{N}(\alpha_N^{-1} - \tau_N).$$

These comparisons provide a strong heuristic argument for supposing that in this case at least the approximations are asymptotically efficient; it seems not unreasonable to suppose that they will have similar properties under more general conditions.

To conclude this section we add a few further general comments.
(1) All of the discussion presupposes that we start from initial estimates of the parameters which are close enough to the true values to be within some 'zone of attraction' of the procedures. While the simulations carried out by Snyder (1972a) suggest a wide region of stability for estimating the parameters in a Poisson process, there is no guarantee that in general the updating equations will converge to appropriate solutions if started from arbitrary initial conditions.

(2) This fact apart, the effect of initial errors will be reduced at rate approximately $1/t$, while the effect of random errors will be reduced at rate $1/t^{\frac{1}{2}}$. This suggests that the procedures should show good stability.

(3) In the classical case of independent observations, it is sometimes possible to introduce a simplification by using the known analytical form of $I(t, z)$, evaluated at $\hat{z}(t)$, as an alternative estimate of the variance terms in equations such as (22) and (23). In principle this approach should still be possible for stationary point processes, if the 'information matrix per unit time' $I(z) = \lim_{t \to \infty} t^{-1} I(t, z)$ can be calculated. Davies has pointed out to me that an expression for this quantity can be obtained in terms of the 'complete intensity function'

$$\lambda^*(t, z) = \lim_{t_0 \to -\infty} \hat{\lambda}(t, z),$$

representing the best estimate of the rate given the complete past history from $-\infty$ to t. In fact we have

$$I(t, z) = -E\left[\frac{\partial^2 L(t, z)}{\partial z \partial z'}\right] = -E\int_{t_0}^{t} \frac{1}{\lambda} \frac{\partial \hat{\lambda}}{\partial z} \frac{\partial \hat{\lambda}}{\partial z'} \, du.$$

If now we divide by $(t - t_0)$ and let $t_0 \to -\infty$, then $\hat{\lambda} \to \lambda^*$, and for an ergodic process the integral average can be replaced by a further expectation, leading to the expression

$$I(z) = E\left[\frac{1}{\lambda^*} \frac{\partial \lambda^*}{\partial z^*} \frac{\partial \lambda^*}{\partial z'}\right].$$

Unfortunately, this integral seems very difficult to evaluate except in trivial cases, so that we are led back to Monte Carlo or similar procedures, or in effect, back to the same sort of updating equations for the variance terms that we have already considered.

5. Parameter estimation for doubly stochastic processes with Markovian rate function

While the methods outlined in the previous section can be applied in a straightforward manner to stationary and non-stationary Poisson processes (as in Snyder(1972a)), and to renewal processes and their generalizations, a major difficulty arises if an attempt is made to apply them more generally, for example to cluster processes. The difficulty arises because, in order to write down the coefficients D_λ^1, D_λ^2, etc., appearing in the updating equations, the conditional rates $\hat\lambda(t, z)$ and their derivatives must be known explicitly as functions both of the unknown parameters and of the observed points. In general, it may not be possible to obtain $\hat\lambda(t, z)$ in closed form, and even when it is, tracking the evolution of the derivatives may prove a formidable task, requiring reconsideration of the whole data set each time new values of the derivatives are required. Of course in such a case, there would be little point in using the updating procedures of the preceding sections, and a direct evaluation of the maximum likelihood estimates would probably be more expedient.

Although this appears as a major difficulty, there may nevertheless be special features in any given problem which allow some modification of the updating procedures to go forward. In essence, it is a matter of finding some supplementary variables which can themselves be updated in a reasonably simple manner, and by means of which such coefficients as D_λ^1 can be written down to an adequate degree of approximation.

One important class of processes which can be handled in this way is the class of doubly stochastic point processes with Markovian rate function, these forming the main object of study in the papers by Snyder *et al.* The majority of examples considered by those authors relate to the case where the Markov process is of diffusion type, so that the rate functions change continuously with time. Such examples can be handled by a further extension of the Taylor series method, and since they are fully discussed in Snyder's own papers we shall choose instead to illustrate possible extensions of the preceding methods by an example in which the rate function changes discontinuously. Discussions of such processes have been given by Yashin (1970) and Rudemo(1973),but so far as we know the parameter estimation problem has not been tackled explicitly before.

The simplest example of this kind, which will suffice for our purposes, has a rate process which alternates between two values, and therefore may be written in the form

$$(27) \qquad \lambda(t) = m + \rho\chi(t)$$

where $\chi(t) = \pm 1$. The unknown parameters in the process are then the quantities m and ρ determining the two rates, and the parameters μ_1 and μ_2 governing the lengths of stay in the states $+1$, -1 respectively. Since the rate process is Markovian, these must have exponential distributions, with densities of the form $\mu e^{-\mu x}$, $x \geq 0$.

In examples of this type it is the process $\chi(t)$ which plays the role of supplementary variable. To keep track of the development of $\lambda(t)$ we therefore need not only current estimates of m and ρ, but also current estimates of the probability distribution of $\chi(t)$, which when $\chi(t)$ is Markovian can be obtained from a modified version of the forward Kolmogorov equations. Current estimates of the remaining parameters μ_1 and μ_2 are needed to write down these forward equations.

The updating equations can then be obtained in two stages. First, we write down the equations which would be obtained by treating $\chi(t)$ as if it were a further unknown parameter entering into the expression for the rate function; thus in the present example we have effectively five quantities and their covariances to update by means of Equations (17)–(20). As a second stage, the updating equations for all those quantities involving $\chi(t)$ must be modified to take into account the fact that $\chi(t)$ is evolving at the same time as we are updating our estimates. The approximations involved in writing down the updating equations are much the same as before: thus we neglect higher order terms in the increment, and also neglect their third and fourth cumulants. Since $\chi(t)$ is never asymptotically normal, this represents a slightly cruder approximation than before, but in fact only mixed cumulants involving $\chi(t)$ need to be considered, and it does not appear that neglecting these will constitute a serious source of error.

Let us list the variables in the order m, ρ, $\chi(t)$, μ_1, μ_2, and use the notation $\hat{m}(t)$, $\hat{x}(t)$, $\hat{\sigma}_{m\rho}(t)$, etc., to denote the current estimates of the parameters and their covariances. Consider first the equations governing the evolution of the estimates between two observed points of the point process. The equations corresponding to (17) and (18) can be written down very readily, using the expressions

$$\boldsymbol{D}_\lambda^1 = (1, \hat{x}(t), \hat{\rho}(t), 0, 0)'$$

$$\boldsymbol{D}_\lambda^2 = \begin{pmatrix} 0 & 0 & 0 & 0 & 0 \\ 0 & 0 & 1 & 0 & 0 \\ 0 & 1 & 0 & 0 & 0 \\ 0 & 0 & 0 & 0 & 0 \\ 0 & 0 & 0 & 0 & 0 \end{pmatrix}.$$

Thus, for example, we find

$$\frac{d\hat{m}(t)}{dt} = -\hat{\sigma}_{mm}(t) - \hat{x}(t)\,\hat{\sigma}_{m\rho}(t) - \hat{\rho}(t)\,\hat{\sigma}_{mx}(t),$$

$$\frac{d\hat{\sigma}_{mm}(t)}{dt} = -2\hat{\sigma}_{m\rho}(t)\,\hat{\sigma}_{mx}(t),$$

etc. Only the equations for $d\hat{x}(t)/dt$ and $d\hat{\sigma}_{\theta x}(t)/dt$ (where θ stands for any one of the remaining four parameters) need further consideration, since

$$\begin{aligned} \hat{\sigma}_{xx}(t) &= \mathrm{Var}\,(\chi(t)|dN(x)) \\ &= E\,[\chi(t)^2|dN(x)] - \{E\,[\chi(t)|dN(x)]\}^2 \\ &= 1 - \hat{x}(t)^2, \end{aligned}$$

in view of the special character of $\chi(t)$.

The equation for updating $\hat{x}(t)$ can be handled as follows. We have, writing $\cdot\,|dN(x) \cup dN(t)$ for a conditioning on observations on the point process over both (t_0, t) and the incremental interval $(t, t + dt)$,

(28)
$$\begin{aligned} E[\chi(t + dt)\,|\,dN(x) \cup dN(t)] = \\ E[\chi(t + dt) - \chi(t)\,|\,dN(x) \cup dN(t)] + E[\chi(t)\,|\,dN(x) \cup dN(t)]. \end{aligned}$$

The second term on the right represents the evolution of the estimate of $\chi(t)$ due solely to the extra observations over $(t, t + dt)$, and is governed by the equations we have already considered: thus for $dN(t) = 0$

$$E[\chi(t)\,|\,dN(x) \cup dN(t)] =$$

$$E[\chi(t)\,|\,dN(x)] - \{\hat{\sigma}_{mx}(x) + x(t)\hat{\sigma}_{\rho x}(t) + \hat{\rho}(t)\,[1 - \hat{x}(t)^2]\}\,dt$$

where we have substituted $\hat{\sigma}_{xx}(t) = 1 - \hat{x}(t)^2$ in the appropriate version of (17).

The other term in (28) represents the expectation of a quantity which is zero unless $\chi(t)$ changes state in $(t, t + dt)$. Since this occurs only with probability of order dt, the extra conditioning on $dN(t)$ introduces a modification of order dt^2, which can be neglected, so that we can drop the

$dN(t)$ in the conditioning. But then, *given* the values of μ_1, μ_2 and $\chi(t)$, the expectation has the value

$$- \mu_1 dt (\chi(t) + 1) + \mu_2 dt (1 - \chi(t)),$$

since $\frac{1}{2}[\chi(t) + 1]$ also represents $\delta(\chi(t), 1)$. Finally taking expectations over μ_1 and $\chi(t)$ (all conditional on $dN(x)$ over (t_0, t)), we obtain

$$E[\chi(t + dt) - \chi(t) | dN(x)] =$$
$$\{- \hat{\mu}_1(t)[1 + \hat{x}(t)] + \hat{\mu}_2(t)[1 - \hat{x}(t)] - \hat{\sigma}_{x\mu_1}(t) - \hat{\sigma}_{x\mu_2}(t)\} dt.$$

Thus the updating equation for $\hat{x}(t)$ can be written

$$\frac{d\hat{x}(t)}{dt} = \hat{\mu}_2(t) - \hat{\mu}_1(t) - \hat{x}(t)[\hat{\mu}_1(t) + \hat{\mu}_2(t)] - \hat{\rho}(t)[1 - \hat{x}(t)^2]$$
$$- \hat{\sigma}_{mx}(t) - \hat{x}(t)\hat{\sigma}_{\rho x}(t) - \hat{\sigma}_{x\mu_1}(t) - \hat{\sigma}_{x\mu_2}(t).$$

In fact the covariance terms should decay to zero as t increases, and it would probably be an adequate approximation to retain only the first three terms of this expression, which are all of order 1. The equation then reduces to the appropriate special case of the equations given by Rudemo (1973) for updating the estimates $\hat{p}_i(t) = \Pr[\chi(t) = i | dN(x)]$ when the parameters are assumed known, and $\chi(t)$ is a countable state Markov process.

The equations for updating the estimates $\hat{\sigma}_{\theta x}(t)$ can be handled by a similar technique. The additional term required is of the form

$$E\{[\theta - \hat{\theta}(t)][\chi(t + dt) - \chi(t)] | dN(x)\} =$$
$$- \{[1 + \hat{x}(t)]\hat{\sigma}_{\mu_1\theta}(t) + [1 - \hat{x}(t)]\hat{\mu}_{\mu_2\theta}(t) + [\hat{\mu}_1(t) + \hat{\mu}_2(t)]\hat{\sigma}_{x\theta}(t)\} dt.$$

Combining this with the term derived from (18), we obtain, to take $\hat{\sigma}_{mx}$ as a specific example,

$$\frac{d\hat{\sigma}_{mx}(t)}{dt} = - \{[1 + \hat{x}(t)]\hat{\sigma}_{m\mu_1}(t) + [1 - \hat{x}(t)]\hat{\sigma}_{m\mu_2}(t)$$
$$+ [\hat{\mu}_1(t) + \hat{\mu}_2(t)]\hat{\sigma}_{mx}(t) - \hat{\sigma}_{mx}(t)\hat{\sigma}_{\rho x}(t) - \hat{\sigma}_{m\rho}(t)[1 - \hat{x}(t)^2]\}.$$

The expressions for the increments to the estimates past a point of the observed process are more straightforward. In this case the evolution of $\chi(t)$ can be ignored, and Equations (19) and (20) can be used without modification, taking

$$D^1_{\log\lambda} = [\hat{m}(t) + \hat{\rho}(t)\hat{x}(t)]^{-1}(1, \hat{x}(t), \hat{\rho}(t), 0, 0),$$

$$D^2_{\log\lambda} = -[\hat{m}(t) + \hat{\rho}(t)\hat{x}(t)]^{-2} \begin{pmatrix} 1 & \hat{x}(t) & \hat{\rho}(t) & 0 & 0 \\ \hat{x}(t) & \hat{x}(t)^2 - \hat{m}(t) & 0 & 0 \\ \hat{\rho}(t) - \hat{m}(t) & \hat{\rho}(t)^2 & 0 & 0 \\ 0 & 0 & 0 & 0 & 0 \\ 0 & 0 & 0 & 0 & 0 \end{pmatrix}.$$

This completes the derivation of the updating equations for the given process. Unfortunately, the implementation of a computer programme based on these equations would be another project again, and one that we have not had the time or opportunity to undertake. One might anticipate that by treating the parameter estimates as constant in the right hand sides of the differential equations governing their evolution between points of the process, it would be possible to obtain an approximate expression for the increments of the estimates over a complete cycle, much as was done for the special case of the Poisson process in Section 4. Such an approximation would greatly facilitate the numerical computations, but we shall have to defer a discussion of such considerations to a subsequent paper.

Unsatisfactory as this conclusion may be, I hope the paper will at least provoke further discussion of the possible use of updating techniques in the difficult problem of parameter estimation for point processes. I should like to acknowledge the valuable comments of my colleagues Dr R. B. Davies and Mr J. H. Jowett in the preparation of this paper, and to express my appreciation of the opportunity of paying tribute, in however inadequate a manner, to Professor Bartlett's outstanding contributions to many branches of probability and statistics, and not least to the problems of inference on stochastic processes.

References

ALBERT, A. E. AND GARDNER, L. A. (JR.) (1967) *Stochastic Approximation and Nonlinear Regression*. M.I.T. Press Research Monograph No. 42, Cambridge, Mass.

BRILLINGER, D. R. (1972) The spectral analysis of stationary interval functions. *Proc. Sixth Berkeley Symp. Math. Statist. Prob.* **1**, 483–513.

DALEY, D. J. (1974) Various concepts of orderliness for point-processes. *Stochastic Geometry*. (Ed. E. F. Harding and D. G. Kendall), Wiley, London, 148–161.

DAVIES, R. B. (1973) Asymptotic inference on stationary Gaussian time-series,. *Adv. Appl. Prob.* **5**, 469–497.

FORRESTER, R. H. (JR) AND SNYDER, D. L. (1973) Phasetracking performance of direct detection optical receivers. Preprint from Biomedical Computer Laboratory, Washington University, St. Louis.

JOWETT. J. H. (1974) The *a posteriori* distribution of the rate function of a doubly stochastic Poisson process. Preprint from Mathematics Department, Victoria University, Wellington.

LE CAM, L. M. (1960) Locally asymptotically normal families of distributions. *Univ. California Publ. Statist.* **3**, 37–98.

LE CAM. L. M. (1969) *Théorie Asymptotique de la Décision Statistique.* Montreal University Press, Montreal.

PAPANGELOU, F. (1974) On the palm probabilities of processes of points and processes of lines. *Stochastic Geometry.* (Ed. E. F. Harding and D. G. Kendall) Wiley, London, 114–147.

RUDEMO, M. (1973) Point process generated by transitions of Markov chains. *Adv. Appl. Prob.* **5**, 262–286.

SNYDER, D. L. (1972a) Filtering and detection for doubly stochastic Poisson processes. *IEEE Trans. Information Theory IT*–18 91–102.

SNYDER, D. L. (1972b) Smoothing for doubly stochastic Poisson processes. *IEEE Trans. Information Theory IT*–18 558–662.

SNYDER, D. L. (1973) Information processing for observed jump processes. *Information and Control* **22**, 69–78.

SNYDER, D. L. AND RHODES, I. B. (1972) Phase and frequency tracking in direct detection optical communications systems. *IEEE Trans. Communications COM*–20,1139–1142.

YASHIN, A. I. (1970) Filtering of jump processes. *Avtomat. i Telemeh.* **5**, 52–58.

PART VII

PROBABILITY MODELS IN
THE PHYSICAL SCIENCES

Diffusion Models with Relativity Effects

VIOLET R. CANE

Abstract

In this paper models for diffusion in one dimension are obtained which are based on correlated random walks. The equations for diffusion with drift can be transformed into the equations for diffusion without drift (and conversely) by the transformations of Special Relativity Theory. The relationship of these equations to Maxwell's equations for electromagnetic phenomena is discussed.

1. Introduction

If a particle executes Brownian motion on the real line its position $X(t)$ at time t has a distribution whose density function $p(x, t)$ satisfies the diffusion equation

$$(1) \qquad \tfrac{1}{2} \sigma^2 \frac{\partial^2 p}{\partial x^2} = \frac{\partial p}{\partial t} \; ;$$

if the particle starts from the origin, the solution of (1) is

$$p(x, t) = (2\pi\sigma^2 t)^{-\frac{1}{2}} \exp(-x^2/2\sigma^2 t)$$

that is, $X(t)$ has an $N(0, \sigma^2 t)$ distribution. If the movement of the particle is Brownian motion with drift, the diffusion equation is

$$(2) \qquad \tfrac{1}{2} \sigma^2 \frac{\partial^2 p}{\partial x^2} - u \frac{\partial p}{\partial x} = \frac{\partial p}{\partial t}$$

and the distribution of $X(t)$ with the same initial conditions is $N(ut, \sigma^2 t)$. Equation (2) can be reduced to the form of Equation (1) by setting $x' = x - ut, t' = t$, a Galilean transformation.

Brownian motion can be regarded as the limiting form of a simple random walk on the integers (see, for example, ·Feller (1962)) and thus may be simulated approximately by the following method: choose a step length κ and a step time τ and let the particle start at the origin and move a distance κ in each time interval τ, the probability of a step to the right being p and of a step to the left being $q = 1 - p$. Its position after n steps will be given by the sum of n random variables each having mean $\kappa(p - q)$ and variance $\kappa^2[1 - (p - q)^2]$; thus, by the Central Limit Theorem, $X(t)$, for $t = n\tau$, will have approximately an

$$N(\kappa(p - q)t/\tau, \kappa^2[1 - (p - q)^2]t/\tau)$$

distribution. By taking a large number of realizations of this process or, what is the same thing, a large number of particles all starting from the origin,and finding the proportion of them at $\gamma\kappa$ ($\gamma = 0, \pm 1, \pm 2, \cdots$) after n steps we can estimate $p(x, t)$. For Equation (1) we need to take $p = q = \frac{1}{2}$ and $\kappa^2/\tau = \sigma^2$; for Equation (2) we need to take $\kappa(p - q)/\tau = u$ and $\kappa^2[1 - (p - q)^2]/\tau = \sigma^2$. If we write V for κ/τ, the actual speed of the particle, then we must take $p = \frac{1}{2}(1 + u/V)$ and $\kappa V(1 - u^2/V^2) = \sigma^2$, putting $u = 0$ if there is no drift. Suppose however that we obtain simulated solutions to both Equations (1) and (2) using the same κ and V; these will be approximately $N(0, \kappa Vt)$ and $N(ut, \kappa Vt(1 - u^2/V^2))$ and to transform the second into the first by a linear transformation we require $x' = \alpha(x - ut)$, $t' \doteq \beta t$, where $\beta = \alpha^2(1 - u^2/V^2)$, which is not a Galilean transformation. There is the additional difficulty that the simulation of (2) will converge to normality more slowly than the simulation of (1) and may show appreciable skewness for some time.

In the usual discussion of the limiting form of a simple random walk, one imposes the conditions $\kappa \to 0$ and $V \to \infty$; however, for a real particle moving in a real fluid one would expect some upper limit to its speed, so that its motion would be more like the simple random walk than like Brownian motion in the mathematical sense. In the next section a model of diffusion is proposed which leads to simple differential equations, which approximates to the usual diffusion equations under suitable conditions, and which preserves the properties of skewness (if there is drift) and finiteness of range shown by the random walk model.

2. Movement of a particle in a fluid

Suppose that a particle Q moves with constant speed V along the x-axis with occasional change of direction according to the following rules:

Pr (turn in $(t, t + dt)|$moving forward) $= \lambda_1 dt + o(dt)$

Pr (turn in $(t, t + dt)|$moving backward) $= \lambda_2 dt + o(dt)$.

This is a kind of Poisson process with reversals. It is convenient to think of the changes in direction as caused by the fluid in the following way: suppose that the particles of the fluid also move with constant speed V and that across any unit area perpendicular to the x-axis a number F will move in a forward direction, a number B will move in a backward direction, in unit time; then if Q turns because it encounters a particle of the fluid we shall have $\lambda_1 \propto BS, \lambda_2 \propto FS$ (S represents the size of Q and is put in to remind us that different types of Q particle may obey different diffusion equations). The density of the fluid is represented by $F + B$, the current is represented by $V(F - B)$, and the mean velocity is

$$V(F - B)/(F + B) \text{ (or } V(\lambda_2 - \lambda_1)/(\lambda_2 + \lambda_1))$$

which we write as u.

The tidy way to derive the probability density function $p(x, t)$ for the position of Q at time t is to define the moment generating functions

$$M_1(\theta, t) = E(\exp(\theta X(t))|Q \text{ moves forward initially})$$

$$M_2(\theta, t) = E(\exp(\theta X(t))|Q \text{ moves backward initially})$$

Then

$$M_1(\theta, t) = \exp(\theta V t - \lambda_1 t) + \int_0^t \lambda_1 \exp(\theta V y - \lambda_1 y) M_2(\theta, t - y) dy$$

$$M_2(\theta, t) = \exp(-\theta V t - \lambda_2 t) + \int_0^t \lambda_2 \exp(-\theta V y - \lambda_2 y) M_1(\theta, t - y) dy$$

from which we obtain

$$\frac{\partial M_1}{\partial t} + (\lambda_1 - \theta V) M_1 = \lambda_1 M_2$$

$$\frac{\partial M_2}{\partial t} + (\lambda_2 + \theta V) M_2 = \lambda_2 M_1$$

and hence

(3) $$\frac{\partial^2 M_i}{\partial t^2} + 2\bar{\lambda} \frac{\partial M_i}{\partial t} - 2\bar{\lambda} u M_i \theta - \theta^2 V^2 M_i = 0 \qquad i = 1, 2,$$

where $2\bar{\lambda} = \lambda_1 + \lambda_2$, $2\bar{\lambda} u = V(\lambda_2 - \lambda_1)$. The moment generating function

$$M(\theta, t) = E(\exp(\theta X(t))) = \int_{-Vt}^{Vt} p(x, t) \exp(\theta x) dx$$

is some linear combination of $M_1(\theta, t)$ and $M_2(\theta, t)$ and so will satisfy an equation of the same form. This method of solution, however, loses some of the flavour of the model and it is more illuminating to work with the differential equations for the flow.

Let $f(x, t)dx$ be the probability that Q is in the interval $(x, x + dx)$ at time t and moving forward; similarly we define $b(x, t)dx$ if Q is moving backward. Then

$$f(x, t + dt) = f(x - dx, t)(1 - \lambda_1 dt) + b(x, t)\lambda_2 dt \cdot$$

$$b(x, t + dt) = b(x + dx, t)(1 - \lambda_2 dt) + f(x, t)\lambda_1 dt$$

to first order, so that, since $dx/dt = V$,

(4)

$$\frac{\partial f}{\partial t} = -V \frac{\partial f}{\partial x} - \lambda_1 f + \lambda_2 b$$

$$\frac{\partial b}{\partial t} = V \frac{\partial b}{\partial x} + \lambda_1 f - \lambda_2 b.$$

Also $f(x, t) + b(x, t) = p(x, t)$, and we put $f(x, t) - b(x, t) = w(x, t)$. Then

(5)

$$\frac{\partial p}{\partial t} = -V \frac{\partial w}{\partial x}$$

$$\frac{\partial w}{\partial t} = -V \frac{\partial p}{\partial x} + 2\bar{\lambda} u V^{-1} p - 2\bar{\lambda} w,$$

and so

(6)

$$\frac{\partial^2 p}{\partial t^2} + 2\bar{\lambda} \frac{\partial p}{\partial t} = V^2 \frac{\partial^2 p}{\partial x^2} - 2\bar{\lambda} u \frac{\partial p}{\partial x} \; ;$$

if $M(\theta, t)$ is found from (6) it satisfies (3). Note that $Vw(x, t)$, which is the local current, satisfies a similar equation.

This model is a continuous version of a correlated random walk, which has been discussed by Gillis (1955) among others. In such a random walk the probability that the particle will move a step to the right is, say, p_1 if its last move was forward and $q_2(= 1 - p_2)$ if its last move was backward; otherwise it moves to the left. What has been done in the present model is, in effect, to treat q_i as small and replace it by $\lambda_i dt$. The correlated random walk reduces to a simple random walk if $p_1 = q_2$, that is if $q_1 + q_2 = 1$ which could require, in the continuous case, $(\lambda_1 + \lambda_2)dt = 1$; if in Equation (6) we take $\bar{\lambda}$ large and $V^2/\bar{\lambda}$ moderate we shall get an approximation to

Equation (2), which corresponds to a simple random walk. Thus (6) represents some sort of diffusion with drift; the corresponding equation for diffusion without drift is obtained by taking $\lambda_1 = \lambda_2 = \lambda$, so that $u = 0$, and is

(7)
$$\frac{\partial^2 p}{\partial t^2} + 2\lambda \frac{\partial p}{\partial t} = V^2 \frac{\partial^2 p}{\partial x^2}.$$

3. Transformation to eliminate drift

We may now ask what linear transformation will reduce (6) to (7). We must bear in mind that the particle cannot move a distance greater than Vt in time t, so that the solution to either equation must be such that $p(x, t) = 0$ if $|x| > Vt$. If we set $t' = \alpha x + \beta t$, $x' = \gamma x + \delta t$, write $p'(x', t')$ for the transform of $p(x, t)$, and make the coefficients of $\partial p'/\partial x'$ and $\partial^2 p'/\partial x' \partial t$ equal to zero, we find that Equation (6) transforms into

$$\frac{\partial^2 p'}{\partial t'^2} + 2\bar{\lambda}\beta^{-1} \frac{\partial p'}{\partial t'} = V^2 \frac{\partial^2 p'}{\partial x'^2}$$

provided that

(8)
$$x' = \pm \beta(x - ut), \qquad t' = \beta(t - uV^2 x);$$

clearly we require β to be positive. The choice of sign in the expression for x' reflects the fact that, for suitable initial conditions, the diffusion is symmetric when there is no drift; there will be less trouble with the initial conditions however, if we choose the positive sign. Whichever sign we choose the condition on the range is satisfied, that is $|x| < Vt$ implies $|x'| < Vt'$ and conversely, since $V^2 t'^2 - x'^2 = \beta^2(1 - u^2 V^{-2})(V^2 t^2 - x^2)$. The value of β can be chosen arbitrarily since Equation (7) can always be transformed into standard form, with $\lambda = 1$, by taking as the unit of time the expected time between reversals and adjusting the unit of distance to match. It is often convenient to have the Jacobian of the transformation (8) equal to unity; in that case β, or $\beta(u, V)$, has the value $(1 - u^2 V^{-2})^{-\frac{1}{2}}$, and transformations between the system with drift and the system without drift become symmetrical in an obvious way. In fact, if V is equal to the speed of light, c, the transformation is the usual one used in Special Relativity Theory and $\beta(u, c)$ equals $\gamma(u)$.

We still have to check that a transformation of this sort on $p(x, t)$ gives a probability density; clearly $p'(x', t')$ is non-negative for all x' and t', so we need only enquire whether $\int_{-Vt'}^{Vt'} p'(x', t)dx' = 1$, for all t', is a consequence of the fact that $\int_{-Vt}^{Vt} p(x, t)dx = 1$ for all t.

If we write

$$F(\theta, t) = \int_{-Vt}^{Vt} e^{\theta x} f(x, t) dx,$$

$$B(\theta, t) = \int_{-Vt}^{Vt} e^{\theta x} b(x, t) dx,$$

so that the moment generating function of $p(x, t)$, $M(\theta, t)$, is $(F(\theta, t) + B(\theta, t))$, then from Equations (4) we have

$$\frac{\partial F}{\partial t} = (V\theta - \lambda_1)F + \lambda_2 B$$

$$\frac{\partial B}{\partial t} = -(V\theta + \lambda_2)B + \lambda_1 F;$$

the Laplace transforms $F^*(\theta, \phi)$, $B^*(\theta, \phi)$ satisfy

$$(\phi + \lambda_1 - V\theta)F^* - \lambda_2 B^* = \Pi$$

$$(\phi + \lambda_2 + V\theta)B^* - \lambda_1 F^* = 1 - \Pi$$

if Π is the probability that the particle was moving forward at $t = 0$. Set $M_u^* = F^* + B^*$ and $W_u^* = F^* - B^*$; then

$$\phi M_u^* - V\theta W_u^* = 1$$

(9)

$$(\phi + 2\bar{\lambda})W_u^* - (V\theta + 2\bar{\lambda}u V^{-1})M_u^* = U_0 V^{-1}$$

where U_0 has been written for $V(2\Pi - 1)$, the initial mean velocity. If we put θ equal to 0 in (9) we have $M_u^*(0, \phi) = \phi^{-1}$ (in agreement with the fact that $M(0, t) = 1$) and $W_u^*(0, \phi) = (\phi + 2\bar{\lambda})^{-1}(U_0 + 2\bar{\lambda}u\phi^{-1})V^{-1}$ which is the Laplace transform of $V^{-1}[u + (u_0 - u)\exp(-2\bar{\lambda}t)]$. $VW_u^*(0, \phi)$ corresponds to the total flow, which thus tends to u as $t \to \infty$.

Now let

$$M_0^*(\theta, \phi) = \int_0^{\infty} \int_{-Vt'}^{Vt'} \exp(\theta x' - \phi t')p(x', t')dx'dt'$$

$$= \beta^2(1 - u^2 V^{-2})M_u^*(\beta(\theta + uV^{-2}\phi), \beta(\phi + u\theta))$$

using the tranformation (8), with a similar expression for W_0^*. Since $M_u^*(\theta, \phi)$, $W_u^*(\theta, \phi)$ can be found from (9) it follows that $M_0^*(\theta, \phi)$, $W_0^*(\theta, \phi)$ satisfy the equations obtained by replacing ϕ by $\beta(\phi + u\theta)$ and θ by $\beta(\theta + uV^{-2})$ in (9). These can be rearranged as

$$\phi\left(M_0^* - \frac{u}{V}\, W_0^* \right) - V\theta\left(W_0^* - \frac{u}{V}\, M_0^* \right) = \beta\left(1 - \frac{u^2}{V^2} \right)$$

(10)

$$\left(\phi + \frac{2\bar{\lambda}}{\beta} \right)\left(W_0^* - \frac{u}{V}\, M_0^* \right) - V\theta\left(M_0^* - \frac{u}{V}\, W_0^* \right) = \frac{u_0}{V}\, \beta\left(1 - \frac{u^2}{V^2} \right).$$

If we now put θ equal to 0 in these equations we see that

$$\left(M_0^* - \frac{u}{V}\, W_0^* \right) \Big/ \left[\beta\left(1 - \frac{u^2}{V^2} \right) \right] = \frac{1}{\phi}$$

and that any other linear combination of M_0^* and W_0^* involves

$$(\phi + 2\bar{\lambda}\beta^{-1})^{-1},$$

which will give a decay term in the expression of which this is the Fourier transform. Thus if $p(x, t)$, $w(x, t)$ are the probability density functions for position and current, for the process with drift, and if we transform them by (8) to $p'(x', t')$, $w'(x', t')$, the probability density functions for the process without drift must be $k[p' - uV^{-1}w']$ for position and $k[w' - uV^{-1}p']$ for current, where $k^{-1} = \beta(1 - u^2V^{-2})$. From the second equation of (10), with θ put equal to 0, we find that the total flow at time t in the equivalent process without drift is $u_0\exp(-2\bar{\lambda}\beta^{-1}t')$.

If a large number N of particles leave the origin at the same time, with the same initial conditions, $Np(x, t)$ is the expected number in the neighbourhood of x at time t and $NVw(x, t)$ is the expected current there. We can define a kind of local mean velocity $v(x, t)$ by $Np(x, t)v(x, t) = NVw(x, t)$. If $v'(x', t')$ is similarly defined for the transformed process, we have

$$v'(x', t') = (Vw' - up')/(p' - uV^{-1}w')$$

$$= (v - u)/(1 - uvV^{-2}).$$

Thus if V is replaced by c, the speed of light, the local mean velocity transforms in the same way as velocity according to Special Relativity Theory; and if, in addition, β is taken to be $(1 - u^2c^{-2})^{-\frac{1}{2}}$ then the transformation from (x, t) to (x', t') is also in accordance with that theory.

4. Comparison with Maxwell's equations

It is not surprising that relativistic transformations can be used on these diffusion processes since the equations are formally similar to Maxwell's equations for the one-dimensional case. If $H \equiv (0, 0, H)$, $E \equiv (0, E, 0)$ and derivatives with respect to y and z are zero, Maxwell's equations *in vacuo* reduce to

$$\frac{\partial H}{\partial t} = -c \, \frac{\partial E}{\partial x}, \quad \frac{\partial E}{\partial t} = -c \, \frac{\partial H}{\partial x} - 4\pi j,$$

and if we take H proportional to p, E and j proportional to w, these equations correspond to Equations (5) for the case $V = c$, $\lambda_1 = \lambda_2 = \lambda$. The transformations, given in the preceding section, for reducing the case with drift to the case without drift correspond to the usual transformations for E and H, that is

$$E' = \beta\left(E - \frac{u}{c} H\right), \qquad H' = \beta\left(H - \frac{u}{c} E\right).$$

We appear to have a vectorial representation of $p(x, t)$ and $w(x, t)$; this can be justified as follows. Suppose that we have a large number, N, of particles all subject to the same process; then $Np(x, t)$ is the expected number moving in the neighbourhood of x at time t and $Nw(x, t)$ is the net number moving forward along the x-axis. The fact that there are $Np(x, t)$ particles moving parallel to the (x, y) plane can be represented by a vector $(0, 0, Np(x, t))$ and the fact that there are the same number moving parallel to the (x, z) plane can be represented by $(0, Np(x, t), 0)$. Thus we need two vectors to specify that all the particles are moving parallel to the x-axis. However, both pairs of vectors lie in the same directions and so one can be used to describe the total flow and the other the net flow; the choice of the vector which is to carry information about the net flow is made in accordance with conventions about polarization. This description applies to the particles of type Q; we may similarly describe the medium in which the particles move by vectors $(0, 2\bar{\lambda}u/c, 0)$ and $(0, 0, 2\bar{\lambda})$. If there is no drift we have only the magnetic vector $(0, 0, 2\lambda)$. In such a case the solution to the usual equation for the flow of electrons

$$\frac{d}{dt} (mv) = evxH/c$$

shows that (if there is no movement parallel to the z-axis) they move in circles of arbitrary radius, taking a time proportional to $1/H$ to complete each circuit. According to the present model, particles move to and fro taking an expected time $2/\lambda$ to complete two turns. If the process is stationary, for example if the particles move between two reflecting barriers, so that $w(x, t)$ is zero and $p(x, t)$ is constant, the observed behaviour of a set of indistinguishable particles could be explained in either way.

5. Comparison with Ornstein-Uhlenbeck and Wiener processes

The equation for the moment generating function $M(\theta, t)$ of $p(x, t)$, in the case without drift,

$$\frac{\partial^2 M}{\partial t^2} + 2\lambda \frac{\partial M}{\partial t} - \theta^2 V^2 M = 0$$

has solutions of the form

$$M(\theta, t) = A \exp[-\lambda + (\lambda^2 + \theta^2 V^2)^{\frac{1}{2}}]t + B \exp[-\lambda - (\lambda^2 + \theta^2 V^2)^{\frac{1}{2}}]t$$

and the mean and variance of the distribution (most easily found from Equations (9)) are given by

$$\mu(t) = u_0(1 - \exp(-2\lambda t))/2\lambda$$

$$\sigma^2(t) = V^2 t/\lambda - V^2(1 - \exp(-2\lambda t))/2\lambda^2 - u_0^2(1 - \exp(-2\lambda t))^2/4\lambda^2$$

for the stated initial conditions. Thus as $t \to \infty$,

$$E[\exp\theta\{(x(t) - \mu(t))/\sigma^2(t)\}] \to \exp(-\tfrac{1}{2}\theta^2)$$

and the distribution tends to normality. If $u_0 = 0$, that is the particle is equally likely to start by moving forward or backward, the process approximates to a Wiener process with V^2/λ as σ^2. The disadvantage of the Wiener process as a model of Brownian movement is that the observed velocity, $x(t)/t$, is $O(t^{-\frac{1}{2}})$ and so becomes very large for small t. Since, in this model, no observed velocity can exceed V, there is no such difficulty. For small values of t we have, if $u_0 = V$, $\mu(t) = Vt(1 - \lambda t)$, $\sigma^2(t) = 4V^2\lambda t^3/3$ approximately, so that the observed velocity has a mean $V(1 - \lambda t)$ and a variance $4V^2\lambda t/3$. These results are similar to those for the Ornstein-Uhlenbeck process for small t, though very different for large t, since $x(t)/t \to 0$ in probability in this case.

For the process with drift, the mean at time $t, \mu(t)$, is

$$[ut + (u_0 - u)(1 - \exp(-2\bar{\lambda}t))/2\bar{\lambda}],$$

the variance, $\sigma^2(t)$, is $(V^2 - u^2)t/\bar{\lambda}$ apart from constants and decay terms, and $(X(t) - \mu(t))/\sigma(t)$ tends to an $N(0, 1)$ distribution. For small values of t, $\mu(t)$ is approximately $ut + (u_0 - u)(1 - \bar{\lambda}t)t$ and $\sigma^2(t)$ is approximately $4\bar{\lambda}V(V - u)t^3/3$; u_0 will normally be either V or $- V$. Again we have a process which approximates to a Wiener process for large t and to an Ornstein-Uhlenbeck process for small t.

6. Discussion

As Bartlett (1957) has pointed out, a hyperbolic type equation for diffusion implies a constant speed of movement. The assumption of a fixed speed V for the diffusing particle is therefore necessary. The description of the medium in terms of particles moving with the same speed is not necessary, since only the rates of turning are required for developing the model; but it has been useful to the author in trying to extend the method to two and three dimensions. The model was in fact originally developed to describe data obtained from a Bekésy machine; this machine, which is used to detect rapid fluctuations in perceptual thresholds, produces a stimulus (say, a note of constant pitch) which gradually increases in intensity. A subject is instructed to press a button as soon as he hears the sound; the intensity then gradually decreases until the subject, on deciding that he no longer hears it, presses the button again and the intensity begins to increase. The intensity which is midway between two successive turning points is taken as the instantaneous threshold. The assumption of constant speed for this case seems reason-able and a null hypothesis that the subject responds at random at a constant rate leads to Equations (4) with λ_1 and λ_2 equal. If this hypothesis is not tenable one can then proceed to develop a model which allows for a fixed threshold, not a fluctuating one. A reasonable approxi-mation to the way in which a threshold (in the psycho-physical sense) operates is to take the fifty per cent point at the origin, and to allow λ_1, λ_2 to depend on x with $\lambda_1(x) = \lambda + \alpha x$, $\lambda_2(x) = \lambda - \alpha x$; the result is a kind of Ehrenfest model. There is thus at least one situation in which the assumption of a fixed speed is reasonable.

What is perhaps surprising is that the equations obtained should resemble those of electro-magnetic theory. The resemblance could of course be exploited whatever the reason for its occurrence. Simple random walks can be used for Monte Carlo simulation to obtain numerical solutions to problems concerning electrostatic potentials; correlated random walks might be used in the same way to find solutions to electro-magnetic problems. However suppose we regard these models as having some basis in physical fact; Dirac's (1958) relativistic theory of the electron does in fact imply that the electron has fixed speed, and random movements to and fro may be as realistic as simple harmonic motion. Then we find that a description of diffusion through a medium in motion can be transformed into that of diffusion through a medium at rest, and that the transformation is effected by the methods of Special Relativity Theory. This transformation is a purely mathematical device, and does not involve any sort of space or time other than that of the observer watching the diffusion, nor does it require a particular value for the maximum speed. The author has been unable to discover any experiment in which relativistic transformations are used which does not concern either the flow of light or the movement of elementary particles through electro-magnetic fields (which may well constitute a medium). We may ask, does the usefulness of relativity theory justify the philosophical arguments that suggested it?

References

[1] BARTLETT. M. S. (1957) Some problems associated with random velocity. *Publ. Inst. Statist. Univ. Paris* **6**, fasc. 4., 261–270.

[2] DIRAC, P. A. M. (1958) *The Principles of Quantum Mechanics*, Chapter XI. Clarendon Press, Oxford.

[3] FELLER. W. (1962) *An Introduction to Probability Theory and its Applications*, Vol. 1. (2nd. Ed).Wiley and Sons, New York.

[4] GILLIS. J. (1955) Correlated random walks. *Proc. Camb. Phil. Soc.* **51**, 639–651.

Restoration of Deformed Lattice Patterns

ULF GRENANDER

Abstract

The restoration of crystal lattices which have been jittered presents some problems that do not seem to have been previously studied. This is true especially in the multi-dimensional case. It is shown that a statistic suggested by Bartlett can be used for this purpose, and this is done both for Gaussian and general deformation mechanisms. The results are accompanied by some numerical experiments.

1. Introduction

The theory of patterns developed during the last few years by this author and his co-workers (see references) has as one of its goals the restoration of pure images that have been distorted by some deformation mechanism. It was noticed that in the special case of a pure lattice pattern, restoration can be achieved by using a tool presented in Bartlett (1964).

While Bartlett intended this tool to be applied to stationary point processes, the lattice patterns are not stationary. Nevertheless, as we shall see below, it is applicable to the present case too.

Assume that the pure image I is a regular lattice in R^n so that its points have the form

$$(1.1) \qquad X_{\nu_1 \nu_2 \cdots \nu_n} = a + \nu_1 \xi_1 + \nu_2 \xi_2 + \cdots + \nu_n \xi_n \in R^n$$

where a is a *phase vector*, and $\xi_1, \xi_2, \cdots, \xi_n$ are *basis vectors* for the lattice and $\nu_1, \nu_2, \cdots, \nu_n$ are arbitrary integers. Of course the basis vectors are not uniquely determined.

Assume now that the phase and basis vectors are not known and that we can observe only the jittered positions

$$(1.2) \qquad X^{\mathscr{D}}_{\nu_1 \nu_2 \cdots \nu_n} = X_{\nu_1 \nu_2 \cdots \nu_n} + n_{\nu_1 \nu_2 \cdots \nu_n},$$

where the noise vectors $n_{\nu_1 \nu_2 \cdots \nu_n}$ are stochastically independent with a normal distribution with mean vector zero and covariance matrix R. From $I^{\mathscr{D}}$ we want to restore I, in other words get the basis vectors (possibly also the phase vector). The observational set-up will be the following. In a given domain, say a cube Q_L of length L, we observe the jittered lattice points that happen to fall inside Q_L. Superficially this could seem to lead to a regression problem of well-known type since (1.1), (1.2) constitutes a linear model. This is indeed true, but only for low noise level.

If the noise level is considerable, we meet a problem which is an order of magnitude harder. First, the number of observations is not fixed and we do not know in advance which pure image points will fall in Q_L after being jittered. This will require a special analysis.

Second, if the jittering effect is considerable, the ordering can be changed completely: we do not know what subscripts $\nu_1, \nu_2, \cdots, \nu_n$ correspond to a given observed X. This difficulty is of a type that has not been treated in the literature as far as the author is aware. Direct estimation procedures will be computationally impossible if they involve exhaustive search of permutations of subscripts.

The problem may seem intractable but we shall see in the next section that a satisfactory solution can be found, although it is not of the traditional regression form.

We really have a composite deformation mechanism $\mathscr{D} = \mathscr{D}_1 \mathscr{D}_2$. $\mathscr{D}_2$ is the jittering by additive noise as in (1.2) and $\mathscr{D}_1$ is the masking, excluding all observations outside Q_L.

Our analysis must be *permutation invariant* and we shall base it on the function in (2.2) that resembles Fourier analysis but is not really Fourier analysis of the usual type: note that the trigonometric functions are not multiplied by the observations, they occur in the exponent instead.

The analysis must also take into account the masking effect and this will be done by a method constructed for this particular purpose.

We shall start with the simplest case when the background space is the real line and when the noise is Gaussian. The one-dimensional case is actually of small interest since it could be dealt with in a more direct manner; see Section 6. It will be instructive, however, to treat this case first and see what sort of analysis is needed, and then extend this to the two-dimensional problem which is the interesting one.

2. The normal linear case

The deformed image is now the set of points

(2.1) $$I^{\mathcal{D}} = \{X_\nu\} = \{a + \nu\xi + n_\nu \in Q_L\}$$

where Q_L is the interval $(0, L)$. As pointed out above the deformation mechanism $\mathcal{D}$ consists of $\mathcal{D}_1$, additive noise *and* $\mathcal{D}_2$, masking the outside of Q_L. The number of observed points is of course not known in advance. We work with the assumption $n_v = N(0, \sigma^2)$ but this can be extended to more general noise distributions.

Form the 'Fourier transform' as in Bartlett (1964)

(2.2) $$\phi(\lambda) = \frac{1}{L} \sum_{X_\nu \in I^{\mathcal{D}}} e^{i\lambda X_\nu}.$$

It will be convenient to carry out the analysis in the complex form.

First, the expected value $m(\lambda)$ is given by

(2.3) $$m(\lambda) = E[\phi(\lambda)] = \sum_{\nu=-\infty}^{\infty} \frac{1}{L} \int_0^L e^{i\lambda X} \frac{1}{\sqrt{2\pi}\sigma} \exp\left\{ -\frac{(X - \nu\xi)^2}{2\sigma^2} \right\} dX,$$

where we have put $a = 0$; this will be compensated later by multiplication with the factor $e^{ia\lambda}$. Now introduce the function

(2.4) $$p(X) = \frac{1}{\sqrt{2\pi}\sigma} \sum_{\nu=-\infty}^{\infty} \exp\left\{ -\frac{(X - \nu\xi)^2}{2\sigma^2} \right\}.$$

Because of the uniform convergence of (2.4), p is continuous. It is also positive and periodic with the period ξ.

We then get

(2.5) $$m(\lambda) = \frac{1}{L} \int_0^L e^{i\lambda X} p(X) dX$$

and if we introduce the absolutely convergent Fourier series

(2.6) $$p(X) = \sum_{k=-\infty}^{\infty} p_k \exp\left\{ -\frac{2\pi i k X}{\xi} \right\}$$

we can write

$$(2.7) \qquad m(\lambda) = \sum_{k=-\infty}^{\infty} p_k \frac{\exp\left\{iL\left(\lambda - \frac{2\pi k}{\xi}\right)\right\} - 1}{iL\left(\lambda - \frac{2\pi k}{\xi}\right)}$$

with the usual interpretation if the denominator is zero.

We now have two separate cases. First, if λ is the kth multiple of $2\pi/\xi$ then

$$(2.8) \qquad \lim_{L \to \infty} m(\lambda) = p_k.$$

Note that, if we use the definition (2.6) of p,

$$p_k = \frac{1}{\xi} \int_0^\xi p(X) e^{2\pi ikX/\xi} dX = \frac{1}{\sqrt{2\pi}\,\xi\sigma} \int_{-\infty}^{\infty} \exp\left\{ -\frac{X^2}{2\sigma^2} + \frac{2\pi ikX}{\xi} \right\} dX$$

$$(2.9)$$

$$= \frac{1}{\xi} \exp\left\{ -\frac{2\sigma^2\pi^2 k^2}{\xi^2} \right\}.$$

This means that p_k tends to zero fast and decreasingly as $|k|$ increases towards infinity. On the other hand if λ is not a multiple of $2\pi/\xi$ the sum in (2.7) tends to zero. Therefore the mean value function $m(\lambda)$ will look like the graph below.

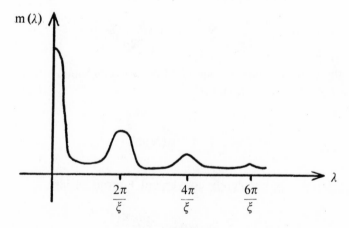

Figure 2.1

We now turn to evaluate the variance

(2.10) $V(\lambda) = E\{|\phi(\lambda) - m(\lambda)|^2\} = E\{|\phi(\lambda)|^2\} - |m(\lambda)|^2,$

still in complex form. We get for the contribution from the term $e^{i(X_\nu - X_\mu)\lambda}$, if $\nu \neq \mu$,

(2.11) $\dfrac{1}{L^2} \displaystyle\int_0^L \int_0^L e^{i(u-v)\lambda} \dfrac{1}{2\pi\sigma^2} \exp\left\{ -\dfrac{1}{2\sigma^2}[(u-\nu\xi)^2 + (v-\nu\xi)^2] \right\} du\, dv$

since only if X_ν and $X_\mu \in Q_L$ do they contribute to $\phi(\lambda)$.

Now we have to sum (2.11) over all ν and μ and would get

(2.12) $\dfrac{1}{L^2} \displaystyle\int_0^L \int_0^L e^{i(u-v)\lambda} p(u) p(v)\, du\, dv = \left| \dfrac{1}{L} \int_0^L e^{iu\lambda} p(u)\, du \right|^2$

except that (2.11) is not valid for $\nu = \mu$. To correct this we have to subtract terms of the form (2.11) for all $\nu = \mu$ and add the correct expression. Doing this we get

$E[|\phi(\lambda)|^2] =$

(2.13) $\left| \dfrac{1}{L} \displaystyle\int_0^L e^{iu\lambda} p(u)\, du \right|^2 + \dfrac{1}{L^2} \sum_{\nu=-\infty}^{\infty} \dfrac{1}{\sqrt{2\pi}\sigma} \int_0^L \exp\left\{ -\dfrac{(u-\nu\xi)^2}{2\sigma^2} \right\} du$

$\qquad - \dfrac{1}{L^2} \displaystyle\sum_{\nu=-\infty}^{\infty} \int_0^L \int_0^L e^{i(u-v)\lambda} \dfrac{1}{2\pi\sigma^2} \exp\left\{ -\dfrac{1}{2\sigma^2}[(u-\nu\xi)^2 + (v-\nu\xi)^2] \right\} du\, dv$

Using (2.10) and (2.5) this reduces to

$V(\lambda) = \dfrac{1}{L^2} \displaystyle\int_0^L p(u)\, du$

(2.14)

$\qquad - \dfrac{1}{L^2} \displaystyle\int_0^L \int_0^L \exp\left\{ i(u-v)\lambda - \dfrac{(u-v)^2}{4\sigma^2} \right\} q\left(\dfrac{u+v}{2} \right) du\, dv$

since

(2.15) $(u-\nu\xi)^2 + (v-\nu\xi)^2 = 2\left(\dfrac{u+v}{2} - \nu\xi \right)^2 + \dfrac{(u-v)^2}{2}$

and we have introduced

(2.16) $q(\alpha) = \dfrac{1}{2\pi\sigma^2} \displaystyle\sum_{\nu=-\infty}^{\infty} \exp\left\{ -\dfrac{1}{\sigma^2}(\alpha - \nu\xi)^2 \right\}$

a periodic, continuous and positive function.

We shall show that $LV(\lambda)$ tends to a limit as $L \to \infty$. It is clear that

(2.17) $\dfrac{1}{L}\displaystyle\int_0^L p(u)du \to$ average of p over a period $= p_0 = \dfrac{1}{\xi}$,

see (2.9).

For the second integral in (2.14) we can write, leaving out one of the
L-factors in the denominator,

(2.18) $\dfrac{1}{2L}\displaystyle\int_{s=-L}^{L} \int_{t\in A(s)} \exp\left\{ is\lambda - \dfrac{s^2}{4\sigma^2} \right\} q\left(\dfrac{t}{2}\right) ds\, dt$

with the change of variables

(2.19) $\begin{cases} s = u - v \\[2mm] t = u + v \end{cases}$

where the 2 in the denominator comes from the Jacobian of the transformation (2.19). The interval

(2.20) $A(s) = \begin{cases} (s, 2L - s) & \text{if } s > 0, \\[2mm] (0, 2L + s) & \text{if } s < 0, \end{cases}$

so that $m(A(s)) \sim 2L$ for fixed s.

We then find by dominated convergence as the limit of (2.18)

average of $q \cdot \displaystyle\int_{s=-\infty}^{\infty} \exp\left\{ is - \dfrac{s^2}{4\sigma^2} \right\} ds =$

(2.21)

average of $q \cdot \sqrt{4\pi}\,\sigma e^{-\sigma^2\lambda^2}$

But from (2.16),

average of $q = \dfrac{1}{\xi}\displaystyle\int_0^{\xi} q(\alpha)d\alpha$

(2.22)

$= \dfrac{1}{2\pi\xi\sigma^2}\displaystyle\int_{-\infty}^{\infty} e^{-\alpha^2/\sigma^2} d\alpha = \dfrac{1}{\sqrt{4\pi}\,\sigma\xi}.$

Combining this with (2.14) we obtain

$$(2.23) \qquad \lim_{L \to \infty} L\ V(\lambda) = \frac{1}{\xi}(1 - e^{-\sigma^2\lambda^2}).$$

This completes the proof of the following theorem.

Theorem 2.1.   To restore the pure lattice image of the deformed image (2.1) we form the function $\phi(\lambda)$ in (2.2). Then, as $L \to \infty$, we have

$$(2.24) \qquad \lim_{L \to \infty} E[\phi(\lambda)] = \frac{1}{\xi}\exp\left\{-\frac{2\sigma^2\pi^2k^2}{\xi^2}\right\} \quad \text{if} \quad \lambda = \frac{2\pi k}{\xi}$$

and

$$(2.25) \qquad \lim_{L \to \infty} E[\phi(\lambda)] = 0 \quad \text{if} \quad \lambda \text{ is not a multiple of } 2\pi/\xi.$$

The variance satisfies

$$(2.26) \qquad \lim_{L \to \infty} L\ \text{Var}[\phi(\lambda)] = \frac{1}{\xi}(1 - e^{-\sigma^2\lambda^2}).$$

The importance of this theorem lies in the fact that it offers us a tool to avoid the complications due both to the masking effect of the second deformation mechanism $\mathscr{D}_2$, and to the lack of knowledge of the 'true' ordering of the points in $I^{\mathscr{D}}$.

The author has been informed in a personal communication from McClure (1973), that the covariances also tend to zero asymptotically in a way similar to (2.26).

In addition, this tool will tell us, if handled properly, how to discover deviations from the model assumed. This will be discussed in Section 3.

The way to use this would be to compute $\phi(\lambda)$ for a reasonably large set of λ-values, depending upon what we know *a priori* about the pure lattice. We would then plot the real and imaginary parts of ϕ and try to locate the maxima of $|\phi(\lambda)|$, especially the first one which should be close to $2\pi/\xi$ if L is large enough. From the ordinates of the first few maxima we can also get some idea of σ from the way the ordinates decrease, see (2.24). Some smoothing procedure could be useful, but we shall not discuss how to do that here.

3. Non-lattice images

Let us now assume that we observe patterns that have not been generated by deforming a linear lattice, but are more chaotic. We shall start by assuming a Poisson process with intensity p generating the set $\{X_\nu\}$. We then get

$$(3.1) \qquad E[\phi(\lambda)] = \frac{p}{L} \int_0^L e^{iX\lambda} dX = p \frac{e^{iL\lambda} - 1}{iL\lambda}$$

which tends to zero for any non-zero value of λ. Hence it exhibits a drastically different behavior from that for lattice images.

The variance can also be obtained by writing

$$(3.2) \qquad \phi(\lambda) = \frac{1}{L} \int_0^L e^{i\lambda x} dN(x)$$

where N is the counting process associated with the Poisson process. Since N is an orthogonal process with $E[dN(x)]^2 = p dx$ we find that

$$(3.3) \qquad \operatorname{Var}[\phi(\lambda)] = \frac{1}{L^2} \int_0^L p dx = \frac{p}{L}$$

which tends to zero with $L \to \infty$. By examining $\phi(\lambda)$ we should be able to find out whether the regular lattice pattern or the more chaotic Poisson model is the right one for the data.

More generally, for a stationary renewal process we obtain a similar result for $m(\lambda)$. Indeed, let the interdistance distribution F be non-arithmetic with mean μ so that the distance from the origin to the first point observed will be

$$(3.4) \qquad F_0(u) = \frac{1}{\mu} \int_0^u [1 - F(v)] dv.$$

Then

$$(3.5) \qquad m(\lambda) = E[\phi(\lambda)] = \frac{1}{L} \sum_{\nu=0}^{\infty} \int_0^L e^{i\lambda x} dF_0(x) * F^\nu *(x).$$

Using a classical result (see Feller (1966), p. 354) we have

$$(3.6) \qquad \sum_{\nu=0}^{\infty} F_0(x) * F^\nu *(x) = \frac{x}{\mu}$$

so that

$$(3.7) \qquad m(\lambda) = \frac{1}{L\mu} \int_0^L e^{i\lambda x} dx = \frac{e^{i\lambda L} - 1}{iL\lambda\mu}$$

just as for the Poisson process.
We have not obtained the variance function in this case.

4. The general one-dimensional case

After the discussion in Section 2 we can now see how to proceed to the non-Gaussian case. Instead of the normal noise we assume, quite generally, that the noise terms in (2.1) have a frequency function f which will be assumed to be even and quadratically integrable. These conditions are not essential but will make the treatment more convenient.
Introducing the function

$$(4.1) \qquad p(x) = \sum_{\nu=-\infty}^{\infty} f(x - \nu\xi),$$

where the series converges almost everywhere, we see that it is non-negative and periodic with period ξ. We can now go ahead as in Section 2 and will leave out those details that are direct generalizations.
We get instead of (2.5)

$$(4.2) \qquad m(\lambda) = \frac{1}{L} \int_0^L e^{i\lambda x} p(x) dx$$

and, as $L \to \infty$,

$$(4.3) \qquad \lim_{L\to\infty} m(\lambda) = \lim_{L\to\infty} \int_0^\xi e^{i\lambda x} \frac{1 + e^{i\lambda\xi} + e^{2\cdot} + \cdots + e^{[L/\xi]2i\lambda\xi}}{L} p(x) dx$$

which tends to zero if λ is not a multiple of $2\pi/\xi$. Otherwise, $\lambda = 2\pi k/\xi$

$$(4.4) \qquad \lim_{L\to\infty} m(\lambda) = \int_{-\infty}^{\infty} e^{(2\pi i k/\xi)x} f(x) dx.$$

For the variance we find analogously to the special case already dealt with,

$$(4.5) \qquad L \, \text{Var}\,[m(\lambda)] = \frac{1}{L} \int_0^L p(u) du - \frac{1}{L} \int_0^L \int_0^L e^{i(u-v)} q(u, v) du dv$$

with

(4.6) $$q(u, v) = \sum_{\nu = -\infty}^{\infty} f(u - \nu\xi)f(v - \nu\xi).$$

Changing variables, the second integral in (4.5) reduces to

(4.7) $$\int_{s = -L}^{L} e^{is\lambda}K_L(s)ds$$

with

(4.8) $$K_L(s) = \frac{1}{L}\int_{u = s}^{L} q(u, u - s)du$$

for $s > 0$ and a similar expression for negative s. Because of periodicity, for any s,

(4.9) $$\lim_{L \to \infty} K_L(s) = \frac{1}{\xi}\int_0^{\xi} q(u, u - s)du = \frac{1}{\xi}\int_{-\infty}^{\infty} f(u)f(u - s)du = K(s).$$

Also, because of the positivity of f, the kernel K_L is dominated by a multiple of the kernel K. But K is L_1, so that

(4.10) $$\lim_{L \to \infty} L \, \mathrm{Var}\,[m(\lambda)] = \frac{1}{\xi}\left[1 - \int_{-\infty}^{\infty} e^{is\lambda}K(s)ds\right].$$

If the Fourier transform of f is denoted by $\hat{f}$, we can express this through the following theorem.

Theorem 4.1. If the noise has an even and quadratically integrable frequency function f we have

(4.11) $$\lim_{L \to \infty} m(\lambda) = \begin{cases} 0 & \text{if } \lambda \text{ is not a multiple of } 2\pi/\xi \\ \frac{1}{\xi}\hat{f}\left(\frac{2\pi k}{\xi}\right) & \text{if } \lambda = \frac{2\pi k}{\xi}. \end{cases}$$

Also

(4.12) $$\lim_{L \to \infty} [LV(\lambda)] = \frac{1}{\xi}[1 - [\hat{f}(\lambda)]^2].$$

5. The two-dimensional lattice pattern

Let the pure image consist of points

(5.1) $$X_{\nu_1 \nu_2} = a + \nu_1 \xi_1 + \nu_2 \xi_2$$

where the phase a and the base vectors ξ_1 and ξ_2 are in R^2. Of course, these vectors are not uniquely determined from the lattice. We also introduce the reciprocal lattice R with the base vectors η_1 and η_2 such that

(5.2) $$\begin{cases} (\eta_1, \xi_1) = (\eta_2, \xi_2) = 1 \\ (\eta_1, \xi_2) = (\eta_2, \xi_1) = 0. \end{cases}$$

The deformed image is again introduced through $\mathscr{D} = \mathscr{D}_1 \mathscr{D}_2$, but the noise terms are now plane vectors with some two-dimensional frequency function f, and $\mathscr{D}_1$ is the masking by the outside of a square Q_L with sides L.

Introduce

(5.3) $$\phi(\lambda) = \frac{1}{L^2} \sum_{X \in I^a} e^{i(\lambda, X)}$$

when λ is a fixed vector in the plane. For the mean value function we obtain

(5.4) $$m(\lambda) = E[\phi(\lambda)] = \frac{1}{L^2} \int_{Q_L} e^{i(\lambda, X)} p(X) \, dX$$

with

(5.5) $$p(X) = \sum_{\nu_1, \nu_2 = -\infty}^{\infty} f(X - \nu_1 \xi_1 - \nu_2 \xi_2)$$

which converges almost everywhere to a non-negative function in R^2 with the periods ξ_1 and ξ_2. Now we fold back p onto one of the fundamental parallelograms P of the original lattice taking into account that

(5.6) $$e^{i(\lambda, X)} = e^{i(\lambda, X_0)} e^{i(\eta, \nu_1 \xi_1 + \nu_2 \xi_2)}$$

with $X_0 \in P$ and $X = X_0 + \nu_1 \xi_1 + \nu_2 \xi_2$ so that

(5.7) $$e^{i(\lambda, X)} = e^{i(\lambda, X_0)} e^{i(h_1 \nu_1 + h_2 \nu_2)}$$

if we express λ in terms of the reciprocal lattice R,

(5.8) $\lambda = h_1\eta_1 + h_2\eta_2.$

This means that if we sum the geometric series over the parallelograms belonging to Q_L (see (4.3) for comparison)

(5.9) $m(\lambda) \sim \dfrac{1}{L^2} \displaystyle\int_P e^{i(\lambda, X_0)} p(X_0) S_L(X_0) dX_0$

so that if $\lambda \notin 2\pi R$

(5.10) $\displaystyle\lim_{L \to \infty} m(\lambda) = 0.$

If $\lambda \in 2\pi R$ so that $\lambda = 2\pi(h_1\eta_1 + h_2\eta_2)$, with integral h_1, h_2,

$$\lim_{L \to \infty} m(\lambda) = \frac{1}{\text{area}(P)} \int_P e^{i(\lambda, X_0)} p(X_0) dX_0$$

(5.11)

$$= \frac{1}{\frac{1}{2}\|\xi_1\| \cdot \|\xi_2\| \cdot \sin\psi} \int_{R^2} e^{i(\lambda, X)} f(X) dX$$

where ψ is the angle between the two base vectors in the original lattice.
   Now, to derive the variance, we have

$$L^2 \text{Var}[\phi(\lambda)] =$$

(5.12)

$$\frac{1}{L^2} \int_{Q_L} p(u) du \quad - \frac{1}{L^2} \int_{Q_L \times Q_L} e^{i(\lambda, u-v)} q(u, v) du dv$$

where u and v are in R^2 and

(5.13) $q(u, v) = \displaystyle\sum_{\nu_1, \nu_2 = -\infty}^{\infty} f(u - \nu_1\xi_1 - \nu_2\xi_2) f(v - \nu_1\xi_1 - \nu_2\xi_2).$

This is quite similar to (4.5), (4.6) and the analysis proceeds analogously, resulting in the direct analogue of (4.10).

   Theorem 5.1.   For a two-dimensional lattice with base vectors ξ_1, ξ_2 and the reciprocal lattice R (see (5.2)) the mean of (5.3) is given asymptotically by

(5.14) $$\lim_{L \to \infty} E[\phi(\lambda)] = \begin{cases} 0, & \text{if } \lambda \in 2\pi R \\ \dfrac{1}{\text{area}(P)}\hat{f}(\lambda), & \text{if } \lambda \in 2\pi R. \end{cases}$$

The asymptotic variance is

(5.15) $$\lim_{L \to \infty} L^2 \text{Var}[\phi(\lambda)] = \frac{1}{\text{area}(P)}[1 - [\hat{f}(\lambda)]^2]$$

where P is the fundamental parallelogram of the original lattice and $\hat{f}$ is the two-dimensional Fourier transform of f.

6. Discussion

In an application the phase a would be unknown, but since this only affects $\phi(\lambda)$ by multiplying it with a factor $e^{i(\lambda, a)}$, which has absolute value one, we would work with $|\phi(\lambda)|$ and search for the largest local maxima. Let us look at the first maximum, $k = 1$, in (4.11) and do it for the one-dimensional case to begin with.

Approximately, we would expect the ordinate to be (for $k = 1$)

(6.1) $$\frac{1}{\xi}\hat{f}\left(\frac{2\pi}{\xi}\right)$$

which should be compared to its approximate standard deviation

(6.2) $$\sqrt{\frac{1}{L\xi}\left(1 - \left[\hat{f}\left(\frac{2\pi}{\xi}\right)\right]^2\right)}.$$

If (6.2) is of the same order of magnitude or larger than (6.1) we cannot expect to locate the maximum. This would happen if

(6.3) $$\frac{\left[\hat{f}\left(\frac{2\pi}{\xi}\right)\right]^2}{\xi^2} \leq \frac{1 - \left[\hat{f}\left(\frac{2\pi}{\xi}\right)\right]^2}{L\xi},$$

which means that

(6.4) $$\hat{f}\left(\frac{2\pi}{\xi}\right) < \sqrt{\frac{\xi}{L + \xi}}.$$

For $n = N(0, \sigma^2)$ we have $\hat{f}(\lambda) = e^{-\sigma^2 \lambda^2/2}$, with

(6.5)
$$\sigma > \frac{\xi}{2\pi} \sqrt{\ln\left(1 + \frac{L}{\xi}\right)}.$$

On the other hand if $n = R(-d, d)$

(6.6)
$$\hat{f}(\lambda) = \frac{\sin d\lambda}{d\lambda}.$$

Hence, using (6.4) we can tolerate the value of d if

(6.7)
$$L > \frac{4\pi^2 d^2}{\sin^2 2\pi d} - 1.$$

If d is small this condition leads to small values of L, of course, but when d approaches $\frac{1}{2}$ the condition blows up. For $d = \frac{1}{2}$ no sample size is sufficient to resolve the pattern. The reason for this is obviously that the function p in (4.1) is now identically constant.

A situation like this will then be harder to deal with, and we shall study it computationally, in the case of two dimensions, in Section 7.

7. The two-dimensional case

The situation in the one-dimensional case is a bit misleading since the direction of the base vector is irrelevant, only its length mattering. One could always estimate the length by L/n where n is the number of observed points.

In two dimensions the difficulty is brought out fully since the directional structure of the lattice is important. As a numerical illustration consider the pure image in Figure 7.1 with

(7.1)
$$\begin{cases} \xi_1 = (1, 0) \\ \xi_2 = (\frac{1}{2}, 2) \end{cases}$$

and the reciprocal base vectors

(7.2)
$$\begin{cases} \eta_1 = (1, -\frac{1}{4}) \\ \eta_2 = (0, \frac{1}{2}) \end{cases}.$$

We shall calculate ϕ for multiples of the vectors η_1, η_2 and of the vectors

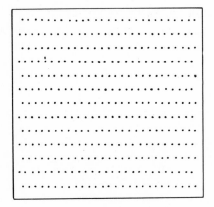

Figure 7.1

$$(7.3) \qquad \begin{cases} \lambda_1 = (.25, \quad .3125) \\ \\ \lambda_2 = (.75, -.0625) \end{cases}$$

displayed in Figure 7.2. We know from Section 6 that rectangular noise can be difficult to deal with and we therefore use it here.

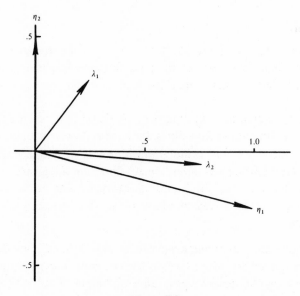

Figure 7.2

The deformed lattice in Figure 7.3 gives for $\psi = \phi/\hat{f}$ the graphs in Figures 7.4a, b, and c corresponding to η_1, λ_1 and λ_2 directions.

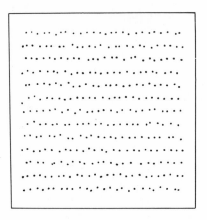

Figure 7.3

This shows that the moderately deformed lattice in Figure 7.3 leads to ψ-functions that have a well-defined maximum near 1 in a, but no obvious maxima in b and c. This is just the behavior that we want.

For a chaotic picture as in Figure 7.5, which displays a highly deformed lattice, the ψ-function in 7.6a along the η_1-direction is satisfactory with its maximum near 1, as is also the graph in the λ_1-direction in 7.6b with no clear maximum. However, along the λ_2-direction the graph in Figure 7.6c has a weak maximum at 1 and a stronger one at 1.5. Hence the deformation was too strong to allow for good restoration with the given sample size.

The restoration technique seems to be able to handle moderate deformations. If the deformations are strong, spurious maxima can occur. The expressions for the mean and variance enable us to say when this can be expected.

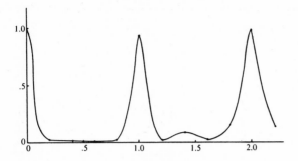

Figure 7.4a

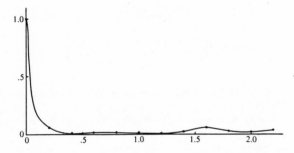

Figure 7.4b

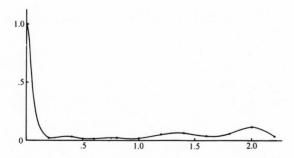

Figure 7.4c

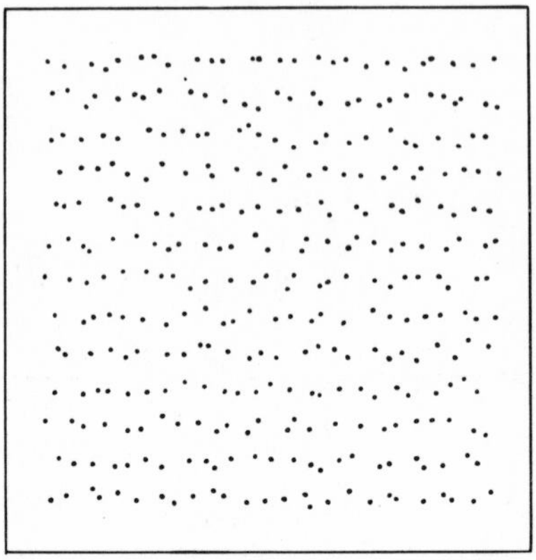

Figure 7.5

References

BARTLETT, M. S. (1964) The spectral analysis of two-dimensional point processes. *Biometrika* **51**, 299–311.

FELLER, W. (1966) *An Introduction to Probability Theory and its Applications*, Vol. II. Wiley, New York.

GRENANDER, U ET AL. *Reports Nos.* 1–32 on pattern analysis. Division of Applied Mathematics, Brown University, Providence, Rhode Island.

MCCLURE, D. E. (1973) Personal communication.

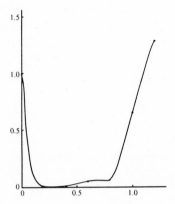

Figure 7.6a

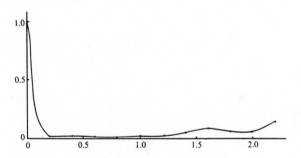

Figure 7.6b

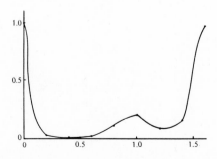

Figure 7.6c

Quaternions, Haar Measure and the Estimation of a Palaeomagnetic Rotation

P. A. P. MORAN

Abstract

Representing a rotation in three dimensions by a unit tensor quaternion and supposing that the errors in the measurements of a number of vector directions follow Fisher's distribution, the maximum likelihood estimator of a rotation is obtained. It is shown that the natural Haar measure for three-dimensional rotations is mapped 1:2 onto the natural Haar measure for random directions in 4-space. The natural Haar measure for rotations in 4-space is also mappable onto the product measure of the Haar measures for two separate random directions in 4-space.

1. Introduction

This paper consists of two parts, the first being concerned with the statistical problem of estimating a rotation, and the second suggested by the method used to solve the first, with some geometric results on rotations in three and four dimensions.

Suppose that a number of different directions in three-dimensional space are known, and that after being subjected to the same but unknown rotation, they are measured with independent errors. We then wish to estimate the unknown rotation from the observed directions.

Choose some fixed set of coordinates in three-dimensional space and suppose that the n known directions, before rotation, are represented by unit vectors with coordinates (x_{1i}, x_{2i}, x_{3i}) $(i = 1, \cdots, n)$. After rotation we suppose that they become the (unknown) unit vectors (y_{1i}, y_{2i}, y_{3i}) $(i = 1, \cdots, n)$. These are now measured with an error so that in fact we observe unit vectors (X_{1i}, X_{2i}, X_{3i}) $(i = 1, \cdots, n)$.

295

The most natural assumption we can make about the error is that the difference between the observed vectors and their true values is distributed in Fisher's 'normal' distribution. This asserts that the angle, α say, between the two vectors is distributed on the interval $(0, \pi)$ with probability density

(1) $$\frac{k}{2 \sinh k} \exp(k \cos \alpha) \ \sin \alpha.$$

From this it follows that the cosine of the angle α of error is distributed with density

(2) $$\frac{k}{2 \sinh k} \ \exp(k \cos \alpha).$$

Using this as an assumed error distribution we wish to estimate the rotation.

This problem arose in a geophysical situation in which a number of geomagnetic directions were known at a certain epoch and were measured, with error, at a later time. I am indebted to Dr. R. Duncan for bringing this problem to my notice. See Hargraves and Duncan (1973) for a situation where such a problem arises.

2. The estimation of the rotation

Since the azimuth of the error is assumed uniformly distributed, it is sufficient to consider the joint likelihood of the cosines of the angles between the observed vectors and the vectors into which the original vectors are rotated. The logarithm of the likelihood L is then, apart from a constant, given by

(3) $$\log L = n \log k - n \log \sinh k + k \sum_i (X_{1i}y_{1i} + X_{2i}y_{2i} + X_{3i}y_{3i}).$$

Denote the sum in this expression by S. We now need to choose a parametrisation of the rotation which will enable us to maximise $\log L$.

Consider first the use of Euler's angles. We shall use Whittaker's (1937) notation, though other notations are sometimes used. The angular parameters are taken to be θ, ϕ, ψ, where $0 \le \theta \le \pi$, $0 \le \phi$, $\psi < 2\pi$, and can be given a geometric interpretation. Then the vector (x_{1i}, x_{2i}, x_{3i}) is rotated into the vector (y_{1i}, y_{2i}, y_{3i}) by being premultiplied by the proper orthogonal matrix

$$
(4) \quad
\begin{pmatrix}
\cos\phi\cos\theta\cos\psi & \sin\phi\cos\theta\cos\psi & -\sin\theta\cos\psi \\
-\sin\phi\sin\psi & +\cos\phi\sin\psi & \\
& & \\
-\cos\phi\cos\theta\sin\psi & -\sin\phi\cos\theta\sin\psi & \sin\theta\sin\psi \\
-\sin\phi\cos\psi & +\cos\phi\cos\psi & \\
& & \\
\cos\phi\sin\theta & \sin\phi\sin\theta & \cos\theta
\end{pmatrix}.
$$

An alternative parametrisation is obtained if we suppose that the rotation is one through an angle V about an axis with direction cosines l, m, n. This is also given in Whittaker. The premultiplying matrix is then

$$
(5) \quad
\begin{pmatrix}
\cos V & lm(1-\cos V) & ln(1-\cos V) \\
+l^2(1-\cos V) & -n\sin V & +m\sin V \\
& & \\
lm(1-\cos V) & \cos V & mn(1-\cos V) \\
+n\sin V & +m^2(1-\cos V) & -l\sin V \\
& & \\
ln(1-\cos V) & mn(1-\cos V) & \cos V \\
-m\sin V & +l\sin V & +n^2(1-\cos V)
\end{pmatrix},
$$

where the four constants have the additional constraint that $l^2 + m^2 + n^2 = 1$.

However for statistical purposes the most convenient representation is given in terms of the components of a quaternion (u_0, u_1, u_2, u_3). This is known to represent a rotation combined with an expansion or contraction; the simplest exposition of the theory is given by Klein (1932). If we wish to make the matrix represent a rotation without change of scale, we impose the additional constraint that $u_0^2 + u_1^2 + u_2^2 + u_3^2 = 1$. Then, using a slightly different notation from Whittaker, the proper orthogonal matrix representing the rotation is given by

$$
(6) \quad
\begin{pmatrix}
u_0^2 + u_1^2 - u_2^2 - u_3^2 & -2(u_0 u_3 - u_1 u_2) & 2(u_0 u_2 + u_1 u_3) \\
2(u_0 u_3 + u_1 u_2) & u_0^2 - u_1^2 + u_2^2 - u_3^2 & -2(u_0 u_1 - u_2 u_3) \\
-2(u_0 u_2 - u_1 u_3) & 2(u_0 u_1 + u_2 u_3) & u_0^2 - u_1^2 - u_2^2 + u_3^2
\end{pmatrix}.
$$

In this representation (u_0, u_1, u_2, u_3) and $(-u_0, -u_1, -u_2, -u_3)$ correspond to the same rotation so that we have a two to one mapping of the surface of a four-dimensional sphere into the manifold of all proper rotations. The u's can be expressed in terms of the Euler angles by formulae given in Whittaker, and in terms of (V, l, m, n) by the following equations:

(7) $u_0 = \cos\frac{1}{2} V, \quad u_1 = l \sin\frac{1}{2} V, \quad u_2 = m \sin\frac{1}{2} V, \quad u_3 = n \sin\frac{1}{2} V.$

Now consider the maximisation of the likelihood (3). It is clearly sufficient to maximise first with respect to the rotation and then with respect to the accuracy parameter k. Write $S_{ij} = \Sigma_k X_{ik} x_{jk}$. Then the sum in (3) is given by

$$S = (u_0^2 + u_1^2 - u_2^2 - u_3^2)S_{11} - 2(u_0 u_3 + u_1 u_2)S_{21}$$

$$+ 2(u_0 u_2 + u_1 u_3)S_{13} + 2(u_0 u_3 + u_1 u_2)S_{21}$$

(8) $$+ (u_0^2 - u_1^2 + u_2^2 - u_3^2)S_{22} - 2(u_0 u_1 - u_2 u_3)S_{23}$$

$$- 2(u_0 u_2 - u_1 u_3)S_{31} + 2(u_0 u_1 + u_2 u_3)S_{32}$$

$$+ (u_0^2 - u_1^2 - u_2^2 + u_3^2)S_{33}.$$

To obtain the maximum, we differentiate

(9) $$L_1 = S - \lambda(u_0^2 + u_1^2 + u_2^2 + u_3^2 - 1)$$

with respect to u_0, u_1, u_2, u_3 and λ. We then obtain the set of equations

$$(S_{11} + S_{22} + S_{33} - \lambda)u_0 + (S_{32} - S_{23})u_1 + (S_{13} - S_{31})u_2 + (S_{21} - S_{12})u_3 = 0$$

$$(S_{32} - S_{23})u_0 + (S_{11} - S_{22} - S_{33} - \lambda)u_1 + (S_{12} + S_{21})u_2 + (S_{31} + S_{13})u_3 = 0$$

(10)

$$(S_{13} - S_{31})u_0 + (S_{12} + S_{21})u_1 + (-S_{11} + S_{22} - S_{33} - \lambda)u_2 + (S_{23} + S_{32})u_3 = 0$$

$$(S_{21} - S_{12})u_0 + (S_{31} + S_{13})u_1 + (S_{23} + S_{32})u_2 + (-S_{11} - S_{22} + S_{33} - \lambda)u_3 = 0$$

These have a non-null solution when λ is a root of the corresponding characteristic equation. Since the matrix is symmetric it must have four real roots whose sum is zero since the trace is zero.

Having found the largest root, we solve the equations using the normalising condition that $\Sigma u_i^2 = 1$. This gives the maximum likelihood solution for the rotation. Differentiating (3) with respect to k we can then estimate k by solving the equation obtained by equating this derivative to zero.

Having found the maximum likelihood solutions for the u_i, they can be turned into the maximum likelihood estimators for θ, ϕ, ψ or for V, l, m, n

by the above-quoted equations. To obtain the asymptotic variance-covariance matrix it is best to use θ, ϕ, ψ since the estimators then have a trivariate non-singular distribution, and their variance-covariance matrix is obtained by inverting the matrix of second derivatives of log L with respect to these. This will contain the estimate of k.

Another method of estimating a rotation has been given by Mackenzie (1957), but without using the quaternion representation which greatly simplifies the algebra and easily gives asymptotically efficient estimators of the second order moments of the asymptotically trivariate normal distribution.

3. Rotations and Haar measure

The fact that quaternions greatly simplify the statistical estimation of a rotation suggests that they may be of use in studying the theory of random rotations. In three dimensions the theory for three dimensions, due to Deltheil, is described in Kendall and Moran (1963) and in Miles (1965). Here the condition is imposed that the probability of a set of rotations is invariant under any rotation of the space. The probability measure is therefore a Haar measure under the group of rotations. In terms of the parametrisation used in (5), this Haar measure turns out to be given by supposing that the vector (l, m, n) of the axis of rotation is uniformly distributed in all directions so that the point (l, m, n) is uniformly distributed on the surface of a 3-sphere, and the angle of rotation, V, is distributed on the interval $(0, 2\pi)$ with the density $\pi^{-1} \sin^2 \frac{1}{2} V$, independently of (l, m, n). Note that V does not have a uniform distribution.

If we now consider the parametrisation used in (6) we can see from (7) that this is equivalent to supposing that the unit vector, (u_0, u_1, u_2, u_3), in 4-space, is uniformly distributed in all directions, and that the vectors (u_0, u_1, u_2, u_3) and $(-u_0, -u_1, -u_2, -u_3)$ are made to correspond to the same rotation in 3-space. That the measures correspond is then easily verified from (7). Thus we reach the elegant result that the set of all rotations in 3-space with its appropriate Haar measure can be represented by the set of all directions in 4-space with its appropriate Haar measure, remembering that opposite directions are identified.

This provides another and easier way to construct a random rotation from normal random variables than that given in Kendall and Moran (1963). We take four independent random variables X_1, X_2, X_3, X_4 which are normally distributed with zero means and the same standard deviation. Taking $u_i = X_i(\Sigma X^2)^{-\frac{1}{2}}$, we obtain the direction cosines of a uniformly distributed direction in 4-space; then, regarding these as the elements of a quaternion and using them in (6), we obtain a random rotation in 3-space.

As an oddity we may mention that it follows from this that if X_1, X_2, X_3, X_4 are any such identically distributed independent normal variates then

$$(11) \qquad (X_1^2 + X_2^2 - X_3^2 - X_4^2)(X_1^2 + X_2^2 + X_3^2 + X_4^2)^{-1}$$

and

$$(12) \qquad 2(X_1 X_2 - X_0 X_3)(X_1^2 + X_2^2 + X_3^2 + X_4^2)^{-1}$$

are uniformly distributed in rectangular distributions on the interval $(-1, 1)$. Moreover if we take any row of the matrix (6) and replace the u's by such X's we obtain three quantities which are jointly distributed in a spherically symmetrical (but not normal) distribution in 3-space.

4. Rotations in 4-space

James (1954) has pointed out that the group of proper orthogonal matrices in n-space has $\frac{1}{2}n(n-1)$ parameters, and that its Haar measure transforms into a uniform measure on a $\frac{1}{2}n(n-1)$-dimensional variety in n^2-space. Thus in the above case we have a mapping into the $3 = \frac{1}{2}n(n-1)$-dimensional surface of a sphere in $4 = n + 1 < n^2$-space. The group of rotations in 4-space must therefore map into a $6 = \frac{1}{2}n(n-1)$-surface in a space of dimension $n^2 = 16$ or less. In fact Cayley showed that rotations in 4-space can be represented by two quaternions, both with unit tensors so that the sums of the squares of their components is unity. The simplest exposition of this theory is given in Klein (1932).

Using $1, i, j, k$ as the quaternion units we represent a point, x, in 4-space by $x_0 + ix_1 + jx_2 + kx_3$. Write

$$(13) \qquad p = u_0 + iu_1 + ju_2 + ku_3,$$

$$(14) \qquad q = v_0 + iv_1 + jv_2 + kv_3.$$

Then a general rotation in 4-space is defined by the transformation of x into $p \cdot x \cdot q$ where the dot denotes quaternion multiplication. Thus the set of all rotations in 4-space is mapped into a six-dimensional space which is the Cartesian product of the three-dimensional surfaces of two 4-spheres in 4-space. In this mapping, it is necessary to make the additional convention that the point (p, q) is identified with the point $(-p, -q)$.

Now consider the associated Haar measure. This has to be invariant under any further rotation. Such a rotation can be represented by another pair of quaternions p', q', (with unit tensors). The resulting rotation will then be given by

$$(15) \qquad p' \cdot p \cdot x \cdot q \cdot q' = (p' \cdot p) \cdot x \cdot (q \cdot q').$$

Thus it is clear that if we take into account the fact that (p, q) is identified with $(-p, -q)$, the uniform Haar measure for rotations in 4-space can be represented by the product of the uniform Haar measures on the surfaces of two 4-spheres in two different 4-spaces, Similarly to the three-dimensional space, this provides an easy way to construct a random rotation in 4-space from eight independent and identically distributed normal variates with zero means. We may summarise by saying that random rotations in 3-space correspond to random directions in 4-space, and random rotations in 4-space to independent pairs of random rotations in 4-space.

In spaces of dimension higher than four, quaternions do not seem to be useful. Possible lines of research in this direction are suggested in a paper by Littlewood (1948).

References

FISHER, R. A. (1953) Dispersion on a sphere. *Proc. Roy. Soc.* A **217**, 295–305.

HARGRAVES, R. B. AND DUNCAN, R. A. (1973) Does the mantle roll? *Nature* **245**, 361–363.

JAMES, A. T. (1954) Normal multivariate analysis and the orthogonal group. *Ann. Math. Statist.* **25**, 40–75.

KENDALL, M. G. AND MORAN, P. A. P. (1963) *Geometrical Probability.* Griffin, London.

KLEIN, F. (1932) *Elementary Mathematics from an Advanced Standpoint. Vol. I. Arithmetic, Algebra, Analysis.* (translated by E. R. Hedrick and C. A. Noble). Macmillan, London.

LITTLEWOOD, D. E. (1948) Invariant theory under orthogonal groups. *Proc. London Math. Soc.* (2) **50**, 349–379.

MACKENZIE, J. K. (1957) The estimation of an orientation relationship. *Acta Cryst.* **10**, 61–62.

MILES, R. E. (1965) On random rotations in R^3. *Biometrika* **52**, 636–639.

WHITTAKER, E. T. (1937) *A Treatise on the Analytical Dynamics of Particles and Rigid Bodies.* Cambridge University Press.

A Highway Traffic Model

HERBERT SOLOMON

Abstract

The trajectory of a car traveling at a constant speed on an idealized infinite highway can be viewed as a straight line in the time-space plane. Entry times are governed by a Poisson process with intensity parameter λ leading to all trajectories as random lines in a plane. The Poisson distribution of number of encounters of cars on the highway is developed through random line models and non-homogeneous Poisson fields, and its parameter, which depends on the specific random measure employed, is obtained explicitly.

1. Introduction

In a paper published in the Fifth Berkeley Symposium on Mathematical Statistics and Probability, Bartlett [1] studied line processes in two dimensions. Traffic flow data served as motivation for his analysis. At about the same time, other authors such as Rényi [2] began to investigate traffic flow models. This author and Wang [3] studied models of traffic flow on a highway in a paper delivered at the Sixth Berkeley Symposium. In that article the structure and properties of Poisson fields of random lines in a plane were employed to provide a more systematic development of models by Rényi, Weiss and Herman [4] and others. It is fitting therefore to return to this topic in this volume and give a somewhat simplified and more instructive proof of the main result in Solomon and Wang.

It is possible to view the trajectory of a car produced by its time and space coordinates on the highway as a straight line in a plane if the car travels at a constant speed once it enters the highway and then never leaves the highway. We assume no change in a car's velocity when it overtakes another car, or is overtaken by another car. The Poisson process is the random device governing car entrance times or equivalently car positions, and the speed distributions for each vehicle are assumed to be identically and independently distributed (i.i.d.). Thus we can view the trajectory of any car as a random line in the plane and we will shortly formalize this notion. The intersections of these random lines in the plane will represent time and space coordinates where an overtaking occurs.

Let one of the vehicles be an observer car (arbitrary line). The number of intersections of the arbitrary line (observer car) by the other lines determines the number of overtakings of slower cars made by the observer car plus the number of times it was overtaken by faster cars. We will develop this distribution and also the distribution of faster car overtakings of the observer car and overtaking of slower cars by the observer car. This requires a formulation for a non-homogeneous Poisson field of random lines from which a different proof of Rényi's theorem and the Weiss and Herman result can follow.

2. Development

First we formalize the notion of straight lines distributed 'at random' throughout the plane. We will describe the plane in terms of (t, x) coordinates, where subsequently the t axis will be employed to register time of arrival of cars at a fixed point on a highway and the x axis will in similar fashion report on spatial positions of cars on a highway at a fixed point in time. The time invariance property for Poisson processes will insure that the conditions will prevail at any point in time. Any line in the (t, x) plane can be represented as

$$(2.1) \qquad p = t \cos \alpha + x \sin \alpha, \qquad -\infty < p < \infty, \ 0 \leqq \alpha < \pi,$$

where p is the signed length of the perpendicular to the line from an arbitrary origin 0, and α is the angle this perpendicular makes with the t axis. Note that if the intersection of the perpendicular with the line is in the third or fourth quadrant, p is taken to be negative. A set of lines $\{(p_i, \alpha_i) : i = 0, \pm 1, \pm 2, \cdots\}$ constitutes a Poisson field under the following conditions.

(1) The distances $\cdots \leqq p_{-2} \leqq p_{-1} \leqq p_0 \leqq p_1 \leqq p_2 \leqq \cdots$ of the lines from an arbitrary origin 0, arranged according to magnitude, represent the coordinates of the events of a Poisson process with constant parameter,

say λ. Thus, the number of p_i in an interval of length L has a Poisson distribution with mean λL.

(2) The orientations α_i of each line with a fixed but arbitrary axis (say the t axis) in the plane are independent and obey a uniform distribution in the interval $(0, \pi)$.

Thus, a reasonable representation of random lines in the plane is that of the Poisson field. This definition of randomness for lines in the plane also has the property that the randomness is unaffected by the choice of origin or line to serve as t axis, since it can be demonstrated that except for a constant factor $\int dp\,d\alpha$ is the only invariant measure under the group of rotations and translations that transform the line (p, α) to the line (p', α'). We will return to this structure and its characteristics, but now we employ it as a point of departure to initiate discussion of a non-homogeneous Poisson field of random lines. To achieve this we will relax Condition (2) above and ask only that the α_i be identically and independently distributed (i.i.d.).

For ease in the algebra of our traffic flow models, we will employ instead of α_i an angle formed by the intersection of the t axis with a line in the plane and we label this θ where $v = \tan \theta$. Also we will only be concerned with those lines where p_i falls in the second or fourth quadrant since this will yield all positive car velocities. The inclusion of the p_i in the first and third quadrant does not complicate the mathematical development, but they are not relevant. Thus, $\alpha = \frac{1}{2}\pi + \theta$ and the lines of interest will now be parametrized by (p, θ) where

$$(2.2) \qquad p = -t \sin \theta + x \cos \theta, \qquad 0 \le \theta < \tfrac{1}{2}\pi.$$

Equation (2.2) takes care of the sign of p, for it insures that p will be positive if it is in the second quadrant and negative in the fourth quadrant.

The set $\mathcal{L}$ of lines $\{(p_i, \alpha_i): i = 0, \pm 1, \pm 2, \cdots\}$ becomes a non-homogeneous Poisson field if we require invariant measure only under translation, and we look into this situation because it will be helpful in our traffic flow models. Under this constraint, we now have the same conditions except that the orientation angles α_i of each line are i.i.d. random variables with common distribution function in the interval $(0, \pi)$. Thus, $\int dp\,d\alpha$ is no longer the appropriate measure and the origin can be arbitrarily chosen at any point on a specific and fixed t axis because invariance is preserved now only under translation.

The orientations θ_i are independent and identically distributed with common distribution F in the interval $(0, \pi/2)$, and further the sequence of values $\langle \theta_i \rangle$ is independent of $\langle p_i \rangle$. This is equivalent to the statement that the velocities of cars, namely $v_i = \tan \theta_i$, are independent and identically distributed with common distribution G on $(0, \infty)$ and thus $\langle v_i = \tan \theta_i \rangle$ are independent of $\langle p_i \rangle$.

When $\theta_0 = 0$, $p_0 = 0$, the traffic flow is characterized by a distribution of time intercepts on the t axis; when $\theta_0 = \pi/2$, $p_0 = 0$, the traffic flow is characterized by a distribution of cars spaced along the x axis. For any other value of θ, the traffic flow is measured along a trajectory line. In the traffic literature, trajectories for low density traffic flow (no delays in overtaking) may be assumed to be linear in the time-space plane. Thus in any development, we must employ the appropriate measure to character-ize distributions of traffic flow in such matters, for example, as distribu-tion of number of overtakings. For our purposes where Poisson processes are the underpinning for traffic flow in both spatial and temporal proces-ses, the evaluation of the appropriate Poisson intensity parameter will be paramount as will be the relationships between these parameters for different measures.

3. Basic result

As noted above, each line is parametrized by (p, θ), where $0 \le \theta \le \pi/2$, and p is the length of the perpendicular from the origin to the line. It is given a positive sign if the line cuts the t axis at time $t_0 > 0$, and a negative sign if it cuts the t axis at time $t_0 < 0$. A glance at Figure 1 will indicate cars faster and slower than the observer car.

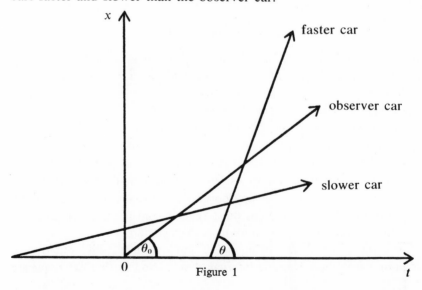

Figure 1

Label N_L the number of cars intersecting the observer car before the point $t = L \cos \theta_0$, $x = L \sin \theta_0$, i.e., in the line segment L of the line $l = (0, \theta)$ stretching from the origin to the point. Let N_p denote the number of cars with the opportunity to intersect the observer car on this stretch. Then N_p is the number of cars with $-L \sin \theta_0 < p < L \cos \theta_0$.

Now any one of these N_L vehicles actually is overtaken or overtakes, given its θ, if

(i) $0 < \theta < \theta_0$ and $0 < -p < L \sin(\theta_0 - \theta)$ or $-L \sin(\theta_0 - \theta) < p < 0$
(ii) $\theta_0 < \theta < \pi/2$ and $0 < p < L \sin(\theta - \theta_0)$.

Graphically we have

(i)

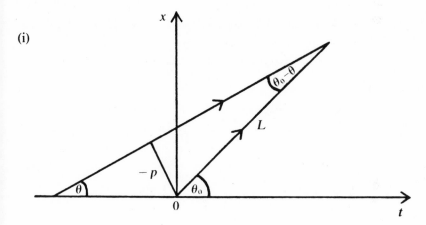

Figure 2

(ii)

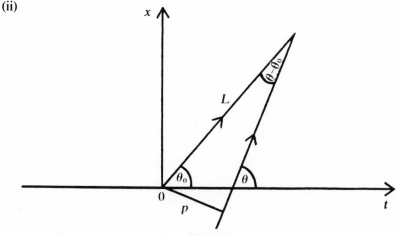

Figure 3

Define $\mu = P\{N_L = 1 | N_p = 1\}$, then

$$\mu = P\{0 < \eta < L \, | \, \exists \text{ exactly one random line } (p, \theta) \text{ with} \\ -L \sin \theta_0 < p < L \cos \theta_0\}$$

and

$$\mu = \left[\int_0^{\theta_0} \int_{-L \sin(\theta_0 - \theta)}^0 + \int_0^{\pi/2} \int_0^{L \sin(\theta - \theta_0)} \right]$$

$$dF(\theta, p \, | \, \exists \text{ exactly one random line } (p, \theta) \text{ with} \\ -L \sin \theta_0 < p < L \cos \theta_o).$$

Now the distribution of θ is independent of the distribution of p and the condition depends only on p. Moreover the conditional distribution of p given $-L \sin \theta_0 < p < L \cos \theta_0$ is uniform on the interval $(-L \sin \theta_0 . L \cos \theta_0)$ since the p's are from a Poisson process.

Therefore we may write

$$\mu = \left[\int_0^{\theta_0} \int_{-L \sin(\theta_0 - \theta)}^0 + \int_{\theta_0}^{\pi/2} \int_0^{L \sin(\theta - \theta_0)} \right] \frac{dp}{L \cos \theta_0 + L \sin \theta_0} \, dH(\theta)$$

or

$$\mu = \int_0^{\theta_0} \frac{L \sin (\theta_0 - \theta)}{L \cos \theta_0 + L \sin \theta_0} \, dH(\theta) + \int_{\theta_0}^{\pi/2} \frac{L \sin (\theta - \theta_0)}{L \cos \theta_0 + L \sin \theta_0} \, dH(\theta).$$

The number of cars N_L is the number of cars with $-L \sin \theta_0 < p < L \cos \theta_0$. Because of our Poisson assumption, N_L is Poisson with parameter $\lambda (L \cos \theta_0 + L \sin \theta_0)$. A random member of this set has probability μ of actually overtaking or being overtaken and so the number of such overtaking occurrences is Poisson with parameter

$$\mu \lambda L (\cos \theta_0 + \sin \theta_0) =$$

$$\lambda L \left\{ \int_0^{\theta_0} \sin (\theta_0 - \theta) dH(\theta) + \int_{\theta_0}^{\pi/2} \sin (\theta - \theta_0) dh(\theta) \right\}$$

Since $v = \tan \theta$, we label $G(v)$ as the distribution of the velocity and replace $dH(\theta)$ with $dG(v)$. Also

$$\sin(\theta_0 - \theta) = \frac{\sin \theta_0}{(1 + v^2)^{\frac{1}{2}}} - \frac{v \cos \theta_0}{(1 + v^2)^{\frac{1}{2}}}$$

and

$$\sin(\theta - \theta_0) = \frac{v \cos \theta_0}{(1 + v^2)^{\frac{1}{2}}} - \frac{\sin \theta_0}{(1 + v^2)^{\frac{1}{2}}}.$$

Thus,

$$\mu(\cos \theta_0 + \sin \theta_0) = \int_0^{\tan \theta_0} \frac{\sin \theta_0 - v \cos \theta_0}{(1 + v^2)^{\frac{1}{2}}} dG(v)$$

$$+ \int_{\tan \theta_0}^{\infty} \frac{v \cos \theta_0 - \sin \theta_0}{(1 + v^2)^{\frac{1}{2}}} dG(v),$$

$$\mu(\cos \theta_0 + \sin \theta_0) = \cos \theta_0 \left[\int_0^{v_0} \frac{v_0 - v}{(1 + v^2)^{\frac{1}{2}}} dG(v) + \int_{v_0}^{\infty} \frac{v - v_0}{(1 + v^2)^{\frac{1}{2}}} dG(v) \right].$$

Therefore the intensity of the Poisson process generated by faster cars overtaking the observer car is

$$\lambda' = \lambda L \cos \theta_0 \int_{v_0}^{\infty} \frac{v - v_0}{(1 + v^2)^{\frac{1}{2}}} dG(v),$$

and the intensity of the Poisson process generated by the observer car overtaking slower cars is

$$\lambda'' = \lambda L \cos \theta_0 \int_0^{v_0} \frac{v_0 - v}{(1 + v^2)^{\frac{1}{2}}} dG(v).$$

From this basic result arising from a merger of geometrical probability and non-homogeneous Poisson processes, all the models developed by Rényi, Weiss and Herman, and others can be derived as demonstrated in Solomon and Wang [3].

References

[1] BARTLETT, M. S. (1967) The spectral analysis of line processes. *Proc. Fifth Berkeley Symp. Math. Statist. Prob.* 3, 135–153.

[2] RÉNYI, A. (1964) On two mathematical models of the traffic on a divided highway. *J. Appl. Prob.* 1, 311–320.

[3] SOLOMON, H. AND WANG, P. C. C. (1972) Non-homogeneous Poisson fields of random lines with applications to traffic flow. *Proc. Sixth Berkeley Symp. Math. Statist. Prob.* 3, 383–400.

[4] WEISS, G. AND HERMAN, R. (1962) Statistical properties of low-density traffic. *Quart. Appl. Math.* 20, 121–130.

PART VIII

PROBABILITY MODELS IN
THE HUMANITIES

Stochastic Models for Type Counts in a Literary Text

J. GANI

Abstract

This paper studies a Markov chain model for type counts $\{X_n\}$ in a literary text. First, a homogeneous Markov chain in discrete time is considered. This is then embedded in a continuous time Poisson process; the probability generating function for the resulting continuous time Markov chain is obtained. Expectations and variances of type counts are found for different values of the token count and various sizes M of an author's vocabulary; these results are finally tested against known data for three of Shakespeare's plays.

1. Introduction

In a recent study of textual type and token counts, that is, counts of words used for the first time and of all words used in a literary text, Brainerd (1972) has postulated a simple non-homogeneous Markov chain model for the type count. Suppose that X_n, the number of word types in n word tokens of text, forms a Markov chain such that

$$\Pr\{X_n = i + 1 \mid X_{n-1} = i\} = f(n - 1, i),$$

(1.1)

$$\Pr\{X_n = i \mid X_{n-1} = i\} = 1 - f(n - 1, i) \quad (i = 1, \cdots, M; n > 1)$$

denote the relevant transition probabilities of the process. One may then write for the column vector $\Pr[X_n = 1, X_n = 2, \cdots, X_n = M - 1, X_n = M]'$

(1.2)

$$
\begin{bmatrix}
1 - f(n-1,1) & 0 & & \\
f(n-1,1) & 1 - f(n-1,2) & & 0 \\
\cdot \ \cdot \ \cdot \ \cdot \ \cdot \ \cdot \ \cdot \ \cdot \ \cdot \ \cdot \ \cdot \ \cdot \ \cdot \ \cdot \ \cdot & & \\
& 0 & f(n-1,M+1) & 1 - f(n-1,M)
\end{bmatrix}
\Pr
\begin{bmatrix}
X_{n-1} = 1 \\
X_{n-1} = 2 \\
\cdots \\
X_{n-1} = M
\end{bmatrix}
$$

313

for all $n > 1$, or more briefly $P^{(n)} = F(n-1)P^{(n-1)}$, where M is the total working vocabulary of the text writer. It is assumed that $\Pr\{X_1 = 1\} = 1$; clearly $f(n-1, i) = 0$ and $\Pr\{X_{n-1} = i\} = 0$ for every $i > n - 1$.

While the chain characterised by the transition probabilities (1.1) is in general non-homogeneous, Brainerd assumed, in order to simplify its structure, that $f(n, i) = g(n)$ for $n > 0$, with $g(0) = 1$ for convenience. He was then able to derive a recurrence relation for the probability generating function (p.g.f.) $G(n, v) = \sum_{i=1}^{n} \Pr\{X_n = i\} v^i$ ($|v| \leq 1$), of the type count; this was shown to satisfy the difference equation

$$G(n, v) = \{1 + (v - 1)g(n - 1)\} G(n - 1, v) \qquad (n > 1),$$

from which the result

(1.3)
$$G(n, v) = \prod_{j=0}^{n-1} \{1 + (v - 1)g(j)\}$$

followed. Using this, the mean and variance of X_n were found to be

(1.4)
$$E(X_n) = \sum_{j=0}^{n} g(j), \quad \mathcal{V}(X_n) = \sum_{j=0}^{n-1} g(j) \{1 - g(j)\}.$$

In the case where $g(n) = e^{-\alpha n}$, for example, these expressions reduced to

(1.5)
$$E(X_n) = \frac{1 - e^{-\alpha n}}{1 - e^{-\alpha}}, \quad \mathcal{V}(X_n) = \frac{1 - e^{-\alpha n}}{1 - e^{-\alpha}} - \frac{1 - e^{-2\alpha n}}{1 - e^{-2\alpha}}.$$

A more realistic and complicated model can be formulated by recognising the natural subdivision of words into two basic groups (see Yule (1944) and Williams (1970)). The large Group I of substantive words consists of nouns, adjectives, verbs and adverbs, while the small Group II of mainly auxiliary words includes 6 subgroups: pronouns, prepositions, conjunctions, auxiliary verbs, articles and interjections. Yule estimated that the number of words in Group I listed in the 1933 Edition of the *Shorter Oxford English Dictionary* was approximately 100,000, while Group II consisted of about 500 words all together.

In his second model, Brainerd (1972) suggested that a writer composing text might select word tokens from the 6 subgroups of Group II multinomially with probabilities β_i ($i = 1, \cdots, m$; $m = 6$), the remaining word types being selected from Group I in the previously described manner. Once again, in this case, $G(n, v)$ can be derived explicitly in the form (1.3), but with

(1.6) $$g(n) = \left[\sum_{i=1}^{m} (1 - \beta_i)^n \beta_i \right] + \alpha (1 - \alpha + \alpha e^{-\lambda})^n$$

where $\alpha = 1 - \sum_{i=1}^{m} \beta_i$, and λ is some positive parameter. The mean and variance of X_n can then be found readily. Other models relating word types to their frequencies of occurrence have also been postulated; for an interesting comparison of two such models, the reader is referred to Lanke (1974).

The purpose of this paper is to consider an alternative homogeneous Markov chain in discrete time for the type count X_n; the transition probabilities of this chain are based on an assumption different from Brainerd's. It is found that the expectation and variance of the type count can be more readily calculated if the original chain is first embedded in a continuous time Poisson process. The probability generating function of the resulting continuous time Markov chain is obtained, and from it the expectation and variance of the type count are derived. Numerical values for these are computed; some general conclusions are drawn on the adequacy of the model, using known data on Shakespeare's plays.

2. A homogeneous Markov chain in discrete time for the type count

Let us suppose that the transition probabilities in (1.1) are now given by

(2.1) $$f(n, i) = \alpha (M - i) \qquad (i = 1, \cdots, M),$$

where M is the author's total vocabulary, and $\alpha > 0$ is an intensity parameter such that $\alpha M \leqq 1$. Brainerd mentions in his paper (1972) that this form was suggested by D. McNeil; briefly, it assumes that the probability of a new word type is proportional to the number $M - i$ of unused types. McNeil studied this problem in a paper published in 1973, which I regrettably did not see until very recently. In it, he has derived the p.g.f. of X_n by a simple direct method, discussed the estimation of M, and argued the relevance of Zipf's law. Our alternative procedure makes use of classical methods for Markov chains in discrete and continuous time. The results are effectively equivalent, but our different approaches emphasise different structural aspects of the same model. The problem considered is identical to that of sampling with replacement from a population of M distinct items, where the probability of sampling a new item at the nth draw given that i distinct types have previously been drawn is $\alpha (M - i)$. The Markov chain for the type count now becomes homogeneous, and it is possible to derive its vector $P^{(n)}$ of probabilities $[\Pr\{X_n = i\}]_{i=1}^{M}$ fairly simply.

The transition probability matrix $F(n - 1)$ is constant, of the form

$$(2.2) \quad F = \begin{bmatrix} 1 - \alpha(M-1) & 0 & & & & \\ \alpha(M-1) & 1 - \alpha(M-2) & 0 & & & \\ 0 & \alpha(M-2) & 1 - \alpha(M-3) & 0 & \cdots & \\ & & \cdots\cdots\cdots\cdots\cdots & & & \\ & & 0 & 2\alpha & 1-\alpha & 0 \\ & & & 0 & \alpha & 1 \end{bmatrix},$$

where α must clearly take values in $0 < \alpha \leqq M^{-1}$. The eigenvalues of F are

$$(2.3) \qquad \lambda_i = 1 - \alpha(M - i) \qquad (i = 1, \cdots, M),$$

with associated post-vectors b_i such that

$$b'_i = [0, \cdots, 0, 1, -(M - i), \cdots, (-1)^{M-i}],$$

$$b_{ji} = (-1)^{j-i} \binom{M-i}{j-i} \quad (j = 1, \cdots, M),$$

and pre-vectors

$$a_i = \left[\binom{M-1}{i-1}, \cdots, (M-i+1), 1, 0, \cdots, 0\right], \quad a_{ij} = \binom{M-j}{i-j} \quad (j = 1, \cdots, M).$$

It is assumed that $\binom{k}{r} = 0$ if $r < 0$; thus $b_{ji} = 0$ for $j < i$, and $b_{ii} = 1$, while $a_{ii} = 1$ and $a_{ij} = 0$ for $j > i$.

The matrix F can now be expressed in the canonical form

$$(2.4) \qquad F = [b_1, \cdots, b_M] \begin{bmatrix} \lambda_1 & & & \\ & \cdot & & \\ & & \cdot & \\ & & & \cdot \\ & & & & \lambda_M \end{bmatrix} \begin{bmatrix} a_1 \\ \cdot \\ \cdot \\ \cdot \\ \cdot \\ a_M \end{bmatrix} = B\Lambda A.$$

If $\Pr\{X_1 = 1\} = 1$ as before, so that

$$P^{(1)'} = [1, 0, \cdots, 0]$$

it follows from (1.2) that

(2.5) $$\boldsymbol{P}^{(n)} = \boldsymbol{F}\boldsymbol{P}^{(n-1)} = \boldsymbol{F}^{n-1}\boldsymbol{P}^{(1)} = \boldsymbol{B}\boldsymbol{\Lambda}^{n-1}\boldsymbol{A}\boldsymbol{P}^{(1)}.$$

From this, after some algebraic manipulation, the probabilities $P_j^{(n)}$ can be derived as

(2.6) $\quad P_j^{(n)} = \Pr\{X_n = j\}$

$$= \binom{M-1}{j-1} \sum_{i=1}^{j} \binom{j-1}{j-i}(-1)^{j-i}[1 - \alpha(M - i)]^{n-1} \quad (j = 1, \cdots, n).$$

Attempts to express their p.g.f. $G(n, v) = \sum_{j=1}^{n} P_j^{(n)} v^j$ ($|v| \leq 1$) in a simple form from (2.6) prove difficult; likewise, $E(X_n)$, $\mathscr{V}(X_n)$ are not readily obtainable otherwise than by lengthy summations. One is therefore led to ask whether simpler forms for these may be found by embedding the Markov chain in a continuous time process. If, for example, the chain were embedded in a Poisson process with parameter $\lambda > 0$, the probabilities of the type count process would then be

(2.7) $\quad \Pr\{Y(t) = n, X(t) = j \mid Y(0) = X(0) = 1\} = e^{-\lambda t}\dfrac{(\lambda t)^n}{n!} P_j^{(n)} \quad (t \geq 0),$

where $Y(t)$, $X(t)$ are respectively the token and type counts up to time t, and $P_j^{(n)}$ is given by (2.6). We shall now consider this process.

3. Embedding the Markov chain in a continuous time process

Let us assume that text writing is a continuous process in time $t \geq 0$, and that the token count $Y(t)$ at t forms a Poisson process with parameter $\lambda > 0$. For simplicity, we consider a word to be written instantaneously at the moment it is first penned. If $X(t)$ is the type count at time t, then embedding the previous Markov chain in this Poisson process, we define the infinitesimal transition probabilities of the process $\{Y(t), X(t)\}$ by

$$\Pr\{Y(t + \delta t) = n + 1, \ X(t + \delta t) = i + 1 \mid Y(t) = n, \ X(t) = i\}$$
$$= \lambda\alpha(M - i)\delta t + o(\delta t)$$

(3.1) $\Pr\{Y(t + \delta t) = n + 1, X(t + \delta t) = i \mid Y(t) = n, X(t) = i\}$
$$= \lambda\{1 - \alpha(M - i)\delta t\} + o(\delta t)$$

$$\Pr\{Y(t + \delta t) = n, X(t + \delta t) = i \mid Y(t) = n, X(t) = i\} = 1 - \lambda\delta t - o(\delta t).$$

Using standard arguments, we may readily derive the forward Kolmogorov equations of the process as

$$\frac{d}{dt} P_{ni}(t) = -\lambda P_{ni}(t) + \lambda P_{n-1,i}(t) \ [1 - \alpha(M - i)]$$

(3.2) $$+ \lambda P_{n-1,i-1}(t) \alpha(M - i + 1)$$

$$(1 \leqq i \leqq M, \ 1 \leqq n < \infty)$$

where $P_{ni}(t) = \Pr\{Y(t) = n, X(t) = i \,|\, Y(0) = 1, \ X(0) = 1\}$, $P_{n-1,0}(t) = 0$ for every $n \geqq 1$ and $P_{ni}(t) = 0$ for all $i > n$.

If the p.g.f. of the process is denoted by

$$\phi(u, v, t) = \sum_{n=1}^{\infty} \sum_{i=1}^{n} u^n v^i P_{ni}(t) \qquad (|u|, |v| \leqq 1)$$

subject to the initial condition $\phi(u, v, 0) = uv$, we can show directly from (3.2) that it will satisfy the first order partial differential equation

(3.3) $$\frac{\partial \phi}{\partial t} = \lambda [(u - 1) + \alpha M u(v - 1)] \phi - \lambda \alpha u v(v - 1) \frac{\partial \phi}{\partial v}.$$

This can be solved in the usual manner using Lagrange's method. The auxiliary equations are

(3.4) $$\frac{dt}{1} = \frac{du}{0} = \frac{dv}{\lambda \alpha u v(v - 1)} = \frac{d\phi}{\lambda [(u - 1) + \alpha M u(v - 1)] \phi};$$

these yield the integrals

$$u = c_1, \quad \left(\frac{v}{1 - v}\right) e^{\lambda \alpha u t} = c_2$$

(3.5)

$$\phi(u, v, t) = v^M \left(\frac{1 - v}{v}\right)^{(u-1)/\alpha u} \psi \left(\frac{v}{1 - v} e^{\lambda \alpha u t}, u\right)$$

where c_1, c_2 are constants, and ψ is an arbitrary function.

From the initial condition, we see that

$$\phi(u, v, 0) = uv = v^M \left(\frac{1 - v}{v}\right)^{(u-1)/\alpha u} \psi \left(\frac{v}{1 - v}, u\right)$$

whence, writing $z = v/(1 - v)$ we obtain

$$\psi(z, u) = u z^{(u-1)/\alpha u} \left(\frac{z}{1 + z}\right)^{1-M}.$$

Finally, substituting $\psi((v/(1 - v))e^{\lambda \alpha u t}, u)$ in (3.5), we derive after some algebra the p.g.f.

$$\phi(u, v, t) = uve^{\lambda t(u-1)}[e^{-\lambda\alpha ut} + v(1 - e^{-\lambda\alpha ut})]^{M-1}$$

(3.6)

$$= \sum_{n=1}^{\infty} u^n G(n, v, t).$$

We now show, as might have been expected, that

$$G(u, v, t) = e^{-\lambda t}\frac{(\lambda t)^{n-1}}{(n-1)!}G(n, v)$$

where $G(n, v)$ is the p.g.f. of the probabilities $P_j^{(n)}$ of (2.6).

For we can readily expand the bracketed expression in (3.6) as a binomial to give

$$\phi(u, v, t) = uve^{\lambda t(u-1)}\sum_{j=0}^{M-1}\binom{M-1}{j}v^j(1 - e^{-\lambda\alpha ut})^j e^{-\lambda\alpha ut(M-1-j)}$$

$$= uve^{\lambda t(u-1)}\sum_{j=0}^{M-1}\sum_{i=0}^{j}\binom{M-1}{j}\binom{j}{i}(-1)^{j-i}v^j e^{-\lambda\alpha ut(M-1-i)}$$

(3.7)

$$= \sum_{n=1}^{\infty}u^n v e^{-\lambda t}\frac{(\lambda t)^{n-1}}{(n-1)!}\sum_{j=0}^{M-1}\sum_{i=0}^{j}\binom{M-1}{j}\binom{j}{i}$$
$$\times (-1)^{j-i}v^j(1 - \alpha(M-1-i))^{n-1}$$

$$= \sum_{n=1}^{\infty}u^n e^{-\lambda t}\frac{(\lambda t)^{n-1}}{(n-1)!}G(n, v).$$

We see that this last generating function can be rewritten in the form

$$G(n, v) = v\sum_{j=0}^{M-1}\sum_{i=0}^{j}v^j\binom{M-1}{j}\binom{j}{i}(-1)^{j-i}(1 - \alpha(M-1-i))^{n-1}$$

(3.8)

$$= \sum_{j=1}^{M}\sum_{i=0}^{j-1}v^j\binom{M-1}{j-1}\binom{j-1}{i}(-1)^{j-i-1}(1 - \alpha(M-1-i))^{n-1}$$

$$= \sum_{j=1}^{M}\sum_{i=1}^{j}v^j\binom{M-1}{j-1}\binom{j-1}{i-1}(-1)^{j-i}(1 - \alpha(M-i))^{n-1}$$

and is thus clearly the p.g.f. of the probabilities in (2.6).

The simplest method of evaluating the mean and variance of $X(t)$ given $Y(t) = n$ is to use the p.g.f. (3.6) rather than the more complicated (3.8). Since

$$E\{X(t)|Y(t) = n\} = \frac{\text{coefficient of } u^n \text{ in } \partial\phi(u, 1, t)/\partial v}{\text{coefficient of } u^n \text{ in } \phi(u, 1, t)},$$

we obtain, after some simple algebra

$$E\{X(t)|Y(t) = n\} = M - (M - 1)(1 - \alpha)^{n-1}$$
$$(3.9)$$
$$= (1 - \alpha)^{n-1} + M[1 - (1 - \alpha)^{n-1}].$$

Similarly, we have that

$$\mathcal{V}\{X(t)|Y(t) = n\} = \frac{\text{coefficient of } u^n \text{ in } \dfrac{\partial^2 \phi}{\partial v^2}(u, 1, t) + \dfrac{\partial \phi}{\partial v}(u, 1, t)}{\text{coefficient of } u^n \text{ in } \phi(u, 1, t)}$$

$$(3.10) \qquad\qquad\qquad - E\{X(t)|Y(t) = n\}^2$$

$$= (M - 1)[(1 - \alpha)^{n-1}\{1 - (1 - \alpha)^{n-1}(M - 1)\} + (M - 2)(1 - 2\alpha)^{n-1}].$$

Let us compare (3.9) and (3.10) with the values of the mean and variance for Brainerd's case in which $g(n) = e^{-\alpha n}$. When α is small, so that $e^{-\alpha} \sim 1 - \alpha$, the expressions (1.5) yield

$$E(X_n) \sim \frac{1 - (1 - \alpha)^n}{1 - (1 - \alpha)} = (1 - \alpha)^{n-1} + \frac{1}{\alpha}[1 - (1 - \alpha)^{n-1}],$$

$$(3.11) \quad \mathcal{V}(X_n) \sim \frac{1 - (1 - \alpha)^n}{1 - (1 - \alpha)} - \frac{1 - (1 - 2\alpha)^n}{1 - (1 - 2\alpha)} = (1 - \alpha)^{n-1} - (1 - 2\alpha)^{n-1}$$

$$+ \frac{1}{\alpha}[1 - (1 - \alpha)^{n-1}] - \frac{1}{2\alpha}[1 - (1 - 2\alpha)^{n-1}].$$

Thus, if $\alpha = M^{-1}$ the expectations of the type counts for large M are approximately the same for Brainerd's and the present models; the variances of the type counts, however, are different.

4. Numerical values for the expectation and variance of the type count

In order to understand more concretely the type count model analysed in Sections 2 and 3, we evaluate numerically the expectation (3.9) and variance (3.10) of the type count. The parameter α will be set equal to M^{-1}, and the working vocabulary M assigned values ranging from 10,000 to 40,000; for an educated man, M is estimated at 20–30 thousand words. Let us first consider the expectation (3.9) for a token count of n; when $\alpha = M^{-1}$ this reduces to

$$(4.1) \qquad\qquad M[1 - (1 - M^{-1})^n].$$

The table below gives values of this expectation for $n = 10,000$, 15,000, 25,000, 50,000, 100,000, 200,000 and 300,000 and 6 values of the vocabulary size M. The expectations are rounded off to the nearest digit.

TABLE 1

Expectations of the type count for different token counts n

	$M = 10,000$	20,000	25,000	30,000	35,000	40,000
$n = 10,000$	6321	7870	8242	8504	8699	8848
15,000	7769	10553	11280	11804	12200	12509
25,000	9179	14270	15803	16962	17866	18590
50,000	9933	18358	21617	24334	26613	28540
100,000	10000	19865	24542	28930	32990	36717
200,000	10000	19999	24991	29962	34885	39731
300,000	10000	20000	25000	29999	34993	39978

If one calculates from (4.1) the value of the token count n for which the type count equals $.95M$, that is the length of a text required to exhaust 95% of an author's working vocabulary, we find that n takes the values 29,956, 59,913, 74,892, 89,875, 104,846, 119,829 for $M = 10,000$, 20,000, 25,000, 30,000, 35,000 and 40,000 respectively. Very roughly, this means that $n \sim 3M$ before 95% of the author's vocabulary is used up.

The standard deviation of the type count for a token count of n can be expressed from (3.10), with $\alpha = M^{-1}$, as

$$\{M[(1 - M^{-1})^n - M(1 - M^{-1})^{2n} + (M - 1)(1 - 2M^{-1})^n]\}^{\frac{1}{2}}.$$

It is readily seen that this standard deviation is zero when $n = 1$, as well as when $n \to \infty$. The table below gives values of the standard deviation for token counts $n = 10,000$, 20,000, 25,000, 30,000, 35,000, 40,000, 45,000, 50,000, 55,000 and the same 6 values of the vocabulary size M as before. Values of the standard deviation are rounded off to two decimal places.

TABLE 2

Standard deviations of the type count for different token counts n

	$M = 10,000$	20,000	25,000	30,000	35,000	40,000
$n = 10,000$	31.18	33.08	32:12	30.97	29.82	28.73
20,000	.28.35	44.09	46.35	47.15	47.17	46.78
25,000	24.19	45.13	49.30	51.48	52.49	52.80
30,000	19.97	44.42	50.40	54.00	56.10	57.23
35,000	16.15	42.60	50.16	·55.13	58.33	60.34
40,000	12.90	40.10	48.97	55.17	59.45	62.36
45,000	10.21	37.23	47.11	54.40	59.68	63.46
50,000	8.04	34.21	44.83	53.03	59.21	63.82
55,000	6.31	31.18	42.28	51.22	58.20	63.56
100,000	.67	11.37	20.39	30.08	39.56	48.37
300,000	0	.08	.39	1.17	2.57	4.69

It is clear that, compared with the expectations in Table 1, the standard deviations σ_n of the type count in Table 2 are small enough to be negligible. Numerical computations indicate that these σ_n achieve their maxima for values of $n \sim 1.25M$ when $\sigma_n \sim .319M^{\frac{1}{2}}$.

5. Some concluding remarks

Like Brainerd (1972), we are interested in testing our results on Shakespeare's vocabulary. On the basis of our model, we would conclude that after writing 310,000 words of text, Shakespeare must nearly have exhausted his working vocabulary (see our Table 1). The size of this vocabulary has been estimated from Mrs. Cowden Clarke's *Complete Concordance to Shakespeare* (1845) as approximately 25,000 words. If, for example, one examines three of Shakespeare's tragedies, *King Lear, Troilus and Cressida* and *Othello*, whose average length is 25,541 words, one finds that they contain an average of 4,067 types. Since 54% of a Shakespearean text consists of Group I words, this means that approximately 13,729 of the 25,541 words would belong to Group I. (As there are only 500 words in Group II, these can be neglected.) If our model were applicable to Group I words, we would find that the expected values of the type count for $n = 14,000$, $M = 25,000$ is about 7,500. This is far larger than the actual type count of 4,067. We are thus led to the conclusion that the model is over-simplified and not appropriate in its present form.

In a paper (1975) to be presented to the E.M.S. and 7th Prague Conference, I have extended this model to the case where Group I words are subdivided into their 4 subgroups of nouns, adjectives, verbs and adverbs. Preliminary calculations indicate that the expected type count for Group I words is now reduced; the more complex model thus appears to be more realistic, though still not entirely adequate. I would conjecture that only a model taking account of syntactic structure and the relationship between consecutive words and sets of words would prove fully realistic. Such a model has yet to be considered.

Acknowledgements

My thanks are due to Professor D. Sprott, Dr. K. Shah and Mrs. Shirley Elliott of the University of Waterloo for their help in computations. I should also like to thank Dr. J. Lanke for drawing my attention to other current work in linguistic analysis, and to Professor Mark Kac for reminding me that A. A. Markov developed Markov chains as a mathematical tool for the study of linguistic structure in Pushkin's *Evgeny Onegin.*

References

BRAINERD, B. (1972) On the relation between types and tokens in literary text. *J. Appl. Prob.* **9**, 507–518.

GANI, J. (1975) A Markov chain for type counts in vocabulary subgroups. *Trans. 7th Prague Conference* (to appear).

LANKE, J. (1974) On the relation between two empirical laws in language statistics. *Research Report*, Department of Mathematical Statistics, University of Lund.

MCNEIL, D. R. (1973) Estimating an author's vocabulary. *J. Amer. Statist. Assoc.* **68**, 92–96.

WILLIAMS, C. B. (1970) *Style and Vocabulary: Numerical Studies.* Griffin, London.

YULE, G. U. (1944) *The Statistical Study of Literary Vocabulary.* Cambridge University Press.

Some Problems in Mathematical Genealogy

DAVID G. KENDALL

Abstract

After a general review of symmetric reversibility for countable-state continuous-time Markov chains the author shows that the birth-death-and-immigration process is symmetrically reversible and further that it remains so even when the description of the present state is refined to include a list of the sizes of all 'families' alive at the epoch in question. This result can be useful in genealogy because the operational direction of time there is the negative one. In view of the symmetric reversibility, some of the questions which face the genealogist can be answered without further calculation by quoting known results for the process with the usual ('forward' instead of 'backward') direction of time.

Further topics discussed include social mobility matrices, surname statistics, and Colin Rogers' 'problem of the Spruces'.

1. Introduction

In this paper I discuss a group of problems which may be introduced by quoting the title of a recent lecture by Mr. Colin Rogers [17]:

'And there were other Spruces in the village, but they were not related to us.'

The practical genealogist, whether professional or lay, will at once recognise the situation crystallised in the above quotation. Everyone is nicely linked up, and one proceeds to move back a generation in time only to find that there were then two contemporary male Spruces each having the same first name and so, presumably, not brothers. Do they both belong to the family of interest? After much further research one finds

325

that they do (perhaps they are second cousins), and one happily proceeds a little farther back in time, only to find that a similar phenomenon occurs once again. And so on.

Related problems are referred to in Edwards' paper [3] and in the discussion of 'time machines' which followed it, and it is well brought out there that an appropriate attack would be to formulate an evolutionary branching process in *reversed time*. The details are tricky, but I noticed recently that there is one rather special version of the problem which admits of a complete and even elegant solution, and it is this which I shall sketch here. The model employed is very far from being a realistic one, but the solution may suggest techniques of value from a data-analytic standpoint, useful both in the problem mentioned above, and also perhaps in the numerous other areas (manuscript filiation, linguistic evolution, molecular biology, etc.), in which evolutionary trees of some form play an important structural role. It is also my hope that we may gain a better idea of how to tackle the formidable problem of making sense of statistics relating to the distribution of family names. A few years ago, when there was no substantial body of numerical evidence apart from that collected in the last century by Guppy [5], the need for such techniques was hardly felt. But very recently, the situation has been completely changed by the work of Redmonds [16] and others, and statisticians may shortly find themselves seriously embarrassed by the lack of appropriate techniques for the study of valuable information accumulated at great labour and expense.

Our work will start with a recapitulation of what is known about the birth-death-and-immigration (BDI) stochastic process introduced in [7] (see also [8]), although essential priority for this kind of construction goes to McKendrick whose pioneer paper [14] seems to have been forgotten soon after its publication in 1914. After some generalities, we shall then structurally decompose the population described by the BDI process into 'families', and also carry out a time-reversal. The mathematical techniques employed are nearly all recorded in the literature but cannot be said to be 'well known', so that I think the results must be new. Readers may however want to note that some other aspects of 'family structure within a branching process' have been quite extensively studied (see Bühler [2], and the papers there referred to). It is possible, but perhaps not likely, that something similar to the present work might be found in the enormous literature in which such matters are discussed from the standpoint of genetics. Again it is likely (but whether possible or not I cannot say) that

related material might be found in [19], a source which I have unfortunately not been able to consult.

2. The simple BDI process

The BDI process is characterised by three positive numbers:

λ, the birth-rate per head per unit of time;
μ, the death-rate per head per unit of time;
κ, the immigration rate per unit of time.

It is chiefly famous because of its association with the negative-binomial
distribution, for which it provides one of at least three different generating
models. The most detailed mathematical study of it was given by
Professor Bartlett and myself in [1] (based on a hectic correspondence
carried out mostly on postcards). There (see also [9] and [10]) the
characteristic functional for the stochastic fluctuations in the age-
distribution was determined explicitly. We shall make no use of that here,
because we shall ignore questions of age (and, indeed, of sex); in the
present discussion our emphasis will be rather on *relationship*.

As a stochastic process, BDI is time-homogeneous Markov, with a
countable set of states labelled as $0,1,2,\cdots$ (the current state $N_t = n$ when
the population size is n), and as such it is uniquely characterised by its
Q-matrix with elements

$$(1) \qquad q_{ij} = p_{ij}{}'(0+) \qquad (i,j = 0,1,2,\cdots),$$

where $p_{ij}(t)$ is a generic transition probability from state i to state j with
time lapse t. The Q-matrix for BDI is readily seen to be stable (each q_{ii} is
finite), conservative (each row-sum is zero), and *regular* (the equations
$Qy = y$ have no non-trivial non-negative bounded solution; the reader
may like to verify this). We recall that the regularity condition (given the
harmless conditions of stability and conservativeness) is necessary and
sufficient for Q to determine one and only one Markov process satisfying
(1), so that (1) (i.e., the specification of the Q-matrix) defines an honest
Markov process for us when and only when we have regularity. We
further recall that the regularity condition is equivalent to the intrinsic
condition that

$$(2) \qquad \Pr\{\text{infinitely many jumps in a finite time} \,|\, i\} = 0$$

for every choice of the initial state i. When Q is not regular, we can still build up the stochastic motion in a local sense, but now (2) will fail for at least one starting-point i, and for such i we shall have

$$\sum_j p_{ij}(t) < 1 \qquad \text{for all } t > 0.$$

This description of what happens when Q is not regular is often vividly (and correctly) described by saying that, for certain starting-points i, the system with a positive probability performs an unbounded number of jumps in a finite time and then 'runs out of instructions'.

An obvious feature of BDI is that all states form a single intercommunicating class, so that they all enjoy the same class-properties. Now we know [8] that

$$p_{00}(t) = \left(\frac{\lambda - \mu}{\lambda e^{(\lambda - \mu)t} - \mu} \right)^{\kappa/\lambda},$$

and so by the usual test we see that BDI is positive-persistent for $\lambda < \mu$, null-persistent for $\kappa \leqq \lambda = \mu$ and transient in all other cases. (The distinction between $\kappa \leqq \mu$ and $\kappa > \mu$, when $\lambda = \mu$, does not seem to have been noticed before* and is rather interesting, although it will not concern us here.) *We shall assume throughout that $\lambda < \mu$, so that we shall always be in the positive-persistent case.* Thus the system will enter and infinitely often re-enter every state (in particular, the 'empty' state 0); also we shall have

$$L_j = \lim_{t \to \infty} p_{ij}(t) > 0 \qquad \text{for all } j,$$

and $\Sigma L_j = 1$. As the notation implies, L_j will not depend on the starting-state i. If we choose an initial distribution

(3) $$\Pr\{N_0 = n\} = L_n \qquad \text{(all } n\text{)},$$

then we can extend the definition of BDI to the whole time-axis $(t: -\infty < t < \infty)$, and we shall have $\Pr\{N_t = n\} = L_n$ for all n and t.

3. Some properties of Markov processes

We now turn to some general properties which hold for any countable-state continuous-time temporally homogeneous Markov processes which we shall quote from [11] and [12]. We assume always that the process is

---

* It may of course be a trivial consequence of general criteria given by Karlin and McGregor.

generated by a *regular* conservative stable Q-matrix, so that it makes sense (as otherwise it would not) to try to characterise various properties of the process in terms of the q_{ij}'s.

First, the whole set of states will form one intercommunicating class (that is, the process will be 'irreducible') *if and only if,* for every choice of i and j (distinct), there exists a non-negative integer r and states h_1, $h_2, \cdots, h_r$ (distinct from one another and from i and j) such that

(4) $$q_{ih_1} q_{h_1h_2} \cdots q_{h_rj} > 0.$$

It is easy to verify that this is true of BDI.

Next, suppose that the system *is* irreducible. Then all states are persistent or not together, and 'positive' or not together. Let 0 denote any convenient reference state, at our choice. Then the states will be persistent *if and only if* the equations and inequalities

(5) $$x_0 = 1, \quad x_i \geqq 0 \ (i \neq 0),$$
$$\sum_i x_i q_{i0} \leqq 0,$$
$$\sum_i x_i q_{ij} = 0 \text{ for all } j \neq 0,$$

possess no solution for which $\Sigma x_i q_{i0}$ is *strictly negative*. Note that the equations and inequalities (5) necessarily do have solutions, and indeed the family of solutions admits a unique least member in the sense of componentwise ordering; naturally only this 'least' solution needs to be looked at, when applying the test.

It is also useful to know that in the persistent case the equations and inequalities associated with (5) then have one and only one solution (which we shall denote by m) and that $m_1, m_2, \cdots$ satisfy (5) with *equality*.

Now suppose that the class of states is persistent. Then it will be positive *if and only if*

(6) $$\sum_j m_j < \infty,$$

in which case we shall have

(7) $$\lim_{t \to \infty} p_{ij}(t) = m_j / \Sigma m_a \qquad \text{for all } i,$$

and on writing $.L_j$ for this limit we can extend the process to the whole time axis if we agree to take $\Pr\{N_t = n\} = L_n$. Note that necessarily every

L_n is positive. The reader may care to amuse himself by checking in this way the positive-persistence of BDI when $\lambda < \mu$.

The statements associated with (5) can be supplemented, when the system (regular, etc.), is merely known to be irreducible, by the useful fact that the (non-vacuous) set of non-negative solutions to the inequalities

(8) $$\sum_i x_i p_{ij}(t) \leqq x_j \qquad (t \geqq 0; j = 0, 1, 2, \cdots),$$

is *precisely the same* as the set of non-negative solutions to the inequalities

(9) $$\sum_i x_i q_{ij} \leqq 0 \qquad (j = 0, 1, 2, \cdots).$$

This fact was proved in [11].

Next suppose we merely know that the (regular, etc.), system is irreducible and that it possesses a non-null (and so positive) invariant measure m; that is, that there exist positive numbers m_j such that

(10) $$\sum_i m_i p_{ij}(t) = m_j \qquad \text{for all } j \text{ and } t.$$

(In the persistent case such an m necessarily exists and is essentially unique; in the transient case it may or may not exist, and if it exists it need not be unique. We make no assumption for the moment about the convergence or otherwise of the series Σm_j.) Then relative to a perhaps infinite measure-space we can extend the definition of the system to the whole time-axis in such a way that the measure of the event $\{N_t = j\}$ is m_j, for all j and t. This will be interpretable as a Markov process if and only if it happens that $\Sigma m_j = 1$, in which case the time-reverse will necessarily also be a Markov process, *but it may be a structurally different one*; indeed, the transition probability from state i to state j over a (reversed) time lapse t will be

$$m_j p_{ji}(t)/m_i,$$

instead of $p_{ij}(t)$. The two will be equal if and only if

(11) $$m_j p_{ji}(t) = m_i p_{ij}(t) \qquad \text{for all } i, j, \text{ and } t.$$

In such a case we say that the (irreducible) Markov process is *symmetrically reversible*, and we can extend this terminology to the case when Σm_j is divergent, provided that we make the suitable interpretations. Notice that in speaking of symmetric reversibility one must always say with respect to *which* invariant measure m one is working, unless one happens to be in the persistent situation (where m is essentially unique).

Notice also that (11), on summing over j, automatically gives

$$\sum_j m_j p_{ji}(t) = m_i \qquad \text{for all } i, j \text{ and } t,$$

so that (11) *by itself* tells us that the positive vector m is invariant and that the process is symmetrically reversible with respect to it.

Now when $i \neq j$, the division of (11) by t and the limit process $t \downarrow 0$ jointly give

(12) $$m_j q_{ji} = m_i q_{ij} \qquad \text{for all } i \text{ and } j$$

(of course (12) holds trivially when $i = j$). *Suppose that we merely know that* (12), *with all m_j's positive, holds for some irreducible regular conservative stable process.* Then the irreducibility criterion tells us at once that the m_j's (up to a constant multiplier) can be uniquely calculated from Q via (12), and summation over j further tells us that

$$\sum_j m_j q_{ji} = 0 \qquad \text{for all } i.$$

This is an instance of (9) and so implies that m is subinvariant (like x at (8)), but, as noted in [11], page 427, a stronger statement holds: m is actually *invariant*. The 'proof' in [11] is wrong, but one can get the result by using both the 'backward' (BIR) and 'forward' (FIR) integral recurrences of Feller. We know that $p_{ij}(t)$ is the limit of a monotonic increasing sequence $f_{ij}^r(t)$, where

$$f_{ij}^1(t) = \delta_{ij} e^{-q_i t},$$

$$f_{ij}^{r+1}(t) = \delta_{ij} e^{-q_i t} + \sum_{h \neq i} \int_0^t q_{ih} f_{hj}^r(u) e^{-q_i(t-u)} \, du, \qquad \text{(BIR)}$$

and

$$f_{ij}^{r+1}(t) = \delta_{ij} e^{-q_j t} + \sum_{h \neq j} \int_0^t f_{ih}^r(u) q_{hj} e^{-q_j(t-u)} \, du. \qquad \text{(FIR)}$$

If we start with f^1 as defined above, each recurrence generates the same sequence (f^r), and this has the limit property already stated. Now it is obvious that

$$m_i f^1_{ij}(t) = m_j f^1_{ji}(t), \qquad \text{for all } i \text{ and } j, \text{ and all } t,$$

and if we assume that the statement

$$m_i f^r_{ij}(t) = m_j f^r_{ji}(t), \qquad \text{for all } i \text{ and } j, \text{ and all } t,$$

holds for some $r \geq 1$, then on multiplying (BIR) by m_i and using (12) and the inductive hypothesis, we find from (FIR) that

$$m_i f^{r+1}_{ij}(t) = m_j f^{r+1}_{ji}(t), \qquad \text{for all } i \text{ and } j, \text{ and all } t,$$

whence on letting r tend to infinity we find that

$$m_i p_{ij}(t) = m_j p_{ji}(t) \qquad \text{for all } i, j, \text{ and } t.$$

Then by summing over i we see that m is actually invariant, as was claimed, and moreover that the process is symmetrically reversible with respect to this invariant measure.

Thus for an irreducible regular conservative stable Q-matrix, the relation (12) is *necessary and sufficient* for the generated process to have m as an invariant measure with regard to which it is symmetrically reversible, and moreover this invariant measure is essentially uniquely determined by (12). It is natural to ask, whether one can find a necessary and sufficient condition (nsc) to be satisfied by the elements of the Q-matrix, in order that (12) should hold for *some* positive m. Such an nsc is known and was given in [11]; it is a generalisation of an earlier result of Kolmogorov [13], where we denote the nsc by

$\mathcal{K}$: *for each j, for each $r \geq 2$, and for each set of r states $h_1, h_2, \cdots, h_r$ distinct from j and from each other, we have*

$$q_{jh_1} q_{h_1 h_2} \cdots q_{h_r j} = q_{jh_r} q_{h_r h_{r-1}} \cdots q_{h_1 j}.$$

We shall use $\mathcal{K}$ below, but in most cases it is more convenient to work directly with (12).

Finally, let the (regular, etc.,) process be irreducible: suppose that (12) holds and that the positive vector m determined by (12) further satisfies $\Sigma m_j < \infty$. Then we can normalise m to make $\Sigma m_j = 1$, and we have

$$\sum_i m_i p_{ij}(t) = m_i \qquad \text{for all } i \text{ and } t,$$

so on letting $t \to \infty$ we get (using now dominated convergence)

$$(\Sigma m_i) p_{ij}(\infty) = m_i,$$

whence we can deduce the positive-persistence of the process without further calculation; we do *not* have to work through the laborious test for persistence.

Now look back at the BDI process, for which of course

$$q_{i,i+1} = \kappa + \lambda i,$$

(13)

$$q_{i,i-1} = \mu i,$$

for which all other non-diagonal q_{ij}'s are zero, and for which the diagonal q_{ii}'s are determined by conservativeness. The structure of the Q-matrix is thus tri-diagonal, and in such a case condition $\mathcal{H}$ is trivially satisfied; the process is thus symmetrically reversible with respect to the invariant measure determined by

$$m_j q_{j,j+1} = m_{j+1} q_{j+1,j},$$

that is, by

$$m_{j+1}/m_j = (\kappa + \lambda j)/(\mu + \mu j).$$

This last ratio tends to λ/μ as j tends to infinity. Positive-persistence now follows at once because we are assuming $\lambda < \mu$, so that Σm_j converges by the ratio-test. This illustrates the value of the remarks in the preceding paragraph.

We have gone through the above general arguments in some detail because they are not readily accessible anywhere, and because we are now about to use them in a much more complicated situation. Before turning to this we make a strictly parenthetical comment. It has been noted [18] that the Markov chain associated with social mobility is approximately symmetrically reversible with respect to its (unique) invariant measure. Now we *could* say that this is just an instance of what physicists call 'detailed balancing', and indulge in some meaningless but pious reference to social entropy or what not. But a moment's reflection shows that this would be quite absurd. What social forces could possibly match the cases of tinkers' sons becoming tailors with an almost exactly equal number of instances of tailors' sons becoming tinkers? The observed phenomenon thus seems to defy intuition, *unless* perhaps the explanation lies along the following lines.

Social mobility is really a continuous rather than a discrete process; suppose then that the social mobility matrix should really be thought of as a transition matrix for a continuous-time Markov process with a finite number of states. Such a process will be characterised by its Q-matrix, and the transition matrix will be symmetrically reversible if and only if the Q-matrix satisfies $\mathcal{H}$. The phenomenon we have to explain has now been reduced to the level of Q-matrices. But here, a possible explanation suggests itself. Suppose that it is possible to arrange occupations in a serial order in such a way that the trajectories of social mobility are equivalent to a step-by-step walk backwards and forwards along this sequence. Were that so, and it is not a preposterous suggestion, then the Q-matrix would be tri-diagonal and so would automatically satisfy $\mathcal{H}$, and the symmetric reversibility which is approximately observed would be completely accounted for in a comprehensible manner. When opportunity offers, I hope to look into this question in more detail; it is only mentioned here to show how tri-diagonality can account for a completely 'accidental' appearance of 'detailed balancing'.

4. A more complex BDI process

We are now ready to introduce the more sophisticated version of BDI which is the real object of study in this paper. Suppose that at some initial epoch it just happens that $N_t = 0$. Then the population size will stay at zero until an immigration occurs, at which moment it will rise to unity. We shall regard this as the initiation of a *family*, and the future additional members of this family will be all the offspring derived from the initiating individual, whether directly or indirectly. Because $\lambda < \mu$, we know that the family will almost surely eventually become extinct, so that a family is here an entity which comes into being with an immigration, fluctuates in size with the subsequent births and deaths that relate to it, and disappears with the death of a family-member who just happens then to be the sole survivor.

At any one time there may be any finite number of families in existence. When there are several families of the same size we shall not here distinguish between them (although in a later treatment this might be desirable and advantageous); we simply record, as the *state* $Z_t = z$ *of the system* at time t, the numbers of families of sizes $1, 2, 3, \cdots$, respectively. We also include, as part of the specification of the state of the system, the number k of persons in each one of the largest families extant, and so the symbol Z_t for the state of the system at time t will always be either of the form

(14) $z = (k; m_1, m_2, \cdots, m_k)$ (where $k \geqq 1$, and $m_k \geqq 1$),

or

(15) $z = (0)$.

Thus $Z_t = z$ (as at (14)) means that there is at least one family of size k extant at time t, and that m_1 families are singletons, m_2 are of size two, $\cdots$, and m_k of size k, there being no families of any greater size than this. The numbers $m_1, \cdots, m_{k-1}$ may be any non-negative integers, but with the conventions we are using *we must always have* $m_k \geqq 1$. This is for $k \geqq 1$. When (15) holds we shall write $k = 0$; this symbol will be used to indicate that the whole population size is equal to zero. The whole set of symbols of the form (14) or (15) is countable, so that we can use it to label the states of a countable continuous-time temporally homogeneous Markov process, which we will define by specifying all the non-zero off-diagonal elements of its (stable) Q-matrix. The remaining elements of the Q-matrix will be zero if off-diagonal and not otherwise specified, while those on the diagonal will be determined by the condition of conservativeness. We shall, of course, have to verify that this Q-matrix is *regular* before we can legitimately pretend that it defines our system for us. This matter will be attended to in due course.

We now go steadily through all possible types of transition '$z \to w$' and state the value of q_{zw} in each case.

Group A : immigrations

   (a) $z = (0)$; then $w = (1; 1)$, and $q_{zw} = \kappa$.

   (b) $z = (k; m_1, \cdots, m_k)$; then $w = (k; m_1 + 1, m_2, \cdots, m_k)$, and $q_{zw} = \kappa$.

Group B : births

   (a) $z = (k; m_1, \cdots, m_k)$ and the birth occurs in a family of size j, where $j < k$. Then $w = (k; m_1, \cdots, m_j - 1, m_{j+1} + 1, \cdots, m_k)$, and $q_{zw} = \lambda j m_j$.

   (b) z is as above, and the birth occurs in a family of size k. Then $w = (k + 1; m_1, \cdots, m_k - 1, 1)$, and $q_{zw} = \lambda k m_k$.

Group C : deaths

   (a) $z = (1; 1)$; then $w = (0)$, and $q_{zw} = \mu$.

   (b) $z = (k; m_1, \cdots, m_k)$ and the death occurs in a family of size 1, where either $k > 1$, or $k = 1$ and $m_1 > 1$. Then $w = (k; m_1 - 1, \cdots, m_k)$, and $q_{zw} = \mu m_1$.

   (c) z is as above, and the death takes place in a family of size j, where $j > 1$, and either $j < k$, or $j = k$ and $m_k > 1$. Then we must have $w = (k; m_1, \cdots, m_{j-1} + 1, m_j - 1, \cdots, m_k)$, and $q_{zw} = \mu j m_j$.

   (d) z is as above, the death takes place in a family of size k, where $k > 1$, and there is only one such family (i.e., $m_k = 1$). Then we must have $w = (k - 1; m_1, \cdots, m_{k-1} + 1)$, and we shall have $q_{zw} = \mu k m_k (= \mu k)$.

We now have to test this Q-matrix for regularity. Its stability is evident. An algebraic approach is entirely possible, but the following argument is far more attractive. When $Z_t = (0)$ let us write $W_t = 0$, and when $Z_t = (k; m_1, \cdots, m_k)$ let us write $W_t = \Sigma jm_j$. We then obtain a 'lumped' system such that the Q-matrix respects the 'lumping', and the lumped system is in fact none other than the original BDI, which we already know to be regular. Every transition in the unlumped system will produce a transition in the lumped system, and *vice versa*, and we already know that the lumped system cannot perform infinitely many transitions in a finite time, because its Q-matrix is regular. The same must then obviously be true of the unlumped system, and so its Q-matrix must be regular, too. Our construction is therefore legitimate; that is, the new Markov process obtained by refining the description of the 'state' of the system can equally well be defined by the new Q-matrix.

5. Properties of the stochastic process $\{Z_t : t \geq 0\}$

We now investigate some of the properties of the system $(Z_t : t \geq 0)$. First we notice that any two states z and z' are mutually q-accessible; that is, one can travel from z to z', and also *vice versa*, by a finite chain of transitions of the kind enumerated in Section 4, every one of which will be associated with a non-zero q-value. Thus all states of the system form a single intercommunicating class; that is, the system is irreducible.

Next we observe that this class (the whole set of states) must certainly be a persistent one, because state 0 is persistent for BDI when $\lambda < \mu$, and state 0 for BDI is in one-to-one correspondence with state (0) for the new system; hence (0) is persistent, and as persistence is a class-property, all states are persistent.

The proof that each state for the new system is positive follows the same lines. We know that state 0 is positive for BDI (because we are assuming that $\lambda < \mu$), and so, for BDI,

$$\lim_{t \to \infty} p_{00}(t) > 0.$$

From this it follows at once that for the new system,

$$\lim_{t \to \infty} p_{(0)(0)}(t) > 0,$$

and so state (0) is positive, whence all states are positive. Let then $\lim_{t \to \infty} p_{zw}(t) = M_w$, so that each M_ω is positive and $\Sigma M_w = 1$ and also

$$\sum_z M_z p_{zw}(t) = M_w \qquad \text{for all } z, w, \text{ and } t.$$

Then, as explained earlier, we can extend the definition of our system to the whole time axis $(-\infty, \infty)$ in such a way that it remains temporally homogeneous, and

$$\Pr(Z_t = z) = M_z \qquad \text{for all } t \text{ and } z.$$

6. Symmetric reversibility and family size

We now ask whether this extended system is symmetrically reversible, or not. The question can be answered directly by testing condition $\mathcal{H}$, and this is how the fact that our system *is* symmetrically reversible was discovered. After the event, however, it is slightly less painful (and perfectly legitimate) to cite the value of M_z and verify that it satisfies (12); this is sufficient because of the theory summarised in Section 3. Notice that we have already shown that our new system is persistent, so that it cannot have more than one invariant measure, up to a constant factor, and therefore if (12) *can* be satisfied, it can *only* be satisfied by some multiple $m = L$ of the measure $M_z = \lim_{t \to \infty} p_{xz}(t)$ introduced in Section 5. That is, we can prove symmetric reversibility and identify the unique invariant measure M_z by the same calculations. We now carry out this programme.

Let us define $L_z = 1$ if $z = (0)$, and for all other values of z let

$$(16) \qquad L_{(k;m_1,\cdots,m_k)} = (\kappa/\lambda)^{\Sigma m_j} (\lambda/\mu)^{\Sigma j m_j} / (\Pi j^{m_j} \, \Pi m_j !).$$

I claim that this definition of L_z yields a solution to (12). In order to verify this we need only consider transitions of the form $A(a)$, $A(b)$, $B(a)$, $B(b)$, for the four transitions of Group C are inverse to these. We have to verify that

$$\frac{L_w}{L_z} = \frac{q_{zw}}{q_{wz}}$$

for each of the four types of transition that have to be considered. The verification is straightforward and may be left to the reader. If we let L denote the sum of the numbers L_z (this sum is necessarily finite, since $L_z = M_z/M_{(0)}$, because of the arguments above), then we shall have

$$(17) \qquad M_z = \Pr\{Z_t = z\} = L_z/L \qquad \text{for all } z \text{ and } t,$$

and so

$$\lim_{t \to \infty} p_{zw}(t) = L_w/L \qquad \text{for all } z \text{ and } w.$$

It will of course be convenient if we can find a closed expression for L, and this task turns out to be easier than might at first be supposed. To see how this is to be done, recall first that a symbol

$$(k; m_1, \cdots, m_k)$$

is not 'well formed' (i.e., does not label anything in the state-space) unless $m_k > 0$. But if we set $m_k = 0$ in the right-hand side of (16), what we get is obviously the value of

$$L_{(h\,;m_1,\cdots,m_h)},$$

where m_h is the first non-zero member of the sequence

$$m_{k-1}, m_{k-2}, \cdots, m_1,$$

if there is one such; if every member of that sequence is zero, then what we get is 1, i.e., $L_{(0)}$. From this it follows that

$$L_{(0)} + \Sigma' L_{(1;m_1)} + \Sigma\Sigma' L_{(2;m_1,m_2)} + \cdots + \Sigma \cdots \Sigma\Sigma' L_{(k\,;m_1,\cdots,m_k)}$$

$$= \Sigma\Sigma\cdots\Sigma L_{(k\,;m_1,\cdots,m_k)},$$

where the last summation in each term on the left *excludes* the value zero, while in the multiple summation on the right the value zero is to be included in all of the summations. It follows from this identity that

$$L = \lim_{k \to \infty} \sum_{m_1} \sum_{m_2} \cdots \sum_{m_k} L_{(k\,;m_1,\cdots,m_k)} \,,$$

where here the summations are *unrestricted*. But these summations are easily effected, and give

$$(18) \qquad L = \lim_{k \to \infty} \exp\left(\frac{\kappa}{\lambda} \sum_{j=1}^{k} \frac{(\lambda/\mu)^j}{j}\right) = \left(1 - \frac{\lambda}{\mu}\right)^{-\kappa/\lambda}.$$

In (16), (17) and (18) we have an explicit formula for *the stationary distribution of the symbol z expressing the partition of the population size in BDI over the constituent families.* We also have, as the main result of the present paper, the following theorem.

Theorem I. The family-size process is symmetrically reversible with respect to its (unique) invariant measure (M_z).

As the three parameters λ, μ, and κ here occur only in the combinations

$$(19) \qquad \alpha = \kappa/\lambda, \qquad \rho = \lambda/\mu < 1,$$

it will be convenient to write the stationary distribution of the state of the *family-size* (FS) process as follows:

$$(20) \qquad \Pr\{Z_t = (k\,; m_1, m_2, \cdots, m_k)\} = \frac{\alpha^M \rho^N}{\prod j^{m_j} \prod m_j!} (1 - \rho)^\alpha.$$

Here, as usual, either $k = 0$ and there are no m's, or $k \geq 1$ and $m_k \geq 1$ (the earlier m's being free to take on the value zero). The statistics M and N are defined by

(21) $\qquad M = \Sigma m_j \qquad$ (total number of families),

and

(22) $\qquad N = \Sigma j m_j \qquad$ (total population size).

Notice however that if we happen to make a mistake and use too large a value of k, the right-hand side of Formula (20) will still make sense and will give the correct probability for the state of the FS process; we shall simply accumulate extra factors of the form j^0 and 0! in the denominator, and extra terms 0 in M and N. Therefore we can now, if we please, adopt the labelling

(23) $\qquad Z_t = (m_1, m_2, \cdots)$

for the state of the FS process, with the understanding that this means (0) if all the m's vanish, and that it means $(k; m_1, \cdots, m_k)$ if all m's after the kth vanish, m_k itself being positive. It will be a convention that the infinite sequence at (23) is to contain only finitely many non-zero terms. But now we can write

(24) $\qquad \Pr\{Z_t = (m_1, m_2, \cdots)\} = \prod_{j \geq 1} e^{-\beta_j} \frac{\beta_j^{m_j}}{m_j!},$

on transforming Equation (20). Here

(25) $\qquad \beta_j = \alpha \frac{\rho^j}{j}.$

This new formula (24) admits a rather astonishing interpretation. Consider the sequence of independent random variables X_j $(j = 1, 2, \cdots)$, where X_j has a Poisson distribution with parameter β_j.

We shall have

$$\Sigma \Pr\{X_j \neq 0\} = \Sigma (1 - e^{-\beta_j}) < \infty,$$

and so by the Borel-Cantelli lemma it will follow that, with probability one, all but finitely many of the X's will be equal to zero. Therefore we can legitimately reformulate our result as the following.

Corollary 1. *For the FS process, the random variables $X_j(t)$ giving the numbers of families of size j extant at time t (for $j = 1, 2, \cdots$) are independent Poisson variables with parameters*

(26) $E(X_i(t)) = \alpha \rho^j/j.$

From Theorem I we at once deduce that

$$E(M) = \alpha \log\frac{1}{1-\rho}, \qquad \text{var}(M) = E(M),$$
$$E(N) = \alpha\rho/(1-\rho), \qquad \text{var}(N) = \alpha\rho/(1-\rho)^2,$$

and

(27) $\text{cov}(M, N) = \alpha\rho/(1-\rho).$

Evidently M and N are sufficient statistics for the parameters α and ρ. Immediately from these formulae we get the following interesting result.

Corollary 2.

(28) $E(M) = \alpha \log\left(1 + \dfrac{E(N)}{\alpha}\right).$

This tells us broadly how many families we may expect to find in a population of given size. The 'law' (28) is closely connected with earlier results of Fisher [4] and others (cf., e.g., [7]) on the number of species in an animal or plant 'catch' of given size. The present derivation is obviously laterally linked to the earlier ones, but has the advantage of being based on a more clearly formulated model.

It is now useful to consider the likely numerical sizes of our parameters in practice. We have insisted that $\lambda < \mu$, so that $\rho < 1$, but one would expect ρ to be 'only just' less than unity in the interesting cases. In considering α we must note that if $\dot{T} = 1/\mu$ temporarily stands for a typical life-length of an individual, then $\lambda T \approx 1$ will be the number of 'children' born to him, and $\alpha = (\kappa T)/(\lambda T)$ is thus about equal to the expected number of 'immigrants' during a typical lifetime. When considering complete populations within a small spatial boundary, there is no reason to expect this ratio α to be vastly smaller or vastly larger than unity. Thus the controlling numerical factor will there be the approach of ρ to unity, the effect of which will be to make both M and N large, with large variances and also with a large covariance. In family-name studies, on the other hand, α *will be small* unless the area covered is very large, and the balance between α and $1-\rho$ will thus be most important. Asymptotics based on these considerations are likely to be fruitful, but will not be pursued here.

We note that, for a given $E(N)$, $\alpha \to 0$ implies (via Formula (28)), that $E(M) \to 0$. This is a quantitative expression of the intuitively obvious fact that low relative immigration rates imply a small number of (mostly large) families.

7. Time reversal and the FS process

We now consider some of the consequences of symmetric reversibility for the stochastic process FS. We note the following table which shows the effect of time-reversal on the various possible incidents and the way we would describe them.

Direct FS process	Reversed FS process
1) An immigration.	A family becomes extinct.
2) A birth to a family.	A family loses one of its members, but does not become extinct.
3) A family loses one of its members, but does not become extinct.	A birth to a family.
4) A family becomes extinct.	An immigration.

Now the problem we considered in Section 1 was that of encountering an apparently unlinked homonym when proceeding backwards in time (which is the direction of genealogical progress). This can be an instance of either item 3) or item 4) in the above table. Suppose (as was envisaged in Section 1) that we are considering only people called SPRUCE, and that at time t we have linked them all into a family of size k, so that the state of the FS process at this epoch is

$$(k; 0, 0, \cdots, 1).$$

On stepping back through time dt, we encounter one new SPRUCE, and so the preceding (natural time) state of the process must have been either

(i) $\qquad\qquad (k + 1; 0, 0, \cdots, 1),$

or

(ii) $\qquad\qquad (k; 1, 0, 0, \cdots, 1).$

Here the first alternative means that we have picked up a SPRUCE whom in due course we shall succeed in linking up with the others, while the second alternative means that we have picked up a totally independent family of SPRUCES who quite truly 'are not related to us'. If we now switch to reversed time, and use the symmetric reversibility of the FS process, we see *without any Bayesian pretensions* that

$$\Pr\{(i)\} = \lambda k / (\lambda k + \kappa),$$

$$\Pr\{(ii)\} = \kappa (\lambda k + \kappa).$$

That is, the odds in favour of ultimate linking being possible are as $k : \alpha$. The lesson is, that *genealogists should be optimists*, unless they are sweeping such an enormous area that α is of the order of k.

It will be obvious that this paper raises many interesting new problems, which it will be worth while pursuing in greater detail elsewhere. For example, one quickly obtains

Corollary 3. The joint probability-generating function for the number of families M and the population size N is

$$(29) \qquad \frac{(1-\rho)^{\alpha}}{(1-\rho y)^{\alpha x}},$$

and

Corollary 4. When M and N are given, the conditional distribution of the family-size statistics X_1, X_2, $\cdots$ is of the form

$$\Pr\{X_j = m_j \text{ for } 1 \leqq j \leqq N - M + 1\}$$

$$(30)$$

$$= C(N, M) \prod_{j \leqq N-M+1} \left(\frac{1}{j}\right)^{m_j} \frac{1}{m_j!},$$

all X_j's with $j > N - M + 1$ necessarily being equal to zero.

The exploitation of these last two results requires adequate asymptotics on the factor $C(N, M)$ for N (and perhaps also M) large. It is trivial to obtain an explicit expression for $C(N, M)$ in terms of the coefficient of ξ^M in the polynomial

$$\xi(\xi + 1)(\xi + 2) \cdots (\xi + N - 1),$$

but, as Hammersley pointed out long ago [6], these are awkward numbers to get a grip on, when N may be in the hundreds. Tempting though these problems are, the wish not to offend the most genial of all possible editors forces me temporarily to break off at this point, while expressing my immense satisfaction at being allowed to participate in this congratulatory volume dedicated to the man who first started me thinking about stochastic growth processes with the remark, 'There is a rather impressive thesis by a young Dane called Arley...' nearly thirty years ago.

Appendix. On a theorem of Quenouille

We know that the distribution of the total population size in BDI is negative-binomial; thus Corollary 1 tells us that the negative-binomial distribution generated by

$$\frac{(1-\rho)^{\alpha}}{(1-\rho s)^{\alpha}}$$

admits a countably infinite factorisation in the sense of Paul Lévy in which the jth factor ($j = 1, 2, \cdots$) is the distribution of jU_j, where U_j is a Poisson random variable with parameter $\alpha \rho^j / j$; we note that this sequence of Poisson parameters is a constant multiple of the terms in a logarithmic series. This result looks strikingly familiar; it recalls a well-known theorem of Quenouille [15] which asserts that if M has a Poisson distribution, and if we consider M independent 'colonies' each of which contains a number of individuals distributed according to Fisher's logarithmic series distribution, then the total population size (the union of all the colonies) will be distributed as a negative-binomial. When we compare the two results, we note that in each case the final population size is negative-binomial, and that in each case the Poisson and logarithmic series play a role, albeit in different orders.

In fact, at the univariate level at which we are working in this present discussion (where we are looking at the FS process at just one epoch of time) the two results are essentially equivalent, and the same situation is just being described in two different ways. We shall see that this bivalence has nothing whatever to do with the logarithmic series distribution: it is a characteristic of the Poisson law.

To elucidate this, let $\{p_j\}$ be *any* probability distribution over $(1, 2, \cdots)$ and let c be any positive number. We set up a sequence of independent Poisson random variables Y_j ($j = 1, 2, \cdots$) where $E(Y_j) = cp_j$, and we note that

$$\Pr\{Y_j \neq 0\} = 1 - e^{-cp_j}.$$

These last quantities form the terms of a convergent series, and so by the Borel-Cantelli lemma we see that (almost surely) all but finitely many of the Y_j's will be equal to zero; we therefore cut back the probability space so that this last statement actually holds 'surely'. Let M be the sum of the Y_j's (this will be finite), and let us construct a population consisting of Y_j colonies of size j (for each $j = 1, 2, \cdots$). Say that in fact $Y_1 = m_1$, $Y_2 = m_2, \cdots, Y_k = m_k$, $Y_j = 0$ for all j beyond k; the probability of this will be

$$\prod_{1 \leq j \leq k} e^{-cp_j} \frac{(cp_j)^{n_j}}{m_j!} \cdot \prod_{j > k} e^{-cp_j}.$$

Also the probability distribution of M will be $e^{-c} c^M / M!$, and if we divide one by the other, we obtain the distribution of the Y_j's *conditional upon* M; this will therefore be

$$\binom{M}{m_1, m_2, \cdots, m_k} p_1^{m_1} p_2^{m_2} \cdots p_k^{m_k},$$

where $\Sigma m_j = M$. But this last expression is just the coefficient of $s_1^{m_1} s_2^{m_2} \cdots s_k^{m_k}$ in the expansion of

$$(\Sigma p_j s_j)^M ;$$

i.e., the situation is the same as if we had first chosen M as a Poisson variable of expectation c, and then picked M independent colonies whose individual sizes had the $\{p_j\}$-distribution.

Other interesting re-interpretations of Corollary 1 have been pointed out to me by Dr. B. M. Brown and Professor P. Whittle, who have observed that the occurrence of the Poisson distribution there is essentially just a consequence of the Poisson character of the immigrations.

References

[1] BARTLETT, M. S. AND KENDALL, D. G. (1951) On the use of the characteristic functional in the analysis of some stochastic processes occurring in physics and biology. *Proc. Camb. Phil. Soc.* **47**, 65–76.

[2] BÜHLER, W. J. (1972) The distribution of generations and other aspects of the family structure of branching processes. *Proc. Sixth Berkeley Symp. Math. Statist. Prob.* **3**, 463–480.

[3] EDWARDS, A. W. F. (1970) Estimation of the branch points of a branching diffusion process. *J. R. Statist. Soc.* B **32**, 155–174.

[4] FISHER, R. A., CORBET, A. S. AND WILLIAMS, C. B. (1943) The relation between the number of species and the number of individuals in a random sample of an animal population. *J. Animal Ecol.* **12**, 42–58.

[5] GUPPY, H. B. (1890) *The Homes of Family Names in Great Britain.* London.

[6] HAMMERSLEY, J. M. (1951) The sums of products of the natural numbers. *Proc. London Math. Soc.* (3)**1**, 435–452.

[7] KENDALL, D. G. (1948) On some modes of population growth leading to R. A. Fisher's logarithmic series distribution. *Biometrika* **35**, 6–15.

[8] —— (1949) Stochastic processes and population growth. *J. R. Statist. Soc.* B **11**, 230–264 and following discussion.

[9] —— (1950) Random fluctuations in the age-distribution of a population whose development is controlled by the simple birth and death process. *J. R. Statist. Soc.* B **12**, 278–285.

[10] —— (1952) Les processus stochastiques de croissance en biologie. *Ann. Inst. H. Poincaré* **13**, 43–108.

[11] —— (1959) Unitary dilations of one-parameter semigroups etc. *Proc. London Math. Soc.* (3)**9**, 417–431.

[12] —— (1971) *Markov Methods.* (Cambridge lectures, as yet unpublished.)

[13] KOLMOGOROV, A. N. (1936) Zur Theorie der Markoffschen Ketten. *Math. Ann.* **112**, 155–160.

[14] MCKENDRICK, A. G. (1914) Studies in the theory of continuous probabilities, with special reference to its bearing on natural phenomena of a progressive nature. *Proc. London Math. Soc.* (2) **13**, 401–416.

[15] QUENOUILLE, M. H. (1949) A relation between the logarithmic, Poisson, and negative binomial series. *Biometrics* **5**, 162–164.

[16] REDMONDS, G. (1973) *Yorkshire: West Riding (English Surnames Series*, 1). Phillimore, London.

[17] ROGERS, C. (1973) Unpublished lecture. (See *Yorks. Archaeol. Soc. Family History Newsletter* **5**, 5.)

[18] BERGER, J. AND SNELL, J. L. (1957) On the concept of equal exchange. *Behavioral Science* **2**, 111–118.

[19] WHO, J. *Recollections and Anticipations.* Unpublished MS, n.d., possibly available (uncatalogued) in Bodleian Library, Oxford.

The reader may also care to consult

KENDALL, D. G. (1975) Branching processes before (and after) 1873: the genealogy of genealogy. *Bull. London Math. Soc.* To appear. (This contains further comments on mathematical problems in genealogy, surname statistics, etc.)

PART IX

BIOMATHEMATICS
AND EPIDEMIOLOGY

The Use of the Cross-Ratio in Aetiological Surveys

P. ARMITAGE

Abstract

The use of the cross-ratio as a measure of association in a 2×2 table is closely related to Bartlett's (1935) definition of interaction in a higher-order table. Inference about aetiological associations from case-control studies is most naturally done in terms of the cross-ratio, as a measure of relative risk. Standard methods of statistical analysis, for the comparison and combination of relative risks and for matched pairs, are reviewed, and some new results noted.

1. Introduction

Maurice Bartlett's work on the mathematical theory of epidemics of communicable diseases is justly renowned and admired, and will be described elsewhere in this book. I wish to draw attention to a less direct influence which he has had on epidemiological theory and practice, in a rather different field of enquiry.

Statisticians who regard epidemiology as the theory of epidemics are sometimes surprised to find that epidemiologists (who ought to know) take a much broader view of their subject. 'Epidemiology', according to MacMahon and Pugh (1970), 'is the study of the distribution and determinants of disease frequency in man'. Two points may be noted about this definition: the subject is essentially statistical in nature; and it is not confined to communicable diseases. Non-communicable diseases now play a predominant role in the pattern of ill-health experienced in highly developed countries and are increasingly important in developing countries. They are often 'chronic' in nature and must usually be studied by carefully designed surveys of contrasted population groups.

MacMahon and Pugh refer in their definition to 'determinants of disease frequency'. In the absence of randomized experimentation it is usually difficult to pin-point factors which are clearly *causative*, but a good deal of effort goes into aetiological surveys which identify associations between disease frequency and various factors. The question of causation has usually to be approached by bringing together evidence of various sorts and applying scientific judgement.

Perhaps the commonest form of aetiological survey is the 'case-control' study, in which a group of patients suffering from a specified disease is contrasted with a group of controls without the disease, comparisons being made of the frequencies of various attributes in the two groups. For any one factor a 2×2 table can be formed:

			Disease		
			$+$	$-$	
		$+$	a	c	$a + c$
(1)	Factor				
		$-$	b	d	$b + d$
			$a + b$	$c + d$	n

Frequently the investigator will choose equal numbers of cases and controls, so that $a + b = c + d = \frac{1}{2}n$. The aim is to test the existence of, and to measure the size of, an association between disease and factor. Further questions are raised if data from several studies, or from different sections of the same study, are to be combined or contrasted. If there are t sets of data like those shown above, they can be represented by a $2 \times 2 \times t$ contingency table, and a difference between the degree of association in the t 'layers' can be regarded as a second-order interaction in this 3-dimensional table. How is it to be measured?

2. Interaction in higher-order contingency tables

Almost all discussions on this topic refer back to Bartlett's (1935) paper on the $2 \times 2 \times 2$ table. In this paper Bartlett suggested that the hypothesis of no second-order interaction should specify that the cross-ratio of expected frequencies in, say, the row-column classification was the same for layer 1 as for layer 2. Other definitions are possible, but will not be reviewed here; see, for example, Lancaster (1969 a, b), Plackett (1969) and Darroch (1974). The implication of Bartlett's definition is that, in each component 2×2 table, an appropriate measure of association is the cross-ratio statistic. In the table shown in Section 1, this statistic is

(2) $$\hat{\psi} = ad/bc.$$

Again, there is room for argument, although $\hat{\psi}$ has the attractive general property of being invariant to multiplication of the frequencies in any row or column by a constant; any statistic with this property is a function of $\hat{\psi}$ (Edwards (1963)). Good (1963) provides a justification in terms of maximum entropy. Our present concern, though, is not with the general advocacy of $\hat{\psi}$, but to discuss its particular use in case-control studies.

3. The cross-ratio as a measure of relative risk

The cases and controls will almost certainly not be selected randomly from any well-defined populations, but they can be regarded as broadly representative of larger populations of cases and controls. As a model we shall suppose that random selection *has* taken place, with different sampling fractions for cases and controls (presumably higher for cases than for controls). Suppose the combined population is subdivided in the following proportions:

		Disease		
		$+$	$-$	
	$+$	P_1	P_3	$P_1 + P_3$
Factor				
	$-$	P_2	P_4	$P_2 + P_4$
		$P_1 + P_2$	$P_3 + P_4$	1

Then the risk of being disease positive is $P_1/(P_1 + P_3)$ for a person who is factor positive, and $P_2/(P_2 + P_4)$ for one who is factor negative.The ratio of risks is thus $P_1(P_2 + P_4)/P_2(P_1 + P_3)$. Now, in many situations, the disease is relatively rare, so that P_1/P_3 and P_2/P_4 are small. The ratio of risks will then be very nearly

$$\psi = P_1 P_4 / P_2 P_3,$$

the 'cross-ratio', 'odds ratio' or 'relative risk'.

Now, in the case-control study, following the notation of Section 1, a/b and c/d are consistent estimators of P_1/P_2 and P_3/P_4 respectively. The observed relative risk, $\hat{\psi}$, is therefore a consistent estimator of ψ which, as we have seen, is close to the ratio of risks. The important point is that the *ratio* of risks can be estimated from a case-control study; the absolute values and their difference cannot be satisfactorily estimated without a knowledge of the sampling fractions of cases and controls. Early references to this approach are Cornfield (1951), (1956); the argument seems to be implicit in certain earlier calculations of relative risk (e.g., Doll and Hill (1950)).

The convenience of the parameter ψ in relation to case-control studies does not imply that, for a particular disease/factor pair, ψ necessarily remains constant under different circumstances and for different types of people. There seems to be little evidence to show whether, for example, the ratio of risks is in practice more nearly invariant than the difference.

Inference about ψ can conveniently be based on the distribution of the entries in (1) conditional on the marginal totals: a hypergeometric distribution if $\psi = 1$, and a generalized hypergeometric otherwise (Cornfield (1956)). Asymptotically $\ln \hat{\psi}$ may be taken to have a variance estimated by

$$(3) \qquad \frac{1}{a} + \frac{1}{b} + \frac{1}{c} + \frac{1}{d} \, ,$$

or by the expression obtained from (3) by replacing the observed frequencies by those expected for a specific value of ψ. Cornfield (1956), Gart (1962a) and Gart and Zweifel (1967) have discussed methods of obtaining approximate confidence limits and an approximately unbiased estimator. For a Bayesian approach see Lindley (1964).

4. The comparison and combination of relative risks

The investigator may wish to study the association between disease and factor separately within sub-groups, formed either from entirely different studies or by subdividing the population in any one study according to certain factors such as age and sex. It may be useful to contrast the relative risks estimated from the different sub-groups, and, if they are sufficiently homogeneous, to form a pooled estimate.

A natural approach is to estimate a supposed common value of ψ by maximum likelihood (ML) and to test for heterogeneity by a generalized likelihood ratio χ^2 test. The ML solution is iterative (Gart (1962)) and can be accomplished either by iterative scaling methods (Brown (1959)) or by using methods appropriate for a general linear logistic model (Cox (1970)).

The large-sample variance formula (2) leads to asymptotically efficient weighted mean estimates and associated heterogeneity tests (Gart (1962b)). An even simpler estimator is the Mantel-Haenszel statistic (Mantel and Haenszel (1959)):

$$(4) \qquad R = \frac{\Sigma \, (a_i d_i / n_i)}{\Sigma \, (b_i c_i / n_i)} \, ,$$

where the subscript refers to the ith subgroup, and the summation is from 1 to t. This method often gives results surprisingly close to the method of taking a weighted mean of the $\ln \hat{\psi}_i$'s. D.G. Clayton, in a private communication, has pointed out that the Mantel-Haenszel estimator appears at the first iteration in one of the methods of obtaining the ML solution, and one might therefore expect the various estimators mentioned here to be close together in practice.

One important form of subgrouping is by matched pairs, when for example each case is matched with a control subject for a number of variables such as age, sex and socio-economic characteristics. The logistic model (Cox (1958), (1970)) leads to the use of discrepant or 'untied' pairs, as in McNemar's test. If ψ is assumed to be constant for all pairs, r pairs have a positive case and negative control and s pairs have a negative case and positive control, then the ML estimator of ψ conditional on the value of $r + s$ is $\hat{\psi}_M = r/s$, and methods of inference using the binomial distribution are available. Interestingly enough, the Mantel-Haenszel estimator R coincides with $\hat{\psi}_M$ in this situation.

Most of the topics discussed so far are fairly well covered in the literature; see Gart (1971) for a recent review. There follow two specific results which may have escaped notice.

5. Random pairing

Suppose pairs are formed at random, for example by deliberate matching on variables which in fact are unrelated to the factor in question. It would clearly be efficient to ignore the pairing and to use the consistent estimator $\hat{\psi}$ as in (2). Is anything lost by using $\hat{\psi}_M$, which is also consistent?

Denoting the expected values of a, b, c and d by α, β, γ and δ, writing V for the asymptotic variance of $\ln \hat{\psi}$ (using (4) with expected frequencies), and V_M for the corresponding asymptotic variance of $\hat{\psi}_M$, we find

$$V_M - V = \frac{(\beta - \delta)(\beta\gamma - \alpha\delta)}{\alpha\beta\gamma\delta}$$

which ≥ 0, equality holding if $\psi = 1$. Thus, the use of $\hat{\psi}_M$ is inefficient in random pairing unless $\psi = 1$.

6. The effect of pooling subgroups

Suppose the relative risk ψ takes the same value in each of a number of subgroups. The subgroups may be different studies, they may be formed by values of covariates or they may be matched pairs. What can be said about the relative risk in the population formed by pooling the subgroups? Seigel and Greenhouse (1973) (whose paper contains references to other discussions on this topic) consider two strata, with random matching within each, and find that the pooled relative risk is asymptotically biased towards unity. The phenomenon has often been noted in the literature, without proof.

Consider a more general formulation. Suppose there is matched pairing, and that for the ith pair the probabilities of the two subjects being positive or negative for the factor are as follows:

		Case	Control
	+	p_{1i}	p_{2i}
Factor			
	−	q_{1i}	q_{2i}
		1	1

where $p_{1i}q_{2i}/p_{2i}q_{1i} = \psi > 1$.

In the pooled population, the estimated relative risk converges in probability to

$$(5) \qquad \psi' = \psi \frac{\Sigma q_{1i}\theta_i \Sigma q_{2i}}{\Sigma q_{2i}\theta_i \Sigma q_{1i}} = \frac{\psi\bar{\theta}}{\bar{\theta}'},$$

where

$$\theta_i = p_{2i}/q_{2i}, \qquad \bar{\theta} = \Sigma q_{1i}\theta_i/\Sigma q_{1i}$$

and

$$\bar{\theta}' = \Sigma q_{2i}\theta_i/\Sigma q_{2i}.$$

$$(6) \qquad \bar{\theta}' = \bar{\theta} = \sum \theta_i \left\{ \frac{q_{2i}}{\Sigma q_{2i}} - \frac{q_{1i}}{\Sigma q_{1i}} \right\},$$

and $q_{2i}/q_{1i} = (1 + \theta_i\psi)/(1 + \theta_i)$, which is an increasing function of θ_i. High values of θ_i in (6) will thus be multiplied by positive terms inside the brackets, and low values by negative terms, giving a positive value to (6). Hence, from (5), $1 < \psi' < \psi$, in agreement with Seigel and Greenhouse's result.

References

BARTLETT, M. S. (1935) Contingency table interactions. *J. R. Statist. Soc. Suppl.* **2**, 248–252.

BROWN, D. T. (1959) A note on approximation to discrete probability distributions. *Information and Control* **2**, 386–392.

CORNFIELD, J. (1951) A method of estimating comparative rates from clinical data. Applications to cancer of the lung, breast and cervix. *J. Nat. Cancer Inst.* **11**, 1269–1275.

CORNFIELD, J. (1956) Some aspects of retrospective studies. *J. Chron. Dis.* **11**, 523–534.

COX, D. R. (1958) Two further applications of a model for binary regression. *Biometrika* **45**, 562–565.

COX, D. R. (1970) *The Analysis of Binary Data.* Methuen, London.

DARROCH. J. N. (1974) Multiplicative and additive interaction in contingency tables. *Biometrika* **61**, 207–214.

DOLL, R. AND HILL, A. B. (1950) Smoking and carcinoma of the lung. Preliminary report. *Br. Med. J.* **2**, 739–748.

EDWARDS, A. W. F. (1963) The measure of association in a 2×2 table. *J. R. Statist. Soc.* A **126**, 109–114.

GART, J. J. (1962a) Approximate confidence levels for the relative risk. *J. R. Statist. Soc.* B **24**, 454–463.

GART, J. J. (1962b) On the combination of relative risks. *Biometrics* **18**, 601–610.

GART, J. J. (1971) The comparison of proportions: a review of significance tests, confidence intervals and adjustments for stratification. *Rev. Inst. Internat. Statist.* **39**, 148–169.

GART, J. J. AND ZWEIFEL, J. R. (1967) On the bias of various estimators of the logit and its variance with application to quantal bioassay. *Biometrika* **54**, 181–187.

GOOD, I. J. (1963) Maximum entropy for hypothesis formulation especially for multidimensional contingency tables. *Ann. Math. Statist.* **34**, 911–934.

LANCASTER, H. O. (1969a) *The Chi-squared Distribution.* Wiley, New York.

LANCASTER, H. O. (1969b) Contingency tables of higher dimensions. *Bull. Inst. Internat. Statist.* **43**, 143–151.

LINDLEY. D. V. (1964) The Bayesian analysis of contingency tables. *Ann. Math. Statist.* **35**, 1622–1643.

MACMAHON, B. AND PUGH, T. F. (1970) *Epidemiology. Principles and Methods.* 2nd ed. Little, Brown, Boston.

MANTEL, N. AND HAENSZEL, W. (1959) Statistical aspects of the analysis of data from retrospective studies of disease. *J. Nat. Cancer Inst.* **22**, 719–748.

PLACKETT, R. L. (1969) Multidimensional contingency tables: a survey of models and methods. *Bull. Inst. Internat. Statist.* **43**, 133–142.

SEIGEL, D. G. AND GREENHOUSE, S. W. (1973) Validity in estimating relative risk in case-control studies. *J. Chron. Dis.* **26**, 219–225.

Approaches to the Control of Infectious Disease

NORMAN T. J. BAILEY

Abstract

Maurice Bartlett's work on the mathematical theory of epidemics, recurrent epidemics and endemicity over the years 1953–66 has helped to stimulate a wide range of applied studies of practical importance. This paper reviews contemporary trends in the control of infectious disease. Historically, the subject started in response to very practical problems, but subsequent developments showed an increasingly marked divergence between general theory and practical applications. In recent years, however, improvements in parameter estimation, asymptotic and stochastic approximation, the modelling of individual diseases, advances in computerized simulations, the construction of resource allocation models, the use of control theory, etc., have been gradually leading to a synthesis of the utmost importance to public health action. Models can now be fitted to specific field data; alternative intervention strategies involving immunization, prophylaxis or treatment can be evaluated; and the incorporation of realistic epidemiological models in a wider decision-oriented system dynamics setting may soon help to solve broader strategic problems on the policy level.

1. Introduction

In a most valuable series of papers covering the years 1953–1966, Maurice Bartlett made a series of substantial contributions to the mathematical theory of epidemics, recurrent epidemics and endemicity. Of special importance is the explanation of the *undamped* sequence of epidemics, frequently observed in measles, in terms of an appropriate

This review is based on a paper originally presented to the 8th International Biometric Conference, Constanța, Romania, 26–30 August 1974.

stochastic formulation—as compared with the *damped* trains of oscillations predicted by deterministic theory (Soper (1929)). Bartlett's work was accordingly not only a skilful investigation of certain theoretical models, but it also provided considerable insight into phenomena which had puzzled epidemiologists for nearly 25 years—unless they were prepared to accept the unfortunately erroneous belief of Soper that allowance for an incubation period (and by implication the introduction of other realistic features as well) could lead to undamped oscillations.

Bartlett ((1957) and later) also succeeded in accounting for the phenomenon of fade-out in communities below a certain critical size. Broad qualitative explanations could be provided for a wide range of population data on measles in both the U.K. and the U.S.A., with subsequent applications to various semi-isolated communities (e.g., Black (1966)).

It is therefore appropriate to review the contributions made by the rapidly expanding theory of infectious disease not only to the scientific understanding of and insight into the mechanisms of disease spread, but also to the systematic development of more effective methods of public health control.

By 'infectious disease' is meant the whole range of infectious or contagious diseases that are communicated from one individual to another, either directly from person to person, or indirectly through an intermediate host, and involving a variety of infectious organisms such as viruses, bacteria, protozoa, parasitic worms, etc. Further, we are primarily concerned with epidemiological modelling to deal with the population dynamics of the spread of disease, although in some diseases, especially those involving parasites, a certain amount of attention may have to be given to modelling the underlying physiological processes as well. But, in considering the public health control of disease, a wider range of models may have to be developed, such as resource allocation models or system dynamics representations, for which the epidemiological modelling is only one of the inputs.

If the full potentialities of mathematical theory are to be realized in practical applications, there must be much closer cooperation between those whose primary concern is with modelling and those whose main responsibility is with decision-making and the implementation of control strategies.

A 'Symposium on Quantitative Epidemiology', dealing largely with communicable disease problems, was organized by WHO in Moscow,

23–27 November, 1970. Amongst the objectives there was an explicit 'intention... to bring academic mathematical research on communicable disease in closer contact with applied problems in public health intervention and control'. At a subsequent international meeting, namely the IASPS Symposium held during the Third Congress of Bulgarian Mathematicians, Varna, 6–15 September, 1972, there was also a session on mathematical epidemiology. In the special discussion that followed, there was general support for the proposal initiated by the Chairman, Professor D. G. Kendall, that there should be closer cooperation between university research workers interested in epidemic theory and WHO medical officers and scientists concerned with practical problems.

Such proposals take time to promote and organize. On the more theoretical side, the writer (Bailey (1975)) has revised and enlarged his original book on epidemic theory. The new version lays special emphasis on an orientation towards practical applications, adopting the view that general theory is only worthwhile insofar as it tends to provide an understanding of and insight into real epidemic phenomena. In addition, informal arrangements have been made, to begin with, between WHO and the Manchester-Sheffield School of Probability and Statistics so as to provide a more direct link between practical statistical work on communicable disease and the kind of theoretical undertakings that are most easily pursued in a university setting.

The present review is a further attempt to foster the integration of theory and practice in the communicable disease field. It describes briefly a number of current trends in the modelling of infectious diseases with the intention of indicating some of the major interests and priorities for future work.

2. Historical setting

Although we are principally concerned here with present trends, together with their future implications, it is of some importance to reflect briefly on the historical development of the subject. Both the early statistical work of Graunt and Petty in the 17th century on the occurrence of infectious disease, and the mathematical investigations of Daniel Bernoulli in the 18th century into the effectiveness of variolation against smallpox, were clearly rooted in a desire to understand and control real phenomena. Again, the attempts in the 19th century to predict the course of epidemic outbreaks through empirical curve-fitting were also immediately related to practical problems.

It was only at the beginning of the 20th century that consistent efforts, beginning wth Hamer and Ross, were made to develop mathematical theories of the population dynamics of infectious disease spread, based on certain notions of an underlying mechanism. Initially, at any rate, the mass of biological and sociological factors was effectively subsumed under a single principle that was virtually identical with the Law of Mass Action.

Since that time there has been a gradual emergence of two major kinds of activity. The first is a constantly increasing flow of primarily mathematical papers, pursued largely for their own intrinsic mathematical interest, though sometimes providing insight into real public health problems. The second is more down to earth, and involves attempts to model specific diseases. Unfortunately, through a lack of specific information on relevant parameters, investigators often have to confine themselves to studying typical models, applicable for example to developing countries in a general way, backing up their work by computerized simulation studies.

Current trends accordingly reflect these two chief components, but also reveal the directions in which an effective synthesis is beginning to develop. The real stimulus comes from the need to be able to influence in a rational way public health decision-making on the control of serious diseases that affect many hundreds of millions of people in the world to-day. When mathematical modelling is directed towards theoretical problems, which if solved would have practical implications for the control or eradication of disease, then it can be both intellectually satisfying and socially valuable.

3. General theory

From the standpoint of the present paper we are concerned with general theory insofar as it is liable to produce insights of practical consequence. Of course, everyone has his own opinion as to what is useful, and what is of purely academic interest. To try to identify the latter here in clear terms would be invidious, but it may be helpful to give an indication of the general principles that can be discerned.

Thus early work, for example by Hamer (1906), showed that the rise and fall of an epidemic was a natural consequence of the homogeneous mixing of infectives and susceptibles, with the transmission of disease following the Law of Mass Action. Again, the idea of a threshold which has to be exceeded if a disease is to maintain itself goes back to the work of Ross (1911) on malaria, but a fully-fledged theory with a clearly enunciated threshold theorem had to wait for the investigations of Kermack and McKendrick ((1927) and later).

While most of these studies were largely deterministic in character, stochastic versions were elaborated later adding several new touches of realism (Whittle (1955)). Stochastic models were also very successful in explaining the frequent occurrence in measles of a maintained *undamped* sequence of repeated outbreaks (Bartlett (1953) and later). Earlier deterministic work by Soper (1929) produced models with only *damped* trains of waves. Bartlett also succeeded in accounting for the observed phenomenon of fade-out in communities below a certain critical size.

Threshold behaviour has also been established for spatial models, e.g., the deterministic threshold theorem of Kendall (discussion on Bartlett (1957)), or the subsequent work of Kendall (1965) and Mollison ((1970) and later) on the occurrence of epidemic waves in a one-dimensional population. Stochastic simulation studies by Bailey (1967) have illustrated the steady advance of epidemic waves from a focus, involving the existence of a threshold blurred by probability effects.

It must, however, be admitted that an enormous amount of detailed mathematical analysis has been carried out on two rather elementary models, namely the simple and general stochastic epidemic models. That vast theoretical complexities can arise from rather simple models is intriguing in itself, but what are the practical implications? For one thing, it frequently happens that very diverse effects can occur purely by chance. This enjoins great caution in attributing special epidemiological causes, such as abnormal virulence or infectiousness, when interpreting practical data.

It is also reasonable to claim that simple problems should be dealt with first, introducing additional complications only as the ability to handle various techniques increases. Thus the theory of probability-generating functions, epidemic curves, duration times, asymptotic approximations, estimation techniques, etc., first developed in the context of the simple epidemic, can be seen as essential prerequisites to the study of more realistic models. Unfortunately, the expected generalizations do not always materialize, but a solid body of useful alternative approaches is being built up.

As a result, increasing attention is being paid to the use of approximating stochastic systems and asymptotic approximations. Some asymptotic threshold theorems seem to require such specialized conditions for their validity that doubts have been expressed about the usefulness of the results. On the other hand, the approximating system approach, initiated by Kendall (1956) and recently revived by Ludwig (1973), shows considerable promise. Such methods, judiciously combined with appropriate computerized calculations, may in fact eventually lead to useful approximate statements being made about actual communities, and not merely about idealized general models.

The development of general theory also permits the study of a variety of realistically-oriented modifications, such as departures from homogeneous mixing, the existence of heterogeneous subgroups in a population, the consequences of carrier individuals, the introduction of time-dependent parameters, the influence of migration, etc. Again, there are many important though difficult problems of parameter estimation. A start has been made by Bailey and Thomas (1971) providing a maximum-likelihood technique for analyzing real data, for which a general stochastic epidemic model might be appropriate. But much remains to be done in determining the validity of the method, in developing adequate goodness-of-fit tests, and in making extensions to more realistic models.

It seems reasonably certain that the broad 'strategic' models, which sacrifice realistic precision in order to clarify general principles, do in fact have a major role to play in developing our understanding of infectious disease phenomena. These models can make underlying assumptions more explicit, sharpen discussion of controversial issues, indicate gaps in our knowledge and help to evaluate in advance proposed investigations of a more directly practical and realistic nature. At the same time extreme care is required to ensure that such work does have genuine practical relevance, and is not merely a time-wasting, academic exercise.

4. Applications to small groups

From general theory we turn to specific applications. The first real successes were in the interpretation of family data on measles, starting with the work of Greenwood (1931). The appearance of successive generations of cases in relatively small groups could be explained by assuming that the infectiousness of measles was concentrated around a single point of time, and that the incubation period was relatively constant. Probability considerations led to the expected occurrence of chains of related binomial distributions. And, subject to certain modifications, such as an allowance for variations in infectiousness between households, the models were shown to fit observed data extremely well (see Bailey (1975)).

The chain-binomial approach enabled the estimation of parameters of epidemiological and biological significance, and so increased scientific understanding of the disease process involved. However, for many diseases, the assumptions of concentrated infectiousness and constant incubation period were very over-simplified. A modification by Bailey (1954) envisaged a variable latent period followed by an infectious period extended in time. This was successful in explaining measles data that were analysed in finer detail. More recently, Bailey and Alff-Steinberger (1970) recast the analysis in a form more suitable for computerized handling, and reduced computation times from several weeks to the same number of minutes. Applications were also made to family data from Hamburg on infectious hepatitis, and to a single outbreak of smallpox in a small Nigerian village community.

Relatively little practical use has been made of simple chain-binomials in recent years. The development of the more realistic models is being held up by technical difficulties. The stochastic process involved is basically non-Markovian. For very small groups, e.g., family sizes of up to three individuals, the probabilities of all observable patterns can be enumerated directly. But with larger groups this has proved intractable, although an approximate method of doubtful validity has been proposed.

Here then is a major problem that should be pursued. Perhaps a more effective analysis of the model could be developed, allowing parameter estimation to be carried out on a wide range of diseases for which data are, or could easily be made, available. The idea of including supplementary variables to construct a related multi-dimensional Markov process is completely workable in theory, but so far appears to be computationally unmanageable. Perhaps some modifications might be made to the model itself which would lead to a more tractable form.

5. Applications to populations

An important trend in recent years has been the application of modelling to the evaluation of proposed alternative intervention strategies. This has entailed the quantitative study of the population dynamics (mostly deterministic) of more or less endemic situations in large communities, using fairly simple multi-compartmental models. The mathematics is frequently intractable in purely analytic terms, but considerable support has been obtained from simulations.

The most impressive developments have taken place in the field of tuberculosis control. This started with the three-category model of Waaler, Geser and Andersen (1962), involving non-infected individuals, infected non-cases and infected cases. The idea was to compare, for appropriate population numbers and transition-rates between categories, the consequences of existing trends for different strategies e.g., no control; adequate treatment of some of the active cases; and BCG vaccination. Extensions and refinements were made by many subsequent writers, including Brøgger, Feldstein, Lynn, Mahler, Piot and ReVelle (see Bailey (1975), Section 16.2). The majority of these writers assumed that the total number of susceptibles was very large and remained virtually constant. However, some strategies, especially if very effective in a heavily infected population, might well change the number of susceptibles drastically.

ReVelle and Lynn therefore developed a more realistic nine-category model, whose behaviour was specified by nine non-linear ordinary differential equations. Variables relating to BCG vaccination, prophylaxis and treatment were to some extent under control. By using a special device the model was adapted to fit into a linear programming format. For a specified programme of case reduction over a given period, of 20 years say, optimization could select the least costly forms of control.

Similar work has been undertaken recently by Cvjetanović, Grab, Sundaresan and Uemura (see Bailey (1975), Section 16.3) for a range of diseases including typhoid fever, tetanus and cholera.

The main difficulty about all this work so far is that it usually applies only to a given disease in some hypothetical community, which may nevertheless be typical of an important class of communities, e.g., in developing countries. Although the models can certainly be used to sharpen discussion of planning disease control and of optimizing resource allocation, much more needs to be done to derive results that are specific to given communities. This involves being able to estimate at least those parameters which are likely to be highly community-specific, and also carrying out tests of the adequacy of the models in fitting available data.

From a practical point of view new developments in this whole area are urgently required. Not only do we need to be able to carry out detailed scientific enquiries of the kind referred to for individual communities, but we also need to develop short-cut methods that can be used operationally within limited periods of time for the purposes of assisting decision-makers to choose between alternative allocations of resources.

6. Parasitic diseases

One of the most important areas for infectious disease theory in the world to-day is concerned with endemic parasitic disease. Although, for the most part, the classic epidemic scourges of history may be past, the prevalence of *each* of several parasitic diseases can be counted in hundreds of millions. The total load of morbidity due to malaria, schistosomiasis (bilharzia), hookworm disease, filariasis, etc. is staggering.

Since we are now concerned with at least one intermediate host in addition to the substantive host, man, the modelling is liable to be more complicated than the relatively simple diseases of the last section. Moreover, it is common in parasitic diseases for the actual parasitic density in man to be an important factor as well: it is not enough to consider simply being infected or not being infected.

Mathematical work in malaria goes back to Ross's studies in 1911, in which there were two basic deterministic equations describing the rates of growth of the infected human and mosquito populations in terms of the relevant transfer and removal rates. More detailed mathematical studies were later made by Lotka (1923), and the whole subject made enormous strides forward due to the well-known epidemiological and mathematical investigations of Macdonald ((1950) and later). The phenomenon of super-infection (simultaneous, distinct, broods of parasites in one individual) was introduced into the models. The importance of different levels of immunity and the huge seasonal variations in mosquito population densities were recognized, but *not* adequately treated.

In general, the position reached in dealing with populations was roughly that of Section 5. Typical, hypothetical populations, though of an over-simplified kind, could be investigated. But there were difficulties in applications to the epidemiological realities of any given community, with concomitant uncertainties about the implications for local decision-making as to control measures.

Recent work by Dietz, Molineaux and Thomas (1974) has broken fresh ground. They use a seven-category compartmental model incorporating such factors as superinfection, immunity structure, seasonal fluctuations, etc., and have applied the model to data from a specific group of 16 villages (totalling about 5,000 individuals) in a WHO research project in Northern Nigeria. To make the treatment more manageable, reasonable values were assumed for eight parameters, while three of greater uncertainty were estimated from the data. Within these limits, a satisfactory goodness-of-fit was obtained. This is highly encouraging, and the work is proceeding to see whether qualitative forecasts as to the effects of certain interventions (drug treatment of people, spraying of mosquitoes) are realized or not.

So far as other parasitic diseases are concerned, investigations are much less developed. The disease that has received most attention over recent years is schistosomiasis, the main contributors being Hairston (1962), (1965), Macdonald (1965), Leyton (1968), Linhart (1968), Tallis and Leyton (1969), and Goffman and Warren (1970). More detailed theoretical developments of potentially great practical importance have been made by Nåsell (1972) and Nåsell and Hirsch (1971), 1972), (1973).

This work is clearly still in a formative stage, but there would be tremendous advantages in pursuing the investigations to the point where models could be fitted to data from specific communities, with a view to facilitating choices between alternative control strategies. Similar remarks apply of course to other major parasitic diseases as well.

7. Public health control

The general orientation of this review has been quite deliberately in the direction of increasing our understanding of infectious disease dynamics so as to facilitate intervention and control. And we have already discussed the type of models that can be used to help decide between alternative public health strategies, involving immunization, prophylaxis, treatment, etc.

Vaccination, for example against smallpox, has come in for rather specific criticism. In the twenty year period 1950–1970, no cases were imported into the United States, thanks to stringent public health measures. But millions of people were vaccinated—14 million in 1968 alone, of whom 572 suffered from confirmed complications, including nine deaths. In that year the total cost of the preventive measures was $150 million. Obviously, the price paid in dollars and in deaths far outweighed the possible risks. A thorough mathematical treatment of this situation was undertaken by Becker (1972), and could be applied elsewhere. He showed how a decision to discontinue vaccination (actually decided for smallpox in the USA only in 1971) could be made at the earliest possible moment so as to minimize the total number of deaths due to the disease itself and to preventive measures taken against it.

The potentialities of modelling for planning and evaluating alternative interventions, especially in regard to the simulation of control measures and the application of cost-effectiveness and cost-benefit analysis, are considerable (see Cvjetanović (1972)). The next stage in the development of such approaches is the utilization of the mathematical methods of standard control theory, using for example Pontryagin's Principle. Work has been developed in this direction in recent years (1968 and onwards) by Abakuks, Gupta, Hethcote, Jacquette, Morton, Rink, Sanders, Taylor, Waltman and Wickwire. The extent to which such applications can really be made realistic is still open to question and requires more investigation. There are several features, such as the cost of estimating the numbers of susceptibles in the population, and of determining other relevant parameters, that still need to be taken into account, before specific applications could be made in practice. There is also the question of whether such theory *should* be used in concrete instances, or whether its main contribution is likely to be in providing general insight into the handling of decision-making from a control theoretic standpoint.

8. System dynamics models

If the sort of modelling discussed in this review is to have its full impact on public health practice then a number of more general quantitative issues have to be faced. First of all, in many developing countries with limited resources, there is not just one major infectious disease, but several, all to some extent interacting because individuals weakened by one disease more easily fall a prey to another. Moreover, a lot of diseases can be partially controlled by many factors other than specific treatments or preventive measures, such as better nutrition, health education, improved sanitation, clean water supplies, elimination of vectors, rising economic standards, etc.

Substantially to reduce the colossal toll taken by parasitic diseases in the world to-day requires far more than an understanding of epidemiological dynamics. As is well known, the decision to improve agriculture by building dams and constructing artificial lakes for irrigation purposes has turned out to be counter-productive in some countries, since the artificial lakes give rise to snail populations that act as intermediate hosts for the spread of schistosomiasis. The handling of such problems involves the development of multi-disciplinary models which incorporate epidemiological models as one of several inputs.

A major trend, which is currently attracting considerable attention, is the attempt to apply system dynamics approaches to problems of policy analysis and to broad organizational studies. The objective here is to increase understanding of a whole range of interlocking phenomena, including health aspects, and to construct projections to guide the choice between alternative feasible strategies.

Although the modelling of infectious disease is only one of the inputs into such a more comprehensive system, some knowledge of the latter may be essential to determine a correct framework for the former. A scientifically valid and statistically adequate model of a widespread infectious disease might turn out to be quite useless in practice if it had nothing to say about the choice between the only interventions that were in fact available. Conversely, the priority and financial support to be attached to a proposed major effort in epidemiological modelling may well depend on the contribution this would make to a wider decision-oriented systems model.

9. Conclusion

In conclusion I should like to say how delighted I am to have this opportunity of recognizing in a formal but sincere way the substantial contributions made by Maurice Bartlett to our understanding of the population theory of the spread of infectious disease. The theoretical insights he has achieved have not only enabled Bartlett himself to pursue applied studies of practical importance, but have also inspired countless others in their quest for the means to control and eliminate one of the most ferocious causes of human suffering throughout the world to-day.

References

ABAKUKS, A. (1973) An optimal isolation policy for an epidemic. *J. Appl. Prob.* **10**, 247–262.

BAILEY, N. T. J. (1954) A statistical method of estimating the periods of incubation and infection of an infectious disease. *Nature* **174**, 139–140.

BAILEY, M. T. J. (1967) The simulation of stochastic epidemics in two dimensions. *Proc. Fifth Berkeley Symp. Math. Statist. Prob.* **4**, 237–257.

BAILEY, N. T. J. (1975) *The Mathematical Theory of Infectious Diseases.* Griffin, London. To appear.

BAILEY, N. T. J. AND ALFF-STEINBERGER, C. (1970) Improvements in the estimation of latent and infectious periods of a contagious disease. *Biometrika* **57**, 141–153.

BAILEY, N. T. J. AND THOMAS, A. S. (1971) The estimation of parameters from population data on the general stochastic epidemic. *Theor. Pop. Biol.* **2**, 253–270. (Summarized in *Adv. Appl. Prob.* **3**. 211–214.)

BARTLETT, M. S. (1953) Stochastic processes or the statistics of change. *Appl. Statist.* **2**, 44–64.

BARTLETT, M. S. (1956) Deterministic and stochastic models for recurrent epidemics. *Proc. Third Berkeley Symp. Math. Statist. Prob.* **4**, 81–109.

BARTLETT, M. S. (1957) Measles periodicity and community size. *J. R. Statist. Soc. Ser.* A **120**, 48–70.

BARTLETT, M. S. (1960a) *Stochastic Population Models in Ecology and Epidemiology.* Methuen and Co. Ltd., London.

BARTLETT, M. S. (1960b) Some stochastic models in ecology and epidemiology. In *Contributions to Probability and Statistics: Essays in Honor of Harold Hotelling* (eds. I. Olkin *et al.*), 89–96. Stanford University Press.

BARTLETT, M. S. (1960c) The critical community size for measles in the United States. *J. R. Statist. Soc. Ser.* A. **123**, 37–44.

BARTLETT, M. S. (1961) Monte Carlo studies in ecology and epidemiology. *Proc. Fourth Berkeley Symp. Math. Statist. Prob.* **4**, 39–55.

BARTLETT, M. S. (1964) The relevance of stochastic models for large-scale epidemiological phenomena. *Appl. Statist.* **13**, 2–8.

BARTLETT, M. S. (1966) Some notes on epidemiological theory. In *Research Papers in Statistics: Festschrift for J. Neyman* (ed. F. N. David), 25–36. Wiley, New York.

BECKER, N. G. (1972) Vaccination programs for rare infectious diseases. *Biometrika* **59**, 443–453.

BLACK, F. L. (1966) Measles endemicity in insular populations: critical community size and its evolutionary implications. *J. Theor. Biol.* **11**, 207–211.

BRØGGER, S. (1967) Systems analysis in tuberculosis control: a model. *Amer. Rev. Resp. Dis.* **95**, 421–434.

CVJETANOVIĆ, B. (1972) Use of mathematical models in the planning and evaluation of control measures against infectious diseases. *J. Egypt. Pub. Hlth Assoc.* **47**, 121–128.

CVJETANOVIĆ, B.,GRAB, B. AND UEMURA, K. (1971) Epidemiological model of typhoid fever and its use in planning and evaluation of antityphoid immunization and sanitation programmes. *Bull. Wld Hlth Org.* **45**, 53–75.

CVJETANOVIĆ, B.,GRAB, B., UEMURA, K. AND BYTCHENKO, B. (1972) Epidemiological model of tetanus and its use in the planning of immunization programmes. *Int. J. Epid.* **1**, 125–137.

CVJETANOVIĆ, B., UEMURA, K., GRAB, B. AND SUNDARESAN, T. (1973) Use of mathematical models in the evaluation of the effectiveness of preventive measures against some infectious diseases. *Proc. Sixth Int. Sci. Meeting, Int. Epid. Assoc.* **2**, 913–933.

DIETZ, K., MOLINEAUX, L. AND THOMAS, A. (1974) A malaria model tested in the African Savannah. *Bull. Wld Hlth Org.* **50**, 347–357.

FELDSTEIN, M. S., PIOT, M. A. AND SUNDARESAN, T.K. (1973) Resource allocation model for public health planning. *Bull. Wld Hlth Org.* **48**, Supp., 3–108.

GOFFMAN, W. AND WARREN, K. S. (1970) An application of the Kermack-McKendrick theory to the epidemiology of schistosomiasis. *Amer. J. Trop. Med. Hyg.* **19**, 278–283.

GREENWOOD, M. (1931) On the statistical measure of infectiousness. *J. Hyg. Camb.* **31**, 336–351.

GUPTA, N, K. AND RINK, R. E. (1971) A model for communicable disease control. *Proc. 24th Ann. Conf. Eng. Med. Biol.* Las Vegas.

GUPTA, N. K. AND RINK, R. E. (1973) Optimal control of epidemics. *Math. Biosci.* **18**, 383–396.

HAIRSTON, N. G. (1962) Population ecology and epidemiological problems. In *CIBA Foundation Symposium on Bilharziasis* (ed. C. E. W. Wolstenholme and M. O'Connor), 36–62. Churchill, London.

HAIRSTON, N. G. (1965a) On the mathematical analysis of schistosome populations. *Bull. Wld Hlth Org.* **33**, 45-62.

HAIRSTON, N. G. (1965b) An analysis of age-prevalence data by catalytic models. A contribution to the study of bilharziasis. *Bull. Wld Hlth Org.* **33**, 163–175.

HAMER, W. H. (1906) Epidemic disease in England. *Lancet* **1**, 733–739.

HETHCOTE, H. W. (1970) Note on determining the limiting susceptible population in an epidemic model. *Math. Biosci.* **9**, 161–163.

HETHCOTE, H. W. AND WALTMAN, P. (1973) Optimal vaccination schedules in a deterministic epidemic model. *Math. Biosci.* **18**, 365–381.

JAQUETTE, D. L. (1970) A stochastic model for the optimal control of epidemics and pest populations. *Math. Biosci.* **8**, 343–354.

KENDALL, D.G. (1956) Deterministic and stochastic epidemics in closed populations. *Proc. Third Berkeley Symp. Math. Statist. Prob.* **4**, 149–165.

KENDALL, D. G. (1965) Mathematical models of the spread of infection. In *Mathematics and Computer Science in Biology and Medicine.* H.M.S.O., London, 213–225.

KERMACK, W. O. AND MCKENDRICK, A. G. (1927–39) Contributions to the mathematical theory of epidemics. *Proc. Roy. Soc.* A **115**, 700–721. (Part I, 1927.) *Proc. Roy. Soc.* A **138**, 55–83. (Part II, 1932.) *Proc. Roy. Soc.* A **141**, 94–122.(Part III, 1933.) *J. Hyg. Camb.* **37**, 172–187. (Part IV, 1937.) *J. Hyg. Camb.* **39**, 271–288. (Part V, 1939.)

LEYTON, M.K. (1968) Stochastic models in populations of helminthic parasites in the definitive host, II: sexual mating functions. *Math. Biosci.* **3**, 413–419.

LINHART, H. (1968) On some bilharzia infection and immunization models. *S. Afr. Statist. J.* **2**, 61–66.

LOTKA, A. J. (1923) Contributions to the analysis of malaria epidemiology. *Amer. J. Hyg.* **3**, (Suppl. 1), 1–121.

LUDWIG, D. (1973) Stochastic approximation for the general epidemic. *J. Appl. Prob.* **10**, 263–276.

LYNN, W. R. AND REVELLE, C. S. (1968) Workshop on model methodology for health planning, with particular reference to tuberculosis. *Amer. Rev. Resp. Dis.* **98**, 687–691.

MACDONALD, G. (1950a) The analysis of infection rates in diseases in which superinfection occurs. *Trop. Dis. Bull.* **47**, 907–915.

MACDONALD, G. (1950b) The analysis of malaria parasite rates in infants. *Trop. Dis. Bull.* **47**, 915–938.

MACDONALD, G. (1952a) The analysis of the sporozoite rate. *Trop. Dis. Bull.* **49**, 569–586.

MACDONALD, G. (1952b) The analysis of equilibrium in malaria. *Trop. Dis. Bull.* **49**, 813–829.

MACDONALD, G. (1953) The analysis of malaria epidemics. *Trop. Dis. Bull.* **50**, 871–889.

MACDONALD, G. (1955) The measurement of malaria transmission. *Proc. Roy. Soc. Med.* **48**, 295–301.

MACDONALD, G. (1957) *The Epidemiology and Control of Malaria.* Oxford University Press, London.

MACDONALD, G. (1965a) The dynamics of helminth infections, with special reference to schistosomes. *Trans. Roy. Soc. Trop. Med. Hyg.* **59**, 489–506.

MACDONALD, G. (1965b) On the scientific basis of tropical hygiene. *Trans. Roy. Soc. Trop. Med. Hyg.* **59**, 611–620.

MACDONALD, G. (1965c) Eradication of malaria. *Pub. Hlth Rep.* **80,** 870–880.

MACDONALD, G. (1973) *Dynamics of Tropical Diseases.* Oxford University Press, London.

MACDONALD, G., CUELLAR, C. B. AND FOLL, C. V. (1968) The dynamics of malaria. *Bull. Wld Hlth Org.* **38,** 743–755.

MACDONALD, G. AND GÖCKEL, C. W. (1964) The malaria parasite rate and interruption of transmission. *Bull. Wld Hlth Org.* **31,** 365–377.

MAHLER, H. T. AND PIOT, M. A. (1966a) Essais d'application de la recherche opérationnelle dans la lutte antituberculose. I: formulation des problèmes, rassemblement des données, choix de modèles. *Bull. INSERM* **21,** 855–881.

MAHLER, H. T. AND PIOT, M. A. (1966b) Essais d'application de la recherche opérationnelle dans la lutte antituberculose. II: programmation linéaire: problèmes conceptuels et d'application. *Bull. INSERM* **21,** 1021–1045.

MOLLISON, D. (1970) Spatial propagation of simple epidemics. Ph. D. Thesis, Statistical Laboratory, Cambridge University.

MOLLISON, D. (1972a) Possible velocities for a simple epidemic. *Adv. Appl. Prob.* **4,** 233–257.

MOLLISON, D. (1972b) The rate of spatial propagation of simple epidemics. *Proc. Sixth Berkeley Symp. Math. Statist. Prob.* **3,** 579–614.

MORTON, R. AND WICKWIRE, K. H. (1974) On the optimal control of a deterministic epidemic. *Adv. Appl. Prob.* **6,** 622–635.

NÅSELL, I. (1972) Mathematical models of some parasitic diseases involving an intermediate host. Ph. D. Thesis, New York University.

NÅSELL, I. AND HIRSCH, W. M. (1971) Mathematical models of some parasitic diseases involving an intermediate host. *Report No.* IMM393. Courant Institute of Mathematical Sciences, New York.

NÅSELL, I. AND HIRSCH, W. M. (1972) A mathematical model of some helminthic infections. *Comm. Pure Appl. Math.* **25,** 459–477.

NÅSELL, I. AND HIRSCH, W. M. (1973a) The transmission dynamics of schistosomiasis. *Comm. Pure Appl. Appl. Math.* **26,** 395–453.

NÅSELL, I. AND HIRSCH, W. M. (1973b) The transmision and control of schistosome infections. Working Proceedings of NATO Conference on 'Mathematical Analysis of Decision Problems in Ecology', Istanbul, 9–13 July 1973.

REVELLE, C. (1967) The economic allocation of tuberculosis control activities in developing nations. Ph. D. Thesis, Cornell University.

REVELLE, C., FELDMANN, F. AND LYNN, W. (1969) An optimization model of tuberculosis epidemiology. *Management Sci.* **16,** B190–B211.

REVELLE, C. LYNN, W. R. AND FELDMANN, F. (1967) Mathematical models for the economic allocation of tuberculosis control activities in developing countries. *Amer. Rev. Resp. Dis.* **96,** 893–909.

REVELLE, C. AND MALE, J. (1970) A mathematical model for determining case finding and treatment activities in tuberculosis control programs. *Amer. Rev. Resp. Dis.* **102,** 403–411.

ROSS, R. (1911) *The Prevention of Malaria* (2nd edn.) Murray, London.

SANDERS, J. L. (1971) Quantitative guidelines for communicable disease control programs. *Biometrics* **27,** 883–893.

SOPER, H. E. (1929) Interpretation of perodicity in disease-prevalence. *J. R. Statist. Soc.* **92,** 34–73.

TALLIS, G. M. AND LEYTON, M. K. (1966) A stochastic approach to the study of parasite populations. *J. Theor. Biol.* **13,** 251–260.

TAYLOR, H. M. (1968) Some models in epidemic control. *Math. Biosci.* **3**, 383–398.

WAALER, H. T., GESER, A. AND ANDERSEN, S. (1962) The use of mathematical models in the study of the epidemiology of tuberculosis. *Amer. J. Publ. Hlth* **52**, 1002–1013.

WHITTLE, P. (1955) The outcome of a stochastic epidemic—a note on Bailey's paper. *Biometrika* **42**, 116–122.

The Deterministic Spread of a Simple Epidemic

H. E. DANIELS

Abstract

An approximation technique is developed for studying the deterministic spread of a simple epidemic which avoids a difficulty inherent in the diffusion approximation. Travelling wave solutions are found and calculated for various contact distributions. The solution developing from an isolated infective is also briefly discussed.

1. Introduction

This paper was stimulated by the recent studies of Kendall [4] and Mollison [6], [7] on the advance of an epidemic using a deterministic model. Its purpose is to suggest a technique by which approximate solutions can be found for non-linear models like the so-called simple epidemic. Such results as we find mostly verify the conclusions of Mollison arrived at by general topological arguments. The merit of the present approach is that it can give an approximate solution which not only faithfully describes the behaviour of the epidemic but also reproduces the correct critical velocity, a property which is lost if a diffusion approximation is used. In this paper the method is used to calculate travelling waves for the one-dimensional epidemic for various forms of contact distribution. The spread of a simple epidemic from an initial infective is only briefly discussed here. A fuller treatment will be given in a subsequent paper.

My interest in the problem was originally aroused by Bartlett's pioneering work on the spatial development of an epidemic, summarised in Chapter 8 of his book *Stochastic Population Models* [1].

2. Spread of an epidemic along a line

Suppose that a population is distributed with constant density N along a line, and that at a point S on it at time t the density of infected individuals is $Y(s,t) = Ny(s,t)$, where $y(s,t)$ is the relative density of infectives at s. The probability of a susceptible being infected by an infective at distance u from it is $\alpha dt dF(u)$ in time t to $t + dt$: $dF(u)$ is called by Mollison the contact distribution. The corresponding infection rate is αN, and we shall take $\alpha N = 1$, thereby incorporating it in the time scale. The deterministic equation for a simple epidemic without removals is then

$$(2.1) \qquad \frac{\partial y(s,t)}{\partial t} = \{1 - y(s,t)\}\bar{y}(s,t)$$

where

$$(2.2) \qquad \bar{y}(s,t) = \int_{-\infty}^{\infty} y(s - u, t)dF(u)$$

and $0 \leqq y \leqq 1$. For simplicity $dF(u)$ is assumed to be symmetrical with moment generating function $\Psi(\theta) = \int_{-\infty}^{\infty} \exp(\theta u)dF(u)$.

In a similar problem concerning the advance of a dominant gene, Fisher [3] and Kolmogoroff, Petrovsky and Piscounoff [5] replace the convolution $\bar{y}$ by the diffusion approximation $y + k\partial^2 y/\partial s^2$ and Kendall uses the same device in his treatment of the epidemic with removals. Mollison [6] avoids this approximation by the ingenious choice $dF(u) = \exp(-|u|/\beta)du/\beta$ which enables him to reduce (2.1) to a non-linear vector differential equation of the first order. Although it cannot be solved explicitly it provides important general information about wave forms. In particular Mollison proves that for each velocity c exceeding a critical value c_0 there is a unique wave form, and that the diffusion approximation gives misleading information about c_0.

3. The linear problem

We begin by considering the simpler situation where there is an unlimited population of susceptibles appropriate to the stages of a simple epidemic. As Bartlett has pointed out, it also applies to the early stages of an epidemic with removals, conditional on the epidemic having properly established itself. This problem can be solved by standard methods and it forms a convenient starting point for developing the technique to be applied to the simple epidemic. Since in this case N is infinite it is better to replace $y(s,t)$ by the actual density of infectives, $Y(s,t) = Ny(s,t)$. Then (2.1) reduces to

$$(3.1) \qquad \frac{\partial Y(s,t)}{\partial t} = \int_{-\infty}^{\infty} Y(s - u, t)\, dF(u),$$

a linear equation which can be handled by transform methods.

We shall study two types of solution, (i) a travelling wave moving with velocity c which maintains its shape, and (ii) the solution developing in time from a single infective at $s = 0$.

A wave travelling with velocity c must have the form

$$(3.2) \qquad Y(s,t) = f(s - ct) = f(z)$$

say, where $f(z)$ is a solution of

$$(3.3) \qquad -cf'(z) = \int_{-\infty}^{\infty} f(z - u)\, dF(u).$$

We need only consider $c > 0$ (the situation is symmetrical when $c < 0$). The simplest way of solving (3.3) is to try $f(z) = \exp(-\theta z)$. This will satisfy (3.3) provided θ is a root of the equation

$$(3.4) \qquad c = \Psi(\theta)/\theta.$$

Hence travelling waves are possible for every $c \geqq c_0$ and for no $c < c_0$, where c_0 is the minimum value of c such that

$$(3.5) \qquad c_0 = \Psi(\theta_0)/\theta_0 = \Psi'(\theta_0).$$

Provided $dF(u)$ dies away at least exponentially, there are two real roots $0 < \theta_1 < \theta_2$ of (3.4) for each $c > c_0$ and waves with velocity $c > c_0$ must have the form

$$(3.6) \qquad f(z) = P_1 \exp(-\theta_1 z) + P_2 \exp(-\theta_2 z).$$

When $c = c_0$, the solution is

$$(3.7) \qquad f(z) = (P + Qz)\exp(-\theta_0 z)$$

but since $f(z) \geqq 0$ for all z the term in z is not admissible. For the same reason we must have $P_1 \geqq 0, P_2 \geqq 0$ in (3.6).

Suppose now that there is a single infective initially at $s = 0$. As we are working with densities the initial condition is taken to be $Y(s,0) = \delta(s)$. It is readily found that

$$(3.8) \qquad M(\theta,t) = \int_{-\infty}^{\infty} e^{\theta s} f(s,t)\,ds = \exp\{\Psi(\theta)\}$$

and the required solution is

$$(3.9) \qquad Y(s,t) = \frac{1}{2\pi i} \int_{-i\infty}^{i\infty} \exp\{t\Psi(\theta) - s\theta\}\,d\theta.$$

The inversion cannot usually be performed explicitly, but when t is large one may either use a central limit approximation, following Bartlett, or the more accurate saddle point approximation

$$(3.10) \qquad Y(s,t) \sim \frac{\exp\{t\Psi(\hat{\theta}) - s\hat{\theta}\}}{\{2\pi t\,\Psi''(\hat{\theta})\}^{\frac{1}{2}}} \{1 + O(t^{-1})\},$$

$$t\Psi'(\hat{\theta}) = s.$$

The solution is symmetrical about $s = 0$ and we shall consider only $s > 0$.

As the shape of $Y(s,t)$ changes with time, it is necessary to decide on a definition of the rate of advance of the epidemic. In the analogous two-dimensional situation Bartlett [1] defined it to be the rate of increase of the radius beyond which there is a given total number of infectives, using the central limit approximation. In our case this amounts to using a diffusion approximation to (2.3), taking $\Psi(\theta) = 1 + \frac{1}{2}\sigma^2\theta^2$ in (3.8) and obtaining exactly

$$(3.11) \qquad Y(s,t) = \frac{\exp\{t - s^2/2t\sigma^2\}}{\sigma(2\pi t)^{\frac{1}{2}}}.$$

(The approximation (3.10) is also exact for this $\Psi(\theta)$.)

The distance $\pm s_1$ excluding a number n of infectives satisfies

$$(3.12) \qquad \tfrac{1}{2} n = e^t \{1 - \Phi(s_1/\sigma t^{\frac{1}{2}})\}$$

where Φ is the standard normal integral. If there is a limiting velocity $c = s_1/t$ for large t it must be found from the asymptotic form of (3.4), which is

(3.13)
$$n \sim \frac{\sigma}{c}\left(\frac{2}{\pi t}\right)^{\frac{1}{2}}\exp\{t - c^2 t/2\sigma^2\}.$$

This gives

(3.14)
$$c = \sigma\sqrt{2} + O(t^{-1}\log t).$$

However, the saddle point approximation leads to a different result. From (3.9) we have

(3.15)
$$\tfrac{1}{2}n = \int_{s_1}^{\infty} Y(s,t)ds = \frac{1}{2\pi i}\int_{-i\infty}^{i\infty}\exp\{t\Psi(\theta) - s_1\theta\}d\theta/\theta.$$

Its saddle point approximation for large t is

$$\tfrac{1}{2}n \sim \frac{\exp\{t\Psi(\hat{\theta}) - s_1\hat{\theta}\}}{\hat{\theta}\{2\pi t\Psi''(\hat{\theta})\}^{\frac{1}{2}}}\{1 + O(t^{-1})\},$$

(3.16)
$$t\Psi(\hat{\theta}) = s_1,$$

provided $\hat{\theta}$ is not small, which is ensured if s_1 is the same order as t. The value of $c = s_1/t$ satisfying (3.16) is

(3.17)
$$c = \Psi'(\hat{\theta}) = \Psi(\hat{\theta})/\hat{\theta} + O(t^{-1}\log t).$$

Consequently as t becomes large, $\hat{\theta} \to \theta_0$ and c tends to the minimal velocity c_0 defined in (3.5). In general this is not the same as $\sigma\sqrt{2}$, as Mollison has emphasised.

The discrepancy arises because, to exclude a *fixed* number of infectives, s_1 has to move progressively further into the tail of the distribution as t increases, and the relative accuracy of the normal approximation deteriorates there. It also follows easily from (3.10) that $Y(s,t)$ becomes proportional to $\exp\{-\theta_0(s - s_1)\}$ near $s_1 = c_0t$ as t becomes large, so that its shape becomes independent of t, as is proper for an advancing wave, though its height attenuates like $t^{-\frac{1}{2}}$.

4. An alternative aproximation technique. Travelling waves

We now approach the problem by an alternative approximation technique, previously described by Daniels [2]. This leads to the same results in the linear situation just discussed, but it has the advantage of being applicable to non-linear situations such as the simple epidemic. It consists in seeking an approximation to $l(s,t) = \log Y(s,t)$ in the following way. In terms of $l(s,t)$, (3.1) is

$$\frac{\partial l(s,t)}{\partial t} = \int_{-\infty}^{\infty} \exp\{l(s-u,t) - l(s,t)\}dF(u)$$

$$(4.1) \qquad = \int_{-\infty}^{\infty} \exp\left\{-u\frac{\partial l}{\partial s}\right\}\left\{1 + \tfrac{1}{2}u^2\frac{\partial^2 l}{\partial s^2} + \cdots\right\}dF(u)$$

$$= \Psi\left(-\frac{\partial l}{\partial s}\right) + \tfrac{1}{2}\Psi''\left(-\frac{\partial l}{\partial s}\right)\frac{\partial^2 l}{\partial s^2} + \cdots.$$

By including successive terms in (4.1) one obtains a sequence of approximating equations. The solution at each stage is used in the next equation to give a solution which one hopes will be a better approximation to $l(s,t)$.

A procedure of this kind usually implies the existence of a small parameter in terms of which the magnitude of the successive terms can be measured, using standard perturbation methods. In the case of an epidemic developing in the time from an initial infective, t is regarded as large and time can be rescaled to introduce the necessary small parameter. In the case of a travelling wave one could assume that c is large, but it is found that the method seems to work well over the whole range of $c \geq c_0$ owing to the successive derivatives being small. We shall therefore adopt a pragmatic approach, justifying the method by the fact that it leads to a solution having the right properties. Of course this is no substitute for a proper mathematical analysis, but it does enable us to look ahead a little.

As before, the travelling wave is first discussed. Writing

$$l(s,t) = g(s - ct) = g(z) = \log f(z),$$

(4.1) becomes

$$(4.2) \qquad -cg' = \Psi(-g') - \tfrac{1}{2}\Psi''(-g')g'' + \cdots.$$

The first approximation $g_1(z)$ satisfies

$$(4.3) \qquad -cg_1' = \Psi(-g_1').$$

The solution is

$$(4.4) \qquad g_1 = -\theta z + A$$

where θ is one of the roots θ_1, θ_2 of (3.4) and A is an arbitrary constant. The second approximation $g_2(z)$ satisfies

(4.5)
$$- cg_2' = \Psi(- g_2') + \tfrac{1}{2}\Psi''(- g_2')g_2''.$$

Assuming the last term is small we replace g_2 by g_1 in it. Since g_1'' and higher derivatives of (4.4) all vanish it could be concluded that (4.5) and all subsequent equations yield the solution (4.4), which is therefore exact. This is true, but it is not the whole story.

Let $g_2 = g_1 + m$ and suppose that m is small. Then, to the first order in m, (4.5) gives

(4.6)
$$\{\Psi'(\theta) - c\}m' = 0$$

so that provided $c - c_0$ is not small, $m' = 0$ and g_2 is essentially the same as (4.4). But if $c - c_0$ is small the coefficient of m' is of the order of terms neglected and we have to retain these. For simplicity consider $c = c_0$. Retaining m'' and $(m')^2$ in the expansion of (4.5) we get

(4.7)
$$- c_0 m' = - \Psi'(\theta_0)m' + \tfrac{1}{2}\Psi''(\theta_0)(m')^2 + \tfrac{1}{2}\Psi''(\theta_0)m''$$

which reduces to $m'' = - (m')^2$ and has the solution $m = \log(P + Qz)$. Hence $f_2(z) = (P + Qz)\exp(- \theta_0 z)$ which recovers (3.7) exactly. The case where $c - c_0$ is small is not much more difficult to deal with and yields (3.6) with θ_1, θ_2 replaced by approximate values near θ_0.

This situation has been examined in some detail because similar considerations arise with the simple epidemic near its critical velocity.

5. Solution for a particular initial distribution

We turn now to the solution developing from the initial distribution $Y(s,0) = \delta(s)$. The first approximating equation is

(5.1)
$$\frac{\partial l_1}{\partial t} = \Psi\left(- \frac{\partial l_1}{\partial s} \right).$$

Writing $\partial l_1/\partial s = - \theta$, $\partial l_1/\partial t = \Psi(\theta)$, we get the complete integral

(5.2)
$$l_1(s,t) = t\Psi(\theta) - \theta s + A,$$

θ and A being arbitrary constants. (It is really (4.4) in another guise.) We would like to write $A = A(\theta)$ so that the one-parameter envelope of (5.2) satisfies the initial conditions and is therefore the required first approximation $l_1(s,t)$. Unfortunately when t is small $\partial^2 l/\partial s^2$ may be large and the approximation is not valid. $A(\theta)$ cannot therefore be determined in this way: all we can say is that

$$(5.3) \qquad l_1(s, t) = t\Psi(\theta) - s\theta + A(\theta),$$

$$(5.4) \qquad 0 = t\Psi'(\theta) - s + A'(\theta).$$

The second approximate equation is

$$(5.5) \qquad \frac{\partial l_2}{\partial t} = \Psi\left(-\frac{\partial l_2}{\partial s}\right) + \tfrac{1}{2}\Psi''\left(-\frac{\partial l_2}{\partial s}\right)\frac{\partial^2 l_2}{\partial s^2}.$$

Assuming $l_2 - l_1 = m$ is small, replacing l_2 by l_1 in the last term and ignoring $(\partial m/\partial s)^2$ we get

$$(5.6) \qquad \frac{\partial m}{\partial t} + \Psi'(\theta)\frac{\partial m}{\partial s} = -\tfrac{1}{2}\Psi''(\theta)\frac{\partial\theta}{\partial s}.$$

Using (5.4) to calculate $\partial\theta/\partial s$, and transforming (5.6) to new variables θ, t it is found that

$$(5.7) \qquad \left(\frac{\partial m}{\partial t}\right)_\theta = -\frac{\Psi''(\theta)}{2\{t\Psi''(\theta) + A''(\theta)\}}.$$

Hence

$$(5.8) \qquad m = -\tfrac{1}{2}\log\{t\Psi''(\theta) + A''(\theta)\} + B(\theta).$$

Our object is not to develop the method as a self-contained technique, but to use known results for the linear problem to help solve the non-linear problem of the simple epidemic. The saddle point approximation (3.10) makes the correct allowance for the initial behaviour. It requires us to take $A(\theta) = 0$, $B(\theta) = -\tfrac{1}{2}\log 2\pi$, in which case

$$l_2(s, t) = t\Psi(\theta) - s\theta - \tfrac{1}{2}\log\{2\pi t\Psi''(\theta)\},$$
$$(5.9)$$
$$0 = t\Psi'(\theta) - s.$$

Then (5.9) can be used as the solution to which the corresponding $l_2(s,t)$ for the simple epidemic must reduce during its early stages of development.

6. The non-linear problem

The equation for the simple epidemic is

$$(6.1) \qquad \frac{\partial Y(s,t)}{\partial t} = \{1 - N^{-1}Y(s,t)\} \int_{-\infty}^{\infty} Y(s-u,t)dF(u).$$

We shall continue to work with Y rather than y in order to link up with the previous case. With $l(s,t) = \log Y(s,t)$, (6.1) becomes

$$(6.2) \qquad \frac{\partial l}{\partial t} = (1 - N^{-1}e^l) \left\{ \Psi\left(-\frac{\partial l}{\partial s}\right) + \tfrac{1}{2}\Psi''\left(-\frac{\partial l}{\partial s}\right)\frac{\partial^2 l}{\partial s^2} + \cdots \right\}.$$

Again, the case of a travelling wave is first discussed. Write $s - ct = z$, $l(s,t) = g(z) = \log f(z)$. The first approximate equation for g is

$$(6.3) \qquad -cg_1' = (1 - N^{-1}e^{g_1})\Psi(-g_1').$$

The most direct way of finding g_1 is to solve for g_1' and integrate, but it is more convenient to introduce the parameter $g_1' = -\theta$. From (6.3),

$$(6.4) \qquad g_1 = \log N\left\{1 - \frac{c\theta}{\Psi(\theta)}\right\},$$

and

$$(6.5) \qquad -\theta = \frac{dg_1}{dz} = \frac{c\{\theta\Psi'(\theta) - \Psi(\theta)\}}{\Psi(\theta)\{\Psi(\theta) - c\theta\}}\frac{d\theta}{dz},$$

which yields

$$(6.6) \qquad z = c\int \frac{\{\Psi(\theta) - \theta\Psi'(\theta)\}d\theta}{\theta\Psi(\theta)\{\Psi(\theta) - c\theta\}}.$$

The solution is given in parametric form by (6.4) and (6.6).

Because the integrand of (6.6) has poles at $\theta = 0$, θ_1, θ_2, θ can only be allowed to range over one of the intervals $(0, \theta_1)$, (θ_1, θ_2), $(\theta_2, \bar{\theta})$ where $\bar{\theta}$ is the upper limit of θ. We can exclude (θ_1, θ_2) since g_1 must be real. Of the other two, only $0 < \theta < \theta_1$ allows z to range over the whole real line. It is therefore the appropriate interval for a travelling wave and (6.6) is taken to be

$$(6.7) \qquad z = c\int_a^\theta \frac{\{\Psi(u) - u\Psi'(u)\}}{u\Psi(u)\{\Psi(u) - cu\}}du,$$

where a is an arbitrary value in $(0, \theta_1)$. As θ varies from 0 to θ_1, z varies from $-\infty$ to $+\infty$ and $f_1 = \exp g_1$ varies from N to 0.

The solution should reduce to (4.4) when $N \to \infty$. This is most readily verified by writing (6.7) in the alternative form (obtained on integration by parts),

$$(6.8) \qquad z = -\frac{g_1(z)}{\theta} + \frac{g_1(0)}{a} - \int_a^\theta \log N \left\{ 1 - \frac{cu}{\Psi(u)} \right\} \frac{du}{u^2}.$$

If $c - c_0$ is not small, $\theta_1 - \theta$ and $\theta_1 - a$ have to be $O(N^{-1})$ for $f_1 = \exp g_1$ to be of moderate size. It then follows that $z = (g_1(0) - g_1)/\theta_1 + O(N^{-1})$ which tends to (4.4) with $\theta = \theta_1$. When $c - c_0$ is small the argument is more complicated but the result is the same.

Mollison proved that for every $c \geqq c_0$ there is a unique travelling wave for the simple epidemic. We have verified that it reduces, when $N \to \infty$, to the exponential travelling wave with the *lower* root θ_1 of (3.4).

The second approximate equation is

$$(6.9) \qquad \frac{-g_2'}{(1 - N^{-1} e^{g_2})} - \Psi(-g_2') = \tfrac{1}{2} \Psi''(-g_2') g_2''.$$

Suppose that c is not near c_0. Write $g_2 = g_1 + m$, replace g_2 by g_1 in the last term, and ignore $(m')^2$, m^2, m''. Then

$$(6.10) \qquad -\frac{cm'}{(1 - N^{-1} e^{g_1})} - \frac{c g_1' N^{-1} e^{g_1}}{(1 - N^{-1} e^{g_1})^2} m + \Psi'(-g_1') m'$$

$$= \tfrac{1}{2} \Psi''(-g_1') g_1''.$$

Since $g_1'' = -d\theta/dz$, one can use (6.5) and (6.4) to express (6.10) in terms of θ as

$$(6.11) \qquad \frac{dm}{d\theta} - \frac{m}{\theta} = \frac{\theta \Psi''(\theta)}{2\{\Psi(\theta) - \theta \Psi'(\theta)\}}.$$

Hence

$$(6.12) \qquad m = \tfrac{1}{2} \theta \int_a^\theta \frac{\Psi''(u)\, du}{\{\Psi(u) - u \Psi'(u)\}}.$$

As a check we observe that when N is large, $\theta_1 - \theta$ and $\theta_1 - a$ have to be $O(N^{-1})$, assuming $c - c_0$ is not small, and hence that $m \to 0$ as $N \to \infty$ as was previously found. Notice also that when $\theta \to 0$, $m \to 0$, so that the second order correction vanishes as f_1 approaches N.

The choice of a as the lower limit of integration was arbitrary. A different choice would add an amount $k\theta$ to m, where k is some constant. Since $k\theta = -kg_1'$ this is merely equivalent to replacing z by $z - k$ in $g_1(z)$, or $g_2(z)$, to the same order.

When $c - c_0$ is small the expansion leading to (6.11) may be expected to become invalid as $\theta \to \theta_0$ since the denominator on the right is then small. (The situation is similar to the one discussed at the end of Section 4.) But fortunately this only occurs at those values of z for which f_1 is small, and the calculations in the next section show that m remains small over most of the effective range of z even when $c = c_0$.

7. Computations for travelling waves

Travelling waves were computed using the above formulae for three contact distributions: the double exponential, the Gaussian and the diffusion approximation. Scaled to unit standard deviation these have $\Psi(\theta)$ equal to $1/(1 - \frac{1}{2}\theta^2)$, $\exp\frac{1}{2}\theta^2$, $1 + \frac{1}{2}\theta^2$ respectively, and the corresponding critical velocities c_0 are $3\sqrt{6}/4 = 1.837$, $\sqrt{e} = 1.649$ and $\sqrt{2} = 1.414$. The natural quantity to consider is the relative density $\phi(z) = N^{-1}f(z)$. Following Mollison the results are presented in terms of $T = -z/c = t - s/c$ rather than z, a form more suited to the growth of the epidemic in time at a fixed point s. The origin of z or T was chosen to make $\phi(0) = \frac{1}{2}$. It is easy to see that when $c \to \infty$ the solution reduces to the logistic function $1/(1 + e^{-T})$ in all cases.

For the double exponential Mollison [6] computed the exact solution numerically from his differential equation, for velocities c_0 and $2c_0$. He found that even at the minimum velocity c_0 the form of ϕ was remarkably close to that of $1/(1 + e^{-T})$, a result which must surely have a simple explanation. Table 1 shows our calculations of ϕ_1, ϕ_2 and $1/(1 + e^{-T})$ for the three contact distributions. (In the diffusion case, (6.7) easily integrates explicitly: in the other two cases it was found more convenient to integrate it numerically. In all cases (6.12) has a simple explicit integral.) We find in the three cases that ϕ_2 is very close to $1/(1 + e^{-T})$ and that $\phi_2 - \phi_1$ is small over the whole range. The latter fact, and the agreement with the logistic function in the double exponential case, gives one confidence in the approximation technique.

TABLE 1

Travelling wave approximations at the critical velocity c_0 for three contact distributions

	Double exponential				Gaussian				Diffusion		
T	ϕ_1	ϕ_2	$1/(1+e^{-T})$	T	ϕ_1	ϕ_2	$1/(1+e^{-T})$	T	ϕ_1	ϕ_2	$1/(1+e^{-T})$
−4.152	.0061	.0139	.0156	−3.613	.0103	.0224	.0263	−3.663	.0055	.0165	.0250
−3.303	.0196	.0337	.0357	−3.043	.0235	.0416	.0455	−3.172	.0131	.0306	.0402
−2.745	.0403	.0591	.0607	−2.612	.0422	.0656	.0683	−2.794	.0244	.0479	.0577
−2.316	.0676	.0893	.0902	−2.256	.0666	.0925	.0948	−2.475	.0400	.0685	.0776
−1.958	.1013	.1241	.1242	−1.944	.0967	.1242	.1252	−2.191	.0604	.0927	.1006
−1.645	.1409	.1632	.1624	−1.662	.1324	.1600	.1595	−1.852	.0861	.1207	.1356
−1.361	.1859	.2065	.2049	−1.398	.1737	.1999	.1981	−1.679	.1177	.1530	.1573
−1.095	.2360	.2533	.2517	−1.147	.2205	.2440	.2411	−1.436	.1555	.1898	.1921
−0.840	.2907	.3048	.3026	−0.902	.2725	.2922	.2886	−1.197	.2000	.2317	.2321
−0.591	.3500	.3583	.3576	−0.660	.3295	.3447	.3408	−0.955	.2516	.2789	.2779
−0.341	.4124	.4180	.4166	−0.415	.3912	.4014	.3978	−0.703	.3103	.3320	.3311
−0.089	.4785	.4798	.4794	−0.162	.4572	.4622	.4595	−0.451	.3764	.3911	.3892
0.179	.5475	.5450	.5459	0.103	.5272	.5271	.5258	−0.177	.4495	.4569	.4559
0.466	.6191	.6133	.6156	0.391	.6005	.5961	.5966	0.121	.5294	.5294	.5301
0.788	.6927	.6848	.6883	0.714	.6768	.6691	.6714	0.456	.6154	.6089	.6121
1.168	.7681	.7592	.7636	1.097	.7555	.7461	.7500	0.853	.7066	.6957	.7011
1.661	.8447	.8366	.8410	1.594	.8360	.8269	.8312	1.565	.8020	.7896	.7965
2.438	.9202	.9150	.9200	2.375	.9177	.9115	.9149	2.162	.9002	.8911	.8967
2.875	.9481	.9443	.9483	2.919	.9506	.9465	.9488	2.743	.9401	.9337	.9395
3.590	.9740	.9733	.9733	4.051	.9835	.9820	.9829	3.852	.9800	.9776	.9792

Similar calculations, not shown here, were made for $c = 2c_0$. The results came intermediate between those for $c = c_0$ and $c = \infty$.

8. Time-dependent solution for a particular initial distribution

Finally we briefly discuss the solution developing in time from $Y(s, 0) = \delta(s)$. A full treatment will appear in a subsequent paper. The first approximate equation is

$$(8.1) \qquad \frac{\partial l_1}{\partial t} = (1 - N^{-1}e^{l_1})\Psi\left(-\frac{\partial l_1}{\partial s}\right).$$

A complete integral of (8.1) can be found from the wave solution (6.4), (6.6) by writing $z = s - ct + b$ and regarding c and b as arbitrary constants. But it turns out that for the solution to reduce to (5.9) when $N \to \infty$ we must take the range $\theta_2 < \theta < \bar{\theta}$ in this case. Using the form analogous to (6.8), the complete integral is

$$(8.2) \qquad l_1 = \log N \left\{ 1 - \frac{c\theta}{\Psi(\theta)} \right\},$$

$$(8.3) \qquad ct - s - b = \frac{l_1}{\theta} - \int_\theta^{\bar{\theta}} \log N \left\{ 1 - \frac{cu}{\Psi(u)} \right\} \frac{du}{u^2}.$$

The required solution of (8.1) is the appropriate envelope of (8.2), (8.3) with $b = b(c)$. As before it is found that $b = 0$ is a suitable choice. The envelope requires that $\partial l_1/\partial c = 0$. On differentiating (8.3) with respect to c (remembering that θ is a function of c) and using (8.2) it is found that

$$(8.4) \qquad t = \int_\theta^{\bar{\theta}} \frac{du}{u\{\Psi(u) - cu\}},$$

and using the alternative form

$$(8.5) \qquad ct - s = c \int_\theta^{\bar{\theta}} \frac{\{\Psi(u) - u\Psi'(u)\}}{u\Psi(u)\{\Psi(u) - cu\}},$$

we also get

$$(8.6) \qquad s = c \int_\theta^{\bar{\theta}} \frac{\Psi'(u)du}{\Psi(u)\{\Psi(u) - cu\}}.$$

The three equations (8.2), (8.4) and (8.6) give the required first approximation l_1 in terms of the two parameters c and θ. Computation can be carried
out by calculating l_1, s, t over the range of θ at given values of c and
interpolating to find how l_1 varies with s for given t.

We shall not discuss the second approximation here—it can be found
much as before, though the details are more complicated.

References

[1] BARTLETT, M. S. (1960) *Stochastic Population Models*. Methuen, London.

[2] DANIELS, H. E. (1960) Approximate solutions of Green's type for univariate
stochastic processes. *J. R. Statist. Soc.* B **22**, 376–401.

[3] FISHER, R. A. (1937) The wave of advance of advantageous genes. *Ann. Eugen.* **7**,
355–369.

[4] KENDALL, D. G. (1965) Mathematical models of the spread of infection. *Mathematics and Computer Science in Biology and Medicine*. Medical Research Council. 213–225.

[5] KOLMOGOROFF, A. N., PETROVSKY, I. AND PISCOUNOFF, N. (1937) Étude de
l'équation de la diffusion avec croissance de la quantité de matière et son application à un
problème biologique. *Bull. de l'Univ. d'État à Moscou.* **A1** fasc. 6, 1–25.

[6] MOLLISON, D. (1972) Possible velocities for a simple epidemic. *Adv. Appl. Prob.* **4**,
233–257.

[7] MOLLISON, D. (1972) The rate of spatial propagation of simple epidemics. *Proc.
Sixth Berkeley Symp. Math. Statist. Prob.* **3**, 579–614.

The Distribution of DNA
in Exponentially-Growing
Cell Populations

P. D. M. MACDONALD

Abstract

This paper illustrates a simple method of deriving distributions for samples from cell populations in exponential growth. The distribution of the elapsed proportion of the DNA-synthetic phase of the cell cycle is derived and used to find the distribution of DNA content in a random sample of cells. Allowing for a normally-distributed measurement error, the resulting distribution agrees well with DNA distributions observed empirically. The statistical analysis of DNA distributions, and the interpretation of the distributional parameters in terms of cell population kinetics, are discussed and illustrated with an example.

1. Introduction

The work described in this contribution owes much to Bartlett, both directly, for his own work on models for cell populations, and indirectly, for the time I spent as his student, benefitting from his mathematical intuition and appreciating his use of mathematics to simplify the analysis of biological problems.

The earliest investigations into the mitotic cell cycle divided the cycle into two main phases: mitosis, which is the visible act of cell division, and interphase, the period between mitoses. While it is apparent that a cell must synthesize DNA to replicate its chromosomes during interphase, chromosomes are not usually visible under a light microscope during this phase. Two techniques that have been developed to study this DNA-synthetic activity are thymidine labelling and Feulgen staining. Thymidine is a specific precursor of DNA. Making tritiated thymidine (H^3Tdr) available to a cell population will radioactively label any cells then

387

synthesizing DNA, and individual labelled cells can be detected later by autoradiography. The Feulgen reaction stains DNA specifically. The Feulgen dye content of a cell after staining is proportional to its DNA content, and the dye content of individual cells can be measured by miscrospectrophotometry or microdensitometry. Cleaver (1967) gives a comprehensive review of fundamental work with these methods.

After it was established that DNA synthesis generally occurs during a discrete period within interphase (Howard and Pelc (1953)), it became conventional to study the cell cycle as a sequence of four phases called G_1, S, G_2 and M, where S denotes DNA synthesis, M denoted mitosis and G_1 and G_2 are 'gap' phases. Cell proliferation can be modelled by a multiphase branching process and interest has centered on the average durations of the four phases (see, for example, Barlow and Macdonald (1973)).

Unless the proliferative characteristics of the cells are changing rapidly or strong external factors are forcing synchrony of each generation, a cell population will approach a steady state of asynchronous, exponential growth. Typically, this state may be attained reasonably well after just a few generations. Certain characteristics of the population then become stable; for example, the distributions of age-in-phase or age-in-cycle and the relative proportions of cells in the different phases. The stable distributions can be deduced from an appropriate mathematical model for cell proliferation and, from this basis, data from thymidine-labelling or Feulgen-staining experiments on exponentially-growing cell populations can lead to inferences about the proliferative characteristics of the cells.

Experimental evidence has led some workers to classify cells as 'proliferating' and 'nonproliferating', although this concept is difficult to define precisely (Cleaver (1967), Steel (1968), Clowes (1971). Suppose that we are observing a cell population and see a cell divide. One or both of its daughter cells will probably divide again after a period of time. The length of this period will vary from one cell to another and this variability defines the distribution of cycle duration for the proliferating cells. There may also be cells which never come into division, even when observed for a time which is very long relative to that distribution, and these are the nonproliferating cells. The presence of nonproliferating cells explains why population doubling times are often much longer than their corresponding average proliferative cycle durations. The conceptual difficulty is in distinguishing between nonproliferating cells and cells which happen to have very long cycles, particularly when the nonproliferating cells have not lost the capacity to divide but may be brought into division very quickly by some stimulus to the population. The proliferating cells constitute a fraction of the population which has been called the 'growth fraction' in the literature. I shall adopt the more explicit term 'proliferative fraction' and postulate a distribution of cycle duration to characterize the proliferating cells.

It should be safe to assume that any cell observed in mitosis is a proliferating cell. Hence an experimental technique such as the fraction-labelled mitoses curve, in which only mitotic cells are observed, will yield inferences about the proliferative cells alone (Macdonald (1970), (1974)). In particular, the distribution of cycle duration of the proliferating cells can be estimated by this technique.

In some cell populations it may also be safe to assume that cells synthesizing DNA are proliferating cells. However, nonproliferating cells may sometimes undergo endomitotic cycles, replicating their chromosomes but not dividing, to become endopolyploid. Endopolyploidy can be detected by a Feulgen-staining experiment to determine the distribution of DNA content. Assuming a cell to be diploid, its normal DNA content in G_1 is denoted by $2C$ and its normal DNA content in G_2 and M is then $4C$. DNA measurements are subject to some error, and a typical distribution of DNA content will show peaks corresponding to $2C, 4C, 8C, 16C, \cdots$, up to the highest level of ploidy found (which will be $4C$ if no endoreduplication occurs). Cells in S and endo-S will contribute some probability between the peaks and the shape of this contribution will depend on the kinetics of the population. Gregor (1969) analysed such a distribution by fitting a mixture of normal distributions, but not considering the underlying structure of the distribution.

Various authors have considered DNA distributions with no endopolyploidy and estimated the relative proportions of cells at the G_1, S and $G_2 + M$ levels of DNA content by inspecting the histogram (Cleaver (1967)). Reddy *et al.* (1973), working with an exponentially-growing population with no nonproliferating cells, found such results to be consistent with those obtained from a fraction-labelled mitoses curve. Dean and Jett (1974) devised a method for analysing the DNA distribution, using a second-order polynomial to represent the distribution of DNA in cells sampled from the S phase and assuming the measurement error to be normally distributed.

This paper shows how an exact mathematical expression may be derived for the distribution of DNA in a cell population experiencing exponential growth with no endoreduplication. The main assumption is that a scale of measurement can be chosen so that the DNA content of a cell in S is, in that scale, linearly related to the fraction of S which has already elapsed. For example, DNA contents should be measured on a linear scale if the rate of synthesis is constant throughout S, or on a logarithmic scale if the rate of synthesis increases proportionally with DNA content. It is also assumed that, in the scale chosen, the measurement error is normally distributed with constant variance. In practice, these assumptions will usually be satisfied to a sufficiently close approximation. Methods of estimating the parameters of the DNA distribution are then considered. In experiments where the same population, or a replicate population, was also studied by thymidine labelling, the results of the two techniques may be combined to deduce what proportion of the nonproliferating cells have completed DNA synthesis.

2. Limiting age distributions for a multiphase branching proceess

Bartlett (1969), (1970) and Brockwell and Kuo (1973) have studied the asymptotic properties of a multiphase branching process with correlated phases. Macdonald (1973) derived the limiting distributions from results previously established for a single-phase branching process (Harris (1963)). The present work is based on certain of these distributions and the notation of Macdonald (1973) will be followed. The assumptions and results which will be needed are quoted below, without proof.

Successive cycles are assumed to be independent. Subscripts 1, 2, 3, 4 denote phases G_1, S, G_2, M, respectively, and are combined to denote combined phases: 12, for instance, denotes phase G_1 and S combined. The subscript 1234, denoting a complete cycle, is usually omitted. A superscript* will denote Laplace transformation. The durations of the four phases in one cycle are distributed according to some probability density function $\phi_{1,2,3,4}(u_1, u_2, u_3, u_4)$. After a mitosis, on average, A daughter cells remain in the proliferative population. Clearly, $A \leq 2$ and the limiting distributions will not exist unless $A \geq 1$. If $A > 1$, the population will approach a state of exponential growth with Malthusian parameter k given by the positive root of the equation

(1) $$A\phi^*(k) = 1,$$

where

$$\phi^*(k) \equiv \phi^*_{1,2,3,4}(k, k, k, k)$$

is the Laplace transform of the probability density function for total cycle duration.

The joint probability that a cell chosen at random from an exponentially-growing population is in Phase 2, having spent time u_1 in Phase 1 and attained age x in Phase 2, and is to remain an additional time y in Phase 2, then spend times u_3 and u_4 in Phases 3 and 4, respectively, is given by

$$(2) \qquad \frac{A}{A-1} \, ke^{-k(u_1+x)} \, \phi_{1,2,3,4}(u_1, x + y, u_3, u_4)du_1 \, dx \, dy \, du_3 \, du_4.$$

This is an example of the basic formula, from which any required distribution may be derived.

The duration of Phase 2, for a cell sampled just as it enters that phase, is given by y conditional on $x = 0$. Hence the probability density function is

$$(3) \qquad h_2(y) = \int_0^\infty e^{-kv} \phi_{1,2}(v, y)dv / \phi^*_1(k),$$

where ϕ_1 and $\phi_{1,2}$ are appropriate marginal distributions of $\phi_{1,2,3,4}$. Note that h_2 and ϕ_2 will differ unless Phases 1 and 2 are statistically independent. For a phase such as 12, however, which starts at the beginning of the cycle, $h_{12} \equiv \phi_{12}$.

Factorizations of the form $h^*_{23}(k) = h^*_2(k)h^*_3(k)$ hold, but, in general, only for argument k. In many respects, the dependent-phase process defined by $\phi_{1,2,3,4}$ gives rise to the same age and phase structure in the population as does an independent-phase process defined by h_1, h_2, h_3, h_4. Hence experiments which involve sampling from the population may lead to inferences about the h_i distributions, but not about the ϕ_i distributions. However, the moments of h_i differ from those of ϕ_i by $O(k)$, if they differ at all.

The fractions of the proliferative population in Phases 1, 2 and 34 are given by

$$(4) \qquad P_1 = \{A/(A-1)\}\{1 - h^*_1(k)\}$$

$$(5) \qquad P_2 = \{A/(A-1)\} \, h^*_1(k)\{1 - h^*_2(k)\}$$

$$(6) \qquad P_{34} = \{A/(A-1)\} \, h^*_{12}(k)\{1 - h^*_{34}(k)\},$$

respectively. For most cell populations, $k \ll 1$ and the approximation

$$(7) \qquad h_i^*(k) = \exp\{-\mu_i k + \tfrac{1}{2}\sigma_i^2 k^2 + O(k^3)\}$$

may be useful, where μ_i and σ_i^2 denote the mean and variance, respectively, of h_i.

3. The elapsed proportion of a phase

Suppose that a cell has been selected at random from an exponentially-growing population. Given that it is in the S phase, we are interested to know what proportion of its total S phase has already elapsed. The distribution of this proportion is derived from the basic formula (2) as the conditional distribution of $r = x/(x + y)$, given that the cell is in S.

Dividing (2) by (5) to condition on the cell being in S, letting $u_2 = x + y$, and integrating out u_1, u_3 and u_4, gives the joint probability density of x and u_2 as

$$(8) \qquad ke^{-kx}h_2(u_2)/\{1 - h_2^*(k)\}, \qquad 0 \le x \le u_2, \qquad 0 \le u_2 < \infty.$$

Setting $r = x/u_2$ and integrating out u_2 then gives the required probability density:

$$\rho(r) = k \int_0^\infty u_2 e^{-ku_2 r} h_2(u_2) du_2 / \{1 - h_2^*(k)\}$$

$$(9)$$

$$= -kh_2^{*\prime}(kr)/\{1 - h_2^*(k)\}, \qquad 0 \le r \le 1,$$

where the prime denotes differentiation.

Since $\mu_2 > 0$ and $\{1 - h_2^*(k)\} > 0$, and it follows from the definition of $h_2^*(s)$ that

$$(-1)^\nu h_2^{*(\nu)}(s) > 0, \qquad \nu = 0, 1, 2, \cdots,$$

the density curve $\rho(r)$ will be strictly decreasing, with slope strictly increasing towards zero, whatever the underlying distribution $\phi_{1,2,3,4}$.

Some special cases of $\rho(r)$ are of interest.

(a) *Deterministic phase duration*

If the S phase is deterministic, of duration μ_2, then $h_2^*(s) = \exp(-\mu_2 s)$

and (9) becomes

(9a) $$\theta e^{-\theta r}/\{1 - e^{-\theta}\}, \qquad 0 \leq r \leq 1,$$

where $\theta = \mu_2 k$, which is a truncated negative exponential distribution.

(b) Gamma distribution of phase duration

If h_2 is a gamma distribution with shape parameter $\alpha = (\mu_2/\sigma_2)^2$ and scale parameter $\lambda = \mu_2/\sigma_2^2$, then $h_2^*(s) = (1 + s\lambda^{-1})^{-\alpha}$ and (9) becomes

(9b) $$\theta \left(1 + \frac{\theta r}{\alpha}\right)^{-(\alpha+1)} \bigg/ \left\{1 - \left(1 + \frac{\theta}{\alpha}\right)^{-\alpha}\right\}, \qquad 0 \leq r \leq 1,$$

where $\theta = \mu_2 k$.

Note that θr follows a truncated central F distribution on 2 over 2α degrees of freedom, which approaches a truncated exponential distribution as $\alpha \to \infty$.

(c) General distribution of phase duration, with small k

If μ_2 and σ_2^2 denote the mean and variance, respectively, of h_2, and k is small, the approximation (7) may be used in (9) to give the probability density

(9c) $$\theta \left(1 - \frac{\theta r}{\alpha}\right) e^{-\theta r(1-(\theta r/2\alpha))}/\{1 - e^{-\theta(1-(\theta/2\alpha))}\}, \qquad 0 \leq r \leq 1,$$

where $\theta = \mu_2 k$, $\alpha = (\mu_2/\sigma_2)^2$. The approximation is valid so long as $(1 - \theta/2\alpha) > 0$; that is, $\mu_2 > \frac{1}{2}\sigma_2^2 k$.

As $k \to 0$, or $\theta \to 0$, (9c) approaches (9a). In the limit, (9) becomes a uniform distribution on the interval $(0, 1)$.

(d) Normal distribution of phase duration

A normal distribution may be assumed for h_2, provided that the negative tail is negligible; in practice, $\mu_2 > 2 \cdot 5\sigma_2$ is an adequate criterion. Since

$$h_2^*(s) = \exp\{-\mu_2 s + \tfrac{1}{2}\sigma_2^2 s^2\},$$

we find that $\rho(r)$ is again given by (9c).

4. The distribution of DNA content

Assuming that no endoreduplication occurs, there will be a mixture of cells at the $2C$ level of DNA content, cells at the $4C$ level, and cells in the S phase which are somewhere in between these two levels. Little is known about the pattern of DNA synthesis within the S phase. The relationship between rate of synthesis and DNA content can be determined by exposing cells to tritiated thymidine for a short time, staining the cells by Feulgen's method, and measuring both radioactivity (which indicates rate of synthesis) and dye content (which indicates DNA content) for a sample of cells (Cleaver (1967), Section 5.6). The results suggest that, at least in some cells, the rate of synthesis increases more or less linearly with DNA content, although the rather wide scatter of the experimental points precludes a more detailed conclusion. Hence it might sometimes be reasonable to assume that, when a fraction r of the S phase has elapsed, the cell has DNA content

$$(10) \qquad\qquad d = c\,2^r,$$

where $c = 2C$ is the normal content of a G_1 cell. Alternatively, if DNA synthesis proceeds at a constant rate throughout S, the appropriate relation would be

$$(11) \qquad\qquad d = c(1 + r).$$

The units of d and c will be those of the microphotometer or microdensitometer scale; calibration in terms of mass of DNA will depend on the staining technique as well as the calibration of the instrument.

In general, let us assume that a scale of measurement can be found such that DNA content, measured on that scale, is linearly related to the proportion of the S phase which has elapsed. That is,

$$(12) \qquad\qquad y = c_1 + (c_3 - c_1)r,$$

where r is the elapsed proportion, y is the DNA content at that point, and c_1 and c_3 are, respectively, the G_1 and G_2 DNA contents, on that scale of measurement. For example, if (10) holds, the microdensitometer readings should be transformed to logarithms to the base 2, so that $y = \log_2 d$, $c_1 = \log_2 c$, and $(c_3 - c_1) = 1$. If (11) holds, the appropriate scale is linear, with $y = d$, $c_1 = c$ and $(c_3 - c_1) = c$.

The probability density function for the DNA content of a cell randomly chosen from S is thus found from (9) and (12) to be

(13) $\quad \delta(y) = -\dfrac{k}{c_3 - c_1} h_2^{*\prime}\left(k\dfrac{y - c_1}{c_3 - c_1}\right)\Big/\{1 - h_2^*(k)\}, \qquad c_1 \leqq y \leqq c_3.$

For most cell populations, however, $\theta = \mu_2 k$ is small enough that (9a) gives an adequate approximation to (9), and the density (13) may be approximated by

(13a) $\qquad \delta(y) = \omega e^{-\omega(y - c_1)}/\{1 - e^{-\omega(c_3 - c_1)}\}, \qquad c_1 \leqq y \leqq c_3,$

where $\omega = \theta/(c_3 - c_1)$.

The DNA measurements will be made with some error and usually it will be reasonable to assume that the observed value x is displaced from the true value y by an independent normal error, with mean zero and variance η^2, which does not depend on y. The distribution of DNA measurements on S-phase cells is thus given by the density

(14) $\qquad \beta_2(x) = \displaystyle\int_{c_1}^{c_3} \dfrac{1}{\sqrt{(2\pi)}\eta} \exp\left[-\tfrac{1}{2}\left(\dfrac{x - y}{\eta}\right)^2\right]\delta(y)\,dy.$

In general, this will require numerical integration. However, if (13a) is used for $\delta(y)$, the result

(14a) $\quad \beta_2(x) = \dfrac{\omega e^{-\omega(x - c_1)}}{1 - e^{-\omega(c_3 - c_1)}}\, e^{\frac{1}{2}(\omega\eta)^2}\left\{P\left(\dfrac{c_3 - x}{\eta} + \omega\eta\right) - P\left(\dfrac{c_1 - x}{\eta} + \omega\eta\right)\right\}$

is obtained, where $P(\,\cdot\,)$ denotes the standard normal probability integral. This form of the distribution should suffice for most practical work.

We have assumed that all cells in the population are either at the $2C$ level, in S, or at the $4C$ level. Denote the proportions of cells in these three categories by π_1, π_2, π_3, respectively, where $\pi_1 + \pi_2 + \pi_3 = 1$. DNA measurements on the $2C$ and $4C$ cells will follow the probability densities

(15) $\qquad\qquad \beta_1(x) = \dfrac{1}{\sqrt{(2\pi)}\eta}\, \exp\left[-\tfrac{1}{2}\left(\dfrac{x - c_1}{\eta}\right)^2\right]$

and

(16) $\qquad\qquad \beta_3(x) = \dfrac{1}{\sqrt{(2\pi)}\eta}\, \exp\left[-\tfrac{1}{2}\left(\dfrac{x - c_3}{\eta}\right)^2\right],$

respectively. Thus the observed distribution of DNA measurements will be the distribution mixture

(17) $\qquad\qquad \beta(x) = \pi_1\beta_1(x) + \pi_2\beta_2(x) + \pi_3\beta_3(x).$

An example of this distribution is shown in Figure 1. The distribution involves five independent parameters: π_1, π_2 and ω, which depend on the kinetics of the cell population, and c_1 and η, which depend on the calibration and experimental error of the microdensitometer.

5. The analysis of DNA distributions

The problem of estimating parameters to fit the distribution $\beta(x)$ to experimental data is an example of a distribution mixture problem. However, the assumption that the error variance η^2 is constant avoids pathological complications of the sort noted by Kiefer and Wolfowitz (1956). Unless η^2 is so large that the $\beta_1(x)$ and $\beta_3(x)$ components of the distribution do not appear as separate peaks, any or all of the five independent parameters $\pi_1, \pi_2, \omega, c_1, \eta$ can be estimated very well by maximum likelihood or by the method of Bartlett and Macdonald (1968). The two additional parameters of the distribution are c_3, which can be computed from c_1, and $\pi_3 = 1 - \pi_1 - \pi_2$.

If there are no nonproliferating cells, then $\pi_1 = P_1$, $\pi_2 = P_2$ and $\pi_3 = P_{34}$. If μ, the average duration of a cycle, is known, and the variances of the phase and cycle durations are not large, then the approximations $h_i^*(k) \simeq \exp(-\mu_i k)$ and $k \simeq (\ln A)/\mu$ may be used in (4), (5) and (6) to obtain estimates of μ_1, μ_2 and μ_{34}. The relation $\mu_2 = (c_3 - c_1)\omega/k$ gives an alternative estimate of μ_2.

If there are nonproliferating cells, results of a DNA analysis can be used to supplement a thymidine-labelling experiment and estimate the proportions of nonproliferating cells at the $2C$ and $4C$ levels of DNA content. Let N denote the total number of proliferating cells in the population and let N_i denote the number in phase i. Similarly, let N^0 and N_i^0 denote the total number of nonproliferating cells and the number in phase i, respectively. Assume that $N_2^0 = 0$ and N_4^0; that is, cells in S and M are taken to be proliferating cells. The DNA analysis will give estimates of

$$\pi_1 = (N_1 + N_1^0)/(N + N^0), \quad \pi_2 = N_2/(N + N^0)$$

and

$$\pi_3 = (N_3 + N_3^0 + N_4)/(N + N^0).$$

The mitotic index $MI = N_4/(N + N^0)$ may be measured directly. A thymidine-labelling experiment (see, for example, Macdonald (1974)) will estimate cell-cycle parameters for the proliferating cells, which may be

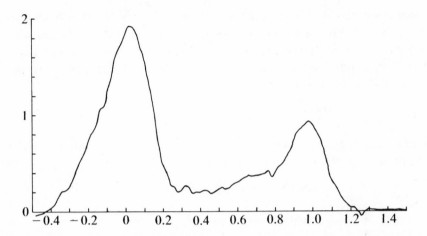

Figure 1(a). log₂ (nuclear DNA content)

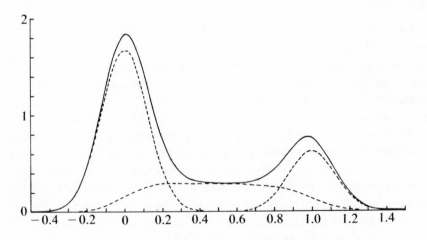

Figure 1(b). log₂ (nuclear DNA content)

Figure 1
(a) Observed and (b) fitted distributions of nuclear DNA content in the stele region of the pea root meristem described in Section 6. The three components of the fitted distribution are shown with broken lines.

substituted into (4), (5), (6) and (7) to estimate $P_1 = N_1/N$, $P_2 = N_2/N$ and $P_{34} = (N_3 + N_4)/N$. The proliferative fraction $PF = N/(N + N^0)$ can then be estimated from the relation $PF = \pi_2/P_2$, or, if the labelling index $LI(\tau)$ has been determined just after a pulse of label of duration τ, by the relation $PF = LI(\tau)/P_2(\tau)$, where

$$P_2(\tau) = \{A/(A - 1)\} h_1^*(k)\{1 - e^{-k\tau}h_{12}^*(k)\}$$

is approximately equal to P_2 but inflated by a non-zero pulse duration. The required proportions are then given by

$$N_1^0/N^0 = \{\pi_1 - PF \times P_1\}/\{1 - PF\}$$

and

$$N_3^0/N^0 = \{\pi_3 - PF \times P_{34}\}/\{1 - PF\}.$$

The above is just an outline of one possible analysis. The analysis used in a particular case must depend on the types of experiments performed and the reliability of the data.

6. Example

Dr. P. W. Barlow has permitted me to quote some unpublished data from an experimental study on the effects of an ethylene atmosphere on the early development of pea roots. The meristematic cells of roots 1–2 cm long were of interest. This example is concerned with the cell population in the stele region of the meristem, 0.25 to 0.5 mm from the root cap, in the control group of roots grown without ethylene.

The roots were studied with Feulgen staining and with thymidine labelling. The latter experiment involved continuous labelling in the presence of colchicine, which blocks the mitotic cycle at metaphase. The data were analysed by the method described in Macdonald (1973) but the analysis was extended to allow estimation of the proliferative fraction and to allow for the fact that cells blocked in M tend to lose the mitotic configuration of their chromosome after a few hours and become indistinguishable from interphase cells. We estimated $PF = 1$, and 4.2 hr. for the average duration of blocked M. The estimates of the cell-cycle parameters were, in hr., $\mu = 18.9$, $\sigma = 2.0$, $\mu_1 = 8.2$, $\mu_2 = 5.9$, $\mu_3 = 2.4$ and $\mu_4 = 2.4$. The phase durations were assumed to be gamma-distributed, with common scale parameter, and A was assumed to be 2.

A replicate group of 9 roots was not exposed to thymidine or colchicine, but the stele region of each root was dissected out, fixed, stained by Feulgen's method, and nuclear DNA contents measured by microdensitometry. The microdensitometry readings, in arbitrary units, were transferred to a $\log_2$ scale. The distribution (17) was fitted to the data by direct-search maximization of the log-likelihood function and various parametric hypotheses tested by likelihood ratios.

The parameter values $\pi_1 = P_1 = 0.519$, $\pi_2 = P_2 = 0.288$, and $\theta = \mu_2 k = 0.217$ were taken from the thymidine-labelling experiment and a likelihood-ratio test indicated no significant departure from these values.

As the calibration, scaling and error characteristics of the microdensitometer were unknown, it was necessary to estimate $c_1, \Delta c = (c_3 - c_1)$ and η. It was found that c_1 differed significantly between roots (perhaps because of differences in permeability to the stain) and a separate value of c_1 was estimated for each root. The other parameters were assumed to be the same for all roots. The data from each root were standardized by subtracting the appropriate c_1 and dividing by Δc, then data from all roots, with a total of $n = 459$ cells, were combined to give the empirical density function shown in Figure 1 (a). On the standardized scale, $\eta = 0.123$. The empirical density function was estimated by the method of Bartlett (1963); the formula $h = 3.06 \, n^{-2/15} \eta$ was used to interpolate in Table 1 of Bartlett and Macdonald (1971) to to determine the optimal width of the quadratic kernel.

The fitted distribution is shown, with its three components, in Figure 1 (b). The underlying distribution $\rho(r)$ is shown in Figure 2; since k is small ($k = 0.037$) and α_2 is large ($\alpha_2 = 28$), (9a), (9b) and (9c) give virtually identical curves.

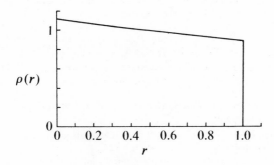

Figure 2

The probability density $\rho(r)$ for the elapsed proportion of the S phase is illustrated with the parameters $\theta = 0.217$ and $\alpha = 28$ from the stele region of the pea root meristem described in Section 6.

The fit is not entirely satisfactory but it is mainly the assumption of a normally-distributed measurement error that is at fault. The logarithmic transformation made the error variance constant, but left the peaks of the empirical distribution negatively skewed. A better fit would be obtained by not transforming the data and, instead, estimating separate error variances for the three components; however, the estimation problem might then be ill-behaved. In other respects, the agreement is remarkably good, especially considering that the cell-cycle parameters were estimated by a very different sort of experiment, and this is evidence that, for practical purposes, the multiphase branching-process model is not an unreasonable model for these cells.

Acknowledgments

I am indebted to Dr. P. W. Barlow of the Agricultural Research Council Unit of Developmental Botany, Cambridge, who provided the problem, the experimental data and many interesting discussions. This research is supported by the National Research Council of Canada.

References

BARLOW, P. W. AND MACDONALD, P. D. M. (1973) An analysis of the mitotic cell cycle in the root meristem of Zea mays. Proc. R. Soc. Lond. B **183**, 385–398.

BARTLETT, M. S. (1963) Statistical estimation of density functions. Sankhyā A **25**, 245–254.

BARTLETT, M. S. (1969) Distributions associated with cell populations. Biometrika **56**, 391–400.

BARTLETT, N. S. (1970) Age distributions, Biometrics **26**, 377–385.

BARTLETT, M. S. AND MACDONALD, P. D. M. (1968) 'Least-squares' estimation of distribution mixtures. Nature, Lond. **217**, 195–196.

BARTLETT, M. S. AND MACDONALD, P. D. M. (1971) Statistical estimation of the derivatives of density functions. Nature Physical Science, Lond. **229**, 125–126.

BROCKWELL, P. J. AND KUO, W. H. (1973) Labelling experiments and phase-age distributions for multiphase branching processes. J. Appl. Prob. **10**, 739–747.

CLEAVER, J. E. (1967) Thymidine Metabolism and Cell Kinetics. North-Holland Publishing Co., Amsterdam.

CLOWES, F. A. L. (1971) The proportion of cells that divide in root meristems of Zea mays L. Ann. Bot. **35**, 249–261.

DEAN, P. N. AND JETT, J. H. (1974) Mathematical analysis of DNA distributions derived from flow microfluorometry. J. Cell Biol. **60**, 523–527.

GREGOR, J. (1969) An algorithm for the decomposition of a distribution into Gaussian components. Biometrics **25**, 79–93.

HARRIS, T. E. (1963) The Theory of Branching Processes. Springer-Verlag, Berlin.

HOWARD, A. AND PELC, S. R. (1953) Synthesis of desoxyribonucleic acid in normal and irradiated cells and its relation to chromosome breakage.Heredity **6**, Suppl. Symposium on chromosome breakage. 261–273.

KIEFER, J. AND WOLFOWITZ, J. (1956) Consistency of the maximum likelihood estimator in the presence of infinitely many incidental parameters. *Ann. Math. Statist.* **27**, 887–906.

MACDONALD, P. D. M. (1970) Statistical inference from the fraction labelled mitoses curve. *Biometrika* **57**, 489–503.

MACDONALD, P. D. M. (1973) On the statistics of cell proliferation. *The Mathematical Theory of the Dynamics of Biological Populations*, eds. M. S. Bartlett and R. W. Hiorns. Academic Press, London. 303–314.

MACDONALD, P. D. M. (1974) Stochastic models for cell proliferation. *Mathematical Problems in Biology, Victoria Conference*, ed. P. van den Driessche. Springer-Verlag, Berlin. 155–163.

REDDY, S. B., ERBE, W., LINDEN, W. A., LANDEN, H. AND BAIGENT, C. (1973) Die Dauer der Phasen im Zellzyklus von L–929–Zellen. *Biophysik* **10**, 45–50.

STEEL, G. G. (1968) Cell loss from experimental tumours. *Cell Tissue Kinet.* **1**, 193–207.

A Stochastic Automaton Model for Interacting Systems

P. TAUTU

Abstract

A stochastic tessellation automaton (STA) is introduced and analysed as an analogue to a stochastic lattice process, called the Markov configuration process. The STA is considered as an (infinite regular) array with interconnected Moore-type automata, each of these representing a B-object interacting with its neighbours. The objective of the paper is to examine some consequences of the analogy between an STA and the Markov configuration process. In addition, the possibility of finding a suitable stochastic grammar arising from the study of this configuration model is briefly considered.

1. Motivation and summary

In an earlier paper (1973), we reported on two stochastic models describing the random evolution of a set of k-coloured objects interacting on an r-dimensional lattice. The basic idea of these models originates in the theory of random processes defined through the interaction of an infinite number of mass points (see, e.g., Spitzer (1969), (1970)), in order to study Markov processes which have as invariant measures some of the classical measures of statistical mechanics. Complex biological processes such as cellular proliferation and differentiation, particularly morphogenesis and carcinogenesis, are the distinctive motivation of our work.

It is the purpose of the present paper to introduce a stochastic cellular automaton with a view to studying various other facets of our models — essentially intended to represent the random behaviour of (initially homogeneous) growing structures. The concept of a cellular automaton was suggested to von Neumann by S. M. Ulam, from whose 22-years-old paper we quote the following problem:

Given is an infinite lattice or graph of points, each with a finite number of connections to certain of its 'neighbors'. Each point is capable of a finite number of 'states'. The states of neighbors at time t_n induce, in a specified manner, the state of the point at time t_{n+1}. This rule of transition is fixed deterministically or, more generally, may involve partly 'random' decisions.

One can define now closed finite subsystems to be called *automata* or *organisms*. They will be characterized by a periodic or almost periodic sequence of their states as functions of time and by the following 'spatial' character: the state of the neighbors of the 'organism' has only a 'weak' influence on the state of the elements of the organism; the organism can, on the contrary, influence with full generality the states of the neighboring points which are not part of other organisms.

One aim of the theory is to establish the existence of subsystems which are able to multiply, i.e., create in time other systems identical ('congruent') to themselves.

As time proceeds, by discrete intervals, one will generate, starting from a finite 'activated' region, organisms of different types (p. 274).

Deterministic cellular-automaton models with reference to the development of filamentous organisms have been introduced by Lindenmayer (1968), and later by many workers (see, e.g., Herman (1969), van Dalen (1971), Salomaa (1973a, b)). These systems were originally conceived as 1-dimensional arrays of interconnected finite automata, each automaton corresponding to a living cell, with the possibility that new automata could be added to the array (cells divide), or deleted from the array (cells die). Our work could suggest a new step in the study of stochastic L-systems.

In the present paper some general features of a stochastic tessellation automaton (STA) are investigated. Section 2 is an introduction where the essential rules of our Markovian configuration models are presented. In Section 3, the definition of an STA, as a natural extension of a deterministic tessellation automaton, is given for both a continuous-parameter STA and its discrete approximation. The relationship between the STA and stochastic grammars is briefly presented in Section 4.

2. Introduction: rules of a stochastic configuration process

In two earlier papers (Tautu (1973), Schürger and Tautu (1975)), two stochastic models of multitype object interactions on an r-dimensional lattice $\mathcal{X}^r, r > 1$, have been studied. These objects have been called B-objects, given the biological motivation of the models.

The lattice $\mathcal{X}^r$ of vectors $x = (x^1, \cdots, x^r)$, $x \in I^r$, is the set of r-tuples of integers and can be thought of as a set of points with integer coordinates in the r-dimensional Euclidean space, with the usual Euclidean distance $|x - y| = 1$ between points (sites) x and y. At each site $x \in \mathcal{X}^r$ a B-object, initially indistinguishable from all others, is located. Instead of the whole lattice $\mathcal{X}^r$ one may consider a finite non-void subset $Z \subset \mathcal{X}^r$, called array, with the same dimension r, and with $|Z| = z$.

The set of rules governing this system of B-objects are the following:

1. *Structural rules*, or rules prescribing the location and the neighbourhood of each B-object, e.g.,

(1a) The rule of unique location: no site on Z can be occupied by more than one B-object at a time.

(1b) To each site $x \in Z$ there corresponds a set $\mathcal{N}(x) = \{x + \nu_1, \cdots, x + \nu_m\}$ of neighbouring sites of x where m is fixed and $\nu_g \in Z^r$, $1 \leq g \leq m$. This means that the neighbourhood of x consists of elements $x + \nu_1, \cdots, x + \nu_m$, where $x + \nu_g = (x^1 + \nu_g^1, \cdots, x^r + \nu_g^r)$, $1 \leq g \leq m$.

(1c) The simple neighbourhood relation is symmetric,

$$x \in \mathcal{N}(y) \Rightarrow y \in \mathcal{N}(x), \qquad x, y \in Z.$$

(1d) The considered structure is homogeneous and isotropic, that is, invariant both under translational shifts and under rotations.

Remark. A neighbourhood relation between two sites $x, y \in Z$ can be an equivalence relation Q, if

(i) $x = y$, or

(ii) $\exists(z_0, z_1, \cdots, z_u)$, $u \geq 1$, $\ni$ $x = z_0$, $y = z_u$ and $z_q R z_{q+1}$, $1 \leq q < u$, $z_q \in Z$,

where R is the immediate neighbourhood relation $z_{q+1} = z_q + \nu_g$, $1 \leq g \leq m$. The partition $Z/Q = \{\Lambda_0, \Lambda_1, \cdots\}$ is called the lamination of the array Z (Yamada and Amoroso (1969)).

2. *Growth rules*, or rules that allow each B-object to produce a replica of itself, e.g.,

(2a) Each B-object in the array has a uniform set of internal states, $S = \{s_1, \cdots, s_n\}$, $n \in N$, specifically called the cell cycle. Each state (or cycle phase) may be considered as a complex of biochemical, physiological and morphological processes. The self-replication of a B-object occurs in consequence of the conclusion of a cycle in state s_n. Both resulting objects are to repeat the cycle from state s_1.

(2b) Each B-objects is of a defined type ('colour') which can be altered to another only at the end of the cycle. The colours constitute a set $K = \{1, \cdots, k\}$ and the colouring process is possible only step by step, that is, from colour i to colour $i \pm 1$. It is supposed that at time $t = 0$ all B-objects on Z have colour 1. Because we have k different colours attributable to a B-object at x, there are $|Z|^k$ different ways of colouring Z.

The state space of a system governed by these rules is therefore the Cartesian product $K \times S = X$. A B-object located at x, of colour $i \in K$ and in cycle phase $j \in S$, will be formally denoted by $\alpha_{ij}(x)$, $(i, j) \in X$. This is said to be the configuration c over Z where c is an arbitrary mapping $c: Z \to X$. A configuration $c(Z)$ specifies what state each B-object on Z is in at a particular time t. If $|Z| = z$, the configuration $c(Z)$ is an ordered z-tuple.

Each $c(Z)$ can be dissected in paradigmatic classes (Grenander (1970)): for instance, the paradigmatic class of all B-objects in state (ij), the paradigmatic class of all B-objects of colour i, etc., denoted by $\mathscr{C}_{ij}, \mathscr{C}_{i\cdot}$, respectively. One of these classes is chosen as the support of $c(Z)$, e.g., $\mathscr{C}_{\cdot n}, \mathscr{C}_{k\cdot}$, or preferably $\mathscr{C}_{kn}$. The sequence $(c(Z, t_0), c(Z, t_1), \cdots)$ is said to be the configuration history.

3. *Competition (interaction) rules*, or rules that allow each new B-object to jump to a neighbouring site. After the replication of a B-object $\alpha(x)$, the replica α' has to leave the 'maternal' site $x \in Z$ (according to rule 1a): it will occupy either a neighbouring site $x + \nu_g \in \mathscr{N}(x)$, $1 \le g \le m$, (killing the B-object already at that site), or a (supposed vacant) boundary site of Z, say $\beta \in \mathscr{Z}' - Z$. In the second case the array is blowing up.

This competition process allows us to consider two models: *Model I*, when the nearest-neighbour competition acts inside the array Z and the number of B-objects remains constant, say z, and *Model II*, when this competition also determines growth over the boundary of Z and the number of B-objects varies in time. In Model I the colouring process plays the main role, whereas in Model II a spatial growth is associated with the process.

In the above-mentioned papers, a stochastic configuration process $\{\gamma_t\}_{t \geq 0}$ with the set $C_X(Z)$ of all possible configurations over $Z \subset \mathscr{L}'$, $0 < |Z| < \infty$ as the state space, has been considered. At $t = 0$, $\gamma_0 = c_0$, the initial configuration. As might be expected, these models show considerable difficulties, especially Model II, just like the entire family of lattice processes. The random configurations of two-state objects* on Z have been considered as a random field with $\Omega = \{0, 1\}^Z$, $Z \subset \mathscr{L}'$, which is called Markovian if it satisfies certain conditions (Spitzer (1971), Hammersley (1972)). This random field can then be interpreted as a probability measure on $C_X(Z)$.

A process $\{\xi_x\}_{x \in Z}$ is a stochastic nearest-neighbour (interaction) process whose definition is possible in two ways: in terms of the joint probability distributions of the binary random variables ξ, (Whittle (1963)), or in terms of conditional probabilities depending only upon the nearest neighbours (Bartlett (1967), (1968), (1971a)). Any valid model satisfying the second definition must also satisfy the first, which has a great degree of generality but also poses intricate questions (Brook (1964), Besag (1972)). We note also the difficulty of proving in all cases the Markovian character of these processes (Holley (1970), Harris (1972), Liggett (1972)).

The increased complexity of our configuration models originates in the distinguishability postulate (k-coloured objects) and in the association of a growth process over the boundaries of Z.

3. The stochastic tessellation automaton

It is easy to realize that a system of interacting B-objects can be studied as a generalized ('coloured') stochastic tessellation automaton**. Only the deterministic theory has been developed (Moore (1962),

---

* E.g., occupied-vacant, infective-susceptible, white-black, etc. For significant biological applications the reader is referred to Morgan and Welsh (1965), Bartlett (1971b), Williams and Bjerknes (1972), Clifford and Sudbury (1973), Richardson (1973).

** For a definition of a 2–dimensional tessellation, see, e.g., Coxeter (1963): A plane tessellation is an infinite set of polygons fitting together to cover the plane just once, so that every side of each polygon belongs also to one other polygon (p. 58).

Yamada and Amoroso (1969) define the tessellation automaton as an infinite regular array of identical finite-state automata, where each machine is connected to its neighbours in a uniform way throughout the array.

Codd (1968), Yamada and Amoroso (1969), Smith (1971)). A probabilistic approach has also been attempted (Burks (1963), Lofgren (1963)) to represent the statistical characteristics of real systems. For biological applications, see Arbib (1966), (1969), Vitányi (1973), Kitagawa (1974), and, certainly, Lindenmayer (1968).

We shall now define the stochastic analogue using the standard treatment. A generalized continuous-parameter stochastic tessellation automaton is a many-sorted structure $\mathfrak{A}(t) = [Z, S, A, B, \pi, \{p(t)\}, t \geq 0]$ iff

(i) Z is the tessellation array of dimension $r \geq 1$, locating B-objects (initially isomorphic) in each polytope;

(ii) S is a finite non-void set of internal states, $S = \{s_0, s_1, \cdots, s_{n-1}\}$, also called the state alphabet;

(iii) A is a finite non-void set of inputs, $A = \{a_1, \cdots, a_l\}$, the inputs alphabet whose elements are called symbols (letters);

(iv) B is a finite set of outputs, $B = \{b_1, \cdots, b_h\}$;

(v) π is an n-dimensional stochastic row vector of the form $\pi = \{\pi_{s_0}, \pi_{s_1}, \cdots, \pi_{s_{n-1}}\}$, called the initial distribution over states (or the initial state designator);

(vi) $\{p(t)\}$, $t \geq 0$, is a rather vague notation which allows us to choose the convenient measurable function in $(0, \infty)$ from the following three:

(1) $p(a; t) = p(s_j, t' | s_i, a, t)$, $s_i, s_j \in S$, $a \in A$, $0 \leq t < t'$, the probability with which $\mathfrak{A}(t)$ in state s_i at time t goes into state s_j at time t' by an input a;

(2) $p(b; t) = p(b, t' | s_i, a, t)$, $s_i \in S$, $a \in A$, $b \in B$, $0 \leq t < t'$, the probability that at time t' the automaton $\mathfrak{A}(t)$ will produce output b, given that at time t it is in state s_i and is fed with input a;

(3) $p_{ij}(a, b; t) = p(s_j, b, t' | s_i, a, t)$, $s_i, s_j \in S$, $a \in A$, $b \in B$, $0 \leq t < t'$, the conditional probability that the automaton $\mathfrak{A}(t)$ will go to state s_j and produce output b at time t', given that at time t it is in state s_i and is fed with input a.

One may clearly assume that, in many cases, a transition from s_i into s_j is induced by a sequence of almost simultaneous inputs and, correspondingly, that a sequence of outputs can be produced by $\mathfrak{A}(t)$ in a short time interval. Let $\mathscr{A}$ be the free semigroup generated by A. The elements of $\mathscr{A}$ are called words (tapes, strings) and if the sequence $a_1, \cdots, a_u$ is in A, then $v = a_1 \cdots a_u$ is in $\mathscr{A}$. Similarly, $\mathscr{B}$ is the free semigroup generated by B with elements $w \in \mathscr{B}$. Both $\mathscr{A}$ and $\mathscr{B}$ also include the empty word ϕ. Clearly, for the words va and wb of equal length $(\mathscr{L}(v) = \mathscr{L}(w),$

$\mathscr{L}(va) = \mathscr{L}(v) + 1$, $\mathscr{L}(wb) = \mathscr{L}(w) + 1$), we have the 'forward' relation

$$p_{ij}(wb, t'|va, t) = \sum_{k=1}^{n} p_{ik}(w, t_1|v, t)p_{kj}(b, t'|a, t_2), \ 0 \le t < t_1 < t_2 < t'.$$

If the sequence $a_1, \cdots, a_u$ occurs at different moments $t_1, \cdots, t_u$, the length of v is $\mathscr{L}(v) = \Sigma_{m=1}^{u} t_m$.

Probabilities (1)–(3) can be defined in terms of their matrix functions. If V is a function from $S \times A \times T$ into $[0, 1]^n$, such that for $(s, a) \in S \times A$

$$V_t(a) = (p_1(a;t), p_2(a;t), \cdots, p_n(a;t)),$$

$V_t(a)$ is an $n \times n$ stochastic matrix with entries $(p(a;t))$, sometimes called the symbol matrix (Page (1966)). We define in a similar way the matrices $W_t(b)$ with entries $(p(b;t))$ and $P_t(b|a)$ with entries $(p_{ij}(a,b;t))$. Clearly,

$$P_t(w|v) = P_t(b_1|a_1)P_t(b_2|a_2) \cdots P_t(b_k|a_k), v \in \mathscr{A}, w \in \mathscr{B},$$

$$\mathscr{L}(v) = \mathscr{L}(w) = k, a \in A, b \in B, 1 \ge 0.$$

with $P_t(\phi|\phi) = I$, the identity matrix.

It is easy to see that matrix $P_t(b|a)$, which defines the input-output relation in the stochastic tessellation automaton $\mathfrak{A}(t)$, is the transition matrix of a continuous parameter Markov chain, preserving all its well-known properties (Chung (1967)). Taking advantage of the known theory, we will employ in the sequel, for the sake of simplicity, instead of $\mathfrak{A}(t)$ its discrete approximation $\mathfrak{A}$, assuming that $\ln P_t(b|a)$ exists for each $a \in A$ and $b \in B$ (see Knast (1969)).

Remarks. (1) The given definition of the stochastic tessellation automaton (STA) would be identical with the standard definition of any stochastic automaton if we ignored the concepts of neighbourhood and of configuration. The corresponding definitions given in Section 2 are then available. This means that

(a) there are inputs which change the colour of a B-object, as outputs which are phase and colour-dependent. Clearly, an element $s \in S$ in the stochastic automaton corresponds to a pair $(ij) \in X$, $1 \le i \le k$, $1 \le j \le n$, defined in Section 2;

(b) if in an STA the B-objects (or B-automata) are interconnected the input alphabet is constituted of two types of symbols: external ('world') inputs and 'carried' inputs, that is, the outputs produced by one or all of its m neighbours.

It follows that an STA is a finite set of interconnected Moore-type automata (Moore (1956)): $\mathfrak{A} = \{\mathfrak{A}_1, \cdots, \mathfrak{A}_z\}$, $z = |Z|$. For each component $\mathfrak{A}_k$, $1 \leq k \leq z$, we have the sets $A_{(k)}, B_{(k)}, S_{(k)}$, and the stochastic matrix $V_{(k)}(a)$. But now the carried or ν-input is a word $u = a_1 \cdots a_m$, $u \in \mathcal{B}^*$, where $\mathcal{B}^*$ is the free semigroup generated by $(B_{(\nu_1)} \cup \cdots \cup B_{(\nu_m)})$. The maximal length of u is m, on the hypothesis that all the neighbours of $\mathfrak{A}_k$ communicate with it. Obviously, if all these inputs are identical $\mathcal{L}(u) = a^m$. It is easy to see that the term 'predecessor' employed by Hartmanis (1962) is equivalent to the nearest-neighbour B-automaton producing a carried input, and that the smallest closed subset of $\mathfrak{A}$ which contains $\mathfrak{A}_k$ is, in fact, the set of the nearest neighbours of $\mathfrak{A}_k$.

The transition probability (1) in the first definition above is actually $p(s'_{(1)}, \cdots, s'_{(z)} | s_{(1)}, \cdots, s_{(z)}, a)$, with $s'_{(k)}, s_{(k)} \in S_{(k)}$, $1 \leq k \leq z$, or, taking into account the notation used in Section 2, $p(c'(Z) | c(Z), a), c', c \in C_s(Z)$.

We say that the set $\{\mathfrak{A}_1, \cdots, \mathfrak{A}_z\}$ is

(i) concurrently connected, if the state s_j at moment t of an automaton $\mathfrak{A}_k$, $1 \leq k \leq z$, depends on the state s_i at moment $t - 1$, the world inputs and the ν-inputs, that is, if there exists a positive probability $p_{ij}(y) = p(s_j | s_i, y)$, $s_i, s_j \in S_{(k)}$, $y = ua$, $a \in A$, $u \in \mathcal{B}^*$ and

(ii) loop-free, if none of $\mathfrak{A}_k$, $1 \leq k \leq z$, is in a cycle.

A Moore-type automaton is an ordered 6-tuple, $\mathfrak{A}_k = [S_{(k)}, A_{(k)}, B_{(k)}, \pi_{(k)}, \{V_{(k)}(y)\}, \rho_{(k)}]$, where $S_{(k)}, A_{(k)}, B_{(k)}$ and $\pi_{(k)}$ have been already introduced, $V_{(k)}(y)$ is the stochastic matrix with entries $(p_{ij}(y))$ and $\rho_{(k)}$ is the output n-dimensional column vector consisting of 0's and 1's only. If the entries are real numbers, $\mathfrak{A}_k$ is called a generalized stochastic automaton.

Interesting hypotheses might be introduced if we assume, for instance that (i) in some final states, say s_{n-1}, the automaton produces no output, becoming 'asocial', or (ii) its output can be received only by neighbours in similar states. Such assumptions modify the structural coherence and stability of the STA. We should point out that using a lamination technique (Yamada and Amoroso (1969)) or a result on percolation processes (Harris (1972)), we may realize a laminated structure with independent laminal subarrays acting in parallel or, by analogy, a countable number of random islands with no interaction between then.

It is to be noted that every Markov chain can be simulated by a Moore-type automaton (Davis (1961)). Therefore, problems such as loop-free decomposition, lumpability, ergodicity, etc. can be treated with the already created probabilistic tools (Gelenbe (1970), Knast (1970)).

If $\mathfrak{A}$ is a generalized stochastic automaton over the alphabet A, a stochastic language is a set $\mathfrak{L}(\mathfrak{A}, \lambda) = \{v : v \in \mathscr{A} \text{ and } \pi V(v) \rho > \lambda\}$, where λ is a real number, $0 \leqq \lambda < 1$, often called the cut-point.

(2) A state s_0, called quiescent (passive, blank) state, has been introduced in the set S of internal states. Its biological equivalent is a particular cycle phase, denoted by G_0, which is conceived as a reservoir from which the living cells could be randomly triggered in order to supply cells for replication. At any time all but a finite number of B-objects are assumed to be in s_0.

(3) The last remark is concerned with the complicated growth problem for our STA. For one-type objects we have Moore's theorem ((1962), p. 23) stating that if n_t is the number of reproduced automata at time t, then there exists a positive number x such that $n_t \leqq xt^r$ where $r > 1$ is the array dimension. A real interesting approach could be the theory of word functions (Paz (1971)), or rather the theory of integral sequential word functions. Growth functions were studied for L-systems (see Salomaa (1973b), pp. 249–251) to determine the length of the nth word generated from the initial word, mimicking the successive sizes of a filamentous organism throughout the development (Salomaa (1973a), Vitányi (1973b)).

A simplified approach is to consider the synchronous apparition of a group of automata in a final state, as a consequence of world inputs. The total number of automata in the array remains fixed (as in our Model I). This is the well-known firing-squad synchronization problem, where results for arrays with dimension $r = 2, 3$ have been recently published (Shinahr (1974)). The expected time for the apparition of a fixed number of objects in a final state has also been studied (Morgan and Welsh (1965), Williams and Bjerknes (1972), Downham and Morgan (1973)). Richardson (1973) has presented an excellent approach to the growth of two-type objects in a plane tessellation.

4. Stochastic grammars for stochastic tessellation automata

We deal here with the grammatical inference problem, that is, with the problem of finding a convenient grammar consistent with the evolution of an interacting system of B-objects. It seems that the setting up of a stochastic model could be a good way of solving this problem. Deterministic grammars explaining biological spatial-temporal growth have been described as developmental systems (Lindenmayer and Rozenberg

(1972)). The generative capacity of these grammars is to some extent diminished, but the complexity increases because rewriting happens simultaneously to all letters of the word under scan and an initial word is assumed as axiom.

It seems that in our case an appropriate grammar must be a multi-dimensional one (and context sensitive) or a method linearizing the pattern. In a fashion familiar to that in the literature, we may define a stochastic grammar as a system $\mathfrak{G} = [X, \alpha, \pi, R]$ where

(i) X is an alphabet consisting of two disjoint subsets: X_1 of non-terminal symbols (variables) and X_2 of terminal symbols;

(ii) α is the starting symbol (axiom or sentence symbol), $\alpha \in X_1$;

(iii) π is a mapping $\pi : X_1 \to [0, 1]$, the initial distribution over X_1;

(iv) R is the finite collection of probabilistic rewriting rules (productions) over X.

The rewriting rules are of the form $p_i(a \to b_i)$, indicating that the 'premise' a can be replaced by the 'consequence portion of the production' b_i with probability p_i.

Generally speaking, we need a picture grammar, if we understand a picture as an array of elements having different colours, which may be regarded as the symbols of X. Theoretically we require rules in R which rewrite arrays as arrays with some local operations on the subarrays. This type of operation is analogous to an isotonic context-sensitive word production.

An appropriate grammar may probably impose more restrictions on the use of rewriting rules, for example, if we assumed that an application of a production could determine with a certain probability which rules are applicable at the next step. This kind of stochastic programmed grammar (Rosenkrantz (1969)), proposed as a convenient formalism for syntactic pattern recognition (Swain and Fu (1962)), is under examination.

References

[1] AHO, A. V. AND ULLMAN, J. D. (1968) The theory of languages. *Math. Systems Theory* **2**, 97–125.

[2] AMOROSO, S. AND GUILFOYLE, R. (1972) Some comments on neighborhood size for tessellation automata. *Information and Control* **21**, 48–55.

[3] ARBIB, M. A. (1967) Automata theory and development. *J. Theor. Biol.* **14**, 131–156.

[4] ARBIB, M. A. (1969) Self-reproducing automata. Some implications for theoretical biology. *Towards a Theoretical Biology* **2**, 204–226. Edinburgh University Press.

[5] BACON, G. C. (1964) The decomposition of stochastic automata. *Information and Control* **7**, 320–339.

[6] BARTLETT, M.S. (1967) Inference and stochastic processes. *J. R. Statist. Soc.* A **130**, 457–477.

[7] BARTLETT, M. S. (1968) A further note on nearest neighbour models. *J. R. Statist. Soc.* A **131**, 579–580.

[8] BARTLETT, M.S. (1971a) Physical nearest-neighbour models and non-linear time series. *J. Appl. Prob.* **8**, 222–232.

[9] BARTLETT, M.S. (1971b) Two-dimensional nearest-neighbour systems and their ecological applications. *Statistical Ecology* **1**, 179–194. Penn. State University Press.

[10] BESAG, J.E. (1972) Nearest-neighbour systems and the auto-logistic model for binary data. *J. R. Statist. Soc.* B **34**, 75–83.

[11] BROOK. D. (1964) On the distinction between the conditional probability and the joint probability approaches in specification of nearest-neighbour systems. *Biometrika* **51**, 481–483.

[12] BURKS, A.W. (1963) Toward a theory of automata based on more realistic primitive elements. *Inform. Proc.* 1962, *Proc. IFIP Congr.* pp. 379–385. (Reprinted in [13], pp. 84–102.)

[13] BURKS, A.W. (ed.) (1970) *Essays on Cellular Automata.* University of Illinois Press, Urbana.

[14] CARLYLE. J.W. (1963) Reduced forms of stochastic sequential machines. *J. Math. Anal. Appl.* **7**, 167–175.

[15] CHUNG, K.L. (1967) *Markov Chains with Stationary Transition Probabilities.* 2nd ed. Springer, Berlin.

[16] CLIFFORD. P. AND SUDBURY. A. (1973) A model for spatial conflict. *Biometrika* **60**, 581–588.

[17] CODD. E.F. (1968) *Cellular Automata.* Academic Press, New York.

[18] COHEN. D. (1967) Computer simulation of biological pattern generation processes. *Nature* **216**, 246–248.

[19] COXETER. H.S.M. (1963) *Regular Polytopes.* 2nd ed. Macmillan, New York.

[20] DAVIS. A.S. (1961) Markov chains as random input automata. *Amer. Math. Monthly* **68**, 264–267.

[21] DOWNHAM. D.Y. AND MORGAN. R.K.B. (1973) Growth of abnormal cells. *Nature* **242**, 528–530.

[22] EDEN. M. (1961) A two-dimensional growth process. *Proc. Fourth Berkeley Symp. Math. Statist. Prob.* **4**, 223–239.

[23] GELENBE. S.E. (1970) On the loop-free decomposition of stochastic finite-state systems. *Information and Control* **17**, 474–484.

[24] GORDON. R. (1966) On stochastic growth and form. *Proc. Nat. Acad. Sci. USA* **56**, 1497–1504.

[25] GRENANDER. U. (1970) A unified approach to pattern analysis *Adv. in Computers* **10**, 175–216.

[26] HAMMERSLEY. J.M. (1972) Stochastic models for the distribution of particles in space. *Adv. Appl. Prob. Suppl.* 47–68.

[27] HARRIS. T.E. (1972) Nearest-neighbor Markov interaction processes on multi-dimensional lattices. *Advances in Math.* **9**, 66–89.

[28] HARTMANIS. J. (1962) Loop-free structure of sequential machines. *Information and Control* **5**, 25–43.

[29] HARTMANIS. J. AND STEARNS. R.E. (1966) *Algebraic Structure Theory of Sequential Machines.* Prentice-Hall, Englewood Cliffs.

[30] HERMAN. G.T. (1969) Computing ability of a developmental model for filamentous organisms. *J. Theor. Biol.* **25**, 421–435.

[31] HOLLEY. R. (1970) A class of interactions in an infinite particle system. *Advances in Math.* **5**, 291–309.

[32] KAMEDA, T. (1968) Generalized transition matrix of a sequential machine and its applications. *Information and Control* 12, 259–275.

[33] KITAGAWA, T. (1974) Cell space approaches in biomathematics. *Math. Biosci.* 19, 27–71.

[34] KNAST, R. (1969) Continuous-time probabilistic automata. *Information and Control* 15, 335–352.

[35] KNAST, R. (1970) Representability of nonregular languages in finite probabilistic automata. *Information and Control* 16, 285–302.

[36] KNAST, R. (1972) Finite-state probabilistic languages. *Information and Control* 21, 148–170.

[37] LIGGETT, T.M. (1972) Existence theorems for infinite particle systems. *Trans. Amer. Math. Soc.* 165, 471–481.

[38] LINDENMAYER, A. (1968) Mathematical models for cellular interactions in development. I, II. *J. Theor. Biol.* 18, 280–299; 300–315.

[39] LINDENMAYER, A. AND ROZENBERG, G. (1972) Developmental systems and languages. *Proc. 4th ACM Symp. Theory Computing*, pp. 214–221.

[40] LOFGREN, L. (1963) Self-repair as a computability concept in the theory of automata. *Proc. Symp. Mathematical Theory of Automata*, pp. 205–222. Polytechnic Press.

[41] MEALY, G.H. (1955) A method for synthesizing sequential circuits. *Bell System Tech. J.* 34, 1045–1079.

[42] MOORE, E.F. (1956) Gedanken-experiments on sequential machines. *Automata Studies. Ann. Math. Studies* 34, 129–153. Princeton University Press.

[43] MOORE, E.F. (1962) Machine models of self-reproduction. *Proc. Symp. Appl. Math.* 14, 17–33. (Reprinted in [13], 187–203.)

[44] MORGAN, R.W. AND WELSH, D.J.A. (1965) A two-dimensional Poisson growth process. *J. R. Statist. Soc.* B 27, 497–504.

[45] ONICESCU, O. AND GUIASU, S. (1965) Finite abstract random automata. *Z. Wahrscheinlichkeitsth.* 3, 279–285.

[46] PAGE, C.V. (1966) Equivalences between probabilistic and deterministic sequential machines. *Information and Control* 9, 469–520.

[47] PAZ, A. (1971) *Introduction to Probabilistic Automata.* Academic Press, New York.

[48] RICHARDSON, D. (1973) Random growth in a tessellation. *Proc. Camb. Phil. Soc.* 74, 515–528.

[49] ROSENKRANTZ, D.J. (1969) Programmed grammars and classes of formal languages, *J. Assoc. Comput. Mach.* 16, 107–131.

[50] SALOMAA, A. (1968) On events represented by probabilistic automata of different types. *Canad. J. Math.* 20, 242–251.

[51] SALOMAA, A. (1973a) On exponential growth in Lindenmayer systems. *Indag. Math.* 35, 23–30.

[52] SALOMAA, A. (1973b) *Formal Languages.* Academic Press, New York.

[53] SANTOS, E.S. (1972) Probabilistic grammars and automata. *Information and Control* 21, 27–47.

[54] SCHÜRGER, K. AND TAUTU, P. (1975) Markov configuration processes on a lattice. *Rev. Roumaine Math. Pures Appl.* To appear.

[55] SHINAHR, I. (1974) Two-and three-dimensional firing-squad synchronization problem. *Information and Control* 24, 163–180.

[56] SMITH, A.R. III (1971) Cellular automata complexity trade-offs. *Information and Control* 18, 466–482.

[57] SPITZER, F. (1969) Random processes defined through the interaction of an infinite particle system. *Lecture Notes in Math.* 89, 201–223. Springer, Berlin.

[58] SPITZER, F. (1970) Interaction of Markov processes. *Advances in Math.* **5,** 246–290.

[59] SPITZER, F. (1971) Markov random fields and Gibbs ensembles. *Amer. Math. Monthly* **78,** 142–154.

[60] STARKE, P. H. AND THIELE, H. (1970) On asynchronous stochastic automata. *Information and Control* **17,** 265–293.

[61] SWAIN, P. H. AND FU, K. S. (1972) Stochastic programmed grammars for syntactic pattern recognition. *Pattern Recognition* **4,** 83–100.

[62] TAUTU, P. (1973) Random systems of locally interacting cells. *3rd Conf. Stoch. Proc. Appl. Sheffield.* (Abstract published in *Adv. Appl. Prob.* **6,** 237.)

[63] TURAKAINEN, P. (1968) On stochastic languages. *Information and Control* **12,** 304–313.

[64] ULAM, S. (1952) Random processes and transformations. *Proc. Intern. Congr. Mathematicians,* **2,** 264–275.

[65] VAN DALEN, D. (1971) A note on some systems of Lindenmayer. *Math. Systems Theory* **5,** 128–140.

[66] VITÁNYI, P. B. M. (1973a) Sexually reproducing cellular automata. *Math. Biosci.* **18,** 23–54.

[67] VITÁNYI, P. B. M. (1973b) Structure of growth in Lindenmayer systems. *Indag. Math.* **35,** 257–263.

[68] WHITTLE, P. (1963) Stochastic processes in several dimensions. *Bull. Inst. Internat. Statist.* **40,** 974–994.

[69] WILLIAMS, T. AND BJERKNES, R. (1972) A stochastic model for abnormal clone spread through epitelial basal layer. *Nature* **236,** 19–21.

[70] YAMADA, H. AND AMOROSO, S. (1969) Tessellation automata. *Information and Control* **14,** 229–317.

[71] YAMADA, H. AND AMOROSO, S. (1971) Structural and behavioral equivalences of tessellation automata. *Information and Control* **18,** 1–31.

List of Contributors

P. Armitage, Department of Medical Statistics and Epidemiology, London School of Hygiene and Tropical Medicine, London, England.

Norman T. J. Bailey, World Health Organization, Geneva, Switzerland.

G. A. Barnard, Department of Mathematics, University of Essex, Colchester, England.

A. Blanc-Lapierre, Ecole Supérieure d'Electricité, Université de Paris, France.

Violet R. Cane, Statistical Laboratory, Department of Mathematics, University of Manchester, England.

W. G. Cochran, Department of Statistics, Harvard University, Cambridge, Massachusetts, U.S.A.

J. W. Cohen, Department of Mathematics, University of Utrecht, Holland.

D. R. Cox, Department of Mathematics, Imperial College of Science and Technology, London, England.

Harald Cramér, Skarviksvagen 33, 182 61 Djursholm, Sweden.

H. E. Daniels, Department of Mathematical Statistics, University of Birmingham, England.

J. Gani, Division of Mathematics and Statistics, C.S.I.R.O., Canberra, Australia.

Ulf Grenander, Division of Applied Mathematics, Brown University, Providence, Rhode Island, U.S.A.

J. M. Hammersley, Institute of Economics and Statistics, University of Oxford, England.

E. J. HANNAN, Department of Statistics, The Australian National University, Canberra, Australia.

DAVID G. KENDALL, Statistical Laboratory, University of Cambridge, England.

J. F. C. KINGMAN, Mathematical Institute, University of Oxford, England.

A. M. KSHIRSAGAR, Institute of Statistics, Texas A&M University, U.S.A.

TOBY LEWIS, Department of Mathematical Statistics, University of Hull, England.

P. D. M. MACDONALD, Department of Applied Mathematics, McMaster University, Hamilton, Ontario, Canada.

PAUL MEIER, Department of Statistics, University of Chicago, Illinois, U.S.A.

P. A. P. MORAN, Department of Statistics, The Australian National University, Canberra, Australia.

C. RADHAKRISHNA RAO, Indian Statistical Institute, New Delhi, India.

C. A. B. SMITH, Department of Human Genetics and Biometry, University College, London, England.

HERBERT SOLOMON, Department of Statistics, Stanford University, California, U.S.A.

LAJOS TAKÁCS, Department of Mathematics and Statistics, Case Western Reserve University, Cleveland, Ohio, U.S.A.

P. TAUTU, Institut für Dokumentation, Information und Statistik, Deutsches Krebsforschungszentrum, Heidelberg, West Germany.

D. VERE-JONES, Department of Mathematics, Victoria University of Wellington, New Zealand.

P. WHITTLE, Statistical Laboratory, University of Cambridge, England.

E. J. WILLIAMS, Department of Statistics, University of Melbourne, Australia.

HERMAN WOLD, Department of Statistics, University of Göteborg, Sweden.

Index